www.wadsworth.com

www.wadsworth.com is the World Wide Web site for Wadsworth and is your direct source to dozens of online resources.

At *www.wadsworth.com* you can find out about supplements, demonstration software, and student resources. You can also send email to many of our authors and preview new publications and exciting new technologies.

www.wadsworth.com
Changing the way the world learns®

From the Wadsworth Series in Broadcast and Production

Announcing
Broadcast Communicating Today

FIFTH EDITION

Carl Hausman
Rowan University

Philip Benoit
Middlebury College

Fritz Messere
State University of New York–Oswego

Lewis B. O'Donnell
State University of New York–Oswego

THOMSON

WADSWORTH

Australia • Canada • Mexico • Singapore • Spain
United Kingdom • United States

THOMSON

WADSWORTH

Publisher: Holly J. Allen
Assistant Editor: Shona Burke
Editorial Assistant: Laryssa Polika
Technology Project Manager: Jeanette Wiseman
Media Assistant: Bryan Davis
Marketing Manager: Kimberly Russell
Marketing Assistant: Neena Chandra
Advertising Project Manager: Shemika Britt
Project Manager, Editorial Production: Mary Noel
Print/Media Buyer: Jessica Reed

Permissions Editor: Joohee Lee
Production Service: Robin Gold, Forbes Mill Press
Text Designer: Robin Gold
Photo Researcher: Myrna Engler
Copy Editor: Robin Gold
Cover Designer: John Odam
Cover Image: Craig McClain
Compositor: Thompson Type
Text and Cover Printer: Phoenix Color Corp

For more information about our products,
contact us at:
Thomson Learning Academic Resource Center
1-800-423-0563

For permission to use material from this text,
contact us by:
Phone: 1-800-730-2214
Fax: 1-800-730-2215
Web: http://www.thomsonrights.com

Library of Congress Control Number: 2003106371

ISBN 0-534-56310-4

Wadsworth/Thomson Learning
10 Davis Drive
Belmont, CA 94002-3098
USA

Asia
Thomson Learning
5 Shenton Way #01-01
UIC Building
Singapore 068808

Australia/New Zealand
Nelson Thomson Learning
102 Dodds Street
Southbank, Victoria 3006
Australia

Canada
Nelson
1120 Birchmount Road
Toronto, Ontario M1K 5G4
Canada

Europe/Middle East/Africa
Thomson Learning
High Holborn House
50/51 Bedford Row
London WC1R 4LR
United Kingdom

Latin America
Thomson Learning
Seneca, 53
Colonia Polanco
11560 Mexico D.F.
Mexico

Spain/Portugal
Paraninfo
Calle/Magallanes, 25
28015 Madrid, Spain

About the Authors

Carl Hausman (Ph.D., the Union Graduate School; post-doctoral fellowship, New York University) is Associate Professor of Communications at Rowan University in Glassboro, New Jersey. Hausman is the author of 20 books, including 9 on the mass media. He has worked in various news and news management positions in radio and television, has worked as a radio producer, staff announcer, and freelance voice-over announcer and has testified before Congress on media ethics issues.

Philip Benoit (M.A., State University of New York at Oswego) is director of Public Affairs at Middlebury College in Middlebury, Vermont. Formerly the director of broadcasting at SUNY Oswego, Benoit has a broad background in radio, television, and public relations. He was executive officer of the American Forces Network in Europe and American Advisor to the Vietnamese Armed Forces Radio Network.

Fritz Messere (M.A., State University of New York at Oswego) is Professor of Broadcasting and Telecommunications and chairman of Communication Studies at SUNY Oswego. Messere has worked in radio and television and has an extensive background in production. He served as external assistant to FCC Commissioner Mimi Dawson and was the Faculty Fellow of the Annenberg Washington Program in Communication Policy Studies.

Lewis B. O'Donnell (Ph.D., Syracuse University) is Professor Emeritus of Communication Studies at SUNY Oswego. O'Donnell, former president of a radio station ownership group, has worked in a variety of management and performance positions in radio and television. He has been awarded the Frank Stanton Fellowship by the International Radio and Television Society and the New York State Chancellor's Award for Excellence in Teaching.

Contents

Preface

We are genuinely excited to bring you this new edition of *Announcing: Broadcast Communicating Today.*

This edition includes much new material on cutting-edge technologies, including the latest in audio and video computer editing, ethics for on-air people, and integration of knowledge into the world of broadcast announcing. It was a pleasure researching and writing the new material, and we hope you enjoy reading it.

Specifically, here is what to look for:

- **Tech Talk** boxes bring you the latest information on trends affecting the on-air communicator, including updated material on the World Wide Web, conducting research over the Internet, illustrations for computer-generated live-assist software, and the latest in digital workstations for radio and TV.

- Stand-alone **Think About It** boxes highlight ethical dilemmas faced by on-air personnel, including "freebies," sensational live-shot coverage, confrontational interviews, and editorializing during news programming.

- Many readers—faculty and students—have asked whether the field of broadcast announcing can be connected in a logical way to the liberal arts. The answer is assuredly yes! In **Connections** boxes, we point out some of the connections to and applications of such disciplines as rhetoric, social science research, logic, ethics, history of technology, and social history of music. When appropriate, we recommend further study in relevant courses. We believe you will find these features relevant and useful for the announcer who wants to bring a broad perspective to his or her work.

- Equipment photos and references to industry trends and events have also been thoroughly updated.

- We've updated practice copy from the Associated Press.

Throughout, we have retained the book's accessible style, which has garnered a steady readership for four previous editions. Featured again in the fifth edition are the popular **Focus on Technique** boxes, which highlight specific guidance on accent reduction, foreign pronunciation, ad-libbing, and radio staff announcing in the world of the modern format, talk radio, and sports play-by-play and color.

We are also pleased to offer an *Instructor's Manual* for this text. This edition of the manual will include invaluable assistance in teaching the course by providing sample syllabi, test questions, and chapter overviews. This will be available on the Wadsworth Communication Web site at http://communication.wadsworth.com/hausman/announcing.

Acknowledgments

We want to thank the following reviewers, who made many valuable suggestions while reading the manuscript for the fifth edition: David M. Guerra, University of Arkansas at Little Rock; Rebecca Kiser, Fort Hays State University; Bruce Manchester, George Mason University; Laura Ackerman Sherwood, University of Nebraska at Kearney; Judith M. Thorpe, University of Wisconsin at Oshkosh; Clayland H. Waite, Radford University. In addition, we would like to thank those reviewers who have helped us with past editions: Steve Anderson, University of Oklahoma; Ed Arke, Messiah College; Phil Blauer, Anchor/Producer, KSEQ-TV (ABC), Palm Springs; Warren Carter, Golden West College; Terry Draper, National Broadcasting School; Lincoln M. Furber, American University; Barry Goldfarb, Monroe Community College; Wayne Jarvis, University of Northern Iowa; Darrell E. Kitchell, Fullerton College; Robert Mendenhall, Southwestern Adventist College; Thomas Mullin, Eastern Wyoming College, Wheatland Program; Robert Musburger, University of Houston; Steven Shields, University of Wisconsin at Whitewater; and Roosevelt Wright, Syracuse University.

Many people have lent their expertise and we'd like to thank Bill Canning, Instructional Technologies at SUNY Oswego, Laura Hand at WSTM-TV Syracuse, Norm Goldstein at the Associated Press, Phil Sanchez at Tascam Corporation, Bob Ellison of Syntrillium Software, Dan Mathers at Clear Channel Communication, Bill Sacia at Automated Data Systems, and Charles Robbins at XM Satellite Radio.

Finally, we would like to thank our publisher, Holly Allen, our production manager, Mary Noel, and all the other people at Wadsworth Publishing who have provided a great deal of experience and expertise to ensure that the final product is as good as we can make it, and that it fully meets the needs of those who will use it.

Foreword

Broadcast announcing is one of the greatest jobs in the world. What other profession allows you to talk with thousands—or millions—of people at a time? But announcing is hard, demanding work, and don't let anybody tell you differently.

You need to sweat the details, think on your feet, and make fast and accurate decisions.

Announcing: Broadcast Communicating Today, Fifth Edition, will help you do just that. The authors—all experienced communicators—have provided a real-world view of the broadcasting business and sound advice and instruction about the skills you need to succeed.

Also, this book will help you develop something that is becoming increasingly critical in today's media—a well-rounded and thoughtful view of the world. The authors have related many useful aspects of history, ethics, and critical thinking to the process of going on mike or camera and getting your message across—while informing, entertaining, and inspiring your audience. And that's exactly what this business is about.

Enjoy this course and good luck with your career.

Spencer Christian

After twelve years of covering hurricanes, floods, and blizzards, Good Morning America's *traveling weatherman, Spencer Christian, is now enjoying a healthier pace of life back home in the Bay Area. He now reports the weather on KGO-TV, ABC 7 in San Francisco.*

The Communicator in Modern Media

*P*ower and magic attend the broadcast media. The mystique was there from the earliest days of broadcast history. Radio waves *could* be explained by science, but people were still fascinated by the idea that voices and music could somehow crystallize out of thin air. A cat whisker moving over a quartz crystal attached to primitive earphones could bring the distant sounds of concert music into the most remote prairie cabin. The simple "crystal set" quickly became a common feature in American homes. It became a popular pastime for families and individuals to don headsets and stare off into space while they used their imaginations to picture the events they were hearing (see Figure 1.1).

As radio developed and flourished, it became possible for virtually the entire nation to participate—in a weekly drama program, a comedy or variety show, a vivid description of a news event—at exactly the same moment. Never before had it been possible for the attention of such vast numbers of people to be focused on the same thing at the same time.

The power of this phenomenon was dramatically demonstrated by the famous Mercury Theater presentation of *War of the Worlds* on October 30, 1938. This dramatized invasion of "Martians" was mistaken for a real news event by millions of frightened listeners. Many people fled in panic from the supposed site of the invasion in New Jersey.

Only a short time later, a young journalist named Edward R. Murrow focused attention on ominous events across the sea (see Figure 1.2). Murrow's broadcasts from London during the war brought the sounds of war to millions of Americans. These sounds created deep empathy with the plight of Londoners who lived with the constant threat of destruction as Hitler's bombs fell on them night after night during World War II.

Many more examples of the broadcast media's dramatic impact can be cited. Live television pictures of the events surrounding the assassination of popular young President John F. Kennedy preceded the shooting of his alleged assassin on live television (see Figures 1.3 and 1.4). TV coverage let

Figure 1.1   People's fascination with early radio focused on the novelty of being able to hear the sounds of distant events immediately. This photo shows two family members in 1921, listening to the first mass-produced receiver for home entertainment.

© Bettmann/CORBIS

Figure 1.2   Edward R. Murrow broadcast reports from London during the German blitzkrieg at the outbreak of World War II. He is shown here at CBS headquarters in London.

© Bettmann-UPI/CORBIS

Figure 1.3   Jack Ruby (right) shoots Lee Harvey Oswald as he was being transferred from city to county jail in Dallas on November 24, 1963.

Figure 1.4   This photo, taken from the NBC-TV screen, shows Lee Harvey Oswald (right), alleged assassin of President John F. Kennedy, gasping in shock as he is shot by Jack Ruby (in the foreground, wearing hat, back to camera). Millions of television viewers saw the event as depicted in this photo.

Figure 1.5   Astronaut Edwin E. Aldrin descends the steps of the lunar module ladder as he prepares to walk on the moon. Fellow astronaut Neil Armstrong took this photo of his colleague.

© Bettmann-UPI/CORBIS

millions of viewers watch as Neil Armstrong made the first human footprint on the moon's dusty surface (see Figure 1.5). Sports coverage turned into a major news story as a devastating earthquake rocked San Francisco's Candlestick Park and much of the Bay Area just as ABC began pregame broadcasting before the third game of the 1989 World Series. Live coverage showed people toppling the Berlin Wall, ending Soviet control of East Germany and challenging it in Eastern Europe. As the attacks on the World Trade Center brought the nation to a standstill, we watched, transfixed in horror by the devastation and human tragedy. For three days, all the major television networks cleared their schedules to provide live coverage of the unfolding events. Recently, as this book went to press, television networks gave unprecedented coverage to the war with Iraq. The list of events is long. (See Box 1.1 and Figures 1.6 and 1.7.) Nearly everyone can relate personal experiences that were made dramatic and memorable by broadcasting's power.

Box 1.1

THE MEDIUM IS THE MESSAGE

The mid-to-late 1990s saw a classic example of what Marshall McLuhan meant by "the medium is the message." Increasingly, television became a live medium, and the on-air performer emerged as an increasingly powerful voice.

What do we mean by "the medium is the message?" The broadcast media became a part of the live, unfolding stories. The trend was firmly established in 1991 when new technology enabled live coverage of the Gulf War, a conflict that played out almost like a video game.

Then came O. J. Simpson (see Figure 1.6). The Simpson chase and trial magnetized the live TV audience and much of the radio audience as well, drawing people around their sets. The *coverage* of the case became a story as big as the case itself.

Figure 1.6

The O.J. Simpson trial in 1995 created continuing drama for TV and radio audiences as live-broadcast coverage made it possible for millions to follow the events from their homes.

SOURCE: AP/Wide World Photos

Continues

Box 1.1   Continued

Figure 1.7   *News coverage of the Monica Lewinsky scandal sparked a vigorous debate about the media's handling of the story.*

SOURCE: AP/Wide World Photos

And when President Clinton confronted allegations of a sexual relationship with White House Intern Monica Lewinsky (see Figure 1.7), the medium again became part of the story and part of the message.

The point? When the medium becomes the message, the obligations of the messenger become more onerous. The broadcast communicator—whose reach is now extended to the Web—must balance a sense of the newsworthy, the fair, and the ethical. And this principle applies to all communicators who reach the public in this increasingly media-saturated society, not just to newspeople.

Gone today is the "romance" that once stirred the imaginations of people huddled over crystal sets, plucking distant sounds from the "ether." We now take for granted our ability to tune into events anywhere in the world. But broadcasting is an even larger part of our daily lives than anyone could have imagined in its earliest days. Radio and television have become our eyes and ears on the world. We stay in touch as we drive, jog, and vacation. Cut off from this link with events, we feel deprived.

Given the amount of time we spend listening to and watching broadcast media, and given their influence on our lives, it's remarkable to realize how recent these developments are. And we do not yet fully understand how these developments have shrunk our globe and changed our prospects.

A Historical Overview

The discovery of electromagnetic waves by nineteenth-century German physicist Heinrich Hertz forms the basis of radio and television broadcasting. Guglielmo Marconi perfected the device that would allow the Hertzian waves to be put to such use. Working in Britain, the Italian inventor and businessman refined the technology, acquired patents, and set up an organizational structure to explore commercial applications for electromagnetic waves.

At the beginning of the twentieth century, the closest thing to instant communication was the telegraph. Marconi's development of radio communication in the early 1900s was viewed simply as a way to remove the need for wires in telegraphy. So the term *wireless* was applied to Marconi's radio technology.

One outgrowth of Marconi's work was ship-to-shore communication. When Marconi expanded his operations from Britain to the United States, this application of his inventions held the major promise of commercial success for his firm.

When the ocean liner *Titanic* sank in the Atlantic in 1912, the ship-to-shore wireless allowed the American public to read in their newspapers about the rescue efforts shortly after they occurred. A young wireless operator, David Sarnoff, sat for long hours at his telegraph key and relayed information from rescue ships to eager newspaper reporters.

Several years later, Sarnoff predicted that radio would become a "music box" that would bring quality entertainment to people far from cultural centers.

Radio's development into Sarnoff's music box was spurred by an invention developed in 1912 by Lee de Forest. De Forest's Audion tube allowed radio to go beyond its role as a wireless telegraph. It was easy to impose on radio waves the simple on-off changes necessary to transmit the dots and dashes of telegraphy. But enabling the medium to carry and then reproduce voice and music was much more complex. De Forest's work made the breakthrough.

Extensive application of de Forest's invention began in the era immediately after World War I. The Roaring Twenties were on the horizon. The "jazz age"

Figure 1.8   Old-style radio studio.

Photo courtesy of NBC/Globe Photos

was dawning, and many radio sets were the playthings of technically skilled tinkerers, but radio equipment was being manufactured for the home, as well. Soon nearly every family could tune in to the sounds of this exciting era.

Schedules in those days were hit or miss, and programs always origi-nated from a studio. Broadcasters took their roles seriously, and performers commonly wore formal clothes when appearing before the microphone (see Figure 1.8). Guest performers were brought in to fill up the broadcast hours. All programs were live. So that performers would not be intimidated by the technology, studios were usually richly furnished to look like sitting rooms. The microphones were often concealed among large houseplants; thus, the term "potted palm era" became a slang designation for this period.

These years gave birth to commercial radio. "Leasing" a radio station's airtime for delivery of a commercial message first took place in New York

City on August 28, 1922. A talky spiel broadcast over WEAF promoted a real estate development in Jackson Heights.

While radio was developing, networks also evolved as distinct entities. By connecting stations and broadcasting the same programs simultaneously, networks could offer high-quality programming on a regular basis. From the stations' standpoint, networks were needed to fill the long program hours that so quickly drained the resources of local operations.

Networks soon dominated radio programming. The first network, NBC, was developed in 1926 and evolved into two separate arms, known as the Red and Blue networks. NBC Blue later split from NBC and became ABC. CBS started in 1928. The networks occupied much of the attention of the U.S. radio listening audience for many years.

As radio developed through the 1930s and 1940s, its promise as a commercial medium ripened. Early advertising in radio used such devices as naming a performing group after the sponsor's product. Every time an announcer introduced the Cliquot Club Eskimos, the sponsor was mentioned. This soft-sell tactic was much favored over the less-dignified direct product pitch. But there were sometimes gross advertising excesses. Bizarre items such as Dr. Brinkley's Famous Goat Gland Medicine and other products were extolled in terms reminiscent of snake oil pitches.

Since then, advertising has dominated the broadcast media. Advertisers associated with stars, and products became known through catchy musical jingles. During radio's heyday in the 1940s and early 1950s, the distinction between program production and advertising blurred. Advertising agencies actually *produced* much of the programming, which was then delivered through the facilities of the stations. And advertising developed the one type of program most closely associated with this era of radio broadcasting—the soap opera still bears the name of its advertising connection.

Soap operas efficiently solved a major problem confronting the broadcast media, namely, the need to fill hour after hour of program schedules with entertainment that would attract audiences. The soap opera let writers work with a basic formula for establishing and developing a daily situation. All that was required was to introduce plot changes in the lives of the characters and to write dialogue that told the story. The extraordinary audience appeal of these imaginary everyday people made the soap opera a staple that has expanded to daytime television and now is a mainstay of evening television as well.

Radio programs of the 1930s and 1940s consisted of the various program types that we see today in modern television. Comedies like *My Friend Irma,* dramas like *Lights Out* and *The Goldbergs,* and westerns like *Gunsmoke* (see Figures 1.9 and 1.10) made up much of the evening programming schedules of the major radio networks.

Many of the most popular programs were sponsored by a single advertiser whose product became associated with the program. Many of the top radio programs were produced by the advertising agencies that handled the

Figure 1.9

Radio drama enacted in NBC radio studio with the aid of a sound effects man and groaning victims (on floor) on "Lights Out."

© Bettmann/CORBIS

Figure 1.10

William Conrad, who went on to television fame in "Cannon" and "Jake and the Fat Man," starred on the radio version of "Gunsmoke," which aired on CBS radio.

© Bettmann/CORBIS

advertising of the sponsors. In some instances, the networks had little control over the programming they supplied to their affiliated stations.

The close association of advertiser and program production and the lack of supervision by broadcasters led to a crisis in the 1950s. The public found out that sponsors, producers, and agencies rigged some ad agency–produced TV quiz programs to inject more drama and excitement into the shows. When the quiz scandal was uncovered, the advertising community lost much of its control over the programming function of broadcasting. And the broadcast industry became more involved in the content of its programs.

Radio journalism initially met resistance from newspapers. Publishers feared that if people could listen to news on radio, they would stop buying newspapers. Although that situation never developed, radio news had great impact in the uneasy days before and during World War II. The ability to transport the listener to the scene of an event and to hear the voices of newsmakers "shrank" the globe and led to a growing awareness that *nations cannot live in isolation from one another.* This revolution in thinking led to the development of the modern broadcast media.

The First Announcers

The people who filled the airwaves with their talents created a tradition in early broadcasting. They developed a specialty that had roots in show business.

The announcer was part salesperson, part master of ceremony, part sophisticated worldly interpreter. Early radio announcers performed a wide variety of tasks. The announcer had to read commercial and news copy, pronounce foreign names, be conversant with classical music, and be knowledgeable about current performers and musical trends.

The announcer was expected to be witty and sophisticated and was perceived as performing, rather than talking, when on the air. By the mid-1930s, radio broadcasting had become the era of the golden-voiced announcer. A deep male voice was considered essential for success in radio.

Delivery was stylized and emphatic. Announcers used a distinctive and instantly recognized style of speaking *that was heard nowhere else but on radio.* Anyone who talked like an announcer in normal conversation would have been considered strange, to say the least. Yet this style was expected and demanded on the air.

How the Modern Media Evolved

By the end of World War II, broadcasting had begun to change dramatically. The emergence of television led directly to developments that characterize contemporary broadcasting.

Television, which became a major force in the early 1950s, turned out to be much more than radio with pictures. Television revolutionized the lives of Americans everywhere. Radio engaged our imaginations and provided stimulus for the theater of the mind, but television allowed us to react with less involvement. It filled empty hours effortlessly. By merely turning a knob, one could be in direct visual touch with arresting activity that occupies the senses. Television spread rapidly.

And what about radio after television captured the U.S. psyche? Many observers felt the radio was on its deathbed. They argued that sound alone could not compete with sound and pictures. The program forms that had been the bread and butter of radio were being usurped by television.

But radio found a new role, a new application of Sarnoff's music box theory. By specializing in the modern availability and popularity of recorded music, and making this music available to the public day and night, radio emerged as a healthy new entity. At the same time, radio news evolved into a short format. News was given in brief doses at frequent intervals so that listeners could tune in and quickly hear about developments. With the newly developed transistor radio, the public found that radio could go anywhere, and the medium became a constant companion, keeping the listener company during driving, picnicking, or studying.

As radio flexed its muscles in this new role, it learned to appeal to advertisers more effectively by targeting specific audience segments. The music selected for programming could attract one segment of the mass audience; then advertisers who wanted to reach this group with a specific message could easily do so.

Developments in Announcing

Announcers of this era began to break away from the stilted formality that had characterized the medium in the 1930s and 1940s. The disc jockeys of the 1950s took their lead from radio personalities like Cleveland's Alan Freed and Philadelphia's Dick Clark. The style was fast paced. The DJ became one of the many elements making up a steady stream of sound that came to be widely known as top-40 radio.

The energy of the style captured the imaginations of American youth and became a focal point of a national youth culture. Rhythm and blues music merged with "hillbilly" music to form rock and roll.

And the role of the radio announcer changed. The DJ became an architect of fun. It was his job (the field was very much male dominated) to inject energy. Rather than merely inform listeners about program elements, it became the announcer's task to fill the spaces between records with zany patter and a fast-paced delivery of time, temperature, and weather interspersed with information about the music and performers that dominated the airways of top-40 stations.

The traditional announcer-host remained a fixture of many stations until the early 1970s, however. The style of this type of on-air personality was much the same as the announcer of the 1930s and 1940s. As the youth culture came to dominate broadcasting, however, the traditional announcer became rare. Today the only vestige of the sophisticated man-about-town style is in the nostalgia sound, typified by the "Music of Your Life" format.

The imprint of the early rock DJs has carried forward into the style heard on modern stations that program the contemporary hit radio (CHR) format.

Meanwhile, television became the mass entertainer, offering something to everyone. At both the local and national levels, news has developed as an entertaining and moneymaking product appealing to a broad audience. Situation comedy, adventures, and other kinds of entertainment rivet vast audiences, and families today gather around an electronic hearth, which one astute social observer has termed "the cool fire."

Current Trends

Today's technology promises to improve the media and the number and variety of program forms that exist. The emergence of the videocassette recorder and the increasing abundance offered by cable and satellite technology provide an array of choices.

It seems safe to predict that modern developments and technology will reinforce certain trends that have emerged:

1. *More program choices, and increased specialization of the programs themselves.* Business reporting, for example, has developed into a distinct specialty, and certain cable and broadcast outlets offer extensive segments devoted to it.

2. *Increased importance of one-to-one contact between announcer and audience, especially in the supersegmented radio markets.* With this development comes the continued decline in the use of the stylized "announcer voice."

3. *The ongoing regulatory debate about the range of expression permissible on broadcast media.* The questions of what constitutes indecency and whether or not such regulatory agencies as the Federal Communications Commission (FCC) can establish standards that don't trample on constitutional guarantees of free expression can affect the program content of both radio and television. Broadcasting that pushes the limits of such expression is likely to experience increasing pressure from the FCC and Congress to conform more closely to the standards of decency shared by the American mainstream.

4. *The ever-increasing importance of news, especially live news.* Technological advances, including portable transmitting units and compact audio and video gear, make further inroads into on-the-spot news

coverage more likely and place additional demands on announcers' ad-libbing skills. For example, during the war with Iraq, network correspondents used satellite picture-phones to transmit live coverage of the battles.

5. *Consolidation in the media, particularly in radio.* Group radio and television station owners have reduced the number of personnel needed to run several stations at once. Automation and economies of scale make it possible to do more with fewer hands.

These and other trends have strongly affected all segments of the broadcast industry, but they relate specifically to the on-air performer in a number of ways.

Era of the Communicator

This book focuses on the communicator in the broadcast media. We use the term *announcer* because it remains in common usage and still serves in industry job descriptions. Eventually this outdated term will be replaced. A modern on-air performer does not simply announce. He or she entertains, converses, informs, and provides companionship, but rarely proclaims a program element in the formal, stylized way of the old-era announcer.

The Communicator's Role

Today's on-air broadcaster is a *communicator,* a catalyst for a message. Whether the message is news, commercial copy, an interview segment, or a game show, the communicator's task is to serve as a conduit for communication between the originator of the message and the audience.

The traditional announcer with the stylized delivery is no longer the backbone of the industry. He has been replaced by professionals who can convey greater intimacy, the image of a real person rather than a disembodied voice or a talking head.

A program director of one major market station, for example, wants air personalities to come across as "next-door neighbors." Another broadcast executive disdains the type of performer who speaks, as if from a pulpit, "to everyone out there in radio-land." One television news director specifies that staff members must show credibility and generate trust.

The communicator in the modern media must use more than good diction and appearance, although these qualities are undeniably important. He or she must also use qualities of personality and physical presence in the job. In addition to being adept at conveying the facts, a news reporter must show that he or she understands the story and is a trustworthy source of news, while communicating the story in a way that holds audience attention.

A communicator-announcer doing a radio commercial can no longer get by with the stylized, rhythmic affectations of the announcers of radio's golden age. Most producers of commercials today, for example, ask announcers to sound natural. That means that the delivery, as such, should not be noticeable. The ideas are the most important aspect, and the announcer's job is to *interpret* and *communicate* them, not *announce* them to all those people in radio-land.

On-air jobs today frequently call for specialized knowledge and skills. In the 1930s and 1940s, the same radio announcer was sometimes expected to host an interview show, do a classical music program, deliver commercials, introduce various types of programs, and read the weather report. Today's broadcast communicator usually is assigned a much narrower range of tasks.

For example, if an early-era announcer had to introduce classical music pieces during a short segment of his shift, he was expected to pronounce the names of the works, the composers, and the artists properly. But a modern radio announcer rarely encounters a brief segment of classical music. If classical music is played, it is generally within the entire format of the station, and the announcer has been hired partly because of his or her in-depth knowledge of the music, its history, and the styles of particular artists. Mere knowledge of pronunciation is not enough. Duties of a modern radio announcer do vary widely, especially in smaller stations, but the tasks are confined to a more focused area. Television on-air duties are typically even more sharply defined than in radio.

This is not to imply that you can succeed by becoming a specialist in one area and learning nothing else. A generalized background is important, for reasons that we point out throughout this text.

Jobs may overlap, especially in smaller stations where a radio staff announcer may double as a TV weather anchor. As you advance in market size, your duties will generally become more specific. Primarily, though, most on-air jobs fall into six basic categories (see Box 1.2).

Responsibilities and Ethics

A communicator has a great deal of responsibility, both to the employer and to the audience. Much has been made of the broadcasting's potential to manipulate. A variety of industry standards and government regulations address this issue.

Like professionals in most fields, the broadcaster must follow principles and standards that guard against misuse or abuse of the power and influence of the media. Considerations of accuracy, fairness, honesty, and integrity apply not only to broadcast journalism, where they are paramount, but to all on-air operations as well. We discuss these considerations as they apply, throughout the book.

Box 1.2

WHAT KIND OF BROADCASTING JOB DO YOU WANT?

Broadcasting has many different specialties in broadcasting, and you will probably find yourself doing one of these jobs:

1. Radio staff announcers, typically thought of as "disc jockeys" (DJs).
2. Radio or television news reporters: general-assignment reporters who file reports from the field, and anchors who deliver news from a studio.
3. Play-by-play sports announcers and sports anchors, in television and radio.
4. TV and radio weather reporters and anchors, who are now often certified meteorologists.
5. Talk-show hosts for radio and television.
6. Specialty announcers, such as commercial voice-over announcers. Stations do not ordinarily hire announcers only to do commercials. Instead, these duties are assigned to staff announcers or freelance announcers and actors. Other specialties include narrators and hosts of movie presentations.

A Career Self-Appraisal

Preparing for a career as an on-air performer begins with an honest appraisal of talents, qualities, and abilities. Strengths and weaknesses must be examined honestly; this is no time for rationalization and excuse making. Make a sincere effort to discover whether you have what is needed to succeed as a broadcast communicator.

Do You Have What It Takes?

It is no disgrace to decide early in life, after a candid look at yourself, that on-air work is not for you. The broadcast announcing course in which you are now enrolled will be the first indicator. If your performance is excellent to outstanding, you stand a chance in this highly competitive field. Keep evaluating yourself as you work through the course and through this text.

PHYSICAL REQUIREMENTS Experience and critique will tell whether you have the physical tools necessary to succeed. For example, although a deep voice with "rounded tones" is no longer essential, and the field is open to women as well as to men, an announcer does need a certain amount of vocal strength and a versatile voice with a pleasing quality. Severe speech impediments, voice problems, or a pronounced foreign or regional accent must be evaluated realistically. If uncorrected or uncorrectable, they will limit your chances of success.

Poor appearance—to which obesity, bad teeth, and skin problems contribute—will certainly interfere with advancement in television. Overall poor health is a detriment on the air because the work is physically taxing and the hours demanding.

EDUCATIONAL REQUIREMENTS   As soon as possible, evaluate your educational preparation. Most broadcasters who hire talent advise that it's important to be broadly educated. Some people who aspire to broadcasting careers make the mistake of concentrating on narrow, vocational courses. But to be an effective communicator, you need to be able to discuss and recognize concepts from a variety of disciplines. The news reporter who is ignorant of political science and history will sooner or later misunderstand a story element and blunder badly on air. A radio announcer who doesn't know how to pronounce and use words will often appear foolish. *Both these flaws will hinder careers,* as will any on-air betrayal of a lack of education.

Whether gained through formal training or through reading and life experience, education is the best tool for success in this industry.

Also, the ability to write well—an outgrowth of the total educational process—is essential for almost all broadcasters.

EMOTIONAL REQUIREMENTS   Whether you are meeting a deadline for a news story or coming up with a funny ad-lib during a music program, you're sure to find stress in broadcasting. For one thing, your job will typically be performed before thousands of people, and that creates stress. Second, "time is money" in broadcasting. Tasks must be performed quickly and accurately to avoid retakes. Broadcasting is a constant race against the clock, and the clock never loses. An announcement slated for 5:59:30 P.M. must be made precisely at 5:59:30, and in most cases it had better be finished exactly at 6:00:00 because that is *precisely* when the news is fed from the network.

The ability to handle stress of this magnitude is critical because for some people stress problems can become emotionally crippling.

Is Broadcasting for You?

It is also important to look honestly at the broadcast industry as a career field, a field that has been described variously as a golden path of opportunity and as a snake pit.

NATURE OF THE BUSINESS   By its very nature, commercial broadcasting is a money-oriented industry. Depending on the level at which you work, you may be paid very well or very poorly. Job security is not particularly good in the industry in general, and it is especially poor for on-air performers. Except for noncommercial radio and television, ratings are money. (Ratings and market studies are also becoming increasingly important to public broadcasting programmers and fund-raisers.) As an on-air performer, you must produce ratings, and you will be looking for work if those ratings don't materialize. To add to the problem, consider that the situation is not always fair: a performer with good on-air abilities may be poorly rated because of inept station programming or an unfavorable time slot. You may come to work one day and find that the station has been sold to new owners who plan a new format, or that the station has replaced live announcers with voice-tracking or that budget cuts have eliminated your job. We have talked with several young television newspeople who were ready to get out of broadcasting because of the uncertainty and insecurity of the field. One news producer had just been hired as part of a "new commitment to news" at a medium-market television station. Three weeks after leaving his former job in another part of the country, he was called in by his new employers and told that his job had been eliminated because of budget cuts.

Careers can take off quickly and rise steadily. You may also, however, find yourself waiting for that big break for years, traveling from station to station. Sometimes that big break comes. Sometimes it doesn't.

BENEFITS AND DRAWBACKS   On the plus side of broadcasting as a career is the sense of importance and the degree of celebrity status that accrue even at lower levels of the business. It is also a job that gives a lot of personal satisfaction, a job that many people do for free.

In the highest levels of broadcasting, the money is excellent, and it is not uncommon to make a good living at the medium-market level. As large corporations increase their involvement in the broadcasting industry, fringe benefits and salaries have been improving at all levels. It is not as common as it once was for radio stations to be staffed entirely by those willing to work at minimum wage, but minimum salaries do exist in small markets nevertheless.

Those who make good salaries have climbed a vast and heartless pyramid. For every announcer in Boston or Chicago, hundreds or thousands of announcers work for poor salaries in small markets while waiting hungrily for an opportunity to move into the big time.

A REALISTIC EVALUATION   Any on-air person knows that there's no greater feeling of accomplishment than that generated by those good days, those magic moments. But there are lows for most of the highs. Hard work may or may not be rewarded. The excitement of the business may make every day a new challenge, but stress may take a serious toll.

So how do you make a choice? There is no pat answer, but we sincerely hope this book will help you decide. When you have finished the chapters

Connections

THE BROADCASTER AND SOCIAL SCIENCES

An on-air performer wields a great deal of influence. In general, people take your word seriously and put great faith in information they receive from the media.

Almost every on-air person can tell a story about an off-hand remark, or one made in jest, that was taken literally by at least one listener or viewer.

Social scientists, researchers who study the behavior of people in societies, have only recently (in the last half-century or so) turned their attention to media effects. The reason for this is that media are relatively new additions to the society. But even though researchers cannot give highly specific formulae for how the media affect society, we know that media are enormously powerful.

An interesting sidelight is that one of the milestones of early communication research was undertaken precisely because a broadcast performer said something in a drama that people took seriously—with some disastrous effects.

Here's the story:

On October 30, 1938, listeners who tuned in to CBS radio heard an announcer interrupt a music program with a bulletin: An unusual cloud of gas had been observed on the planet Mars.

That was interesting, but not earthshaking, and the announcer returned the audience to the concert.

A little later, another bulletin interrupted the music, and the announcer implored observatories to watch the situation carefully.

More music . . . and more bulletins. A "meteorite" had landed in New Jersey. But reporters at the scene saw that it was no mere piece of stone. The top opened up. As a radio newsman reported this, death rays suddenly cut down the observers standing by the impact site.

Martians marched from the spaceship. They devastated the U.S. military sent to stop them. War machines sliced through the cities. Reporters were cut off in mid-sentence by death rays. At last, only the choked and quavering voice of an amateur radio operator remained on air.

"Isn't anybody there? . . . Isn't anybody . . ."

As you certainly have surmised, that was fiction, a radio play based on an H. G. Wells story. But here is a true account of what happened next. You might find it stranger than fiction.

Continues

Connections Continued

RADIO LISTENERS IN PANIC, TAKING WAR DRAMA AS FACT

Many Flee Homes to Escape "Gas Raid From Mars"—Phone Calls Swamp Police

A wave of mass hysteria seized thousands of radio listeners throughout the nation between 8:15 and 9:30 o'clock last night when a broadcast of a dramatization of H. G. Wells's fantasy, "The War of the Worlds," led thousands to believe that an interplanetary conflict had started with invading Martians spreading wide death and destruction in New Jersey and New York.

The broadcast, which disrupted households, interrupted religious services, created traffic jams and clogged communications systems, was made by Orson Welles, who as the radio character, "The Shadow," used to give "the creeps" to countless child listeners. This time at least a score of adults required medical treatment for shock and hysteria.

—*The New York Times*
Monday, October 31, 1938

Why did people believe a radio play recounting, of all things, an invasion of Martians armed with death rays? One fundamental factor was that radio was a relatively new medium, and at the time it had been reliably bringing to a stunned United States reports about the advance of Hitler in Europe. Problems seemed much more distant and less immediate in the days before electronic mass communications. In 1938, the importation of the sounds of war into the living room was improbable, but nevertheless it was real.

So the Martian story came over an unfamiliar conveyance that had, up until this time, provided a quite reliable new view of events in Europe—which, in 1938, seemed about as far away as Mars.

But what truly puzzled observers was that many of the listeners who panicked ignored several explicit announcements by Orson Welles that this was, in fact, a prank and a work of fiction. Nor did they bother to check other radio stations to confirm the incident. What made the incident *particularly* troubling at the time is that the world was on the verge of war, and the power of the media to persuade was a topic heavy on the minds of those who viewed the success of Hitler's propaganda films.

So, why did this happen? What did it say about the effects of media on the populace?

We had been vaguely worried about the effects of media for a couple of decades, beginning shortly after the introduction of motion pictures. There are many stories about moviegoers who were simply dumbfounded to see events unfold, bigger than life, before their eyes. It was widely re-

Continues

Connections *Continued*

ported that when motion pictures were first shown in a rural area, first-time moviegoers shrieked in panic and clambered out of the theater when a stampede of cinematic horses thundered toward them.

That story is probably apocryphal.[1] And that is a perfect illustration of the need for communications research! First, we needed to know if such events really occurred and, secondly, whether motion pictures really could so profoundly affect people's grasp of reality.

Such investigation began in earnest in 1929, when a series of research efforts called the Payne Fund studies were undertaken. The Payne Fund studies attempted to gauge how powerful movies really were, and that research indicated movies had enormous power.

But there was a flaw in the Payne Fund studies. Investigators simply *asked* teenagers if movies had a powerful impact on their life, and the teenagers, possibly wanting to accommodate the researchers, said yes. In hindsight, we can laugh at such mistakes, but hindsight should also allow us to be a bit charitable in our evaluation of past efforts. Social science measurement techniques were then in their infancy, and the notion that *the way a question was asked could drastically influence the outcome of the response* was not yet clear to investigators.

The Payne Fund studies led researchers to believe that the power of movies figuratively pierced into the psyche of the person watching and listening. This notion became known as the "magic bullet" or the "hypodermic needle" theory of media effects. The "hypodermic needle" phraseology reflected the idea that a media manipulator could "inject" beliefs into unwilling subjects.

But do media really have such targeted and powerful effects? Would anyone be vulnerable to a magic bullet? Those questions were important for a number of reasons, not the least of which is that behavior of the masses—if the theories were true—could be manipulated by Svengali-like media-masters who would overtake the evolving media.

Communications scholar Hadley Cantril set to work studying media effects, to see if the magic bullet theory held true. His subject was not movies, but the Martian "invasion."

The *War of the Worlds* radio play (see Figure 1.11) used the technique of a "newscaster" interrupting normal programming to report that strange gas clouds had been sighted on Mars. Later, the music was interrupted again to inform listeners that a strange craft had landed in Grovers

---

[1] Meaning "legendary," or "unsubstantiated even though they have been often repeated." The word means false or counterfeit and comes from a Greek word meaning "hidden."

Continues

Connections Continued

Figure 1.11

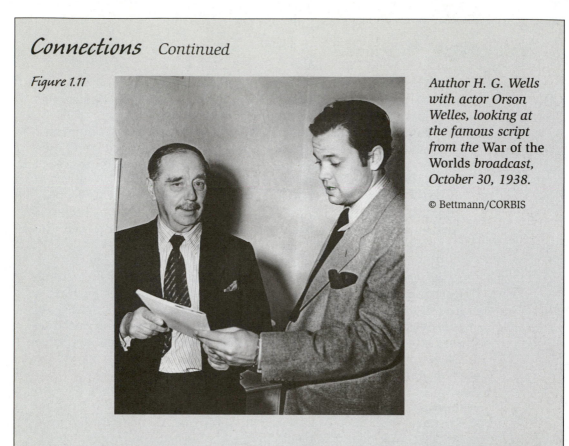

Author H. G. Wells with actor Orson Welles, looking at the famous script from the War of the Worlds *broadcast, October 30, 1938.*

© Bettmann/CORBIS

Mill, New Jersey. (That was a quite a departure from the original British setting of H. G. Wells's story, but Orson Welles—no relation to H. G.—had been driving through New Jersey a day or two before the show and had randomly picked Grovers Mill from a road map.)

Even though there were frequent reminders that this was a dramatization—reminders that carried something of an urgent tone after panicked listeners started calling the radio station—many people still assumed that the events were real. Indeed, a fabric of believability was woven into the narrative; the "newscaster" would conduct a breathless interview with an "expert" and then return the program back to the network . . . only to return moments later, agitated, with reports of Martian war machines on the rampage.

Actually, the vast majority of listeners did not for one second believe that Martians were invading the earth. But why did some people see through the thinly disguised ruse while others disintegrated into a panic?

Cantril found that the *War of the Worlds* scare was a living laboratory for his studies of media effects. After extensive interviews and data

Continues

Connections *Continued*

collection he theorized that it was *level of education and critical thinking skills* by the audience that separated the believers from the nonbelievers. Cantril would later theorize that those skills also enabled people to resist propaganda.

Cantril's studies refuted the magic bullet theory (the conclusion of the Payne Fund studies). Whereas earlier it was believed that media could be used to precisely target anyone, Cantril stated that the effects of media were weaker than first thought and that media manipulation was effective primarily on the unsophisticated and unintelligent.

Given that media affected some people some of the time, *how much* did it affect them and *how* did media go about insinuating these effects? The next major study to examine media effects tackled precisely these questions. Called "The People's Choice," the study was conducted by a team of researchers led by Paul Lazarsfeld.

In 1940, Lazarsfeld's researchers studied voter behavior in Erie County, Pennsylvania. The goal was to determine how media affected the way people decided which candidate to vote for. Specifically, the researchers tracked *change* in voter preference over a six-month period.

The results:

- Political advertising converted only 8 percent of voters from their original positions.

- The major effect of media appeared to be *reinforcing* beliefs originally held. In other words, advertising was more likely to get a committed voter *to believe more strongly* in his or her original choice than to *change his or her mind.* (This was before negative campaign ads.)

- In many cases, advertising did not have a direct effect. Instead, voters were influenced by opinion leaders—powerful people whom they respected—within their community. Media often worked *indirectly* by affecting opinion leaders who in turn affected other members of the community.

Lazarsfeld's study concluded that media had *minimal* effects, and that many of those effects were indirect and difficult to measure. Many scholars today continue to believe in the minimal effects theory.

However, later researchers reexamined strong media theories, and contended that media do have a strong influence, but it is difficult to measure. Most researchers today believe that the media have strong effects, sometimes indirect, and have woven themselves inextricably into our everyday lives.

Tech Talk

WEB TV AND RADIO

The World Wide Web, the graphic section of the Internet, offers a new venue for broadcasters. Audio and (fairly primitive) full-motion video can be transmitted over the Web, and many broadcast outlets find this new medium to be a promising new way to reach audiences. And what's really exciting from the video producer's point of view is that the Web allows one person to create video and "broadcast" or "bitcast" it to the entire planet.

Anyone beginning a career in video is well advised to become Web literate in a hurry, because that is where many future jobs may be created.

A Look at Radio and TV on the Web

During the last few years the fortunes of Web radio have gone up and down. Several years ago, many radio stations started to rebroadcast their signals over the Web in anticipation of creating a new venue for listeners. For example, many people who worked in an office setting with a computer could now tune into their favorite radio stations while at work.

In 2001, the situation changed because the royalties for music that radio stations would have to pay for webcasting skyrocketed. Many radio and television stations pulled the plug on Internet broadcasting. Congress passed new legislation in 2002 that provided for lower royalty payments. As we wrote this text, there was some speculation that radio webcasting would return.

Regardless of whether or not a station broadcasts on the Web almost all radio and television stations maintain strong Web sites. Radio Web sites have information relevant to their listeners, such as restaurant reviews, breaking news, and text features such as the current pop charts on their sites. Stations try to make these sites informational and fun to visit. For example, New York City pop station Z100 integrates a games section along with a webzine related to Z100 programming (Figure 1.12).

Television on the Web generally consists of sites where video clips can be downloaded, such as CNN's large site (www.cnn.com) or "streamed." Although most streaming video produces a small picture of fairly low resolution, newer media players, such as the Quicktime 6 player, are capable of producing higher quality audio and video playback.

C-SPAN, which features many interview programs with "talking head" shots, uses streaming video to replicate portions of its entire broadcast day on its Web site, www.C-SPAN.org.

Continues

Tech Talk   Continued

Figure 1.12   *New York City's Z100 Web site presents an array of information.*

Screen shot courtesy of Clear Channel Radio/WHTZ-FM, NY

Getting Started in Web Broadcasting

First, you need to get on the Web. Most colleges have excellent Web access, and all Internet service providers can set you up with the correct browser software. (A browser is a program that allows you to view Web pages. The most popular are Microsoft Explorer and Netscape Navigator.) If you are a novice to the Web, don't worry. Plenty of starting points are available to help you learn its workings and structure. Try logging onto *Wired Magazine's* Web site at www.wired.com, or look at Yahoo's portal (a gateway to the Web) at www.yahoo.com. Both are good starting places for Web-based adventures.

Continues

Tech Talk Continued

Figure 1.13 *Many news sites such as CNN.com make the Web a news junkie's paradise.*

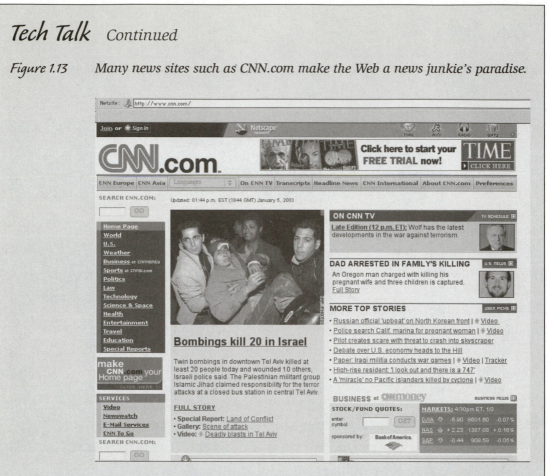

Finding Broadcast Outlets Stations on the Web

Up to speed on the Web? Then the next step is to tune into Web radio and TV. You may need some special additions to your browser (you can download media players at www.webcasting.com), but the easiest way to find out is attempting to tune in. If you're missing the right software, the radio station Web site will usually instruct you about how to download it.

One of the most convenient stops for finding Web radio is the BRS Web Radio home page at www.web-radio.fm/. There you can search for a station by call letters or formats. Another good site is Yahoo Radio

Continues

Tech Talk Continued

Figure 1.14   *Fans of C-SPAN can access its Web site to probe more deeply into C-SPAN's public affairs offerings.*

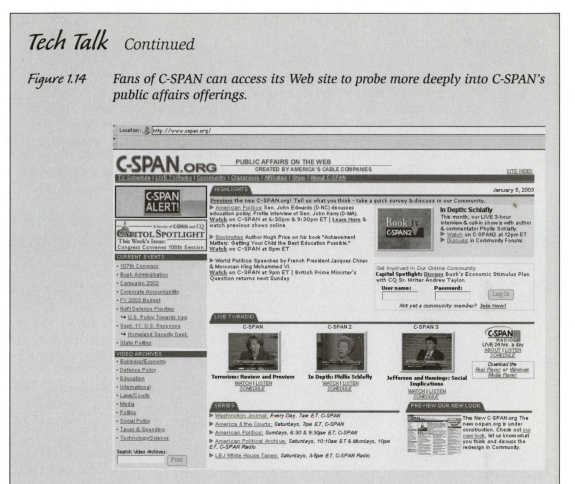

Screen shot courtesy of C-SPAN

(radio.yahoo.com). You can browse this site based on formats or choose from featured music selections. Happy Web surfing!

Software for the Web

Several programs, called streaming media programs, take care of the complex task of transmitting audio, and in some cases video, over the Web. Among the most common are Microsoft Media Player, Apple QuickTime, RealPlayer, and VivoActive. But be sure to tune into a Web site first before you download. The necessary components may already be loaded into your browser.

Continues

Tech Talk   Continued

Putting your radio or TV station on air is a little more complicated than receiving, but modern technology is simplifying the task. The same companies that produce the free listening or viewing software also sell (usually for a quite reasonable price) the necessary software to transmit the signal. Their respective Web sites contain detailed information on the process.

If you are affiliated with a college, you probably have access to a very good internal Web infrastructure, meaning it's likely that you would be able to put your station on the Web with minimal hassle.

and exercises, you should have a realistic picture of what is required and where your particular strengths and weaknesses lie.

If you decide to pursue the profession of on-air broadcasting and performance, you will be entering a field that offers tough standards but wonderful rewards. You, too, will feel the unparalleled excitement of participation in important and significant moments.

The world of broadcasting, in fact, is a great succession of moments, like the ones Edward R. Murrow transmitted in the dark days of the Battle of Britain, and in the social drama reflected in television images of women reservists leaving husbands and children for military duty in the Persian Gulf. Those moments have been captured by a system of modern media that is stunning in its capabilities: we can be anywhere on the globe in an instant, and never be out of touch with entertainment, companionship, or news. Today, the study of media helps us understand the significance of broadcasting these events (see Connections: The Broadcaster and Social Sciences).

The nature of broadcasting continues to evolve. Radio and television stations are experimenting with the World Wide Web as an ancillary channel of information. Tech Talk provides some insight into what's happening.

Improving Your Speaking Voice

*M*ost good broadcast voices are made, not born. True, many announcers have an extra share of native talent, but most of us learn effective vocal skills by practice.

This chapter lays a foundation on which you can build a clear, powerful, and professional-sounding speaking voice. After you have learned mechanics of posture, projection, and diction, you'll be able to practice those fundamentals not only during classroom sessions, but also lifelong, on the job.

These mechanics are important because a good-quality voice is an entry-level qualification for almost any on-air position. In broadcasting, voice quality is one of the first points on which people judge you. In radio, it is just about the only one. Your voice is what you *are* to the listener. This text steers clear of the "rounded tones and golden throat" approach to broadcasting, but having a pleasing voice is important. Remember that the emphasis is on a *pleasing* voice, not necessarily a deep, booming, overpowering voice.

Talent coaches frequently point out that the most successful announcers are those who have learned, one way or another, to refine their speech patterns, often by removing offending regionalisms, and by learning to speak in a well-articulated style. It can take significant effort to overcome speech problems, and most successful anchors and reporters have worked hard to ensure that their speech is clearly understandable.

This chapter suggests ways to make the most of your voice, to use it as effectively as possible. We also discuss ways to eliminate problems that could disqualify you from on-air employment, such as diction problems, poor voice quality, a severe foreign accent, and regionalism.

And we explain how to protect your voice from abuse by relaxing the mechanism. This technique also improves voice quality.

Voice instruction is worthwhile for anyone who speaks for a living, and it is of prime importance to an announcer. Often, voice and diction receive cursory treatment in broadcast performance courses. One reason, perhaps, is the feeling that the only way to deal with speech and voice problems is to get help from a professional therapist. And it's true no broadcasting text could possibly cure stuttering or a severe speech impediment. For such disorders, consult a speech pathologist.

However, many problems broadcasters face are simply the result of bad habits, and this is where a full treatment of the subject can be beneficial. You *can* improve the quality of your voice by practicing some easy exercises. You *can* make your diction more crisp by acquiring an awareness of common problems and by practicing with a tape recorder. Many of the solutions are simple.

How Your Voice Works

The vocal mechanism is a marvelous device and has certainly come a long way from the early days of human evolution, when the apparatus was primarily a sphincter that could be manipulated to form a grunt. We can still grunt, but we can also use the vocal apparatus to form an incredible range of sounds.

When you are working on exercises to develop your voice, it helps to know the structure you are using. For instance, tightness in the throat can be more easily overcome if you understand the musculature of the region. In **diaphragmatic breathing,** it's important to understand just where the diaphragm is and what it does.

You do not need to memorize all the structures of the breathing and vocal apparatus, so we show only the basics. For further information, investigate classes in basic speech production, almost certainly available in your institution. In addition to classes in normal speech production, you will benefit from exposure to singing instruction, even if you entertain no ambitions as a singer and have no talent for singing.

Vocal Anatomy

The mechanism that produces your voice is tied to your respiratory system (see Figure 2.1). This is important to know for a number of reasons, not least of which is the action of your diaphragm. Your lungs extract oxygen from the air, but they don't suck air in or propel it out. That function is performed primarily by your diaphragm, a muscle that extends across the base of your chest. It is connected by fibers and tendons to your sternum (breastbone) in front, to your ribs at the sides, and to your vertebrae in back. When you inhale, your diaphragm contracts, pushing your intestines down and out. That is why your abdomen should expand when you breathe in. When you exhale

Figure 2.1   How you breathe.

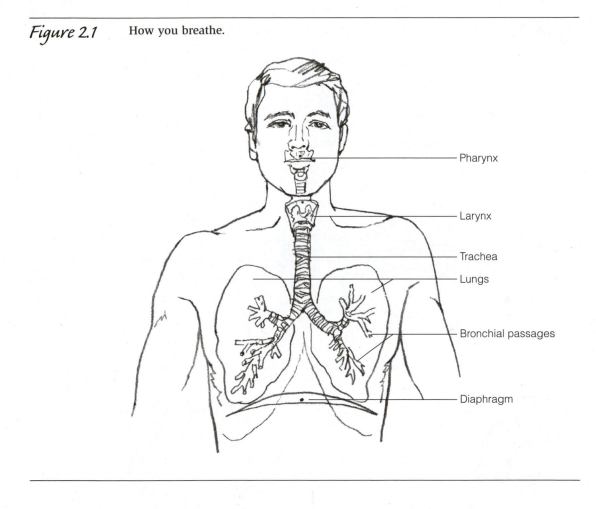

Pharynx

Larynx

Trachea

Lungs

Bronchial passages

Diaphragm

during speech, your diaphragm relaxes and is pushed upward by your abdominal muscles. Air in your chest cavity is compressed and forced out through your *trachea.*

The trachea is the airway leading from your chest to your *larynx.* The trachea is the point at which a number of airway tubes, including the bronchial tubes, are joined together. Bronchitis is an inflammation of the bronchial tubes; through experience with this common malady, most people are keenly aware of the location of the bronchial tubes.

The larynx (see Figure 2.2a) is often called the "voice box." The larynx is cartilage, a tough, somewhat flexible and gristly material. Several different cartilages make up the larynx. The most important are the *thyroid* cartilage, which protrudes from the neck and forms what we call the "Adam's apple" (larger in men), and the *cricoid* cartilage, which connects to the thyroid

Figure 2.2   The larynx. (a) In this roughly tube-shaped structure, vocal cords are suspended across the tube. (b) Vocal cords open during quiet breathing. This is the view you would have looking directly down someone's throat. (c) Vocal cords closed during phonation.

cartilage. These cartilages form a roughly tubular structure in which the vocal cords are suspended.

The vocal cords—more properly called vocal folds, since they're not really cords—are membranes that come together across the cavity of the larynx. There are two folds, and during the process of producing voice, known as **phonation,** they stretch across the cavity. The easiest way to visualize the vocal cords is to see them as if you were looking down someone's throat, as shown in Figure 2.2b.

A number of muscles contribute to speech. The *intrinsic* muscles of the larynx are entirely contained within the larynx. The *extrinsic* muscles are outside the larynx and serve in speech, singing, and swallowing.

Above the larynx is the *pharynx,* the part of the vocal tract that exits into the mouth and the back of the nasal passages. Constricting muscles in the pharynx can close off the respiratory tract above the back of the throat. The pharynx connects with nasal passages above the back of the throat, the part of the throat you would see if you stuck out your tongue and looked in a mirror.

How Voice Is Produced

During normal breathing, the vocal cords are relaxed and are some distance apart, as pictured in Figure 2.2b. But during phonation, the folds meet and actually impede the flow of air through the larynx (see Figure 2.2c). Air escapes through the folds in short bursts only hundredths or thousandths of a second in duration. These bursts cause vibrations in the air. Combinations of tension and air pressure on the vocal cords produce various pitches and loudness.

Each small vibration is amplified to produce voice in the same way a brass instrument amplifies the sound from the mouthpiece. If you took the mouthpiece off a trombone and blew through it, it would produce only a weak, high-pitched squawk, the direct vibration of your lips. But when the mouthpiece is attached to the trombone, the acoustics of the instrument's piping cause an entire column of air to vibrate. Because of this effect, the musical note is heard, full of resonance and power. Likewise, a violin string just produces a scratchy noise when vibrated all by itself. The sounding board and the internal resonance cavities of the violin augment the sound of the string to produce a full, rich tone.

Roughly the same effect occurs in the human voice. The mouth and nasal cavities act as resonators, enhancing some of the harmonics (overtones) of the voice. Even the sinuses and the bones of the skull act as resonators.

Resonation in the nasal cavities is most apparent during the pronunciation of so-called nasal sounds, such as *m, n,* and *ng.* This becomes apparent when you close your mouth and hum; where does the air escape? The buzzing sensation of humming shows that you are producing resonance in the nasal passages.

You don't pass air into the nasal passages all the time. But nasal cavity resonance while saying *m, n,* and *ng* can enhance your voice. Resonance along the entire vocal tract enhances the quality of your voice.

Methods of developing resonance and other qualities of a pleasing voice are discussed later in the chapter.

Evaluating Your Voice and Speech

It is worthwhile to make a clear distinction between voice and speech. Basically, *voice* is the vibration that emerges from the vocal cords and from resonance along the vocal and nasal tracts. *Speech* is how that sound is shaped and arranged within the mouth. The term *speaking voice* applies to the whole effect of voice and speech.

Making an honest evaluation of your voice and speech is one of the most productive things you can do in your career. Any voice or speech deviation is a handicap. Some performers have succeeded despite such deviations, but that is rare.

Evaluate your voice and speech with a tape recorder and, ideally, with a knowledgeable instructor, speech/language pathologist, or vocal coach. You can start with Box 2.1, the Self-Evaluation Checklist, later in this chapter. It is difficult to critique yourself. You hear your own voice through bone conduction or vibration, whereas others hear your voice after it has traveled through the air. Remember the first time you heard yourself on tape? The difference between *your* perception of your voice and the actual playback was probably startling.

But tape playback also has its limitations because we don't discriminate our own speech sounds with precision. Even people with severe lisps sometimes cannot tell they have a problem unless they are trained to listen critically to a taped playback.

Take advantage of critique from instructors and colleagues to identify problem areas, and listen critically to your tapes in an effort to develop self-critiquing skills.

Voice

A pleasing voice is helpful to a broadcaster, but an offensive voice is a real handicap. Voices that "turn off" listeners may result from problems in *quality, delivery,* and *breathing.*

PROBLEMS WITH VOICE QUALITY   Have you ever developed a negative image of someone on the other end of a phone conversation, someone you've never met but have pictured because of his or her voice? Gravelly voices, for example, are not pleasant to listen to and certainly are a detriment for most broadcasters. Here are some of the most common negative voice qualities, possible causes, and suggestions for improvement.

Hoarseness   A raspy sound in the voice, often categorized as a voice that "sounds like it's hurting," is called hoarseness. This vocal sound may be a symptom of a pathological condition and should, if persistent, be checked by a physician. Most hoarseness results from overuse and improper use of the voice, such as cheering at a sports event, and can be compounded by too much tension in the vocal apparatus.

"Thin" voice   When a "thin," weak voice is the result of the way the vocal mechanism is formed, not a lot can be done about it other than to enhance the thin voice as best one can through good vocal habits. Often, though, a thin

quality is the result of a lack of resonance. The two keys to increasing resonance are proper air support, including good posture and relaxation. Also, chronic inflammation and swelling of the nasal passages can cut off resonance. (Try pinching your nose and talking; note how "weak" the voice appears.)

Gravelly voice   Whereas a hoarse voice typically has a strident "breaking" quality to it, the gravelly voice is usually low pitched, does not project, and is not melodic. Gravelly voices sometimes result from a simple lack of projection. Note how gravel-voiced people often slouch and speak with the chin on the chest. Gravelly voices often result from speaking in a pitch that is too low. Better breath support, a higher pitch, and better projection can often ease this problem.

PROBLEMS IN VOCAL DELIVERY   Even when the vocal and breathing apparatus is working properly, a voice can fail to be pleasing because of poor delivery. We'll define five typical problems and give possible solutions.

Monotone   Failure to change pitch results in a monotone delivery. *Pitch* is the listener's perception of the frequency of a sound (its relative highness or lowness), as in the pitch of a note on a musical scale. A monotone can be extremely unpleasant to listen to and conveys the impression that the speaker is bored or boring. Speaking in a monotone can also irritate the vocal cords. A speaker with a monotone should pay more attention to the nuances of the pitch rising and falling.

Poor pitch   Some people try to talk out of their ranges, too high or, as is sometimes the case with male news reporters, too low. One effect on the voice is an unnatural quality. Speaking at an unnatural pitch opens the door for vocal abuse, and a problem that would-be basses don't consider is that constantly talking at the bottom end of their range limits the expressiveness of the voice. When you are at the bottom of the range, you can only go up. Finding a more comfortable and natural pitch often clears up the problem.

Singsong   A singsong delivery is characterized by a rhythm that rises and falls; it's a predictable voice pattern showing artificially wide and pronounced pitch swings—the "disc jockey voice." The problem isn't hard to eliminate once it has been recognized. Adopting a normal speech melody solves the problem.

Ending pattern   Many people end each phrase or sentence on the same pitch or series of pitches. A voice pattern that becomes predictable is boring and can be distracting.

Whininess   A whiny sound is often caused by speaking at a pitch that is too high and elongating vowels. "I toooooold you this would happen . . . look at the mess you've gotten us into noooooowwwwww." Awareness of whiny delivery is the first step in eliminating it, along with assuming a better pitch and shortening vowels. Whininess is also sometimes associated with an overly nasal delivery (too much air being diverted into the nose during speech).

PROBLEMS IN BREATHING   Poor breath control and the related problem of poor posture are often at the root of an unpleasant voice. Even though breathing is an automatic function, there is some technique involved in breathing properly for voice production. The old gym class concept of "throwing your chest out" when you breathe is incorrect and counterproductive. It is the abdomen, and not the chest, that must expand significantly during inhalation for proper speech. Here are some typical problems and suggestions for alleviating them.

Breathy voice   The "Marilyn Monroe" or "breathy starlet" voice may be either a physical or a breathing problem. It can be caused by failure to bring the vocal folds together closely enough during phonation, so that air escapes while you are speaking. A common and more easily corrected cause of a breathy voice, however, is not having sufficient air reserves, so that the speaker "runs out of breath." More attention to proper phonation, proper vocal tension, and possibly professional therapy are indicated, along with better posture and breath support.

Voice with no "carrying power"   Often the result of inadequate support from the abdominal muscles, lack of carrying power is compounded by lack of projection. Projection is simply the process of sending vocal sounds out of your mouth. Breathe diaphragmatically, and pay attention to posture.

Speech

There are different ways to categorize speech problems, and our categorization is not the same as a trained speech pathologist would use. Instead, speech problems are discussed in terms of their occurrence and importance to the on-air talent.

The most common categories of sounds produced within the mouth and vocal apparatus are vowels and consonants. Among the consonants, different parts of the vocal apparatus are used to produce various sounds, including the following.

Fricatives   The source of these sounds is the gradual escape of air through a constriction in the mouth or vocal tract. Major English **fricatives** are *f, v, th, s, z, sh, zh,* and *h.*

Plosives and stops   An explosion of air (*t* and *d* at the beginning of a word) or suddenly stopping air flow (*t* and *d* at the end of a word) will produce these sounds. Major English **plosives** are *p, b, t, d, k,* and *g.*

Frictionless consonants   Included are semivowels, nasals, and laterals. Semivowels, *w, r,* and *y,* have a continuous, vowel-like quality in their pronunciation. An *l* sound is similar but is known as a *lateral,* because the breath exits from the side of the mouth. Another related type of sound is the nasal category: *m, n,* and *ng.*

When the sounds just described are omitted, distorted, added, or substituted for one another, speech problems occur. Here are examples of four typical deviations:

- **Omissions:** Dropping the *k* in "asked" so it sounds like "ast" instead of "askt."

- **Distortions:** Altering the *s* sound so that it comes out more like a *th* (lisp). Vowel distortions are also common, such as saying "pin" for "pen" or "min" for "men." Vowel distortions sometimes are traceable to a regional accent.

- **Additions:** Putting an *r* where it does not belong: saying "soar" instead of "saw."

- **Substitutions:** Saying *d* for *th,* as in "dese" and "dose" for "these" and "those"; or *n* for *ng,* as "bringin." This is sometimes called "dropping the *g,*" an error that also shares some characteristics of an omission.

Difficulties in sequencing sounds constitute yet another type of deviation, defined as follows.

- *Fluency problems (stuttering and cluttering):* **Stuttering** is a problem of rate and rhythm that is best addressed by a professional therapist. **Cluttering,** as an informal definition, involves telescoping sounds together, saying "vejble" for "vegetable."

Omissions, distortions, additions, substitutions, and fluency problems are terms used to identify specific speech deviations. How do they relate to broadcast announcing? Specific speech deviations are components of these overall problems: sloppy diction, regionalism, accents, and cluttering and rate problems.

SLOPPY DICTION   Simple failure to pronounce sounds clearly is sloppy diction. Faults of this type include omissions, such as dropping the final *-ing,* which is a typical transgression. Although "lookin'" might be acceptable in conversational speech, it is not usually acceptable on the air. Sometimes substitutions are simply the result of social or cultural diction habits, such as saying "dis" and "dat" instead of "this" and "that." Substitutions, though, often require professional therapy. A lack of knowledge about the language can lead to additions, too, although this is not strictly a diction problem. For example, the adjective form of "disaster" is "disastrous," not "disasterous." The proper word is "nuclear," not "noo-cue-lahr."

Poor diction is a habit. "Lip laziness" accounts for many cases of sloppy diction, and failure to move the lips and tongue enough for crisp diction is a habit that must be overcome.

Here are some guidelines to help you tighten up sloppy diction.

1. *Self-evaluate.* Listen carefully: do you say "pitcher" for "picture"? Practice correct pronunciations.

2. *Do not "drop" final endings.* Be sure to pronounce *-ing* with an *ng*, not *n*.

3. *Practice giving full measure to all sounds within words.* The word "beasts" has three distinct sounds at the end. Say "beasts," not "beese."

4. *Watch contractions.* Unless you articulate clearly, the negative form of a contraction may sound like the positive form. If the announcer doesn't clearly pronounce the *t* at the end of "can't," the statement "The mayor said he can't remember being told the funds were missing" could be understood as meaning the opposite of the way it is written.

REGIONALISM   Although there is nothing wrong with speaking with a regional accent, regional speech is frequently a handicap to on-air talent. Yes, there are successful news reporters with New England accents, and radio personalities with southern drawls, but these are the *exceptions*, not the rule. A regional accent in New York City, for example, may label you as being from Brooklyn or the Bronx. A pronounced regional accent may even disqualify you from getting a certain job.

FOREIGN ACCENT   A noticeable foreign accent can be a charming and engaging characteristic. In broadcast communication, however, the decoration an accent adds to your personality can be offset by the fact that it severely interferes with clear communication.

In most broadcast situations, a severe foreign accent is considered a detriment that can limit your opportunities and stall your career. If you speak heavily accented English, you should recognize this as a liability to your future as a broadcast communicator and take measures to deal with it. Professionals use a variety of techniques to reduce foreign accents (see the Focus on Technique box).

CLUTTERING AND RATE PROBLEMS   Cluttering, or telescoping sounds, is different from sloppy diction because cluttering typically involves a problem with rate of speech and sometimes a lack of attention to communicating the message. The clutterer often jams words and sounds together because he or she is speaking too quickly. Many otherwise intelligible people become practically incoherent when they read aloud and rattle off the words at breakneck pace, with no phrasing. A clutterer who reads over the air frequently compounds the problem by just reading, not communicating. In other words, proper stress is not given to the words and phrases, so the reading comes out as a mashed-up jumble.

Focus on Technique

ACCENT REDUCTION

Although broadcast executives are more tolerant of foreign and regional accents today than in the past, anything that gets in the way of communication is an obstacle. On a realistic note, you will find that specifically targeted shows, such as *Asia Week,* are the only places you might hear highly recognizable accents.

Accent reduction is difficult but not impossible. But it is very difficult if you try it by yourself, because you simply may not be able to hear your accent. Many Asian speakers, for instance, have trouble hearing the difference between *l* and *r.*

If you want to pursue a career in broadcasting, and if you have a foreign or regional accent, your best option is to consult a speech-language pathologist or a theatrical vocal coach. Speech-language pathologists are voice and diction scientists, and many are skilled in accent reduction. (Ask, though; some might be more interested in reducing stuttering and have little experience in accent reduction.) Theatrical voice coaches are often highly skilled in teaching the building blocks of producing pronunciation; a good coach can not only teach a Swede how to pronounce English with a native U.S. pronunciation but could also teach an American how to speak with a Swedish accent.

If these options are unavailable to you, you can still make progress with a partner, such as a teacher, colleague, or news director, and your *other* partner—a tape recorder. The key is to listen to yourself on tape and listen to the suggestions of your native-speaking partner.

Here are some techniques you can use:

- Tape and listen to network news anchors. They typically speak a more-or-less standard speech. Compare their phrasing with yours. For example, if CNN's Aaron Brown (an excellent model of clear, unaccented speech) says, "floodwaters inundated the Midwest yesterday," play that part of the tape back and copy his pronunciation, rate, and stress.

- Practice the "musical" part of your delivery. Pitch changes and levels of stress are just as important to general American delivery as word pronunciation is. Rhythm and inflection, called *prosody,* not only are tip-offs for foreign accents but change meanings as well.

For example:

She is a light HOUSE keeper.
She is a LIGHT-house keeper.

Continues

Focus on Technique   Continued

Prosody is particularly difficult for Asians, who tend not to vary their patterns as much as do speakers of Germanic languages like English or speakers of Romance languages (Spanish, Italian, and so on).

- To practice proper English prosody, try reading rhythmic poetry aloud. Anything by Edgar Allan Poe is good. Simply by keeping the meter of the poem you will be forced into using native English stress patterns.

In *The Raven,* for example:

ONCE u-PON a MID-night DREAR-y,
WHILE I PON-dered WEAK and WEAR-y . . .

- You will find it awkward *not* to stress the correct words and form the proper rhythm. If you don't mind a little good-natured silliness, try children's books by Dr. Seuss.

- Learn to say pitch changes *within vowel sounds.* If you listen to a native English speaker, he or she will make a considerable pitch change in the *oh* sound that ends "Hello." Generally, the sound will be elongated and drop quite a bit in pitch. Or, if the word is being used as a question:

"Hellooooooooo . . . anybody hooooooome?"
Both *oh* sounds will *rise* in pitch.

This is one of the biggest problems in accent reduction. Asians and many Romance-language speakers (such as Spanish speakers) tend to make their vowels short and flat. Once you realize this, you can begin to mimic the vowel patterns of native pronunciation.

- Move your lips. Ann Madsen Dailey, a speech pathologist with many years of experience in accent reduction training, notes that many accent problems, particularly with Russians, Indians, and Asians, stem from the fact that they do not move their lips enough to form English sounds. The *oh,* sound, for instance, can be difficult for anyone not used to puckering the lips severely enough.

- In general, pronounce the consonants and vowels *as far in the front of your mouth as possible.* This is something of an obscure concept, to be sure, but it basically boils down to this:

As an example, when you say the *n* sound use the tip of your tongue up against the roof of your mouth *near the front teeth.* Chinese and Japanese speakers say the *n* by closing the back of the tongue, and the sound is made in the back of the mouth.

Continues

Focus on Technique Continued

The *ooh* sound in "too" should be made far in front of the mouth, at the lips, which are pursed. Spanish-speaking people tend to make the sound in the back of the mouth. Try it if you are a native U.S. speaker—say "ooh" and don't purse your lips and make the sound short and without variation and you will produce a good imitation of a Spanish accent.

- Strive to move pronunciations farther forward in the mouth, and you will generally achieve more near-native speech.

- Slow down! It is very difficult to maintain your hard-fought native-U.S. pronunciations when you talk too quickly. It takes considerable fine motor coordination for a nonnative speaker to form an American *r,* and if you are speaking too quickly you will not be able to do it.

- There is nothing wrong with having two speech standards—one for the family and the neighborhood and one for the camera. People attempting accent reduction often face opposition and sometimes ridicule from those with whom they have day-to-day contact. That is a natural response—imagine how Americans living in Tokyo would react to other Americans who tried to adopt native-Japanese voice mannerisms. So live with this; you need not try to eradicate your cultural roots. Changing your speech patterns to adapt to the situation is common and reasonable. Doctors, for example, talk differently with other doctors than with their nonmedical friends. You have the same right.

- Improve your vocabulary! Probably the largest difference between native and nonnative speech is the size of the vocabulary. If you are attempting to reduce your accent, you will sabotage your progress when you stumble over unfamiliar words. (Your rhythm and pronunciation will both be affected.) Look up unfamiliar words. Always keep a dictionary handy.

- Drill yourself on the difficult sounds. If *r* is your problem, say lists of words with that sound, and make sure you have an *r* in the beginning, middle, and end. Have a native speaker listen and critique.

A good collection of tapes is available to help you work with accent reduction. Dialect Accent Specialists, Inc. (www.dialectaccentspecialist. com) offers an inexpensive and very good series of video- and audiotapes as well as residency programs.

These deviations reflect problems in **articulation,** meaning the joining and juxtaposition of sounds and words, rather than simple **diction,** which usually refers to the formation of individual sounds.

Cluttering and rate problems are common for people beginning air work. The novice disk jockey sometimes tries to emulate a fast-talking pro who's practiced at speaking at an accelerated rate. These problems are most effectively handled by

1.   Slowing down the rate of reading.
2.   Marking copy for effective understanding and delivery (shown in the next chapter).
3.   Speaking clearly in an effort to communicate ideas, not just read words.

FLUENCY LIMITATIONS AND THE BROADCASTER   On-air performers who have **fluency** difficulties will have difficulty communicating effectively. If words are delivered at breakneck speed and articulation is poor, the effect is like hearing the music from a Broadway musical without the lyrics. The music may not sound too bad, but it is easy to miss the full meaning of the message that the writer intended to convey.

The broadcast announcer has a number of tools that can be used to help convey the full meaning of the words being read. If the rate is too fast or if articulation is poor, however, those tools don't get a chance to perform the functions they should. The effectiveness of *speech melody,* or **inflection,** is totally wasted if it flies by the listener too rapidly. Nuances of meaning are lost and the intended effect of the copy is diminished or eliminated.

An uneven rate of delivery can also cause inaccurate and inconsistent timing. When a television news anchor reads copy that leads into a taped news package, people in the control room need to be able to depend on a consistent rate of delivery. To come up to the proper speed, tape must be started several seconds before the anchor completes the lead-in. So an anchor who slows down at that point will "step on" the opening of the taped segment.

In radio, the increased use of satellite and computer automation means that timing must be more precise than ever before. On many stations in the past, a five-minute newscast could run over or under time by several seconds or more without anyone noticing. But if you know that the satellite programming will start exactly when the minute hand of the clock hits 12, you also know that five minutes is all you have. Anything less than that will create dead air. That tight limit also applies to reading commercial copy and items like station IDs, promos, and weather forecasts.

Similar requirements limit people who do narration and voice-over assignments. Timing must be an element of your delivery that you can control. You must often adjust your rate so that you convey meaning even when conditions force you to vary from your usual rate.

The bottom line is that if you want to be effective as on-air talent in almost any type of assignment, you must know how to read copy precisely to time. Some top professionals can take a piece of copy, ask the producer how much time he or she wants filled, and read the copy in one take so that it hits the time limit exactly. But most of us need some rehearsal first. You must find ways to practice timing so that you can hone your skills.

One effective exercise to improve timing is to divide a piece of broadcast copy into sections, to be read in a stated amount of time. Read the copy over and over until you are able to read through to the end in the designated amount of time. Here's how to set up the exercise.

Copy has about 10 words per line, on the average. Sixteen lines of copy would be about a minute's worth at a reading rate of 160 words per minute—a generally good rate for broadcast announcers.

Take a piece of copy with at least 16 lines, and mark the midpoint—8 lines down—with a mark that is easy to see. Place another mark at the end of the copy—16 lines down. Using a timing device that lets you easily see the number of seconds that have elapsed, read the copy through. See how close you can come to reaching the midpoint at 30 seconds. Did you complete the 16 lines in 60 seconds? Practice this over and over with various pieces of copy. (You can use the copy in Appendix B of this text.) With practice, you'll find that you will develop an awareness of how to read the copy at the proper rate to make it fit the proper time frame.

The point we're making is simple. Don't assume that you can simply ignore speech problems in rate and timing. Your problems may not be severe enough to require professional attention, but even relatively minor difficulties can severely hinder your ability to interpret copy effectively. The exercises at the end of this chapter can help you identify any problem areas you may have. For more help, consult a speech therapist or one of the many books on voice improvement.

One of the most comprehensive books is Utterback's *Broadcast Voice Handbook*.[1] Utterback has a wide background in voice and diction and has helped many professional broadcasters improve their vocal delivery.

Language and the Broadcaster

Using language well is obviously of paramount importance to the broadcaster. Unfortunately, there are no simple and all-inclusive guidelines for proper pronunciation and usage, and categorizing standards and definitions is very difficult. Scholars have debated the issues of dialects and standardized language for centuries without producing a completely definitive standard.

For example, what defines a **dialect**? In most basic terms, it is a variety of a language, but from what exactly does it differ? Is a certain dialect substandard? What is standard?

---

[1] Ann S. Utterback, *Broadcast Voice Handbook*, 3rd ed. (Chicago: Bonus Books and Radio and Television News Directors Association, 2000).

It is useful to look at the language issue in the most basic terms, the terms most directly related to on-air broadcasters. This discussion includes pronunciation, which is obviously germane to a chapter on speech and voice. Also important, and included in this chapter to complete the discussion of language, is an examination of usage.

Two common terms encountered in on-air broadcasting are **standard English** and **general American speech.** Although these descriptions are sometimes used interchangeably, "standard English" is generally taken to mean the English language as it is written or spoken by literate people in both formal and informal usage, whereas "general American speech" can be defined as pronunciation of American English using few or no regional peculiarities. From the standpoint of pronunciation, deviations from general American speech are dialects resulting from regionalism or social circumstances.

REGIONAL DIALECTS   Linguists identify dialects in terms of local and regional peculiarities in pronunciation. There are said to be four main regional dialects in the United States: Northern, North Midland, South Midland, and Southern. There are many distinct variations within these categories.

The exact scope of general American speech has always been elusive, but it has come to be used for all speech except that of New England and the coastal south.[2] Perhaps a better basis for judgment would be **network standard,** the unaccented speech of most newscasters and actors delivering commercials.

An unaccented form of American speech was thought to be spoken in Chicago, although clearly some speakers in Chicago do use regional speech. In the early days of broadcasting, some organizations sent announcers to Chicago in an effort to eliminate regional accents.

Eliminating regionalisms in any manner is not easy. We're so used to hearing our own regionalisms (primarily vowel distortions) that we find it hard to distinguish regional speech from the unaccented speech used by most network newscasters.

An effort must be made to correct regionalisms, though. Vowel distortions caused by regional dialects can be distracting to a listener who, for example, expects to hear "boy," but hears instead "bo-ih" from a southern speaker. And many people find substitutions even more intrusive. The New England trait of adding *r*'s where they don't belong ("pizzer," "bananer") and dropping them where they do belong ("cah," "watah") can irritate listeners unaccustomed to the dialect.

As we noted earlier, you may not be able to distinguish your own regional dialect. If your instructors or colleagues tell you that you have a distracting regionalism, they're probably right. And if you can't identify and

---

[2] David Blair McClosky and Barbara McClosky, *Voice in Song and Speech* (Boston: Boston Music Company, 1984). Used with permission.

correct the regional distortion or substitution on your own, by all means ask a speech professional or coach for help in getting rid of it.

SOCIAL DIALECTS Certain differences in pronunciation are apparent among groups that differ in educational levels or cultural practices. Standard speech is arbitrarily assumed to reflect the highly educated members of a society, so a similarly arbitrary definition pegs other **social dialects** as nonstandard.

George Bernard Shaw satirized the rigid British class system by reflecting its cultural differences in speech patterns. In *Pygmalion*, Shaw made the point that more attention was given to the packaging of the words than to their substance.

Still, it is important for a broadcaster to reflect the social dialect looked on as standard. You must use educated pronunciations and usages. Saying "dese" instead of "these" can reflect a nonstandard social dialect, as can loose pronunciation. "Whatcha gonna do?" is not acceptable speech for a newscaster. The appropriateness of loose pronunciations, however, clearly varies with the situation. You don't commonly intone every sound when asking a friend, "What are you going to do?" In informal situations, some loosening of pronunciation is acceptable.

USAGE The choice and use of words must be considered in evaluating standard language. Standard English, remember, is pegged to the educated speaker or writer. Use of double negatives, such as "haven't got none," is obviously nonstandard.

There is a more subtle point to be considered here, however. Although it is assumed that anyone contemplating a career in the broadcast media has the knowledge and ability to avoid such obvious blunders as "haven't got none," other lapses in grammar and usage can seriously detract from your image as an educated, standard English–speaking broadcaster. What is your impression of an announcer who speaks about a "heart-rendering" movie? The usage is comically incorrect. (If you're in doubt, look up "rendering.")

A lack of knowledge of the language also can mislead. One news reporter, for example, spoke of a city official's "fulsome" praise for a retiring teacher. "Fulsome" is a word that is used as a synonym for "abundant" so often that its original meaning, namely, "offensive or disgusting," is rapidly becoming lost. Similar fates seem to be in store for "presently," "disinterested," and "infer." Use words correctly. Never guess in an on-air situation.

Self-Evaluation

It is important to be aware of any speech or voice problems you may have. Self-evaluation can help you assess your own speech so you can more easily identify and deal with problems that will hinder your progress toward achieving a more professional on-air delivery. Use the checklist in Box 2.1 to get started.

Box 2.1

SELF-EVALUATION CHECKLIST

A speech or voice deviation or a significant deviation from standard English or general American speech can slow the advancement of even the most intelligent broadcaster. It is important to keep an open mind to critiques and evaluations of voice, speech, and language. Although it is often difficult to perceive deviations in your own voice and speech, by constant monitoring with a tape recorder you can train yourself to be your own best critic.

Read through two or three pages of copy or a newspaper article. Then play back the tape and ask yourself,

1. Do I slur any words and sounds together?
2. Are my consonants crisp and clear?
3. Are my *s* sounds too harsh? Do my plosives (*p*'s and *b*'s) cause the mic to pop?
4. Are there any regionalisms or colloquialisms in my speech? Do I say "soar" for "saw," or "youse" for "you"?
5. Do I "drop" endings?
6. Do I read too quickly? Do my words telescope together?
7. Do I have a distracting voice pattern? Do I sound like a bad disc jockey?
8. Is my voice hoarse, harsh?
9. Am I speaking in a pitch range that is too high or too low?
10. Can I *hear* tension in my voice? Does it sound constricted, tight?

Note: Although self-evaluation is helpful, the difficulty of hearing your own mistakes cannot be overemphasized. If at all possible, have an individual analysis of your voice and articulation problems.

Making Your Speaking Voice More Pleasing

The next step is to concentrate on some positive steps you can take for self-improvement. Of primary importance to improving voice quality is posture. Another critical aspect of a pleasant voice is relaxation of the vocal apparatus, which also plays the major role in preventing vocal abuse. Relaxation techniques are discussed in the section titled "Maintaining Your Voice."

The first step in improving your speaking voice is to learn correct posture and breathing.

Diaphragmatic Breathing

The suggestion to "speak from the diaphragm," which is a good one, doesn't make any sense unless the process is explained and understood. Using posture and breathing techniques will require forming good habits and breaking bad habits.

The first habit to cultivate is proper posture, contends David Blair McClosky, an author and voice therapist who has coached presidents and broadcasters.

McClosky recommends a posture in which your feet are spread comfortably apart and your weight is slightly toward the balls of your feet. The key to the proper posture is to get rid of an exaggerated curve in your back. Keep your back straight and tuck your hips in, as shown in Figure 2.3. This posture allows for proper breathing. Virtually all voice coaches point out that the abdomen must expand during breathing, rather than the chest. Although you may have been taught in elementary school to "throw out your chest" when you breathe, that's not good technique. It doesn't let your abdominal muscles and therefore your diaphragm provide adequate support for the column of air in your vocal tract. If you are unclear about this, please take a moment to review the sections on vocal anatomy and physiology.

"Diaphragmatic breathing" is something of a misnomer because we have to use the diaphragm to breathe regardless of what scrunched-up posture we may assume. However, proper diaphragmatic breathing is accomplished when the contraction of the abdominal muscles pushes the diaphragm in and supports the column of air. This can be accomplished only if the abdomen is allowed to expand when the diaphragm pulls down into the abdominal cavity during inhalation.

Proper breathing compels us to abandon some of the typical vanities imposed by current culture, including the notions that we should be wasp-waisted and that men should have swelling chests. For us to breathe properly, the abdomen must expand. Note the action in Figure 2.4 (a and b).

When the abdomen and the diaphragm have expanded, natural exhalation from that position, involving a contracting of the abdominal muscles, will produce the proper effect. Be certain you have used your diaphragm properly. One way to check on diaphragmatic breathing is to stand against a wall and have someone press his or her fist against your abdomen. Proper inhalation will drive that fist away (Figure 2.4c).

Here is one final test to see if you are breathing properly. Assume the correct posture and place your hands on your lower ribs (Figure 2.4d). Inhale. If your ribs move you are expanding your chest instead of your diaphragm.

Figure 2.3   A good posture for speaking. The goal is to minimize back sway and give your diaphragm and abdomen plenty of room for expansion.

Minimize "sway" in back

Tuck hips in

Slightly flex your knees

Figure 2.4 (a) The telltale way to determine whether you're breathing diaphragmatically: before inhaling, place your hand a couple of inches below your breastbone. (b) When you inhale, you should feel and see an expansion of your abdomen. This demonstrates the action of the diaphragm. (c) A good test of whether your diaphragm is being used in breathing is to stand against a wall and have a partner press with his or her fist as shown; inhale and try to push the fist away. (d) If you can detect rib motion, you are breathing from your chest rather than from your diaphragm.

Photos by Philip Benoit

This breathing posture works just as well in a seated position. All that will change is the position of your legs. Keep your back straight and your hips tucked in. Practice minimizing rib motion.

Exaggerated Diction

We've all heard the unnatural, affected delivery of the speaker whose diction is just *too* precise. We raise this issue because some people try to clear up imprecision in diction by swinging to the other extreme, which is probably a marginal improvement at best. Remember, English-speaking people do not pounce on every single sound in a sentence.

The best way to identify too-precise diction is, of course, to listen to a tape. It also helps to watch your mouth as you speak into a mirror. Exaggerated mouth and lip movements are often indicative of exaggerated diction.

Special Considerations for Broadcast Work

Even normal-sounding *p*'s and *b*'s can cause a microphone to pop—that is, to vibrate with an explosive noise because a blast of air has hit the mic element. Sometimes, simple awareness of the problem and practice in controlling the force of plosives is enough. Speaking across the mic, rather than into it, can help. Or you might choose a mic that is less susceptible to popping. All options are discussed in Chapter 4.

Women doing on-air work sometimes encounter resistance from listeners who claim their voices are harder to understand. For some people, especially older listeners with age-related hearing losses, this is true. For reasons dealing with acoustics and the functioning of the hearing mechanism, the impaired ear hears lower-pitched voices better than higher-pitched voices. A reasonable lowering of pitch can sometimes overcome this. Good projection and resonance can also resolve much of the problem.

Finally, be aware that many on-air diction problems can be solved by careful attention to copy interpretation. "Read for meaning," advises Ann Madsen Dailey, an author, consultant, and speech/language pathologist. "Use pauses where appropriate, stress key words, and use natural expression. Very often this can clear up the problems caused by poor habits developed by just 'reading out loud.'"

Maintaining Your Voice

Broadcasters, like teachers and salespeople, often must contend with hoarseness, irritation, or just plain tiredness in the vocal apparatus. Even if the abuse is not serious enough to cause harm, no performer can communicate effectively when his or her voice is reaching the point of failure.

Box 2.2

DIET AND HEALTH TIPS

To get the most from your voice, follow a healthy lifestyle. The vocal mechanisms are physical, after all. Good health practices and proper diet help strengthen the vocal mechanisms and provide the energy that helps you develop an effective vocal delivery. Here are some basic tips that will help you keep fit and avoid the consequences of poor general health:

- *Get plenty of rest.* When your body is tired, the weariness will show up in your voice. A tired voice is usually higher pitched and lacking in strength. Announcers who try to perform with tired voices may wonder if they can even finish the shift. Attempts to "clear" the voice—frequent throat clearing and straining to lower the pitch— just aggravate the problem. The only effective remedy is to get some rest. Better yet, get enough sleep in the first place, and try to find some time for relaxation before starting assignments that require heavy use of your voice.

- *Exercise.* In addition to exercises that work the vocal mechanisms, engage in some form of regular, strenuous physical activity that works the major muscles of the body. This will strengthen your heart and lungs and give you endurance and overall energy. Your vocal delivery will reflect the general condition of the rest of your body. You'll be able to go longer with less strain, and the extra energy will give you a more forceful delivery when you need it. Of course, it is always wise to have a physical examination by a qualified physician before starting a strenuous exercise program—especially if you have been leading a sedentary life.

- *Watch what you eat.* A diet high in fat and low in nutrition contributes to fatigue and susceptibility to illness. The carbohydrates in whole grains and fruit, combined with adequate protein from various sources, will provide energy and help you maintain health. Don't eat too much fat, and pay attention to the nutritional values of the food you eat. If you are overweight, start a weight reduction program that helps you lose pounds over a reasonable length of time. Fad diets can endanger your health, and they usually don't work.

Continues

Box 2.2 Continued

- *Don't smoke.* The constant irritation of heavy smoking can damage the vocal mechanism and greatly impair vocal delivery. Aside from the well-known risks to general health, smoking continually irritates the vocal cords. General irritation of the throat can result in excessive mucus production and the development of a "smoker's cough" that further strains the vocal mechanism. Over time, the general quality of the voice can change as the result of permanent damage to the vocal folds. Eventual lung damage can impair effective breath control and reduce the force of your vocal delivery.

Good health and nutrition are important to on-air performers: They help you improve effectiveness the same way proper physical conditioning contributes to the performance of an athlete. Like athletes, announcers are called on to perform at specific times and places. That means you must perform well *then*—not just at those rare times when your voice sounds perfect. If you have to produce a quality vocal performance on a regular basis, you should try to be as fit as possible at all times. Eating sensibly, exercising moderately, and avoiding behaviors that harm your health will help you make sure your vocal tools are always ready to use to their best effect (see Box 2.2).

Relaxation is the key to maintaining your voice. Proper relaxation also helps produce a pleasant, resonant voice. The exercises recommended in Box 2.3 really do work! Try them, practice them, and make them into a daily regimen.

Vocal Abuse

"Vocal abuse" is any excess strain on the vocal apparatus, most notably on the vocal cords, that produces irritation. Symptoms of vocal abuse include hoarseness, a change in the character of the voice, fatigue or discomfort in the region of the larynx and throat, and a change in the basic pitch of the voice.

Vocal abuse can be chronic or acute. Chronic abuse develops gradually from improper vocal habits and excessive stress in the vocal mechanism. The results of acute abuse come on suddenly, usually from screaming or a very hard period of speaking or singing.

Such abuse can result in a number of physical problems, including

- Formation of vocal cord nodules and polyps
- Excessive "bowing" (taking on a misshapen appearance) of the vocal cords
- Chronic irritation

Box 2.3

SOME EXERCISES TO RELAX YOUR BODY AND THROAT

Professional singers and speakers perform many of these regularly.

1. Roll your head: forward, to the left, backward, to the right, and forward again. Repeat several times in each direction. This helps relax shoulders and neck.

2. Massage the muscles of your face. Work down from your hairline, and let your jaw go slack.

3. Thrust out your tongue several times, then let it hang limply over the bottom lip. Relaxing your tongue is important because the back of your tongue goes right down your throat. Tension here can interfere with vocalization.

4. Massage the area under your chin (Figure 2.5a) until there is no rigidity apparent. Learn to relax these muscles "on cue."

5. Grasp your lower jaw between thumb and forefinger and work it up and down until you overcome any muscular resistance. When you get good at this, you can bounce your jaw up and down with your forefinger (Figure 2.5b).

Figure 2.5

(a) Massaging under the chin.

Photos a, b, and c by Philip Benoit

Continues

Box 2.3 *Continued*

Figure 2.5 (Continued) (b) Working the jaw. (c) Massaging the larynx eliminates rigidity.

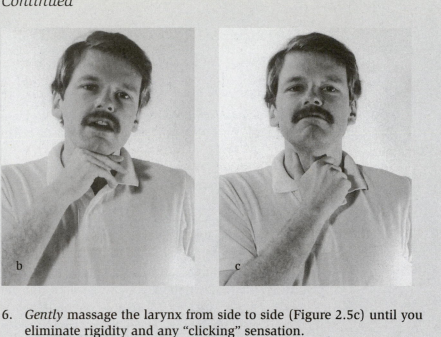

6. *Gently* massage the larynx from side to side (Figure 2.5c) until you eliminate rigidity and any "clicking" sensation.

7. Vocalize the word "hah" gently, using the *ah* sound as in "arm." Start vocalization high in pitch and then slide down the range of pitch. Initiate the vocalization as gradually and gently as you can.

One cause of vocal abuse is an abnormally low pitch. McClosky notes that when he was a university choirmaster and singing teacher in the heyday of the big-voiced announcer, a surprising number of students who reported voice problems to him were enrolled in the college's broadcasting school. They were trying to lower their pitch to the male ideal of those days.

Preventing Vocal Abuse

In addition to speaking in a natural tone of voice, you can protect your voice from abuse in several ways. Neri Holzer, M.D., a Connecticut ear, nose, and throat specialist, offers these suggestions:

1. *Listen to what your larynx and throat are trying to tell you.* The body has several defense mechanisms, including pain and hoarseness. If these symptoms are chronic, reevaluate your speech patterns.

2. *Warm up.* Do some light vocalizing (humming, singing, and so on) before an extended on-air period or other time of vocal stress.

3. *Keep well hydrated.* When tissues lose moisture, they're more susceptible to damage. Have a glass of water on hand.

4. *Use amplification when possible instead of raising your voice.* A radio announcer, for example, can reduce strain on the voice by turning up the volume on the mic channel instead of shouting.

5. *Don't smoke.* Tobacco smoke directly irritates the vocal cords. Smoke indirectly irritates the cords by stimulating coughing.

6. *Avoid extensive use of the voice when you have a cold.* Using your voice then makes you more susceptible to vocal irritation. Also, avoid habitually clearing your throat.

7. *Look at your whole body for signs of tension.* Stress in other parts of the body can cause a reaction in the voice. Similarly, posture has an important role in keeping the vocal mechanism relaxed and working freely.

Vocal Relaxation Techniques

Dr. Holzer's last point is important: having a relaxed body and vocal apparatus relieves much of the strain on the voice mechanism and allows the voice to function better. Voice therapist McClosky contends that relaxation is the precursor to any progress in voice development. Unless you can relax the muscles in your face, tongue, jaw, throat, and neck that interfere with the muscles controlling the vocal cords themselves, he says, "your singing and speaking will be muscle-bound" (see Box 2.3).

Make these relaxation techniques a daily routine, and remember that relaxation exercises can be done at any time. Doing this routine during a break in a tiring recording session, for example, will help your voice immensely.

Summary

Broadcasters need not force their voices into abnormally low pitch ranges. A pleasant voice, rather than a deep voice, is the hallmark of today's professional announcer. An artificially low-pitched voice is unattractive, and it can actually damage the vocal cords.

A basic knowledge of the vocal mechanism lets you identify the function of various parts of the apparatus when doing exercises to improve its function. Vocal cords are suspended in a chamber of cartilage and allow air to escape in short bursts. Those short bursts create a vibration, which is amplified by the vocal tract and nasal passages.

Evaluation of voice and speech is valuable for all on-air performers. Typical voice problems involve poor quality, delivery, and breathing. Typical speech problems are sloppy diction, regionalism, and cluttering.

Connections

RHETORIC

The study of rhetoric, the art and science of using language persuasively and effectively, provides an excellent base for understanding the work of a broadcast announcer.

When rhetoricians study communications, they focus on how communication influences beliefs or actions. And when we engage in any type of communication on radio, on TV, or simply in everyday life, we are often attempting to get our point across, to persuade people to our way of thinking.

Rhetoric in the broadest sense has been in existence since the first human could communicate, but it took its modern form and name during the 5th century B.C. when Greeks began studying oratorical technique, or *rhetorike techne.* In ancient Greece there were no lawyers, so if you were charged with a crime or if you brought an action against another citizen, you were compelled to speak for yourself. A group called the Sophists taught citizens how to make their cases persuasively.

Aristotle codified the field in about 330 B.C. when he compiled his work *Rhetoric.* Aristotle contended that the truth could be found and expressed through a combination of logic and elegance of speech. In this claim he differed from his teacher, Plato, who taught that persuasion could and should be carried out with pure logic.

Many of the concepts Aristotle wrote about are used today in analysis of persuasive communication. In fact, writers, speakers, and performers frequently use these concepts in their works:

How do you "prove" an argument? Aristotle noted that there are three methods. A speaker must demonstrate:

- Ethos—A powerful, credible, believable character.
- Pathos—Style and substance that will stir the emotions of the listener.
- Logos—The use of logic to prove a point. Sometimes the argument is deductive, meaning that it works from general premises to a specific conclusion. Or the argument may be inductive, meaning that it provides many specific examples that lead us to a general conclusion.

Think about how effective broadcast communicators you have heard or seen use these principles. News anchors are often judged on their credibility—their ethos. The top-drawer music announcers relate the music to the emotions of their listeners, communicating pure pathos. And notice how many commercials feature copy that uses selective facts and a

Continues

Connections Continued

convincing announcer to communicate logos and draw the listeners or viewers to an inescapable conclusion.

Note that rhetoric has traditionally had some negative connotations: People sometimes regard it as the knack of persuading people regardless of the facts, the skill to mislead. Indeed, persuasive people can skirt the facts and lead listeners to an unreasonable conclusion. But that is another reason why the study of rhetoric is useful for an on-air person: Knowing how and why we are persuaded allows us to dismantle the arguments and see what makes them tick.

It is also important for on-air personnel to be familiar with standard American English and general American speech and to avoid significant deviations from these standards.

An inappropriate rate of delivery and poor articulation can detract from the effectiveness of your vocal communication. Proper control of delivery rate also helps the announcer read to time limits—an important skill.

The broad task of making the speaking voice more pleasing begins with self-evaluation and isolation of specific problems. Continued work for crisp diction is important, but diction should not be overemphasized. It is also important to be aware of special considerations for broadcast work, such as using microphones properly.

Learning diaphragmatic breathing is the first major step in the long-term process of improving your speaking voice. Learning to relax is the second major step. In addition to preventing vocal abuse (a common problem of on-air broadcasters), relaxation increases resonance and improves the overall tone of the voice. Exercises can relax the vocal apparatus. A program of diet and fitness can help to ensure overall good health, which contributes to your ability to use your voice effectively at all times.

Exercises   In addition to practicing regularly the techniques described in this chapter, you can benefit by doing these exercises.

1. Pronounce the following pairs of words; record them if possible. Is there a distinguishable difference in your pronunciation? There should be.

picture/pitcher	saw/soar
wear/where	best/Bess
park/pock	peas/please
adapt/adept	aunt/ant

bowl/bold	pin/pen
can/kin	ensure/insure
kin/king	bad/bed

An interesting variation of this exercise is to have a colleague or instructor check your pronunciation. An even more useful variation is to use each pair of words in a sentence. See if the distinction between the two similar words is still as clear during conversational speech as when the words are spoken in isolation.

2. Read through a line of poetry or other work and enunciate *every* sound in the sentence. Exaggerate to the point of silliness, but be sure to hit every consonant and vowel precisely. If you don't have poetry on hand, try this: "Speak distinctly, and rise above the babble of the crowd." The point of this exercise is to discover all the "hidden" sounds and variations of sounds we often gloss over.

3. Another type of diction practice is the tongue twister, which can be fun and interesting but probably not of extraordinary value. There was, however, a time when tongue twisters were popular material for radio announcer auditions, perhaps reflecting an overemphasis on mechanics, rather than on communication. Tongue twisters can bring about a healthy awareness of the accuracy of diction, though, so try these:

    Betty Botter bought some butter. But, she said, the butter's bitter, and if I put it in my batter it will make my batter bitter. So Betty Botter bought some better butter and put it in her batter, and the batter wasn't bitter so she opened a tin of sardines.

4. A variation on tongue twisters is a passage containing seminonsense words that must be read for *meaning*. Read the following paragraph so that the meaning is clear to a listener who has not heard it before. It is a very good exercise for showing how control of rate, pause, and inflection conveys meaning.

    Bill Bell builds bells. The bells Bill Bell builds bang and bong on Beele Boulevard. Bill builds bells with brass bell balls. Bell's bell balls build big bells. Bill Bell built brass ball-built bells for the Beal's bull, Buell. Buell's Bell-built brass bell banged when Buell bellowed on Beele and bore Bell's bells bong abroad. Bill Bell's bells, brass-ball-built for Beal's Beele-based bull Buell biased brass bell builders toward Bell brass ball-built bells. Boy![3]

---

[3] Douglas Ehninger, Bruce E. Gronbeck, Ray E. McKerrow, and Alan H. Monroe, *Principles and Types of Speech Communication,* 10th ed. (New York: Scott, Foresman, 1986), p. 398.

THREE

Understanding the Message

The whole point of putting an announcer in a studio with a script to read is to convey a message to a listener or viewer. Whether that message is delivered solely by sound as in radio or with the added use of visual elements as in television, the objective is to translate what the copywriter had in mind, so that the listener ends up with the same idea. The broadcast communicator is responsible for using all the skills and talents he or she can bring to bear to make sure the message is as effective as possible. This chapter addresses the basic responsibility of the broadcast communicator to understand the meaning of the message, and we outline techniques to improve the message's delivery. We will discuss (1) finding key words; (2) determining the mood, the pace, and the purpose of the copy; and (3) understanding that the goal is communicating, not merely reading. We'll also explore ways to mark copy for pronunciation, interpretation, and phrasing.

Getting the Meaning

The "message" is far more than just words. You must consider a variety of emotions and reactions when you look at words on paper, words that must be conveyed with meaning to each member of the audience. To compound the challenge, you must be sure that a faulty reading doesn't mar or blunt the meaning of the message.

An announcer conveys meaning by giving the copy an *interpretation* that communicates, through inflection and emphasis, something beyond the literal reproduction of the words on paper. Perhaps the words must be charged with emotion, or give a sense of excitement. You communicate these ideas *by first getting a clear and precise understanding of the message.* To do so, you must

59

1. Carefully analyze the meaning and purpose of the **copy** (the topic of this chapter)
2. Communicate the words and phrases in such a way that the message has meaning and impact (the topic of Chapter 4)

Although years of experience can result in these two practices "coming naturally," the top professionals in the business never forget the need for understanding and communicating. "The most important ability an announcer can have is to interpret copy correctly," says Bill St. James,[1] host of ABC Radio's program *Flashback* and one of the industry's best-known freelance commercial voices (see Figure 3.1). "You have to be able to read it as the guy who wrote it had it pictured in his head. And the other thing is that, when you get to this level, you have to do more than just read copy. You're expected to breathe life into it, to make it believable and human."

The point is often driven home rather vividly to beginners. Consider, for instance, this businessman's response to hearing a tape of a proposed commercial: "The announcer doesn't know what he's talking about . . . don't you people know anything about my business?"

One prospective news reporter lost a job he wanted very badly. The news director explained why when the audition tape was played back. "Listen to how you read right through this line: '. . . relative calm except for rioting in a black township north of Soweto. . . .' What the hell is this story about? It's about rioting in a *BLACK* township."

Both performers were ineffective because they failed to understand the message.

To understand and communicate the message, you must identify *key words*, identify *pace and purpose*, and *communicate*—rather than just read—the copy.

Key Words

The example we just gave of the news story shows what happens when the performer misses a key word. Finding those key words is the first step in analyzing the thrust of the copy.

Too often performers try to find key words by simply underlining every word that looks relevant. That approach is better than nothing, but if too many words are emphasized, they are no longer key words. Striking a balance is the goal.

One way to get to the heart of a piece of copy is to read it through and identify *three* words that summarize the thrust. This approach can give a surprisingly accurate reflection of which words are most important.

Theater set designers, who must come up with simple structures to convey complex messages, often play the mental game of distilling a play into a

---

[1] Quotes used with permission.

Figure 3.1

Bill St. James hosts ABC Radio's program
Flashback.

Photo by Philip Benoit

paragraph, then a sentence, and then a word. The set is designed around this word. This approach is oversimplified, but it does force you to think about the most basic meanings behind a play or any other form of communication. Key words are *those that accurately convey the meaning of the copy.* So changing key words can change the meaning of the copy.

For example, "Kim won the 10-kilometer run" is a simple statement. If you're looking for key words in that statement, you have to understand the context of the sentence. Is it an expression of amazement at athletic power? Turn it into a question-and-answer form to show it in a framework of a complete thought:

- *"KIM* won the 10-kilometer run? She hasn't trained in months!"

Changing the key word, then, can alter the perceived meaning. Let's complete three more question-and-answer pairs and show how context affects meaning.

- "Kim *WON* the 10-kilometer run? I thought she came in *third."*
- "Kim won the 10-*KILOMETER* run? She said it was a 10-*mile* run."
- "Kim won the 10-kilometer *RUN?* I thought it was a *walk*athon."

Finding the key words may mean going through the original copy several times to clarify for yourself what the author had in mind. This is not a mechanical process, although mediocre announcers make it so. For example, in most commercial copy the performer can rightly assume that words such as "bargain," "inexpensive," "free," "new," "natural," and "modern" are key words, words that are intrinsic to the message and that deserve stress. But those powerful-looking words are not *always* the key words, and a performer can mangle the message by not understanding it in context. How important is the word "new" in the following piece of copy?

> The new line of Smith Shoes will give you a step up as you swing into spring. . . . Look great and feel great in . . .

The most important words here are probably "Smith Shoes," "look great," and "feel great"; "new" is really not important. Also of secondary importance are the words relating to spring. The word "new" is almost redundant because few shoe stores offer old shoes as their spring line. The purpose of this copy is not to communicate the idea that Smith Shoes are new. The purpose is to communicate the idea that Smith Shoes will make you look and feel great and will let you "swing into spring" in an upbeat way.

But let's take another example:

> The new line of Smith Personal Computers, designed with the latest in digital technology . . .

Here, the word "new" assumes paramount importance. After all, a *new* personal computer, in these days of technological one-upmanship, is inherently more valuable than one of an older design.

The point is to avoid a mechanical approach to finding key words. Never assume that the most obvious choices are the words that convey the message.

Much the same caution applies to news copy. In news, there's really no stronger verb than "died." It conveys the most urgent event in our society, the loss of a life. But although there's no question that "four children *died* in a fire at . . ." is the correct interpretation of the copy, the word *died* isn't always the most important word in a message. For example,

> The families of the four children who died in Tuesday's tenement fire are suing the owner of the building . . .

Is "died" the key word here? Not really. The most important words are "families," "suing," and "owner." Putting too much stress on the concept of death makes the listener think that the communicator is calling attention to a contrast between the families of those who died and those who didn't:

> The families of the four children who *died* in Tuesday's tenement fire are suing the owner of the building . . .

According to this reading, the sentence ought to be completed with

> . . . but the families of burn victims who did *not* die are not suing.

To sum up, finding key words is not a simple or mechanical process. It involves a thorough analysis of the copy. Marking key words in the copy helps the performer accurately communicate the thrust of the message.

Mood

Understanding the mood the copywriter wants to project helps you to give an accurate interpretation. By contrast, not understanding the mood can detract from the communication. Projecting an inappropriate mood or making an inappropriate change of mood can baffle the audience. For example, in one familiar situation comedy routine the newscaster mixes up his copy and blunders into a tragic plane crash story with the smile and upbeat tone reserved for the final "light side" piece.

Misreading the mood is seldom that obvious, but it can happen, and it can mar your delivery. So carefully determine the mood. It could be, for instance, any one of the following:

- *Carefree.* "Swing into spring with Smith Shoes . . ."
- *Sincere.* "Are you concerned about your health insurance?"
- *Romantic.* "Dinner by candlelight at the Copper Bottom Restaurant will be one of the most . . ."
- *Somber.* "Twenty-three miners were killed this afternoon in a cave-in north of the city of . . ."
- *Excited.* "Bob Smith Oldsmobile has 30 cars ready to go at below wholesale!"
- *Humorous.* "A bank customer using an automatic teller machine in Los Angeles got more than he bargained for today when the machine spit out ten thousand . . ."

The relatively straightforward task of evaluating the copy for mood is done not so much to determine what mood the particular piece reflects as to find out where *changes* in mood must be expressed. A common problem for inexperienced or ineffective newscasters is not being able to *spot the points in copy where the mood must change.* When mood changes are not spotted in advance, the interpretation becomes inappropriate. At best, the announcer slides through the copy with an overall lack of mood. At worst, he or she catches the error and tries to change the mood at an inappropriate point, losing the real mood and sense of the copy.

Pace

Pace is the rapidity of words, the overall rate of reading, and the rate of reading within phrases. You can make the most effective use of pace after you have acquired an understanding of when and why to vary it. In general, a speeded-up pace conveys a sense of excitement. Sometimes, that excitement can be panicky, harried:

> Time is running out. Yes, you've heard all the talk about business phone systems. . . . All the commercials . . . all the hype. But it's your decision and you've got to make it soon! And you better make it *right.*

But note that a change of pace is needed in the second part of the commercial:

> . . . you'd better make it *right.*

> At Telephone World Business Systems, we've been helping people like you make the right decisions for over twenty years. We've got the

facts—not hype—and we can sit down with you and tailor-make a system that will do the job right.

We know it's a big decision, and . . .

Where would you vary the pace, and why? The first part of the commercial conveys a sense of time running out. That is as urgent a message as you can get. The pace, of course, is very rapid, almost breathless.

But the second part of the spot calls for a slower, more deliberate reading, "At Telephone World Business Systems, we've been helping people like you . . ." signals a change to a slower, deliberate, purposeful pace.

Get into the mind of the writer. What is he or she trying to get across? At this point, it's simply *you can stop panicking and come to Telephone World Business Systems, where we help people in the same situation every day, so calm down!*

An announcer who used the same pace throughout would mutilate this spot and lose much of its impact.

Purpose

What is the copy intended to do? Why was it composed in the first place? When you have answered these questions, you know the copy's purpose. Copy can persuade, inform, entertain, even anger. The communicator must understand the purpose before he or she can transmit the message accurately.

To understand the purpose, you have to understand more than what's on the paper. The more you know about the context for the copy, and the broader your range of knowledge, the better you can interpret the message.

For example, consider the intense advertising campaigns that competing phone systems have engaged in since deregulation opened the door to competition. To help interpret our imaginary Telephone World Business Systems spot, the announcer should be aware that the employee responsible for choosing a new phone system is under a great deal of pressure to make the right decision amid an intense advertising barrage. A valid interpretation must appeal to this theme.

Experienced professionals can lend an important sound to such copy through accumulated skills of emphasis and inflection. Understanding copy, though, will *always* help *anyone's* interpretation.

In addition, the announcer should understand the purpose of individual phrases in relation to the context. What would you perceive to be the purpose of the question "Why did this happen?" Standing on its own, it means little. It assumes varied significance when read in relation to the context. For example,

- "Economists said interest rates fell sharply in the wake of the presidential election. Why did this happen?" Here, "Why did this happen?" is an expression of simple curiosity.

- "Scientists found that the orbit of Pluto varied last year by hundreds of millions of miles. Why did this happen?" Now the question expresses wonderment.
- "Speculation about whether the birds would fly north or south was ended today when they flew west. Why did this happen?" Why did it happen this way, and not the other ways?
- "Ten people died in yesterday's apartment house fire. There were no smoke detectors in the building, which had passed a recent code inspection. Why did this happen?" The question now expresses outrage.

To sum up, understanding the purpose is essential. The next stage of the broadcast performance process—communicating the message—cannot be done effectively unless you know why the copy, sentence, phrase, or word is there in the first place.

Communicating versus Merely Reading

Perhaps the ultimate example of reading instead of communicating was provided by an announcer with a fine voice but a lazy and mechanical approach to his work. The copy was designed to relate the sponsor's product to the weather, and the announcer was supposed to open the spot with *one* of the following *three* options:

- "What a beautiful, sunny day. . . ."
- "Look at all that rain. . . ."
- "We've had more than our share of snow. . . ."

But he read all three, and he failed to understand at first why the program director and the sponsor were so upset with his delivery.

That example is *not* too far-fetched. Similar mess-ups happen every day. Poor on-air performers can make hash out of commercial and news copy because they simply do not take the time to understand the message they want to communicate.

This is the sum of what we discussed in the previous section. A good broadcaster must incorporate key words, mood, pace, and purpose to communicate, rather than just read.

Most of us have heard "announcers" who have decided in their own minds "what announcers sound like." They deliver each message in a mechanical singsong. That is *reading*.

A *communicator* knows how the copy should be read and can get across the intent of the author. He or she does not follow a preset formula but instead approaches each reading with an open mind, looking for the thrust of the material. In most cases, the better performer is not necessarily the one with the better voice, but the one who makes the copy genuine, natural, believable, and true to the intent of the author.

After many years of practice, this ability can become second nature. Good performers develop that second nature by marking copy to indicate key words, pace, pauses, and in some cases mood and purpose. They also include methods of indicating pronunciations of difficult words. Learning to mark copy is one of the most important steps you can take toward improving your performance skills.

Marking Copy

To many, marking copy is more a learning process than a practical tool. Many performers don't mark copy. They rely on experience and ability to carry the situation.

Many announcers do not have the opportunity to mark copy. Commercials are kept in a copybook that is used by all staff announcers and would soon be obliterated if each staffer put individual marks on the copy. Newscasters must often read copy that is prepared by others and that is not assigned to a particular newscaster until moments before airtime. Marking such copy is not practical.

What experienced announcers do, in effect, is to mark copy mentally. Beginners should mark as much copy as possible directly on the paper because the ability to do it mentally takes extensive practice.

However, all on-air people mark unfamiliar pronunciations, and such markings frequently are written right into the typed copy or wire service text. Marking copy for pronunciation is an integral part of understanding the message.

Phonetic Spelling

How do you show how to pronounce an unfamiliar word? Basically, you must come up with notations that will let you or another reader look at the agreed-on code and know how to pronounce the word. Such a system is known as *phonetic spelling.*

There are a variety of phonetic systems, and some are very accurate but very complex. The **International Phonetic Alphabet (IPA),** for example, uses symbols not found in the English alphabet to indicate elements of pronunciation. The IPA is a valuable tool for linguists and other scholars, but its value for broadcast performers is limited for two reasons:

1. Not all broadcasters understand it. The IPA can help someone who knows it to reproduce pronunciations with great accuracy, but most broadcast copy is not written by people who will read it over the air. Even in newsrooms where broadcasters do write most of the news department's copy, much of that copy is read by other newspeople.

2. Many of the symbols in the IPA are not reproducible by standard typewriters, Teletype machines, or computerized word-processing equipment.

Box 3.1

THE ASSOCIATED PRESS PRONUNCIATION GUIDE

	Vowel Sounds				Consonants	
a	bat, apple	oh	go, oval	g	got, beg
ah	father, arm	oo	food, two	j	job, gem
aw	raw, board	ow	scout, crowd	k	keep, cap
ay	fate, ace	oy	boy, join	ch	chair, butcher
e, eh	bed	u	curl, foot	sh	shut, fashion
ee	feet, tea	uh	puff	zh	vision, mirage
i, ih	pin, middle	yoo	fume, few	th	thin, path
y, eye	ice, time, guide	kh	gutteral "k"		

SOURCE: Brad Kalbfeld, *AP Broadcast News Handbook* (New York: McGraw-Hill, 2001), p. 382.

The second problem also rules out the use of diacritical marks, such as those found in the dictionary. Standard typewriters, Teletype devices, and word processors can't reproduce markings such as ă and ī, easily.

Despite its limitations for broadcast applications, however, the IPA is a tool you should be acquainted with. Appendix C gives you a system for learning the rudiments of the IPA quickly. If you take a little time to familiarize yourself with the IPA, you will be able to use it—along with the other tools discussed in this chapter—to unravel nearly any unknown pronunciation you encounter.

As a readily available tool for everyday use, the best alternative seems to be the phonetic spellings used by the Associated Press Radio Network. The AP uses a simple phonetic spelling system to convey how a name or other word sounds. It "goes along with the commonly accepted principles of English usage as to how vowels and consonants are sounded."

When an accent is indicated, the AP places a Teletype apostrophe over the letter or letter group that should be accented. As an example, in the style of the *AP Broadcast News Handbook*,[1] the name Juan Martinez spelled phonetically would appear as *Wahn Mahr-tee'-ness.*

When you are constructing or interpreting a **pronouncer,** as it is called, use standard English usage and the guide shown in Box 3.1, from the *AP Broadcast News Handbook.*

Pronouncers are shown in all wire service copy destined for broadcast use. If you are doubtful about a word and don't have a pronouncer, two very

---

[1] Kalbfeld, Brad, *AP Broadcast News Handbook* (New York: McGraw-Hill, 2001), p. 382.

helpful works are the pronunciation guides prepared by the National Broadcasting Company (NBC) and the British Broadcasting Company (BBC). Newspeople are responsible for determining the pronunciation of names of local newsmakers, a process that often involves making telephone calls to individuals, their families, or business associates.

Marking and Decoding Unfamiliar Words

To be able to approximate unfamiliar English words and words in foreign languages, it is worthwhile to get some exposure to foreign pronunciations. For one thing, some pronunciations can't be approximated by phonetic spelling because the sounds are not commonly used in English. Also, sooner or later you will come across a foreign word and have no way to check it out.

The English-speaking announcer faces some additional problems, other than simply deciphering pronunciations.

PROBLEM   Many foreign words have been anglicized as a matter of convention. In English, we speak of Munich, Germany; to speakers of German, the city is named *München.* Naples, to an Italian, is *Napoli.* Even when the spellings are the same, American pronunciations can differ from those of the original language. Paris, to a Frenchman, is *Pah-ree.'* How does an announcer decide?

A GENERAL STRATEGY   The best strategy is to combine knowledge of pronunciation rules with a good set of reference books, a broad education, and an observant personality. Suppose you need to say,

Our next selection is by Richard Wagner: the prelude to *Das Rheingold.*

Wagner is one of the names that is customarily pronounced with full inflection and adherence to native pronunciation. Most names in classical music follow this custom. Therefore, the *ch* in "Richard" is pronounced as a *k.* The *a,* as is typical of most foreign pronunciation, is close to the *a* in the American word "arm." The *w* takes the Germanic *v* sound. The title of the music needs little decoding except for the *ei* configuration, which is pronounced like the word "eye." Thus we have *Rih-kart' Vahg'-ner, dahs Ryn'-golt.*

Similar analysis can be applied to the following examples or to the copy in the drill section in Appendixes A and B:

The Spanish region of Castile was originally divided into the provinces of New Castile and Old Castile, known as *Castilla la Nueva* and *Castilla la Vieja.*

Note in this example that you would use different inflections when reading the English and Spanish designations of the same regions.

Although not known as the most intellectual of Italian composers, Giacomo Puccini is one of the best known.

To begin your analysis, check the difference in pronunciation between the single *c* in Giacomo and the double *c* in Puccini.

Although this chapter centers on marking and understanding copy, some suggestions on delivering copy involving foreign words and phrases are appropriate to conclude the discussion:

1. *Try never to be caught unaware.* Check copy thoroughly and phoneticize words. Be aware that foreign words can arise in almost any on-air work, not just classical music, international news, or sports. Check proper names with the people named, if possible, because even a common name such as *Gentile* can be and is pronounced *"Jen-teel'-ee"* by some people in certain locations. With some words, you may have little information about the word's origin or pronunciation, so it is wise to flag the word and check with an authoritative source, such as the radio station news director.

   As announcer Norm Howard of KQED-FM in San Francisco put it in one of his broadcasts: "In the course of our work we often have to pronounce unfamiliar and foreign words—the names of opera singers, composers, places and names in the news, words from different ethnic and cultural groups, from alphabets other than Roman. This is all by way of saying that a few minutes ago I mispronounced the name of the polar bear Pike, and I want you to know that it is *'Peek-uh,'* not 'pike.' Such are the hazards . . ."

2. *Do not hesitate before saying the word.* If you hesitate, listeners may think you are wrong *even if you are right.*

3. Bluffing sometimes is necessary, but don't get carried away. One announcer, for example, recalls the time he was reading "cold" a list of boxing title holders, who in the lower weight classes were mostly Latin Americans. He did rather well except for his highly accented rendition of what he thought was the name of the featherweight champion, *"Teet'-lay Vah-caht'-ate,"* which turned out to mean "Title vacated."

Remember that although learning the basic pronunciation rules can help in many situations, there are exceptions to many of the rules. True competence in foreign pronunciation is best achieved by having some familiarity with the actual languages. Several semesters of foreign language courses will be very beneficial in cultivating pronunciation skills.

English words should also be marked and phoneticized. In fact, English is a very irregular language, and a simple set of rules to govern all English pronunciations cannot be devised.

Most lexicographers (writers and compilers of dictionaries) define "acceptable pronunciation" simply as a pronunciation agreed on by convention among educated people. Pay attention to the way knowledgeable speakers pronounce words, and when in doubt about a word, *look it up in a reference book.*

Some pronunciations are especially deceptive, and incorrect pronunciations have worked their way into common usage. See Box 3.2 for examples.

Box 3.2

EXAMPLES OF FREQUENTLY MISPRONOUNCED WORDS

Some really common words are also very commonly mispronounced. Here are some examples:

- *Nuclear.* It's *noo'-clee-yahr*, not *noo'-cue-lahr*.
- *Status. stayt-us* is more widely accepted than *stat'-us*.
- *Data. dayt'-uh* is more widely accepted than *daht'-uh*.
- *Greenwich.* Say *"Gren'-ich"* to designate Greenwich, England, and Greenwich Village in New York City. Some small communities pronounce the same word *"Green'-wich,"* however, which points up the need for checking local usages.

If these words took you by surprise, consult a dictionary or other reference book and check out the following words and place names. Be sure you are pronouncing them correctly and not adding additional sounds. For example, *"ath'-ah-leet"* is a common mispronunciation.

accessory	infamous	radiator	length
impotent	Moscow	Delhi	Yosemite
Spokane	La Jolla	Canaan	Cannes

Marking copy with correct pronunciations is one of the first things you need to do when evaluating material. The next consideration is marking it for proper interpretation, for correct *phrasing*.

Using Symbols to Aid Interpretation

The dictionary defines "phrasing" as a grouping together of words into a unit forming a single thought. Perhaps a more interesting definition from the broadcaster's point of view is the musical concept of phrasing, where many of the passages that combine to form a larger piece can also stand alone, each such passage, or phrase, expressing a more or less complete thought.

Musicians and composers use a variety of symbols to aid interpretation, such as a crescendo (<), indicating a gradual increase in volume, or a "retard" (anglicized contraction of *ritardando*), meaning a slowing of the tempo.

Figure 3.2   Symbols for aiding interpretation.

A broadcaster can do the same. Figure 3.2 shows some useful symbols for marking copy. The next section shows how these symbols can help you communicate the message by phrasing it properly.

Phrasing

Notice how the symbols in Figures 3.3 and 3.4 add to both the understanding and impact of the copy. Key words are identified and their relative strengths indicated. The unfamiliar street name is flagged, and the pronunciation indicated phonetically.

One part of the first sentence in the second paragraph could be confusing if not read as a unit: "the explosion and resulting fire" is bracketed as a grouping.

The examples in Figures 3.4 to 3.7 take the marking process further and add some pauses and nuances. Observe how the jagged line in Figure 3.5 indicates a speeded-up tempo. You want to create a fast, harried mood for the first section. But when the copy must be slowed down, the change is indicated by the series of dots. The performer who marked up this copy realized that the second portion must be read in *deliberate* fashion. Note how in the final phrasing, pauses are used for emphasis: "That's a fixed-rate mortgage (pause), at 11 percent (pause), and no points."

Figure 3.3   A marked news story.

> Two people are dead, four injured, in the wake of a violent
> Mahr-say'
> explosion this morning at 443 Marseilles St. The names of the
> victims are being withheld pending notification of next of kin.
>
> [The explosion and resulting fire] leveled the two-story house.
> Investigators are currently on the scene. One fire official [who does
> not want to be identified] told Eyewitness News that arson is a
> possibility.

The performer who marked up this copy also used a cue for a jingle at this point. He or she might also elect to use that cue mark for timing. The performer could indicate that the remaining copy must be read in a given time period.

Phrasing and Interpretation

Consider how the examples presented show the ways in which phrasing can affect interpretation. The bank commercial was affected (see Figure 3.5) because the pace conveyed two very different moods.

Ineffective readers typically do not blend and match all the phrasing elements in a piece of copy. This frequently results in what might be called "mixed signals," for example, someone on television who is smiling but is clenching his or her fists.

You have to get your signals straight. There is some latitude in phrasing, but slow, deliberate phrasing would be inappropriate for most soft drink commercials, and quick, frenetic phrasing wouldn't work well for an insurance spot.

Rhythm and Inflection

The example of "Kim won the 10-kilometer run" in the section headed "Finding Key Words" illustrates the impact of inflection. Rhythm is also a powerful tool in conveying a message. The pause can create emphasis and, to an extent, suspense. Paul Harvey is an acknowledged master of the long, long pause, which virtually makes the audience beg for the punch line of his news story.

Rhythm incorporates change of pace, which is also a component of understanding and communicating a message.

Figure 3.4   A marked news story.

["From ghoulies and ghosties and long-leggity beasties, and things that go bump in the night .] . . Dear Lord protect us."/So goes an old Irish kitchen prayer.

It's that last item that concerned two local residents late last evening.

[The bump in the night][turned out to be an 18-wheel, semi-tractor-trailer] that crashed through the north wall of the kitchen in the home of John and Marsha Redbone, of 255 Mulberry Street at about 11:00 p.m. last night, while the Redbones watched television in their living room.

Hearing the loud "bump," John Redbone went to investigate. What he found was the front of a large truck protruding through the kitchen wall, with the front tire resting atop the overturned refrigerator.

The truck's driver, Ted Jarvis of Murfreesboro, Tennessee, was not injured.
Murfreezburro

State Police say the truck failed to make it around a sharp bend in the road at the Mulberry Street residence.

The location of that [bend in the road] has caused problems before for the Redbones. Two years ago a truck overturned in the side yard of the residence, dumping its entire cargo of chickens into the nearby swimming pool.

[The Redbones have rejected the idea of placing a guard rail along the edge of the property,] but say they might consider/a sturdy fence.

The Melody of Speech

In many cases it is not difficult at all to visualize the copy as a piece of music. Variations in rhythm, different inflections and emphases, and variations in loudness, intensity, and pitch all combine to provide a total effect.

Figure 3.5   Marked copy for a commercial.

> jibberish
>
> You've been running from bank to bank, you've heard gibberish
> and promises. You need a mortgage and time is running out. Well,
> you can keep on running, or you can walk into Hypothetical Savings,
> where qualified borrowers can get a fixed rate mortgage at 11 percent,
> and no points. That's a fixed rate mortgage/at 11 percent,/and
> no points. (JINGLE) The Hypothetical Savings Bank, member, FDIC.

Figure 3.6   Marked copy for a commercial.

> It's late July./August is right around the corner./It's time to shop for
> fall clothes, but it's hard to get enthusiastic about wool and corduroy,
> when the thermometer is pushing 90 degrees.
>
> [So take a break from your shopping for fall]/and enjoy something
> tall and cool. [Come to the lunch counter at Woolworth's in the Park
> Plaza Mall] and treat yourself to a "Sizzlebuster."
>
> It's not exactly a drink. But it is cool, delicious, and
> refreshing. [The Sizzlebuster is made from six kinds of fruit] mixed with
> ice. There's no sugar added, and each one is mixed fresh at the time you
> order it. [It's a smooth, tasty treat] that makes your whole body feel
> cool and refreshed. [And this week] it's only $1.50.
>
> So if you need a break from summer, and looking at heavy fall
> clothing isn't cooling you off, stop at Woolworth's lunch counter and
> get a Sizzlebuster. It's the cool thing to do.

Figure 3.7   Marked copy for a commercial.

A fine Italian restaurant is hard enough to find today in this world of fast food and grab it and run. And if you want to take time to enjoy the quiet elegance of beautiful surroundings while you dine, you may have given up hope.

But wait./There's Montinerio's [Montinareeos] Casa Italiano, where fine dining is still considered a necessity of life. The finest northern Italian cuisine, expertly prepared by a master chef, is presented to you/in an atmosphere of quiet Victorian elegance. Your food is served with the attention to detail that reflects the Old World grace and style of the finest European restaurants.

So forget the hurry-up world for a while. Put some style back into your life. Come to Montinerio's Casa Italiano and see what life can be like in the slow lane.

Good writers know this, which is why they "write for the ear." Effective communicators recognize the melodic and dramatic features of what is written, and often compose their own words and **melody.** The Gettysburg Address, for example, uses a memorable rhythm. And one noted piece of advertising copy was delivered in an unforgettable way: "We make money the old-fashioned way . . . we *earn* it."

Summary

Communicating a message is the first and most basic responsibility of an announcer. The announcer must think in terms of ideas, not words.

Finding key words in the copy is a tool for understanding meaning and ideas. Getting the meaning of the message involves understanding and identifying mood, pace, and purpose. The goal is to communicate, not just to read.

Key words are not always obvious. Often some analysis and digging are necessary to uncover the true meaning and impact of the piece. Noting key

Tech Talk

RESEARCH ON THE WEB:
A GUIDE FOR ANNOUNCERS

On-air personnel must have a wide range of knowlege, and they are frequently called on to address current events, trends in music, and developments in the industry. The World Wide Web is an incredible resource for staying up-to-date in all these areas.

This is *not intended to be an all-inclusive list* but simply a series of starting points for performers who want to use the Web as a ready reference.

Check out the following sites.

General News and Information

The American Journalism Review's *Newslink* provides links to a whopping 3,500 newspapers worldwide. Newslink also offers an efficient search engine for news stories appearing in selected newspapers, magazines, and broadcast outlets.

www.newslink.org

Gebbie, Inc., a directory publisher, offers an excellent, easy-to-use, and reliable link to most major U.S. newspaper Web editions.

www.gebbieinc.com/dailyint.htm

Time-Warner's *Pathfinder*, a service combing several of the company's publications and services, provides stories from and links to CNN, *Time, People, Fortune,* and *Money.*

www.pathfinder.com/pathfinder/index.html

For a quick scan of the world's and nation's top news, and searches of recent editions, try the *New York Times* . . .

www.nytimes.com/

And the *Washington Post* . . .

www.Washingtonpost.com

Search Engines

A search engine is basically a program that scans the content of Web sites and allows you to find Web sites that contain the key words you specify.

Continues

Tech Talk   *Continued*

An excellent way to start your search is with

www.google.com

For a guided search, try

www.yahoo.com

Library Links

Search the indexes of the Library of Congress at

www.lcweb.loc.gov/

Journalism Links

The Poynter Institute features a wide assortment of links related to journalism along with examples of prize-winning stories and photographs and suggestions for improving writing and coverage. Search at

www.poynter.org

The Project for Excellence in Journalism has a useful site at:

www.Journalism.org

Radio and TV on the Web

Check out the World Wide Web Virtual Library: Broadcasters

http://archive.museophile.sbu.ac.uk/broadcast/

Radio Locator allows you to search for radio stations by call letters, zip codes, or format:

www.radio-locator.com

Billboard Magazine has features about broadcasting and music:

www.billboard.com/billboard/index.jsp

And you can find out a great deal about the TV news industry and see some job ads at

www.tvspy.com

words is part of marking copy. Another important part of marking copy is identifying and decoding unfamiliar words and phrases. Wire service phonetic spelling, although it has its limitations, works well within the constraints of word processors, Teletype machines, and typical newsroom operations.

An announcer should make every effort to become familiar with the principles of foreign pronunciation. In addition to learning some language rules, it is important to know how and when to employ foreign pronunciation and inflection. In most cases it is best to follow the rules of pronunciation of the appropriate language but without trying to use the inflections of a native speaker of that language. Speak as you would imagine an educated American would, assuming some familiarity with the language in question. Never hesitate before you say a foreign word.

Names of contemporary newsmakers are pronounced as the person named wants. Names of foreign cities are pronounced according to conventional American usage. In the specialized field of classical music, however, foreign words receive full native accents and inflections.

The major component of marking copy is using symbols to aid interpretation. These symbols act like a musician's notation and guide the announcer to proper phrasing.

Phrasing—the grouping together of words into units forming single thoughts—affects meaning and communication. Marking copy identifies many of the signposts to meaning and communication. Also, it helps the announcer convey the proper rhythm and inflections of words and the melody of the words.

Exercises

1. Mark up copy from the drill material in Appendix A and B or copy provided by your instructor. Split into groups of four and exchange copy. Compare similarities and differences. Discuss the differences and why you feel markups are right or wrong.

   Next, elect one person to read all four pieces of marked copy, following the markings closely. Others in the group may also do this, depending on time limitations.

2. Using newspaper articles, pick three key words per sentence and write those words down. Do this for an entire article. Many long sentences will have more than three key words, so you will have to use your judgment in identifying the most important words. Be sure to use a straight news article, not a feature or human-interest piece.

   Read your key words aloud to a partner or to the class. Your partner or the class members must try to *reconstruct the story* from the three key words per sentence. When you read aloud, play out the words broadly and give them as much meaning as possible.

3. Write three approximately 30-second commercials for automobiles, and to the best of your ability write them "to ear." Make up whatever details you wish, but structure the commercials around these three concepts:

Commercial 1: To express elegance and love of luxury. Think in terms of rich leathers, classic interiors, and elegant lines.

Commercial 2: Youth, excitement, adventure.

Commercial 3: Practicality, dependability, durability, value to a growing family.

Have a partner or classmate give an interpretation of the commercials that you have written, aloud or on tape. Critique that performer. Work with him or her until you feel that each commercial is done correctly. Compare your critique with the instructor's critique.

FOUR

Communicating the Message

*O*nce he or she understands the basic message, the broadcast communicator must apply those skills to the actual delivery of information. Whether you're reading voice-over copy from a printed script or ad-libbing your way through the morning drive segment of an adult contemporary radio station, the basic requirement is to generate a response from the audience.

In this chapter, we begin by discussing the basic principles of reading copy and then deal with some of the nuances. We discuss ad-libbing in detail. Finally, we'll examine two technical skills that are central to effective delivery of the message: mic technique and camera technique.

Reading Copy

Why bother to sit down before a mic or TV camera and read a piece of copy? The answer is not as simple as it seems because, in addition to good mechanical delivery, a broadcast performer has several goals:

1. To communicate the message accurately

2. To convince the audience, on a *one-to-one* basis, that the performer understands and believes what he or she is reading

3. To breathe life into the message

4. To keep the listeners' and viewers' attention by giving energy to the reading

Accomplishing these goals involves proper use of your voice, a genuine and believable delivery, and the addition of style to the reading.

Using Your Voice

Proper use of your voice will help you considerably in communicating, in being convincing, in breathing life into a message, and in keeping the audience's interest.

A good voice is more than an "announcer voice." Today, you can be successful with what was once thought of as an average-quality voice. In news, the trend has been toward hiring on-air people who act more like journalists and less like performers. The commercial industry often needs voices that express humor or whimsy. Radio station managers and program directors search for true communicators who can reach specific audiences, rather than baritones with "rounded tones."

Two key elements of proper use of your voice were outlined in Chapter 2:

1. A healthy and relaxed vocal mechanism
2. The absence of distracting deviations, such as speech impediments or inappropriate regionalisms

Here we add a third key element:

3. A natural-sounding, genuine delivery

Genuine Delivery

A common beginning mistake is to put on an "announcer voice" and ignore the copy, focusing on the delivery as an end in itself. But even if you remember nothing else from reading this book, remember that the voice is only a tool and the message in the copy is what is important. Your voice *must not distract* from the message.

Some performers use the message as a vehicle for their voices, a practice that is neither productive nor professional. Actor John Carradine once said that one of the most valuable lessons ever taught to him was not to be "in love with my voice."

It is difficult to define the elements of genuine delivery because "genuine" implies a sound as natural and unaffected as possible. And yet, the broadcast studio is not a natural setting, and you certainly would not read copy the way you speak to a friend in a restaurant. Although some people advise announcers to talk as though they were speaking to friends in their living rooms, that's not, in a literal sense, what you want to do.

You must work in an unnatural setting and make your performance *appear* natural. You must make your message *resemble* the manner in which you speak to your best friend. If you listened to a tape of a conversation among friends, you would probably decide that it did not meet broadcast standards, especially in terms of diction and energy level.

A genuine delivery adds excitement and interest to a message without injecting artificiality. Mechanically trying to "punch up" copy can result in a

Figure 4.1 Terry Gross, who hosts *Fresh Air,* an interview program aired on National Public Radio, is noted for her ability to communicate one-to-one with both her guests and her listening audience.

Photo by Philip Benoit

strained, unnatural sound. That strained quality sometimes is a result of not paying attention to the phrasing of the copy. The delivery will sound much more believable if the words and phrases have been carefully analyzed and the copy marked appropriately.

Lack of artificiality is rapidly becoming one of the most desirable qualifications for an on-air performer. Today's performers in both radio and television are people who can communicate one-to-one. No longer do broadcasters *address* the audience. In radio, particularly, you are often being listened to by one person who is alone.

Top performers who conduct interviews on the air have become particularly adept at the kind of personal approach required of broadcasters today. One of the best in this format is Terry Gross (see Figure 4.1), who hosts *Fresh Air,* an interview program heard nationwide on National Public Radio. She is particularly adept at establishing a close rapport with both her guests and her audiences. Although she has an excellent voice, she uses it *conversationally,* putting her listeners at ease as they join her to explore the personalities of her interesting guests.

Style

A style can also be defined as a particular and distinctive characteristic or mode of action. Style is a component of both writing and performing.

It is difficult to draw a line between a stylized delivery and an artificial delivery, and even more difficult to try to cultivate a style that works. Trying too hard can result in an affected, phony delivery.

Yet broadcasters, by the very nature of their work, are required to have something distinctive about their delivery and appearance. On-air people frequently become noted for their styles, and unless a performer has something unusual going for him or her, advancement may be difficult.

There is no comprehensive list of styles, nor should you adopt mannerisms based on the approaches given here. Bear in mind, too, that performers use bits and pieces of various style categories to form their own unique styles.

Don't consciously wedge yourself into a style or copy everything a particular performer does. Do, however, remember that all performers pick up things from their colleagues. No one lives in a vacuum, and the way other professionals work must have an effect on each of us.

This eclecticism has plus and minus sides. Former *Tonight Show* host Johnny Carson admits that some of his style was picked up from the late Jack Benny. The result was obviously successful because Carson hosted the show for more than 20 years. On the other end of the spectrum is the speech pattern of NBC's Tom Brokaw. Brokaw has a very slight lazy 'L' pronunciation that people would *not* want to imitate, but he is a first-class communicator and an outstanding journalist.

Let's look at some style categories and representative performers.

SOPHISTICATED   Diane Sawyer is an example of a performer who projects a sophisticated air. She projects intelligence, culture, and taste in her bearing, her phrasing, and in her appearance. She is one of only a very few performers who manage to present this image without seeming to be a caricature of sophistication.

Sixty Minutes journalists Charlie Rose and Morley Safer also convey airs of cultured intelligence.

AUTHORITATIVE   Someone who projects an air of importance and power comes across as "authoritative," a word that is overused in broadcasting to promote news programming. ABC's Peter Jennings is a good example of authoritative style, as is CBS correspondent Leslie Stahl. ABC News senior correspondent Carole Simpson also delivers news with an authoritative style (see Figure 4.2).

WHIMSICAL   Advertisers often seek performers who can project humor or vulnerability. The whimsical style works well in specific applications. Perhaps

Figure 4.2

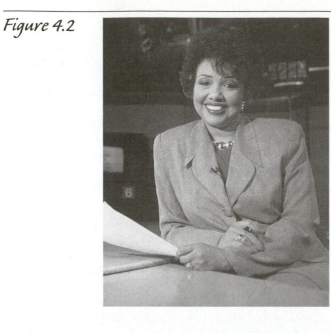

Carole Simpson, senior correspondent for ABC News, is an example of a news anchorwoman with an authoritative style.

© Richard T. Nowitz/CORBIS

Figure 4.3   David Letterman, known for his playful interviewing style, chats with Regis Philbin, another successful talk-show host.

Photo by Zuma Archive/ZUMA Press. Copyright © 2000 by Zuma Archivea Week.

Figure 4.4

Charles Osgood often employs a whimsical style.

Photo courtesy of CBS News

the best example of a host who successfully uses whimsy is CBS *Latenight Show* host David Letterman (see Figure 4.3). You would not, though, customarily find this style in the evening news anchor. There are certain whimsical *elements* in newspeople and people related to the news business, including Charles Osgood (see Figure 4.4) and Andy Rooney.

FOLKSY   Without peer in the "true-to-life" folksy approach to communication is *Today Show* host Al Roker. Roker is a very able performer who conveys great friendliness and personal charm. A performer who can master this style is sometimes able to parlay it into great trust and therefore great sales power. Walter Cronkite, one of the premier newspeople in the history of American broadcast journalism, projected the aura of an intelligent next-door neighbor. Cronkite's use of phrases like "By golly!" when covering a space flight and his overall friendly, informal style gave him tremendous credibility. Former host of CBS's *Sunday Morning,* Charles Kuralt also exemplified the effective use of the folksy style.

KNOWLEDGEABLE/DIDACTIC   *20/20*'s Hugh Downs is noted for the knowledgeable/didactic approach. "Ask Hugh what time it is," Jack Paar once wrote, "and he'll tell you how to build a watch." This schoolteacher approach inspires confidence and curiosity.

Bill Moyers appears rather bookish and has a reputation as an intellectual, which he bolsters by his style. He often analyzes a story in a way no typical hardnews reporter would. Linda Cohn, a superb sportscaster, projects

Figure 4.5   Geraldo Rivera.

Photo by Philip Benoit

this type of image. Perhaps the epitome of the didactic, professorial approach is the analytical approach employed by George Will, who indeed once was a college professor.

AGGRESSIVE OR HARD SELL   Performers who seem to leap out of the radio or television set represent the aggressive approach. Mike Wallace has made a living from this style. Some observers have noted the aggressive manner of Geraldo Rivera (see Figure 4.5). Rivera's bearing and body language convey a sense of energy—even urgency, although he is noted more for an emotional rather than an intellectual approach. Sam Donaldson carries the aggressive approach to its zenith—or nadir, depending on your point of view.

PHYSICALLY APPEALING   When a performer's appearance becomes part of his or her persona, this physical appeal qualifies as a style element. However, an attractive on-air performer does not automatically fit only this one style. In the most blatant of cases, it is not difficult to see why an advertiser would feature Cindy Crawford or Michael Jordan. On a more subtle level, newscasters frequently benefit from an appealing appearance. Although attractiveness was certainly not the primary reason for their success, physical appearance has helped Dan Rather and Paula Zahn.

SINCERE   "C'mon, this is a real problem, so help me out here." Phil Donahue has turned sincerity into something of an industry, and for him it succeeds. The sincere and trustworthy approach also works well for commercial spokespeople such as Nolan Ryan and Catherine Zeta Jones. Former CBS News anchor Walter Cronkite is still recognized as the embodiment of the sincere and trustworthy news figure. Tom Brokaw projects a more vigorous form of sincerity, and Charles Kuralt comes across as a friendly next-door neighbor in cable reruns of his *On the Road* reports.

NOVELTY   Usually people in the novelty category have distinguishing characteristics that make them virtually unique, yet they often have many imitators. Howard Cosell was a perfect example.

COMBINATIONS OF ELEMENTS   The preceding descriptions of the categories are of course not definitive. Many performers cut across style lines, using several elements to hone their particular deliveries. For example,

- *Ted Koppel.* Koppel gives the impression that he plans to get his *Nightline* guests to deal forthrightly with controversial areas, even if it makes them uncomfortable to do so. His style is not threatening. He conveys authority through a combination of sincerity and a knowledgeable approach.

- *Geraldo Rivera.* The style of this controversial television talk show host is remarkably effective in conveying to viewers the impression that he represents them. He uses a "street-smart" image combined with a sincere approach. Rivera alternates the aggressive style of an investigative reporter trying to uncover wrongdoing with the image of a sensitive person who is only putting his guests on the spot because he has to get at some important issues.

- *Bryant Gumbel.* Gumbel (see Figure 4.6) combines a direct, "let's cut to the chase" approach with a thoughtful, reflective style that often came through when he was cohost on the *Today* show and then later as host of CBS' *The Early Show.* His style tends to dominate when he shares the screen with others, a trait that has been criticized by some viewers.

- *Jane Pauley.* Former *Dateline* co-anchor and host of MSNBC's *Time and Again,* Jane Pauley combines elements of a knowledgeable delivery with a sincere approach. This combination allows Pauley to explain complex happenings to the audience without appearing to talk down to the audience and without smugness.

You can certainly apply this same type of analysis to most performers you view and, just as important, to yourself.

DEVELOPING A STYLE   As we have said, developing a style requires a measured approach, not all-out imitation. It is a combination of assessing your own strengths and weaknesses and experimenting with style elements that capitalize on your strengths. We list briefly several methods for developing a style.

Figure 4.6   Bryant Gumbel, seen here with Microsoft's Bill Gates, is an incisive interviewer with a "let's cut to the chase" technique.

SOURCE: CBS Photo Archive

1. Imitate performers who have style elements you would like to adopt. Do this during practice sessions and within the bounds of reason.

2. Before adopting stylistic devices, analyze *why* those styles are successful for the performers who use them. The foregoing section was intended to stimulate such analysis. Ask why the style element bolsters that person's performance.

3. Play up your strengths and make a realistic evaluation of your weaknesses *as you appear to the audience.* Aaron Frankel, Broadway director and acting instructor, points out to students that personal qualities do not always translate to the actor's stage identity. The same holds true for broadcasting. An extremely sophisticated and urbane performer may not *appear* as such on camera or on mic.

4. Experiment. That is what practice is for. If something works, add it to your store of knowledge and experience. If it doesn't work, discard it.

5. Learn from the techniques and successes of others, but do not ape their styles.

Nuances

Many intangibles are associated with communicating a message. Most are subtle, but such nuances often are key elements in getting the message across effectively.

Gestures, energy, and *body language* are some of the more important nuances involved in broadcast communication.

Gestures

As an exercise, try delivering a piece of radio copy while sitting on your hands. It's difficult, or should be. Gestures, even on radio, act to *color* the delivery by their association in our own minds with moods and feelings.

To turn the example around, adding gestures can help radio announcers add expression to their readings. No, the audience can't see the gestures. The audience can, though, sense the announcer's involvement in communicating an idea. Just record a lighthearted radio commercial while smiling and again while frowning. You'll hear the difference.

On television, gestures are obviously more apparent. A television lens magnifies many movements and makes them look exaggerated, so poor use of gestures can also have a negative effect on TV.

For example, restrain your head movement on television. A certain amount of head movement is natural in everyday conversation, especially among animated speakers, but it can be distracting on camera. Be especially conscious of restraining the movement of your head when the TV camera is on a tight shot.

Radio announcers who plan to move into television should restrain their head movement, too. If you have practiced head-bobbing for years in the radio studio, it may be impossible to break the habit when you try to make a transition to television. Avoiding this mannerism from the start is easier than trying to break the habit later on.

Proper gestures, movement, and posture can reflect positively on performance. We address this topic later, in a section on body language.

Energy

For many of us, putting energy into a piece of copy requires conscious effort. Low-key speakers appear fine in most normal conversation but can seem decidedly lackluster on the air.

Here is a gray area where the performer has to consciously "punch up" copy but must avoid artificiality. The only way to arrive at a proper compromise is through practice and critique. During practice, it's perfectly all right to overdo the level of energy. If it appears too "hyped," back off a bit. Fine-tune as you go along.

The most important aspect of energy and liveliness is that you cast yourself in the role of being extremely interested or excited by what the copy is

> ## Box 4.1
>
> ### GUIDELINES FOR PROJECTING ENERGY
>
> 1. Show enthusiasm for the subject.
> 2. Project your voice and personality. As one director puts it, "try to jump right into that lens."
> 3. Vary your pitch and delivery, and be sure to avoid a monotone.
> 4. *Look* involved and interested, even in radio.
> 5. Maintain good posture when on mic or on camera.
> 6. Do not use excessive motion. Motion by itself will not inject energy. Appropriate and controlled gestures will.
> 7. Do not try to inject energy by using a high-speed delivery. Speeding up a monotone won't make it any more interesting.
> 8. Make every effort to appear and to actually be physically vigorous. Successful radio performers sound vigorous, and successful TV performers look and sound vigorous.

saying, just as you would be interested and excited when telling a friend you've gotten a great job. That approach may be overdoing it a bit for some products, and much news delivery requires a more somber attitude. But energy is always an important attribute of a performer's talent, and it is worthwhile to cultivate these qualities. The guidelines in Box 4.1 will help you project energy and liveliness.

On the last point, note that most top television performers actually *are* physically fit. Walter Cronkite was physically active and aggressive. People like Tom Brokaw typify the vitality and energy that health and fitness provide. Cronkite was at one time a race-car driver, and his competitive vigor showed on air. Dan Rather was an energetic, though undersized, college football player, and Tom Brokaw is a runner.

Being in good physical condition never hurts and can help considerably in the effort to give energy to your on-air work.

Body Language

Body language has a powerful effect on a performer's appearance and delivery. It is really a combination of gestures, physical energy, and posture.

Body language reflects your attitude toward the audience. Pay attention to body language and your use of it. Some suggestions are shown in Box 4.2.

Box 4.2

USE BODY LANGUAGE TO YOUR ADVANTAGE

1. Make your body language show that you are open and at ease. Avoid crossing your arms in front of you, a posture that reflects a closed and defensive attitude.

2. Reflect vigor in your posture. Resist the temptation to slump, which is a particular problem faced by TV performers when sitting at a desk.

3. Use body language to project an interested attitude. Leaning slightly forward toward the camera lens gives the impression of energy and interest.

4. Review videotapes of yourself in search of unconscious negatives in your body language. Do you clench your fists while smiling? Do you wet your lips, giving the impression of nervousness even if you are calm?

5. Be aware of how your body language affects others. During an interview program, tenseness on the host's part often communicates itself to the guest.

6. Maintain the posture and breathing habits demonstrated in Chapter 2. Good posture energizes a performance and improves breath support.

Ad-Libbing

Many people think of ad-libbing as a matter of opening the mouth and letting the words flow. Even the most experienced performer, however, is never sure exactly what will come out at a given moment. The result of a too-spontaneous ad-lib is frequently embarrassment.

Most good ad-libbers have worked very hard to develop thought patterns that allow them to draw material together in advance, even only a moment in advance, and to use the material appropriately. Ad-libbing is a kind of role-playing, and even a second's rehearsal in that role gives the performer an advantage.

The ability to ad-lib (literally, to speak "at pleasure") is becoming one of the most important parts of a broadcaster's arsenal. News reporters today must ad-lib more often than ever before, thanks largely to modern live transmission technologies.

Components of an Ad-Lib

The first step in developing ad-lib talents is impossible to master in a quick lesson: it is the state of being well educated and conversational in a variety of fields. An announcer cannot fake knowledge. A news reporter must know the facts, a program host must know something about the guest's topic, and a radio personality must, if he or she ad-libs about local matters, be up on current events.

Step 2 in effective ad-libbing consists of learning how to do a quick encapsulation and rehearsal. Give some thought, even an instant's thought, to what you want to say. Break it into coherent, short, and simple thoughts and phrases. Mentally edit what you want to say. The biggest problem of most ad-libbers is their tendency to ramble on too long. One of the authors of this book, for example, was once assigned to ad-lib a 90-second piece from a crime scene live over the air. Just moments on the scene, and panicked by the thought of having to *fill* 90 seconds, he delivered a rambling, barely coherent report that went on for 6 unbearable minutes. The point? Ninety seconds is not really very long to ad-lib, and the report would have gone much better if the reporter had collected what few facts he did know, assembled them into three or four coherent thoughts, and ad-libbed without trying to fill. This would have turned out to be much closer to the 90-second requirement and would have made much more sense.

The same principles apply to the interview format. Some program hosts are more concerned with showing what they know rather than clarifying what the guest knows, and they ad-lib a halting and seemingly endless recitation of the facts during the show's introduction. *Less is always better when it means the difference between a coherent ad-lib and rambling.*

Here is a review of the principles of good ad-libbing, followed by an example:

1. Plan and encapsulate. Sum up what you want to say in a few mental notes.
2. Deliver the ad-lib in bite-size segments.
3. Keep it short.

Good ad-libbing involves giving a natural appearance to an unnatural action. When we speak in normal conversations, we don't use the well-thought-out phrases of expert reporters. This is graphically brought home to people who read transcripts of what they have said in court testimony or legal depositions. What sounded quite lucid while being spoken seems almost unintelligible and semiliterate when reduced to the written word.

Thus, news reporters ad-libbing live over the air need to organize their material more carefully than if they were describing the scene to someone during a telephone call. Organization and as much pre-air planning as possible are needed. For example, take this scene approximated from a report of a major windstorm.

This is _____ reporting live on the road. . . . It's really difficult driving because of all the debris in the road, and we don't know when the situation is going to be cleared up. The winds were very heavy, and because of all the debris in the road, police are banning travel. Like I said, it's difficult getting around because of the power lines and downed tree limbs . . . so police don't want people on the roads. No one is quite sure when the situation is going to be cleared up . . .

Had the reporter given a bit more thought to the coming ad-lib, the thoughts could have been broken down into three main points:

1. Police have banned travel.
2. Storm damage is heavy.
3. There is no indication of when the situation is going to be cleared up.

Breaking that down might take just 5 seconds, but the result would have been a significantly better report:

This is _____ reporting from the mobile unit, one of the few vehicles on the road now because the police have banned travel in the wake of this evening's windstorm. Debris in the road has made driving virtually impossible . . . the city streets are littered with downed tree limbs and power lines. At present, police aren't able to give any indication of when the situation is going to be cleared up . . .

The same information is presented, and the report is shorter and more logical.

The principle of planning and encapsulating applies to all facets of ad-libbing. A radio staff announcer, for example, might want to ad-lib about the upcoming Fourth of July weekend. Instead of barging headlong into the ad-lib, she thinks, "I'll come out of the music, read the weather, mention how short the summer has seemed so far—it's almost the Fourth of July—then talk about some of the events coming up."

In addition to being an accurate and coherent expression, an ad-lib should be able to pass the test of appropriateness and should be delivered with a professional-sounding flow.

APPROPRIATENESS   Just why do you want to ad-lib? To say something, or to hear yourself talk? Try to avoid the latter option. It never hurts to subject a planned ad-lib to this test. A radio personality whose primary purpose is to entertain still must deal in appropriate ad-libs, which touch on common experiences that have meaning to the listeners. In-jokes concerning station personnel, for example, don't meet this test.

FLOW   Practice eliminating pauses and interjections. Saying "uhh" or making extensive pauses can become annoying to listeners. There is no reason, in most cases, for these delays to collect one's thoughts. Stalling and interjections are primarily nervous habits.

Although the principles just outlined are useful for just about any circumstance, certain tasks require individualized techniques. Let's look at some specific ad-libbing requirements of some typical broadcast performance situations.

Ad-Libbing in Radio

In radio today there is considerably less ad-libbing in general than there once was. Most modern radio music formats promote themselves as providing listeners with "more music, less talk." So a steady stream of patter from a "personality"-oriented announcer or disc jockey is counterproductive.

The key is that "less is more." Most radio shifts today call for the announcer to be the facilitator. It is her or his responsibility to make the program elements flow together and create an atmosphere where the audience feels comfortable. Announcers must blend with the overall sound that identifies the station and the format. Ad-libbing helps in that effort by providing information and by supplying transitions to smooth the process of getting from one program element to another.

In large-market radio, there are usually strict guidelines for announcers who work an airshift on a music program. In most cases, the music is the star. Announcers are expected to talk about things that will interest the particular types of listeners the station is targeted to reach. An oldies station that targets adults between the ages of 35 and 44, for example, wants its announcers to be knowledgeable about the music and the events that occurred when the music was first popular.

Many stations will spend a great deal of money researching the music they play to determine how often a particular cut should come up in the playlist rotation and how the music should be blended to meet the desires of the audience. One major-market announcer who was fond of claiming full credit for attracting listeners to the station was invited by the program director to substitute polka music for his normal fare of contemporary hits to see if his sparkling presence was really the crucial element that held the interest of listeners. He declined the challenge. A talkative announcer who wants to be the center of attention can interfere drastically with a carefully designed music format.

Announcers who are permitted creative leeway are under fewer restrictions for the style and content of the program. In these programs (often aired in morning drive time), the personality is the focus. Personalities in major markets often work with a producer who helps put together ideas for the program and helps in the studio work necessary to make the material work on the air. Even though greater creative latitude is allowed on personality programs, there is no less attention paid to the content of the show. The host of a personality morning show, for example, often spends three or more hours after the airshift preparing for the next day's program.

What does it take to be successful in large market personality radio? Brad Murray, former station manager for Baltimore's WQSR, says you need to be creative, a good writer, and well informed. Many of the comedy elements used on personality shows are based on current topics in the news. The personality must also be sensitive to how far he or she can go in flirting with the boundaries of good taste. Top radio personalities and their producers usually know when they're crossing the line, according to Murray. When they get into questionable areas, they ask for an opinion about whether or not to go with the idea.

Depending on which format you're working with, ad-libbing is either virtually nonexistent, as in some "lite" music stations, or is a major element, as in many contemporary hit radio formats. A brief look at several popular formats will show how widely ad-libbing requirements can vary in radio today.

COUNTRY   Modern country formats are much changed from the hillbilly styles of most country stations of an earlier era. As pointed out in the discussion of staff announcing responsibilities in Chapter 5, today's country music recording industry uses all the mixing techniques used in any other category of music. Aside from the major identifying characteristics of steel guitars and lyrics about truck driving and cheating in love and romance, country music stations don't vary widely from many other formats in their overall sound.

Consult Chapter 5 for the general requirements of the country station staff announcer. At this point we'll focus on the special requirements for ad-libbing in this format.

The overriding principle of effective ad-libbing in a country format is "know the music and the artists who create it." Even though your ad-libbing will be restricted by the same "more music" constraints of all modern music radio, the ad-libs you do use will almost always touch some aspect of the current scene in country music.

If you are new to the category of country music, you'll need to get a quick education. There are several good histories of country music in book form. Check one or two out of the library and bone up.

For actual on-air ad-libbing, here are several principles to guide you:

- *Relate comments to what is going on at the moment on your station.* Don't start talking about the latest Hollywood gossip about Faith Hill if you've just come out of a cut from Tim McGraw's latest album.

- *Don't depend on your memory of items in the news when making comments about the music or the artists.* Bring clips of information to the studio with you so you can briefly review the information before using it on the air. Chances are listeners are already aware of any news, and you'll lose all your credibility with your audience if you get the facts wrong.

- *Never make fun of the music or the artists.* Country music fans are fierce in their loyalties. Many country music fans regard their favorite artists as "family." Attempts by a radio personality to get a laugh by making comments about an artist are not well received. The same, of course, holds true for all music genres to some extent: listeners may also take offense at remarks about performers as diverse as Bob Dylan or Frank Sinatra.

ADULT CONTEMPORARY OR LITE   The concept of the announcer as facilitator of program flow is nowhere more prominent in radio than in the adult contemporary format. Ad-libbing should be used sparingly and often is not even allowed by program directors. Keeping the music flowing is the key here. This format tends to have greater diversity of music styles than many others in radio. It tries to draw from a bit wider spectrum of musical tastes. The theory is that, even if listeners may not particularly like what's playing at the moment, they will often stay around long enough to hear a selection they do like. But there must be music.

Ad-libbing, when permitted, is very brief and usually is based on the weather, traffic reports, or comments on a current movie or a performance by an artist featured in the station's music format.

For ad-libbing purposes, it is not necessary to have the kind of in-depth knowledge of the music that country music announcers need. Usually the adult contemporary formats have oldies mixed in with more contemporary cuts, but oldies are not the featured aspect of the format, so avoid ad-libs taking off from nostalgia that accompanies a selection. The guidelines to keep in mind for ad-libbing in this format are

- *Keep remarks very general.* The audience has a somewhat broader range of interests than those of other formats, so you may risk offending part of the group if you give opinions about anything.

- *Submerge your personality.* The announcer's role as facilitator is aided by a certain amount of anonymity. The music should form the central core of the station's sound. Ad-libs that draw attention to the personality of the announcer detract from this goal.

- *When in doubt, leave it out.* If you have any question in your mind about the appropriateness of an ad-libbed remark, don't say it. You'll seldom be worse off by passing up an opportunity to ad-lib. You may, however, regret having interjected an item that turned out to be inappropriate.

TOP 40 OR CONTEMPORARY HIT RADIO (CHR)   The CHR format, as it exists on most stations, includes more ad-libbing than any other format in radio with the exception of talk radio. The CHR format follows in the tradition of the Top 40 stations of the 1950s, where the personality of the disc jockey figured heavily into the sound of the station. Several varieties of personality type within the CHR category generally break into three basic types:

1. *Rock jock.* This is the modern equivalent of the personality form invented by the famous DJ's of the 1950s. They maintain a steady patter laced with information about the music and the artists. Various items of interest to teens and young adults are interspersed, punctuated by

humor that appeals to those groups. Energy is the hallmark. The overall sound is heavily produced.

2. *Outrageous.* This style skirts the boundaries of good taste, occasionally overstepping the boundary of what some find offensive. Disc jockeys who affect this style typically insult listeners and often make disparaging remarks about well-known people. The sound is characterized by short prerecorded segments with heavy use of sound effects.

3. *Shock jock.* This personality type exists primarily in large markets where the personality can afford to annoy substantial numbers of listeners, many of whom will tune in out of a sense of curiosity about how far the disc jockey will go in his or her effort to shock listeners. The bounds of good taste are frequently crossed, and the only restraints seem to be to make obvious word substitutions for language that would be considered too offensive for broadcast.

The requirements for ad-libbing in the CHR format will of course vary, depending on the particular style. The style of personality will often vary by time slot within the same station. There may, for example, be an outrageous style jock for a "Morning Zoo" program in morning drive time and a standard rock jock for midday. Some general principles can be stated for all three categories within this format.

- *Develop a humor style based on the youth culture.* Take a lead from the *Saturday Night Live* and David Letterman types of humor, but be sure to avoid the appearance of being a rip-off artist, who steals phrasing and material directly from these sources. Check out www.humor.com or other Web sites related to humor. Work on humor that meshes with these styles, but that bears the stamp of your own personality.

- *Keep up with the music and artists that constitute the format.* Read trade press articles about them and keep up to date on news about items such as concert tours, film appearances, and music videos. Integrate this into your ad-libs. This is particularly necessary for the rock jock who relies less on humor and shock to create an effect.

- *Maintain a high energy level in your style.* This is helped by the heavy use of short produced program elements that characterize this format. Prepare a list of ad-lib topics and short items, and take it into the studio with you. Check them off as you use them to avoid repeating items. Keep comments short, and move quickly from item to item.

- *Even in the categories of outrageous and shock jock, there is danger in going too far beyond the limits of the acceptable.* The line is difficult to define, but when you have gone too far, it can mean the end of the job and sometimes the end of your career. The best guideline to avoid going too far is to make it a practice to back off when you sense that you may be overstepping the bounds of what you can get away with—with your audience and your station management.

TALK RADIO   The announcer on talk radio must be able to ad-lib effectively about a wide number of topics. The major key is to be well informed. You should regularly read one or two major national newspapers, a good regional paper, and both general-interest and news magazines. You need to keep up with topics and people who appear on *Nightline, Hardball,* and other public affairs programs on television, and you will have to be generally aware of the books that are drawing a large public following.

In short, the talk show host has to be a well-rounded person who can articulate thoughts with clarity and style. Not an easy assignment, but there are many opportunities for work for those who do it well.

Ad-libbing in this format requires the ability to move quickly from one topic to another and to deal with a wide variety of people. And it's important to keep alert to what callers are saying so you can hit the "dump" button when callers' remarks are not appropriate for the air. Keep the following general principles in mind:

- *Bone up on the topic under discussion.* If you are speaking with a guest expert, familiarize yourself with the guest's background and with the books he or she has written. Read the background on topics in the news or on the Web that are scheduled for discussion.

- *Be careful about expressing opinions.* Unless your assignment calls for a personality who has strong opinions that are supposed to provoke listeners and guests into disagreement and conflict, soft-pedal your opinions. In general, keep your comments as neutral as possible, but don't be afraid to play "devil's advocate" to generate discussion.

- *Don't let yourself come through as a know-it-all.* The most effective host comments in talk radio are made with a certain degree of humility. If you are as well informed as you should be, you will be far more knowledgeable on most topics than the average call-in listener. Never forget, though, that the listener is the most important element of the equation. Treat all callers with respect, but don't get drawn into displays of emotion.

Radio ad-libbing is an art that demands careful attention to context. A reticent talk show host will not succeed, nor will a big-mouth adult contemporary announcer. Many announcers can effectively work in a number of different formats and quickly sense the requirements of ad-libbing. The key is that when it's done effectively, ad-libbing is virtually unnoticeable as such to the average listener. When it draws attention to itself, ad-libbing can detract from the impact of the format in general. The announcer who does so quickly becomes expendable. Adding vivid description can help the announcer bring a scene alive. In Focus on Technique we offer tips to would-be broadcasters.

Ad-Libbing on Television

Several television situations require announcers to ad-lib. On the local level, news, sports, and weather programming often call on announcers to ad-lib.

Focus on Technique

SEE IT ON THE RADIO

One of radio's consummate ad-libbers is WCBS-AM's Rich Lamb. The 20-year veteran of New York all-news radio has covered the installation of a cardinal and the funeral of a first lady, the visits of presidents and the city's final farewell to a firefighter killed in the line of duty.

His word pictures are vivid—and occasionally listeners pay a high compliment (accidentally or on purpose) and note that they've "seen it on the radio" after hearing his coverage.

Here are some tips he offered to student broadcasters:

- *Appeal to the senses.* "Flags snapping in the breeze . . . ," for example, paints a sight-sound picture and grounds the listener in an authentic environment.

- *Put yourself in the mood of the story.* "Mourners are lined ten deep along ten blocks of Fifth Avenue . . ." Say it slowly and quietly, and the story of a firefighter's funeral will carry itself.

- Relating to the point above, *don't be afraid to use natural sound and let the story tell itself.* Lamb's advice: "Sometimes you just have to shut up."

- *Know the specifics.* When Lamb covered the firefighter's funeral, his background knowledge of city politics enabled him to inform listeners that one of the politicians closely involved was a former fire commissioner—a relevant point that affirmed the notion that this particular politician was not simply there to be seen.

- *Know the generalities*—in other words, have a healthy inventory of general knowledge. "A liberal arts education is extremely valuable," Lamb says. "You'll be surprised how much stays in your head and falls out of the right slot exactly when you need it."

Also at the local level are talent assignments involving hosting movie programs and local talk or interview programs. Network-level announcing assignments that require ad-libbing include game show hosts, talk show hosts, sportscasting, and news reporting.

Some general guidelines for each category can help prepare you for the ad-libbing requirements of each of these assignments.

LOCAL   Local news, sports, and weather talent need to be prepared to ad-lib in these general sets of circumstances:

1. *Between segments on the news set.* The concept known as "happy talk" brought ad-libbing to local news programs all over the country. The extremes of that idea, in which the conversation was specifically structured to convey the impression that the on-camera talent were great friends, has given way to brief segments of conversation that simply function as bridges between segments of the program.

2. *In live reporting situations.* The increasingly common use of live reports from the scene of a news event makes it necessary for reporters to ad-lib news reports that once would have been taped and edited for broadcast. Live sports coverage also uses on-air talent to fill in spots between sports action with ad-libbed material.

3. *During weather shows.* The TV weather reporter is the only person on the news set who works without a written script. The basic information is given on the maps and charts, but it is up to the reporter to present the information smoothly.

4. *When hosting television movie programs.* Although this format has almost disappeared, some programs on some local television stations still broadcast feature films in a format that calls for a host to introduce the film and make comments in the spots where there are commercials.

5. *During local talk shows.* Programs in which a host interviews area personalities and visiting celebrities require talent to ad-lib extensively to make the program run smoothly.

NETWORK At the network level, ad-libbing is done by live news and sports reporters, talk show hosts, and game show hosts.

News and sports reporting requirements are similar to those at the local level, although the audience is larger. The same general abilities are required at network and local levels.

Game show hosts have special requirements. Generally, they must create an atmosphere of fun for the participants and the audience.

Talk show hosts at the network level are generally required to interact easily with guests and to move the conversation along so that it stays fresh and entertaining for the audience.

Whether at the network or local level, each of these assignments requires announcers to draw on their experiences to make the unnatural seem natural. Those who succeed in that task draw little attention to their ad-libbing ability. That's the sign that they have succeeded.

It is difficult to draw general guidelines for ad-libbing in these different circumstances, but keep these several principles in mind:

- *Prepare yourself as well as possible before you go on camera.* If you are on the news set, for example, plan ahead with colleagues to establish the general sequence of the conversation. If no one knows what to expect, and everyone tries to jump in to fill up the dead air, viewers will sense the confusion, and the credibility of the whole news team will be in jeopardy. If you are reporting live, list what you will say in sequence. Do the same thing for live sports reports.

- *Don't be a slave to your pre-set plans.* The best ad-libs are indeed "off the top of your head." The trick is not to have blind faith that something will occur to you once you're on the air. If you have prepared properly, you'll have an idea of what you will say when you are expected to ad-lib. If something better occurs to you later, go with it.

- *Try to think ahead about what exactly will take place during the program or program segment you're involved with.* Not all situations requiring ad-libbing are live, but many are. The more you can anticipate what will happen, the more confidence you'll have. Relaxing and feeling confident improve the effectiveness of your ad-libbing. The same goes for taping sessions. There is a certain amount of leeway for error in some ad-lib situations, but the more professional you are in the session the better you'll feel about your performance.

Ad-libbing in performance situations is the ultimate test of a professional. Those who do it well have considerably broader opportunities for advancement in broadcasting than do those who can simply read a prepared script.

We'll discuss ad-libbing more as it fits in with other aspects of various performance situations, in later chapters. For example, there is more on ad-libbing for staff announcing in general in Chapter 5. News ad-libs are explored in the context of overall considerations for on-air work in both radio and television in Chapters 6 and 7, and ad-libbing for commercials is examined in Chapter 10.

Playing to Microphones and Cameras

The rest of this chapter deals with techniques of playing to microphones and cameras. Mic technique and camera technique are major components of basic announcing skills, and they significantly affect a performer's ability to communicate a message.

In broadcasting, the equipment necessary to put the broadcast over the air is a prominent part of the performer's work. The ability of a performer who does not know how to deal with mics or cameras can be seriously compromised by technical errors. By extension, a performer knowledgeable about equipment can enhance his or her performance. Some mics, for example, tend to flatter voices of certain types.

A basic communication model (see Figure 4.7) shows that anything that hinders transmission of a message from sender to receiver is known as *interference*. A performer who is uncomfortable and unfamiliar with the tools of the trade may generate a great deal of interference. Every performer does not have to be a technician. Only a basic knowledge of mics and camera technique is required for skillful on-air work, but that knowledge is essential.

Figure 4.7   A basic communication model.

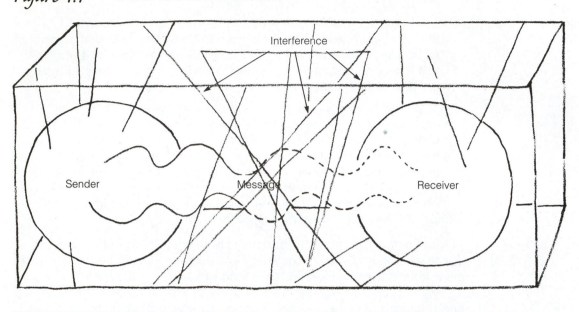

The Microphone

A microphone reproduces sound by means of a diaphragm within the instrument. The diaphragm vibrates in response to sound. Sound is a vibration of molecules in the air or other medium. The diaphragm of the mic responds to that sound in much the same way as our eardrums respond to sound. The mic then converts the vibration of the diaphragm into an electrical signal, which can be transmitted or recorded. The process of converting one form of energy to another is known as **transduction.**

What does this mean to the broadcast performer? Various microphones respond differently to sound. To use the instruments properly, performers should be aware of at least some of these differences.

MICROPHONE TYPES   Mics are classified first according to their internal electronics. The mics most common in broadcasting are the **moving coil, ribbon,** and **condenser** types.

Moving coil: The diaphragm vibrates in sympathy with the sound that activates it. An attached conductor moves through a magnetic field and creates an electrical signal. Moving coil mics, such as the ElectroVoice 635A (see Figure 4.8a), are regarded as rugged and versatile and are used extensively in fieldwork. An ElectroVoice RE20 is a standard studio mic.

Figure 4.8   Examples of the three main types of mics. (a) The EV 635A, a rugged, dependable, moving coil mic. (b) The RCA 77DX, a fine-quality ribbon mic. (c) The Neumann U-87, a popular condenser mic.

a   b   c

Photos (a) and (b) by Philip Benoit. Photo (c) courtesy of Gotham Audio Corporation, New York City.

Ribbon: A thin foil ribbon is suspended between two poles of a magnet. Vibrations move the ribbon; the moving ribbon creates an electrical signal. This mic is not very rugged, but many broadcast performers like a ribbon because it is said to impart a warm, rich quality to the voice. RCA's 77DX (Figure 4.8b) is an old-fashioned ribbon mic still favored by many announcers who find that the ribbon element flatters their voices. But ribbon mics do have their disadvantages, one being an extreme sensitivity to wind. Popping of plosives (*p*'s and *b*'s) is very evident on a ribbon mic.

Condenser: An electrical element called a *capacitor* stores an electrical charge. Actually, "condenser" is an old term for "capacitor" that happened to stick as the name for this type of mic. An electrical charge is applied to the diaphragm and a capacitor plate. The vibration of the diaphragm produces a change in capacitance, which is transduced into an electrical signal.

Condenser mics provide the highest quality of sound reproduction with excellent sensitivity. (A good example is the Neumann mic pictured in Figure 4.8c).

For a performer, this can be an advantage and a disadvantage. Extreme sensitivity provides the intimate "presence" so in tune with many FM radio formats. Conversely, a supersensitive condenser mic picks up a great deal of unwanted sound, such as breathing, mouth noises, and console operation.

PICKUP PATTERNS   Another major consideration in mic technique is knowledge of pickup patterns. The major pickup patterns are omnidirectional, bidirectional, and cardioid.

The **omnidirectional** mic picks up sound from all directions equally well (except from the very rear of the mic, where the actual mass of the unit blocks sound reception). A very simplified representation of the omnidirectional "pickup pattern" is shown in Figure 4.9a. The pickup pattern chart packed with the mic would contain concentric rings representing the relative volume in units of sound intensity called *decibels*. Technical details are beyond the scope of this book, but if you are interested in exploring the role of sound and audio in broadcasting further, we suggest you consult *Modern Radio Production* by Hausman, Benoit, Messere, and O'Donnell, and *Audio in Media* by Alten (see Suggested Readings).

For the performer, an omnidirectional mic is especially useful in handheld operations where background noises are desired, as in many news applications. The **bidirectional** pattern (Figure 4.9b), which is characteristic of the ribbon mic, is sometimes useful in a two-person interview.

"**Cardioid**" means heart-shaped, which describes this pickup pattern (Figure 4.9c). Remember, these patterns extend in three dimensions, so you can approximate a cardioid mic's pickup by imagining it to be the stem of a gigantic apple.

A cardioid pickup pattern is useful to the performer in that it cancels out sound from the rear. That feature is often essential in "combo" operations where a radio staff announcer operates the console and other equipment. If noise from the background were not canceled, the listener would be treated to a wide variety of clicks and thumps.

FREQUENCY RESPONSE   In addition to mic type and pickup pattern, frequency response is an important consideration to on-air performers. **Frequency response** is a complex subject, but basically it means the range of frequencies that can be picked up by an audio system, and because of differences in this response, certain mics emphasize certain pitches and deemphasize others. One notable characteristic of cardioid mics is known as the "proximity effect," an emphasis of bass frequencies as the performer moves closer to the mic. This can be good or bad, depending on the announcer. Some mics emphasize the frequencies that lend clarity to speech, such as the higher frequency sounds of consonants. These types of mic are quite useful when maximum intelligibility is required.

Still other mics have switchable patterns. The user, for example, may select a "flat" response for music (all ranges of frequencies receiving equal

Figure 4.9   Three mic patterns. (a) An omnidirectional pickup pattern—mic picks up sound equally well from all directions. (b) A bidirectional pickup pattern—mic rejects sounds from the sides, hears only front and back. (c) A cardioid (heart-shaped) pickup pattern—mic rejects sound from the rear.

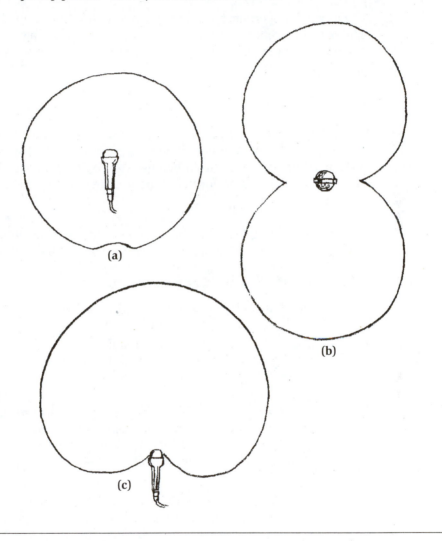

emphasis), or a "bass roll-off," where the bass frequencies are deempha-sized, to defeat the proximity effect and lend greater clarity to speech.

MICROPHONE SELECTION AND USE   Selection and use of microphones can affect the performer's image and appearance. Someone other than the performer usually selects the mics, although experienced announcers do develop a preference for particular mics and use them when available. More important for the entry-level performer is knowing how to translate the information just presented into effective performance. Some practical suggestions are given in Box 4.3.

Learning proper mic technique requires an investment of time and a willingness to experiment. You must also ask questions of engineering and production personnel, who are usually willing to help you with any aspect of mics and their use.

Performing on Camera

The equipment of television places a variety of demands on broadcasters. Mic technique is not very important because mics in TV are usually clipped to the performer or hung from booms. The unblinking eye of the camera, however, can flatter a performer, or poor camera technique can hinder the performer.

PLAYING TO THE LENS   One of the major problems faced by newcomers to TV performance is difficulty in becoming comfortable with the properties of the TV camera lens.

To play to the lens, work as follows.

1. When you look at the lens, *look directly at it.* Even a small diffraction of the angle of your gaze will be very apparent to the viewer.

2. Take an occasional glance at the studio monitor so that you know what kind of shot you are in. When the lens is on a close-up, you must be careful to restrain movement and gestures.

3. Use proper eye movement. Some of us glance to the side when carrying on a conversation. Although not particularly bothersome in normal conversation, this habit is extremely distracting on TV. A camera lens will mercilessly pick up this movement, and the performer may look "shifty-eyed." When you break contact with the lens, it is much better to glance downward than to glance sideways.

The subject of camera changes is addressed more completely in Chapter 7 on television news, but it is worthwhile to note that changing the gaze from one camera to another is a good talent to cultivate. Do not make a glassy-eyed rotation of the head. Instead, pretend you are changing conversation partners at a party.

POSTURE AND BEARING   Movement and posture are important elements of camera technique. To use movement and posture to improve your on-camera appearance, try the following:

Box 4.3

TIPS FOR USING MICROPHONES

1. If you have problems with popping plosives, avoid ribbon mics. With ribbon mics, position yourself and the mic so that you can speak across the diaphragm, not directly into it.

2. Positioning yourself closer to a mic will provide a more intimate feel to your reading. This is particularly true of the supersensitive condenser mics. Be aware that the intimacy can be accompanied by a strong increase in the audibility of mouth noises, such as lip smacking and teeth clicking.

3. Working closer to a mic with a cardioid pattern will lend a deeper quality to the voice. It also may muffle the sound reproduction, which is why some station engineers cover the mic with a thick foam wind filter. The filter mechanically keeps the announcer back from the mic.

4. Wind filters, which come in many shapes and sizes, can sometimes help the announcer who is operating outside in windy conditions or has a problem with popping plosives. These filters, also known as *pop filters,* simply block some air movement.

5. When speaking into a mic, maintain the same relative distance from the instrument. This depends on the piece you may be reading, of course. For an intimate feel you might want to move in closer to the mic, but be sure to maintain that same distance throughout the reading so that the intimate feel is consistent.

6. How close should your mouth be to the mic? The answer depends on your individual speech pattern, the mic itself, and the effect desired. As a *general rule,* 6 inches, about the length of a dollar bill, is a good working distance.

7. You will want to work closer to the mic in noisy situations. Move farther away from the mic if you have a deep, powerful voice and tend to sound muffled during playback.

8. **Hard-sell** pieces generally sound more convincing when the announcer moves back from the mic. The perspective offered more adequately reinforces the hard-sell message than does a close-up, intimate perspective.

1. *Learn a standard stance and practice it.* This is particularly important to announcers who read while seated at a desk. Considerable practice often goes into developing a good-looking and consistent body position. Desk-sitting announcers should practice using the full-front or three-quarters postures (see Figure 4.10). The goal is not to slump and to avoid unnecessary movement, while appearing reasonably relaxed.

2. *Don't fidget.* Excessive blinking, table tapping, and constant wetting of lips will imply that you are ill at ease, even if you are not.

3. *Don't use mechanical expressions.* The "raised eyebrow" that some viewers think implies skepticism may simply be a gesture that the newscaster has affected. Not only does it not mean skepticism, it doesn't mean *anything.*

The newscaster's pasted-on "concerned face" can often appear ludicrous and can be offensive to some viewers who know that you really are not ready to break into tears. Some viewers may feel that a maudlin expression is an insincere attempt to appear emotionally moved by a tragedy that is being reported.

EYE CONTACT   Now that prompting devices (see Figure 4.11) are common in TV stations, maintaining eye contact isn't as difficult as it once was. Devices such as the teleprompter consist of a mirror that is angled over the camera lens. A special camera takes an image of the news copy, and that image is projected onto the mirror. The newscaster or other performer can see the script, but it does not interfere with the camera's view.

You will, though, be required to read directly from copy in many circumstances. TV news, late-breaking events, election coverage, and so forth all require you to read from printed copy and still maintain good eye contact.

Maintaining eye contact involves the ability to read ahead a sentence or two in the copy. This skill is valuable for radio announcers, too, because it allows them to monitor clocks and look at equipment they are operating. Reading ahead also allows you to spot errors in copy and allows a moment or two to adjust. To cultivate eye contact, use the following guides.

1. Practice reading one sentence ahead of the point in the copy you are reading aloud. This is not as difficult as it sounds, and experienced communicators can often digest entire paragraphs in advance of the words they are reading aloud.

   Push yourself during practice sessions to scan as far in advance as possible. Reading ahead helps in more ways than maintaining eye contact because you will be digesting and repeating back ideas rather than words.

2. When reading from a hand-held script, avoid looking up at monotonously regular points. Don't, for example, get into the habit of glancing down at the end of each sentence.

Figure 4.10   Camera positions for announcers. (a) The three-quarters position is frequently used when on-camera talent is seated at a desk. (b) The full front position creates a more direct feel.

a.

b.

Photos by Philip Benoit

Figure 4.11   (a) The teleprompter is fitted over the front of television camera. (b) Software projects large-font letters with the ability to scroll up smoothly.

(a)

3. Although prompting devices have simplified the problem of making eye
    contact, they do require some measure of skill. For one thing, a
    performer using a prompter must avoid staring too directly into the lens.
    It's natural to keep an eye on the lens, though, so remember to glance
    down occasionally.

4. Announcers with poor eyesight need the prompters placed close to
    them. Otherwise, they will stumble over the copy and squint. But per-
    formers with very dark eyes must be wary of having the prompter and

Figure 4.11   (Continued)

(b)

CENTRAL NEW YORK LABOR FEDERATION
TUESDAY AM 10/01/02   AEC
   CENTRAL NEW YORK LABOR UNIONS
ARE POOLING THEIR RESOURCES TO
BETTER PUSH THEIR AGENDA.
   SIX LABOR COUNCILS ACROSS THE
REGION HAVE FORMED THE CENTRAL
NEW YORK LABOR FEDERATION, A-F-L
C-I-O.
   WITH OVER 110-THOUSAND MEMBERS
COLLECTIVELY, PRESIDENT MARSHALL
BLAKE SAYS THE GROUP WILL BE ABLE
TO BETTER ORGANIZE UNIONS, BUILD

Photos by Fritz Messere

the camera lens too close because the movement of their eyes from word to word will be apparent and can be distracting.

ENERGY   One of the most important elements of camera technique and on-air performance in general is the *ability to infuse energy into a performance,* and the most common defect is a lack of that energy. Consider these three remarks overheard or read recently:

- "Be as vibrant as possible," a TV talk show producer recently told a guest for an upcoming segment. "There's something about the medium that robs energy."

- "If you sat next to the announcer on the set," a weather reporter told a trainee as they watched the host of *Good Morning, America,* "he'd blow you away. But on the air he has just the right level of energy. You need that kind of energy in your performance."

- "I am returning your tape," wrote the news director. "Your appearance is good, your voice is outstanding, but your energy level is very low. If you don't care about what you are reading, why should the viewers?"

It is better to inject too much energy than too little. First, what you think is too much might be just enough after the lens and camera have "robbed" the energy. Second, it will be easier to back off than to try to add. Finally, the potential to influence an audience is important to realize. We close this section with a discussion related to the ethics of broadcasting (see Connections).

Summary

In the most basic terms, reading copy involves using the voice to facilitate expression, and communicating the *ideas* with an unaffected delivery. The way the announcer does this involves the element of style. Polished performers often borrow style elements from professionals they admire, and you can do the same. However, developing a style must never be outright imitation.

Many of the announcing skills needed to communicate a message involve nuances. Gestures are a nuance that can improve expression even in radio because they add an intangible element of communication. Gestures must be carefully controlled because the television lens magnifies gestures and they can detract from appearance. Energy is another nuance, and a performer should always infuse energy into on-air work. A third nuance is body language, which can subtly convey many impressions to the audience. A talk show host tensely holding the arms across the chest, for example, will convey the image of a withdrawn and up-tight person, a feeling that may be communicated to the audience and to guests on the program.

An increasingly important basic announcing skill is ad-libbing. To be effective, an ad-lib must be kept brief and must be thought out in advance, even if the announcer can devote only a moment to planning. Break down what you want to say into distinct ideas, and make mental or written notes of those ideas.

Both radio and television performers need to develop the ability to ad-lib. Ad-libbing in radio requires knowledge of the audience and the format. Ad-libs must blend well with other elements of the overall station sound. Today's "more music, less talk" concept requires music show hosts to make ad-libs short and effective. Talk radio hosts need to keep up with current events and to move quickly from one topic to another. Television situations that require ad-libbing include news, sports, weather, talk and interview programs, and hosting movie shows.

Camera and mic techniques are crucial in communicating a message. An announcer who knows how to work effectively within the technical constraints of the media and who can take advantage of the properties of mics and cameras will look and sound better. Microphones have varying electronic elements and pickup patterns. The elements are moving coil, ribbon, and condenser. Patterns are omnidirectional, bidirectional, and cardioid. An example of mic technique involves moving closer to a mic for a more intimate perspective.

Connections

ETHICS

Because questions of ethics pervade almost any discussion of mass media, this book deals with case histories of on-air people faced with ethical dilemmas.

Understanding ethics is vital to an on-air performer for a number of reasons. First, though the on-air performer often receives undue credit for the work of a large team of production personnel, the announcer also receives some of the blame if there is a lapse in factuality or ethics.

Second, you can recover from almost any career stumbling block other than an ethical lapse. Factual mistakes are generally forgiven in time, so if you make a horrible but honest blunder it is not a career-killer. But a reputation for connivance or dishonesty may follow you from market to market and dim your employment outlook.

So what is ethics? There are at least two definitions of ethics, the first being "the branch of philosophy which studies questions of right or wrong." The second definition comprises the more common understanding of the term, and identifies "ethical" behavior with "good" behavior.

The word *moral* is sometimes used synonymously with *ethical,* although morality usually refers not so much to philosophy as much as to prevailing customs. We have a tendency to use the word "moral" in matters dealing primarily with those customs and not with fundamental questions of right or wrong. For example, we would be far more likely to describe marital infidelity as "immoral" rather than "unethical." Another point of usage: "Ethics," when used to refer to the branch of philosophy, is usually treated as a singular noun, such as "Ethics is a controversial subject." If you refer to individual collections of ethical principles—"My personal ethics are quite flexible"—the word takes a plural form.

If you elect to study classical ethics, you'll find that an immediate benefit is the revelation that ethical problems have had essentially the same structure for centuries. In a way, it's comforting to know that you are not the first person to confront a problem.

So here's a simple (and admittedly simplistic) crash course in ethics.

An initial point of analysis, and a widely accepted one, begins with the two camps into which philosophers tend to fall when discussing ethics: they usually are termed *consequentialists* or *nonconsequentialists.* Some gravitate toward the middle, advocating an approach that adds up the pluses and the minuses and produces an average, or *mean,* that

Continues

Connections Continued

Figure 4.12   *One way to conceptualize ethics.*

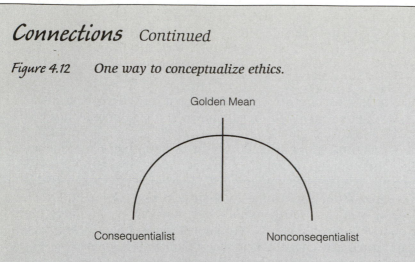

balances the two extremes. Figure 4.12 shows a continuum that illustrates this concept.[1]

Consequentialists generally believe that instead of attempting to judge whether an act itself is right or wrong, the judgment should be predicated on the *outcome.* John Stuart Mill and Jeremy Bentham were noted consequentialists. They advocated a type of consequentialism called "utilitarianism," the course of action that produces the greatest good for the greatest number, or as Mill put it, "the greatest happiness." (Note that this is an oversimplification; Mill and Bentham shared basic ideas but there are differences in their philosophies, which are beyond the scope of this chapter.)

In short, consequentialists will argue that the ends justify the means, and that *motives* are not a particularly relevant factor in that analysis. If someone saves me from drowning, a consequentialist might argue, it makes no difference if he saved me out of the goodness of his heart or because he wanted to get his picture on the six o'clock news. I was saved, and that's all that counts.

Nonconsequentialists, on the other hand, contend that *results* are not the standards by which we should judge an action; *motives* are. Immanuel Kant was the most widely recognized nonconsequentialist, and his philosophies still guide those who advocate adherence to the "categorical imperative." The categorical imperative means that each person

---

[1] This structure and analysis is adapted from Carl Hausman's *Crafting the News for Electronic Media,* Wadsworth, 1992, and Carl Hausman's *Crisis of Conscience: Perspectives on Journalism Ethics,* HarperCollins, 1992.

Continues

Connections   *Continued*

should act as if his or her "maxim should become a universal law." Kant might argue, for example, that you have no right to steal food even if you are lost and starving. Stealing is wrong, he would contend, under *any* circumstances. It cannot *become right* when it proves convenient, because if everyone adopted that handy and painless approach to ethics, we would see theft become rampant as people bent their ethics to fit the situation.

Ethicists who have taken the middle ground essentially put their trust in the individual's judgment. In other words, a person attempting to come up with an ethical solution to a problem would aim for a point halfway between excess and deficiency. Aristotle called this the *golden mean*. He claimed it was the quickest path to excellence, and that virtue is the mean between extremes, a mean that can be determined not by blind adherence simply to consequences, or simply to motives, but to "rational principle . . . that principle by which the man of practical reason would [make a decision]."

Consequentialist, nonconsequentialist, and golden mean thinking are used every day in analyses of ethical problems. Here is an example.

Suppose you are scheduled to anchor the 6 o'clock news and your department becomes embroiled in a controversy about whether or not to use the name of a suicide victim. How could you apply this framework to the decision?

In general, most broadcast news departments do not air the names of suicide victims if those people are essentially private persons and the suicide an essentially private act. That is a *nonconsequentialist* rule, grounded in the quite decent categorical imperative that families have already suffered enough at this point, and there is little to be gained by dragging the name of the victim out into the public spotlight. So we just won't use the name of the victim, ever.

But things don't always work out so neatly. Let's assume that the suicide victim was a popular young man, the captain of the football team, a person who seemingly had everything going for him. A *consequentialist* might argue that this is a case that merits breaking the rules. Why? Because it shatters the myth that only lonely, reclusive people take their own lives. Teenage suicide is indeed a growing problem, and potential suicide victims often drop hints or display symptoms disclosing that they are at risk. Friends and family members who find it impossible to believe that popular kids kill themselves, though, frequently ignore those symptoms. "Sure," a consequentialist might argue, "using the victim's name will cause the family pain, but in the long run we'll save lives."

Continues

Connections Continued

An advocate of the *golden mean* might search for a reasonable middle ground. Perhaps the story could be handled in such a way as to avoid identification of the victim. Family members, if they were willing, could be unidentified and be interviewed in silhouette, and thereby pass along their valuable, albeit tragic, experience to family and friends of other teens.

Those are the most basic approaches to one common ethical dilemma. You will find those rationales (consequentialist, nonconsequentialist, and golden mean) served up at some point during almost every ethical debate. But remember that they are not foolproof formulae. They could hardly be foolproof, since consequentialism and nonconsequentialism are diametrically opposed to each other. But they help to illuminate our thinking patterns by shedding light on whether we are thinking and arguing from a consequentialist, nonconsequentialist or golden mean point of view.

But what's the point of "illuminating our thinking patterns" or determining the rationale from which we are arguing? Simply this: once we understand why we reason a particular way, we can take a step back and gain a clearer perspective of our thought process. We can also, by examining our thinking and the well-established criticisms of *nonconsequentialist, consequentialist,* and *golden mean thinking,* search for flaws in our ethical reasoning.

Here are some examples of ways in which we might sift through our reasoning process.

Nonconsequentialism: Pro and Con

Arguments in favor of nonconsequentialism. Nonconsequentialism is a philosophy with a noble heritage, and within the context of our example (the suicide victim) it offers many strong points. Why should we suddenly decide to break a rule because we *think* it will produce some benefit? What proof can we offer that airing the name of the suicide victim will prevent further suicides?

And another point follows: If we're not going to stick to a rule, what is the point of having it? Rules are meant for the tough choices; you cannot simply choose to invoke them only in the easy cases.

Those are the arguments nonconsequentialists use to bolster their case. But their opponents can peck away at that logic.

Arguments opposed to nonconsequentialism. Critics of nonconsequentialist reasoning argue that clinging to a categorical imperative is, in itself, logically inconsistent. Why? Because a nonconsequentialist says that consequences don't count—but at the same time, he or she is *antici-*

Continues

Connections *Continued*

pating consequences. By imposing a rule prohibiting the use of suicide victims' names, for example, aren't we *predicting* consequences—*assuming* that we will besmirch the name of the victim, disgrace the family, "glamorize" suicide, and so forth?

Also, it is arguable that we are indeed blocking an act of good will—bringing the issue of teenage suicide more directly into the public spotlight—by blind adherence to a rule. Perhaps these are special circumstances that should cause us to change our thinking. We cannot adapt to unfolding situations if we are obsessed with following rules.

Consequentialism: Pro and Con

Arguments in favor of consequentialism. Basically, the previously stated rebuttals to nonconsequentialism serve as the consequentialist's platform when he or she defends the concept that the ends justify the means.

- We should not be hidebound to a set of inflexible rules. We can adapt.
- We can look past the immediate situation and can do what will provide the greatest good for the greatest number.
- We do not anticipate consequences while pretending to ignore them.

Arguments opposed to consequentialism. Consequentialists also take their lumps in ethical analysis, though. As mentioned above, the consequentialist argument about "preventing teenage suicide" sounds appealing, but how do we really know what the outcome will be? Will breaking our rule and running the story deter teenage suicide? Maybe.

Maybe not.

Doesn't it make sense to base our decision on the premises of which we are sure: Our policy which, for good reason, protects the privacy of the families of terribly disturbed people who, confronting their own private demons, take their own lives?

The Golden Mean: Pro and Con

Arguments in favor of golden mean thinking. The best we can hope for is to make a rational decision based upon what we know. Instead of trying to predict the outcomes, and instead of clinging to an inflexible rule, we must add up pluses and minuses and come to a reasonable decision halfway between the extremes.

Arguments opposed to golden mean thinking. While the idea of adhering to a *golden mean* is appealing, self-reference problems are involved. After all, if you are the one making up the two extremes you can still

Continues

Connections Continued

wind up with a distorted mean. ("How many people will I murder today, one or ten? Oh, let's compromise and make it five.")

On a more realistic level, let us also note that a compromise is not always the best solution. Because this is first and foremost a journalism text, we need to point out that there simply *may not be a reasonable middle ground* when reporting an event of this nature. You could not hedge indefinitely; it would be ludicrous to write a story about "the captain of the Central High School football team, whose name is being withheld." Also, if the event occurred in a public place, and many citizens witnessed rescue units dashing to the high school, you would show poor judgment by going on air at noon with a story saying, "a student died by suicide this morning at Central High" and not naming the student. That could start a panic among parents.

Camera lenses pick up and magnify any deviation of the eyes from a direct angle to the lens, so a direct gaze, without eye shifting, is important. The properties of a TV camera also require polished movement and posture. Eye contact bolsters contact with the viewer, and cultivating the ability to read ahead in the copy allows greater eye contact as well as improves communication skills.

The most common mistake in television, and to a great extent in radio, is failure to project enough energy.

Exercises

1. Cast celebrities in the following hypothetical commercials. Write down which celebrities you would choose for each spot, and what elements in their styles will reinforce the particular message to be communicated.

   a. A radio bank commercial specifically geared toward attracting young customers.

   b. A radio bank commercial geared to attracting mature investors with a great deal of money.

   c. Narration (off camera) for a television documentary on the great science fiction movies of the 1990s.

   d. Host (on camera) for a TV special on the earth's volcanoes.

   e. Host (on camera) for a humorous look at small-town America. The host must *not* imply anything demeaning about small towns; the humor must be good-natured.

2. Experiment with different body positions as you read several pieces of copy (from the drill section in Appendix A or B or provided by your instructor). Record the readings on audiotape. Use these modes:

   a. Slouching in a chair

   b. Standing

   c. With gestures

   d. Sitting on hands

   e. Smiling

   f. No expression

3. Practice ad-libbing. Take the following exercises seriously; they can be very effective and useful. Using a portable tape recorder, try the following:

   a. Describe a scene (a busy street corner, looking out a window, a sporting event—anything) for 60 seconds or so. Make it compelling, and more than just a physical description of objects.

   b. Clip an action news photo from a newspaper and ad-lib a description of the scene (about 60 seconds' worth).

   c. Ad-lib a brief commercial from the following facts:

      • There is a Washington's Birthday Sale at the Acme House of Furniture.

      • Everything is marked down 20 percent.

      • There's a complete selection of Nordberg Scandinavian furniture, including teak desks and coffee tables.

      • Acme will be open all day tomorrow from 9 till 9.

   Before you start, let us complicate things a bit. Do this commercial twice: once as you think it should be done for a hit music radio station, and once for a classical music station.

FIVE

Radio Staff Announcing Today

*T*he radio industry is going through a period of unprecedented change in the way it uses announcers. On some radio stations and for certain airshifts, technology has supplanted the staff announcer altogether. For example, many stations use a live announcing team for their morning drive-time show but then switch to voice-tracking for their midday show. For stations that use voice-tracking software, the staff announcer has been replaced with a board operator, a person who may or may not have any announcing experience.

Where staff announcers exist in today's radio station, they do far more than just read copy and introduce records. In addition to informing, persuading, and entertaining, the staff announcer must reinforce the station's overall sound quality and format. Staff announcers provide linkage between the station and the listener.

In some instances, a computer program has replaced the disk jockey's ability to select music within the station format. The program manager may preselect production elements and the rhythm and pacing of the format to reinforce the basic programming strategy of the station. Despite continuing technological innovations, the staff announcer still has to make the station sound cohesive and interesting. If the format happens to be fast-paced contemporary hit radio, for instance, the staff announcer is expected to convey energy and to inject the right amount of humor to provide an entertaining accompaniment to the music.

Modern radio is very specialized. Formats are targeted for well-defined segments of the population. In radio today, on-the-air performance is measured by the announcer's success in attracting listeners among the station's target "demographics" (population). The primary goal of a staff announcer,

Figure 5.1   Nick Butchko, WRVO-FM, Oswego, New York, working "combo."

Photo by Fritz Messere

whether doing a live shift or voice-tracking, is to attract and hold the interest of the audience segment that the station needs for attracting advertisers.

Although reaching those particular audiences is their primary goal, announcers also must know how to operate equipment and how to organize time and perform the tasks integral to on-air work. Small- and medium-market stations usually require the announcer to work in "combo," operating the mixing console (see Figure 5.1) and manipulating discs and tapes, while announcing.

In this chapter, we outline the operational and organizational skills required for effective on-air performance in modern radio.

The Staff Announcer's Job

In a broad sense, the duties of a staff announcer can be classified as *performance, operations,* and *organization.* Although these categories of duties overlap, they categorize the typical staff announcer's job as well as any other classification. Understanding these categories provides valuable insight into some of the operational and organizational tasks that are not heard by the listening audience but that still play an important role in the staff announcer's job.

Much of this chapter centers on programming and technology, rather than on what would strictly be considered announcing, and you may wonder why. Well, programming has been evaluated in such detail because *programming and the role of the performer have become inseparable.* Although 20 years ago an announcer could rely on a good voice and a glib tongue, today a program director can replace a good voice with a computer that provides voice-tracking capability. Therefore, the choice to keep a live announcer on the air is a conscious choice the station management makes. A competent and skilled performer is one who can work effectively within a format and can reach that target audience better than can a technological solution.

Performance

Performance includes introducing music, entertaining with humor, and reading commercials, weather, sometimes news, and routine announcements such as time and temperature, school closings, and so on. It also includes the air personality's general patter, which can range from occasional ad-libs to extended comedy monologues.

Operations

The duties associated with getting program elements over the air by means of station equipment (computers, CDs, microphones, the mixing console, and so forth) are called *operations*. This category involves such duties as the off-air recording for later replay of in-studio programs or material fed via a network line. Taking readings of the station's transmitting gear also falls in this category. Another operational duty assigned to some staff announcers is answering telephones and taking requests. Many radio stations pay close attention to telephone calls, using them as an informal research tool.

Never forget that a heavy responsibility can rest on the shoulders of the on-air person during periods of emergency or natural disaster. On-air staff—and sometimes this means the staff announcers as well as newspeople—must pass along crucial information about storm warnings, floods, and other imminent dangers. Each and every on-air person *must* be familiar with the appropriate contacts at local police, fire, and civil defense agencies. In addition, the radio console operator is generally responsible for monitoring the Emergency Alert System.

Organization

Organizational duties vary from station to station. For stations that use computers to automate the program selection, frequently the music and the commercials have been programmed into the station's computer. The announcer does live announcements at intervals designated in the program (see Figure 5.2). At other stations where music is on CDs or carts, the duties may include pulling music from the station's library in preparation for an airshift and refiling them when the shift is completed.

Generally all announcers who also run the board (combo operation) have other duties that include filling out the station's program logs and lining up commercials and music in advance of airplay.

Typical Duties

With our three categories in mind, let's watch some typical staff announcers at work, focus on requirements of the job, examine the equipment used, and discuss the role of formats in the working world of the staff announcer. The responsibilities of an air personality vary tremendously from station to station. In smaller operations, the announcer may even be responsible for vacuuming the studios. In the top markets, an air personality is just that: an entertainer expected to project a personality, with very few or no operational or organizational chores.

The following job descriptions and working conditions are typical for stations in the market sizes given. All names are fictitious.

SMALL-MARKET COUNTRY AM WITH FM AUTOMATION   Juan is the morning person at this station, which is housed in a prefabricated three-office building in an open field next to the transmitter and antenna. The station serves a city of 19,000.

Juan arrives at the station at 5:30 A.M., relieving the all-night person, who is in charge of tending the automation and doing some production. He signs on the AM at 6:00 A.M. His performance duties include acting as host of the morning music show until 10. He will also **"rip and read"** newscasts during the shift. Commercial reading is an important duty. Juan is known for his ability to ad-lib a commercial, and sponsors furnish him with many fact sheets. At 10 he moderates a half-hour telephone call-in swap shop. From 10:30 until 11 he plays a taped religious program, supplied by an organization that buys the airtime. During the tape, he must cut two or three commercials. When he is relieved at 11, he goes to lunch and later returns to the station for some more production work.

Operational duties include turning on the transmitter, taking transmitter readings at intervals during his shift, running the board for his own program, running the production board when cutting commercials, and operating all the studio equipment. Another responsibility on Juan's shift is to keep the FM automation running. There is very little to do for the automation as the program is downloaded from a satellite and a computer plays the commercials and IDs.

Organizational duties include filling out logs, pulling music for his show, refiling that music after the program, monitoring news computer for headlines

Figure 5.2   Note that the program stops at designated "pause" intervals in this live assist
operation.

OnTheAir Software, used by permission

and weather forecasts, and checking the newspaper for local stories. In addition, Juan must keep neat records of the swap shop program because listeners will call in throughout the day to inquire about advertised items.

Summary: Although not a particularly accomplished performer, Juan is well known in the community. He is expected to be reasonably knowledgeable about the music he plays and to be able to communicate effectively on the air. He is in actuality a "personality," but much of his job involves operations and organizational duties.

SMALL-MARKET FM ADULT CONTEMPORARY   Lisa, a college student, is a part-time staff announcer at this station, which barely survives in a town of 12,000. The station plays mainly contemporary songs, although there is some country and some "easy-listening" music. Physically, the station consists of an on-air studio, a small production studio, and two offices. The news service was removed when the owners fell behind in their payments to the service provider.

Performance duties include acting as a host of a music program and reading an occasional commercial or public service announcement.

Operational duties include running all station equipment. From 7 A.M. until 10 A.M. on Saturday, Lisa will run the board for her own record show, and from 10 until noon she will act as engineer for a Polish music program hosted by a local businessman.

Organizational duties include making standard log entries, filing records and copy, vacuuming the station, and emptying ashtrays and trash cans. Lisa works for minimum wage, as do most of the employees at the station. She receives no benefits of any kind.

Summary: Lisa's primary responsibilities are operational: putting records on air, running the board, and so on. She is not a smooth air personality, nor is she expected to be.

SMALL- TO MEDIUM-MARKET AM/FM STATION   George is an announcer on the FM. He plays easy rock and works the afternoon shift. The station is located in a city of 50,000 and is very successful. Headquartered in a reasonably modern building in the center of town, George's station has modest but modern equipment, all of which is well maintained.

Performance duties include introducing music (which is preprogrammed on a computer), some light patter, and reading commercial copy and weather. Station policy prescribes back-announcing; that is, George gives the name of the song after it has finished.

Operational duties include running the board for his show and for the local news anchor. He also must hit the network newscast at the top of the hour exactly and open the network channel on the board.

Organizational duties include planning music *backsells* (the back-announcing of songs), taking occasional phone calls, and keeping the program log.

Summary: George is expected to maintain a light, pleasant tone throughout, to give brief intros to the music, and to back-announce the songs. Voice quality is important, but there is not much emphasis on personality.

MEDIUM-MARKET ADULT CONTEMPORARY FM   This station has a rigidly programmed music format, and heavy emphasis on news, traffic reports, and other useful information. It serves a city of 250,000. Jay, the afternoon staff announcer, also deals with numerous promotions and contests. His shift runs from 3 P.M. to 7 P.M., although he reports to work at 11 A.M. to handle the heavy production load assigned to him.

Performance duties include heavy ad-libbing, fast humor, and banter with callers who are participating in promotions and contests. Jay reads an occasional commercial, but most commercials are recorded.

Operational duties include the complex job of running the board, which involves handling incoming air traffic reports and frequent prerecorded station identification announcements, inserting commercials, and running the console for the news anchor.

Organizational duties are minimal; music is preselected and programmed into the station computer. Commercials are also programmed on the computer and are sequenced between music sets by the program director.

Summary: Jay is expected to run a tight board, making sure his talk between music sets is smooth and comes over the music outros, and he needs to be an excellent ad-libber. He is a good communicator and provides listeners with an entertaining four hours of music, information, and humor.

MEDIUM- TO MAJOR-MARKET FM MODERN ROCK   Angela works in a very high-tech environment. The equipment is state-of-the-art, and there is a great deal of glass in the spacious studio setup. On Angela's shift, from midnight until 6 A.M., she plays new music and album cuts for a loyal audience in a city of 450,000.

Performance duties include projecting a hip, laid-back style and ad-libbing about the recording artists. She also reads, in her style, short news summaries prepared for her by the late-evening newsperson, who leaves at midnight.

Operational duties include running board, a relatively simple job because most of the music is programmed on the station computer. Angela has some flexibility and can program and play certain requests into the computer's rotation.

Organizational duties include programming the computer and taking requests. Requests must be logged because station management wants to know what listeners want to hear.

Summary: Angela is expected to project a certain personality over the air, the aura of the laid-back aficionado of a particular kind of rock music. In addition, she is required to ad-lib about the music and, therefore, must be extremely knowledgeable.

MAJOR-MARKET ALL-TALK AM   Barbara hosts the 10 A.M. to 2 P.M. shift in a station located in a city of one million. She sits in a fairly small studio separated by glass from her engineer, who runs the console. There is a producer for the show who screens incoming telephone calls. To Barbara's right is a device that identifies each caller by first name and hometown.

Performance duties include conversing with the callers and, indirectly, with the rest of the listening audience, and providing information on the topic being discussed. She conducts interviews and reads commercials.

Although Barbara has very few operational duties, her organizational duties include heavy research into the topics being discussed, including a ritual morning's reading of four major newspapers. Barbara also must be knowledgeable about the topics of discussion with interview guests.

Summary: Barbara is expected to be a lively conversationalist and an interesting person in general. She must be a superb ad-libber and interviewer. Also, she is a true one-to-one communicator, an absolute must in the business of talk radio. A comprehensive knowledge of current events is taken for granted.

MAJOR-MARKET ADULT CONTEMPORARY FM   Bob has the afternoon shift in a network-owned and operated (commonly called an O&O) station in a city of several million. Located in a downtown skyscraper, the studio is lavishly furnished and even equipped with a fireplace, a holdover from the golden days.

Performance duties include introducing music, giving informal patter between cuts, reading commercials, and introducing the news. Bob will cut some other commercials, but not as part of his regular job. He will be paid extra, and very well, for any voice work he does in addition to his airshift. After his shift, Bob will spend another hour voice-tracking programs for two other smaller stations the network owns. He is paid extra for his voice-tracking work.

Operational duties include nothing more than turning on his mic. An engineer in another room runs the console.

Organizational duties are limited to keeping track of the commercial scripts and other announcements handed him by an assistant. After his shift, Bob will read a summary of activities for the stations he will voice-track and then he will record a series of song intros and other patter for the two smaller stations.

Summary: Bob is expected to perform flawlessly. Sponsors pay thousands of dollars for commercials and expect him to bring that copy to life. He has an exceptional and distinctive voice, which has made him wealthy.

THREE RULES OF THUMB   The examples just given do not cover every situation in modern radio staff announcing. They do, however, illustrate three rules that generally prove true—see Box 5.1.

Box 5.1

THE DIVISION OF LABOR IN LARGE AND SMALL STATIONS

1. Facilities and equipment tend to be better in larger stations. Of course, there are poorly equipped, rundown facilities in major markets, and state-of-the-art equipment can be found in smaller markets. But in general owners of stations in larger markets have more money at their disposal, hence, they also have better equipment and physical plants.

2. The staff announcer is responsible for fewer operational and organizational duties in larger markets than is the case in smaller markets.

3. An air personality is expected to be more professional and talented in larger markets. That person usually will have proved his or her abilities in progressively more demanding arenas before reaching a major market.

Job Requirements

The tools and experience necessary for an air personality vary with the particular needs of the station and the size of the market. The format, a concept that is examined in more detail shortly, also shapes the requirements.

Smaller markets often seek the so-called jack of all trades. The reason: small market staff announcers simply do not have the support staffs available in larger markets, and must therefore absorb some of the duties that are relegated to other specialists in larger markets. It is not unusual, for example, for a small-market announcer to double as an engineer. A small-market announcer with no technical training will often be required to perform routine maintenance on equipment, or do production work for the station. Air personalities may also participate in station sales, act as play-by-play announcers, or write copy.

In larger markets, positions are more specialized and require more narrowed and refined talents. The ability to do an interview is useful in small markets, but it is vital to the radio talk show host. What passes for engaging humor in a small market may not captivate audiences in New York, where whole formats evolve around the gag-telling ability of the staff announcer.

Basic requirements for a staff announcer in any market or format include a working knowledge of music and the ability to garner an in-depth knowledge of a particular music style if the situation requires. Familiarity with good grammar and pronunciation is a must. Also important is the ability to work with equipment because almost every staff announcer must start in a small or medium market and run his or her own board. Lack of this ability definitely hinders a career.

A clear, expressive voice, free of speech and vocal defects, is almost mandatory. Some announcers can turn an odd speech pattern into a trademark, but the odds are against anyone with a distracting defect in his or her delivery.

A resourceful personality and the ability to perform well under pressure are definite pluses. A college education is helpful, but rarely specified in the job description. However, being well educated in a general sense is extremely worthwhile for any performer.

Equipment

As mentioned earlier, operation of equipment is a major portion of a staff announcer's job in most small and medium markets, and a "tight board" is important. Mastery of equipment is not the be-all and end-all of staff announcing, however. Being an air personality involves genuine communication, not just manipulating the console. Unfortunately, some air people become fixated on equipment and gimmickry at the expense of developing an engaging personality and real communication skills.

Even production specialists are wise to avoid thinking of hardware and technical operations instead of focusing on concepts and communication of a message. With that point understood, do recognize that confident operation of equipment is important. Here is a short introduction to some of the equipment found in a typical radio station.

CONSOLE   To the uninitiated, the console (see Figure 5.3) is an intimidating and complex collection of switches and slide faders. But although the hardware can be complex, the concept is simple. The console is the Grand Central Station of the control room, and has three main functions: routing signals, mixing signals, and amplifying signals.

Routing   The console is able to take the output of a sound source such as a microphone or CD and send, or route, it to the transmitter or to a computer or DAT (digital audiotape) machine. A variable resistor called a **fader** ("fader pot") governs the loudness of the audio signal. Audio is the electrical signal, which transmits sound.

There is also, in a typical console, an on-off switch that governs the pot. Further details are provided at the end of this discussion.

Mixing   An important duty of the board operator is to mix signals, such as music from a CD or computer and voice from a microphone. The console allows multiple audio sources to be put over the air at the same time. For example, if the computer is brought up on Pot 1, and the microphone on Pot 2,

Think About It

FREE STUFF

Music announcers are often called on to make appearances at events, sometimes acting as master of ceremonies or simply lending publicity to the gathering. In addition to putting in an appearance, the announcer frequently is expected to "plug" the event on-air ahead of time.

Stations have varying rules and procedures about such appearances, and the federal government has drawn up rules governing what sort of "reward" an announcer can receive for saying things on the air or playing certain kinds of music.

The biggest taboo is "payola," meaning cash, drugs, or other gratuity given to an announcer to play certain music. (Giving or accepting payola is not only against station rules, but it can also be a crime, punishable by fines or imprisonment.) The FCC regulations against payola were instituted when it became obvious that some staff announcers were making more than their salaries by playing and plugging music.

Another taboo, rigging contests, was codified in federal regulations after the quiz show scandals of the 1950s. What happened was this: Contestants on quiz shows, placed in "isolation booths," would grimace, bite their knuckles, and publicly wrack their brains to come up with an answer—usually as the clock was ticking off the final second. It all seemed too dramatic to be true. And of course it was.

The advertising agencies that produced the programs were selecting the most telegenic performers and feeding them the answers. Congress and the FCC put a halt to that with Section 509 of the Communication Act of 1934, making it a violation of federal administrative law to fix a contest.

A practice known as "plugola" straddles the line between legality and illegality. There are regulations about plugging (making mention of) products on-air, but as media ethicist Jay Black notes, the process has now become more "refined," particularly in the film industry. Producers seeking authenticity in their movies make extensive use of easily recognized brand name products—cars, soft drinks, beer, cigarettes, junk food, and so on—for which they are paid fees by the product manufacturers and advertisers. The practice has become so widespread that agents openly advertise their product placement services in trade journals, such as *Advertising Age*.[1]

An announcer who makes an occasional appearance at a night club, with his station's approval, and plugs that night club on air is commit-

---

[1] Jay Black and Jennings Bryant, *Introduction to Media Communication*, 4th edition, New York, Brown and Benchmark, p. 550.

Continues

Think About It   *Continued*

ting no crime. But here is a question for consideration: Suppose you find that because of the popularity of your radio program, you can get away with frequent plugs of your favorite club? The club obviously likes having you there, and gives you free drinks. Soon the free drinks become free meals. And soon the free meals become a nightly occurrence.

Do you think you have crossed an ethical line? Do you think that the fact that most staff announcers don't make much money justifies your arrangement? Where would you draw the line?

Figure 5.3   This console features 10 input channels. Slide faders control the volume level for each channel.

Photo by Fritz Messere

the operator, by judgment and experience, will set the correct balance between music and voice.

Amplification: The electrical signal strength of most components in the radio control room is very weak, and the console must amplify these signals

Figure 5.4	Assignment buttons at the top of the fader allow the board operator to select between program and audition channels.

Photo by Fritz Messere

to a level high enough to feed the transmitter or a tape recorder. Line amplifiers in the console boost the incoming signals to usable levels. The various signals can be combined together. The console performs these functions by means of the faders, which are manufactured in the form of vertical sliders. The on-off switch is commonly known as a "key" (even though it may be a button).

An important element to understand regarding console function is the key, which is generally a button that selects or turns the fader on (see Figure 5.4). The **audition channel** and the **program channel** may be separate buttons. Audition is an off-air channel, used for private listening or, in some advanced applications, for off-air production work on the on-air console. The program channel is the on-air channel. When a channel's fader is keyed to program, the audio source it governs is fed to the transmitter. During off-air production work, the program signal is generally fed to a recording device such as a computer or a DAT machine.

An alternative to the audition channel is the cue channel, which feeds a signal to a small speaker usually located in the console, without putting that signal over the air. One useful application for the cue channel is in listening for the point in a song at which the announcer wants to begin a cut. Then the CD can be paused so that at a specified time, the music will begin at the desired point. Another is to cue up request call-ins from one of the station's computers.

Figure 5.5   Smartcaster allows many board operations to be automated.

Courtesy of Smarts Broadcast Systems

COMPUTERS   Computers are the primary playback device in broadcasting for music reproduction today. They may also be programmed to playback commercials and spot announcements. To some extent, computers can also replace the staff announcer when the installed software allows the station to voice-track segments of their programming.

Modern broadcast software such as Smartcaster (see Figure 5.5) and OnTheAir allow a staff announcer to automate many of the functions that used to be done manually by the board operator. On stations that have tightly formatted music playlists, the program director or music director can pre-select the music and the name of each song will appear in the order to be played. Note that the commercial breaks are also programmed into the software program. The pauses displayed in the screen indicate stop sets where the announcer will "backsell" the music selections (see Figure 5.2).

Sound on computers will usually be recorded in either an MP3 (MPEG audio layer 3) or WAV file format.

COMPACT DISCS (CDS)   CDs (see Figure 5.6) use a digital, microcomputer-aided system to play back sounds, so they give what some feel is a truer

Figure 5.6   A compact disc player.

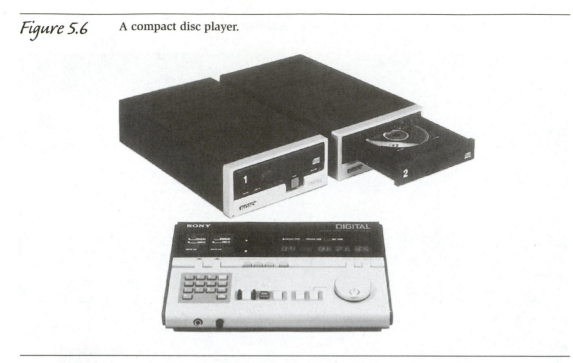

Photo courtesy of Sony Corporation of America

rendition of recorded sound. The compact discs play with display track numbers and track times, so there is less need to cue discs than there was when analog turntables were dominant, and there is less chance of damaging CD recordings. Modern broadcast CD players are easily programmed to play many music cuts over a period of time. Combined with other facets of computerized operation in state-of-the-art on-air studios, CDs have reduced the amount of physical operational detail for modern radio performers. CDs have become virtually indispensable in air and production studios.

New CD recorders are gaining some popularity in the broadcast industry. These machines record as well as play back audio tracks. They use CD-R (recordable compact disc blanks) for recording or playing back standard CDs.

TURNTABLES   Turntables (see Figure 5.7) are essentially record players, but they differ from the home variety in several respects. For example, a broadcast turntable is a heavy-duty unit that has a plate (the part that spins) that can be manipulated by hand to cue a record to a point just before the music starts. Few radio stations use turntables today, but we include them in this discussion because you will still find them in some production set ups.

For the broadcast performer, working with turntables is basically a matter of learning to cue discs properly and to start them smoothly.

Figure 5.7　This turntable can be manipulated by hand to cue a record.

Photo by Fritz Messere

MINIDISCS　Minidiscs are recordable magneto-optical devices (Figure 5.8) that allow the user to perform basic editing functions in addition to recording and playing back audio. In some radio stations minidiscs have replaced broadcast cartridge (cart) machines in news operations. Minidiscs can be cued to play back tracks instantaneously, and each minidisc can record as many as 255 tracks or about 74 minutes of audio.

REEL-TO-REEL TAPE MACHINES　Tape reels come in several sizes, including 10½-, 7-, and 5-inch widths (see Figure 5.9). The tape itself is generally ¼-inch wide for most broadcast applications. Audiotape has a Mylar or acetate base coated with iron oxide—a fancy name for rust. The iron oxide coating can pick up magnetic impulses and store them by means of the arrangement of the particles. The pattern is encoded onto the tape by the heads of the tape machine. Typically, a tape machine (see Figure 5.10) has an erase head, a record head, and a playback head, and the tape crosses the heads in that order.

A variant of the **reel-to-reel** tape machine is the **cassette** recorder (see Figure 5.11). High-quality cassette machines are often found in production and air studios, sometimes used as skimmer decks to record the day's programming.

Portable cassette machines are used extensively in radio news.

CARTRIDGE MACHINES　The cart machine comes in two varieties. The digital cart machine is essentially a hard-disc recorder with features that provide for the easy recording, naming, and selection of audio tracks.

Figure 5.8 Minidiscs can be used for instantaneous playback, making them ideal for broadcast use.

Photo courtesy of TASCAM

Figure 5.9

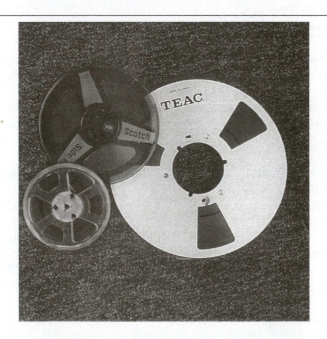

Tape reels come in various sizes; the most common are 5 inch, 7 inch, and 10½ inch.

Photo by Philip Benoit

Play back of the track is instantaneous and cueing is done simply by selecting the name of the track or the track number.

The analog cart machine is a record and playback device that uses a single loop of tape. The broadcast cart does not need to be rewound because

Figure 5.10   Tape heads are arranged as erase, record, and playback (from left to right). As the tape passes through, the erase head deletes the previous recorded information, the record head imparts new information, and the playback head plays the signal back.

Photo by Fritz Messere

it contains a continuous reel of lubricated tape that feeds from the middle of the spool. An inaudible tone automatically stops the tape when it reaches the point where the recording was started.

The advantage of a cart over reel-to-reel tape is that the operator does not have to thread a machine and locate the beginning of the program, or rewind the tape when it finishes. Because the cart machines are so convenient, some stations will cart virtually all commercials and public service announcements.

Other types of equipment are available to an on-air performer, but their use is best addressed in a production course. Production skills are indispensable to a radio staff announcer because the duties of radio performer and producer usually overlap. In fact, the ability to use equipment often plays a major role in the overall effectiveness of the communicator. (Just read through the trade journals and note how many help-wanted advertisements for on-air positions specify expertise in production.) Consider too that if you lack the ability to run the board competently, your performance will be compromised. No matter how good an announcer's voice and delivery may be, constantly flubbed program elements will detract from the message.

Figure 5.11   This type of cassette recorder is used in many radio stations.

Photo by Philip Benoit

Formats and the Staff Announcer

In modern radio, the format identifies stations and differentiates one station from another. One primary duty of a radio staff announcer is to reinforce the station's format.

Formats center on more than the choice of music. The format is built by the style of announcing, by the overall pace of program elements, by the choice of announcers, by the sound of commercials, even by the choice of microphones. Any sound element must reinforce the format.

For example, certain FM radio formats center on the "laid-back" air personality who communicates in an intimate way with the listeners. Stations using this format often equip the air studios with highly sensitive mics that pick up breathiness and mouth noises, important components in projecting the "personal" feel. Also enhancing that feel, of course, is the style of the air personality and how well he or she works within the format.

In the past, a typical announcer had a powerful, versatile voice and was called on to do widely differing tasks. A typical shift might have involved reading news, introducing classical music, hosting a live band show, and reading loftily worded commercials.

Glibness and a good voice often were sufficient qualifications for an announcer's position. Auditions usually consisted of tongue twisters and classical music pronunciations to test the announcer's mechanical ability to render words and phrases.

Today, much more emphasis is placed on communicating a particular message. The news reporter, for instance, is expected to have more than just a voice. He or she must project understanding of the news, a perspective gained only by a professional journalist. Classical music announcers today must show in-depth understanding of the music, not simply the ability to correctly pronounce titles and composers' names.

The specific formats of modern radio call for special abilities and characteristics by the on-air personality. Following are some examples of how an effective on-air communicator must work within a format to reach a particular audience segment.

ADULT CONTEMPORARY (AC)   In what is known as the **adult contemporary** (AC) format, radio station programmers typically try to reach the young adult audience, usually defined as listeners ages 18 to 35 or 18 to 49, depending on the particular *demographic* sought. Demographics are statistical representations of populations.

The demographic data obtained from a study of an audience's density, distribution, and vital statistics are intensely important in the station's overall sales and programming effort. In short, a commercial station's goal is to "capture" a demographic range and sell that distinct audience to advertisers who want to reach a specific group.

An interesting outgrowth of demographics is psychographics, statistical breakdowns of the audience by lifestyle. Researchers have developed such colorful psychographic designations of audience segments as "minks and station wagons," or "shotguns and pickups." In any event, radio stations use demographics and psychographics to shape their sound toward reaching a clearly defined audience.

Although adult contemporary programming varies widely within the format, it usually consists of a mixture of light rock, some former hits, and possibly some easy-listening music. Current popular hits are used, but AC programmers steer away from heavy or experimental rock.

To work effectively within an AC format, consider these suggestions:

1. Avoid artificiality. Extremely patterned, singsong "disc jockey" voices are not popular, nor are voices with odd characteristics.

2. Maintain an even pace, not frenetic but certainly not laid back.

3. Be well organized. AC radio relies heavily on the transfer of information (school closings, notes of community interest, traffic, weather, etc.).

In hiring AC announcers, it is not unusual for program directors and station managers to specify "a performer who can provide companionship." This job description might translate into projecting the personality of a friendly and amusing next-door neighbor. As one program director put it, "the kind of man or woman you'd like to have at your cocktail party."

Focus on Technique

HOW NOT TO BE AN "IRRITANT"

Radio program directors worry as much about people tuning out as about people tuning in—perhaps more. Indeed, "tune-out" is a major factor in constructing the format and in choosing (and retaining) talent.

What this means is that one of the top priorities of a radio staff announcer is to keep from irritating listeners. This usually does not mean simply being personally agreeable; a lot of "shock jocks" would actually be an "irritant" and "tune-out" factor to listeners if they suddenly became mild mannered.

The point: Tune-out happens when listeners don't get what they expect. If they want to hear the music and the jock talks over it, they tune out. If they want to hear the jock talk and he or she doesn't—ditto.

Here are some tips for avoiding what program directors (PDs) call "on-air irritants":

- *Too much hype.* Most staff announcers are toning down their deliveries, and at the time of this writing the "growling voice" and "in your face" delivery was out of favor in all but the hardest-format stations.

- *Too many reminders about how much music you are playing.* Interviews with disaffected listeners confirm that when you continually stop the music to tell people how much music you are playing—TEN HITS IN A ROW!!—you irritate the audience. Remember that every time you say "less talk" you must talk to do it.

- *Endless "pre-sell" on the music sweeps.* "TEN IN A ROW, COMING NOW, YES, TEN IN A ROW, THE MID-DAY SWEEP, AND HERE IT COMES . . ." may induce a listener to push a button before the sweep starts.

- *Laughing at your own in-jokes.* Air people sometimes like to convince themselves they are funny by chuckling endlessly with the weather reporter, but this doesn't always seem entertaining to the listener.

- *Stepping on the end of songs.* Listeners may actually want to hear the ending and will resent you talking over it or dumping out of it completely. Research shows listeners are irritated by missing the ends of such current hits as "Landslide" by The Dixie Chicks; the ending is consistently nipped off. Other examples include "She Hates Me" by Puddle of Mudd and "Disease" by Match Box Twenty.

Continues

Focus on Technique Continued

- *Stepping on a "cold" ending.* On a related note, don't talk over the end of songs that end cold.

- *Getting tricky with the call letters.* Radio stations often use "handles," such as "Mix 101," that have no real relation to their call letters. As a result, when stations give the required legal ID (a direct statement of the call letters and station location) at the top of the hour, the announcers often try to bury it in a heavily produced montage that touts the station's "handle." This annoys listeners. Just say the call letters and don't make an enormous production of it.

- *Always talking over the beginning instrumental and butting up to the start of the vocal.* Focus groups say this is an irritant, and it is often heard as the announcer's self-indulgent exercise.

HIT RADIO   The category that used to be referred to as Top 40 but now is commonly called contemporary hit radio, or **CHR,** is oriented toward the younger listener. Often, stations are zeroing in on the 12 to 24 age bracket. The format is fast paced, with many different program elements interjected in short periods of time. A jingle may be followed by a commercial, which butts up to a very short station promo, which overlaps the beginning of the music cut, while the announcer "talks up" to the vocal (see Figure 5.12).

To be effective in hit radio, an announcer should

1. Project a very high energy level.

2. Have a good working knowledge of the music. The hit radio announcer won't be required to engage in lengthy discourses on the performers, but knowledge of new releases and up-and-coming acts is necessary. Ignorance of the music and musicians will quickly become evident. Remember, many of the listeners to this format read fan magazines, memorize jacket liner notes, and attend concerts by the performing artists. Internet sites such as Billboard (www.billboard.com) and the College Music Journal (www.cmj.com) can provide useful information.

3. Handle control room equipment smoothly. A great deal of practice is necessary, because the "tight board" is essential in this fast-moving radio type.

If you opt for a career in hit radio, remember that you must be able to sustain enthusiasm for the format and for the music. Trends in music come and go, and even announcers in their early twenties often find their

Figure 5.12   Ted Long and Amy Robbins have won consistently high ratings with their morning show on WNTQ, Syracuse, New York.

Photo by Fritz Messere

tastes moving away from current hits. But on-air enthusiasm must always be evident.

COUNTRY   There are several formats for **country** music. One old style was typified by twanging guitars and whining vocals. Some of those elements can still be found in country, but for the most part the format has moved closer to the mainstream of popular music, featuring more sophisticated arrangements and orchestral backgrounds to supplement the guitars. Country can run the gamut from folk to hillbilly to bluegrass to what some programmers refer to as countrypolitan—country music oriented toward a primarily urban audience.

Suggestions for country music air personality work include the following:

1. Study the music and artists. Many listeners are devoted fans, so the announcer must have good working knowledge. The *Journal of Country Music* is a good publication to look at (www.halloffame.org/jcm/).

2. Have genuine interest in and appreciation for the music. Enthusiasm for country music is hard to fake.

3. Develop an understanding of factors that relate to rural life. This is not to be construed as implying that all country music listeners are farmers. They are not. Some of the most successful country music stations in the nation, in fact, are located in large cities. However, country music has strong roots in agricultural settings, and many country stations serve rural people. If you do serve a rural area, remember that farming today is a big, sophisticated business, and a modern farmer is just as likely to read the *Wall Street Journal* as the dairy association newsletter.

Country music can be a satisfying format in which to work because country personalities often attain celebrity status in their markets. This means that an announcer in this format should have a strong desire to communicate and an interest in individuals and the community.

EASY LISTENING   Formats for so-called **easy-listening** music have evolved in many directions, from "elevator style" background music to more lively programming that incorporates some of the more melodic current hits. Many **lite** formats qualify as easy listening. Typically, the music is heavily orchestrated, but now a wider playlist with vocals by artists like Elton John, Phil Collins, and Celine Dion is being incorporated into the format.

Here are some hints to help you function successfully in an easy-listening format:

1. Develop a resonant and pleasant voice. "Mellowness" is one of the more popular qualities stressed by programmers of this format. Also, a mature-sounding voice is an asset because many listeners to this format are 35 years old and older.

2. Develop the ability to read with great accuracy. Ad-libbing is less important than in other formats because most material is read. But those spots must be delivered with precision because copy is slotted less frequently and sponsors typically pay a premium for commercials that will stand out.

3. Always maintain a friendly, personal approach. The "friendly communicator" has become something of a buzzword in the easy-listening category.

Easy listening may involve nothing else from the announcer but time and temperature checks, or it can entail a full-scale, albeit low-key, music show. Good voice and diction are especially important in this format.

ALBUM-ORIENTED ROCK (AOR)   Although long record cuts and heavy rock are staples, within the AOR format are a myriad of music types and demographic targets.

Probably no other format is involved in such precise "narrowcasting," or targeting of a very specific audience segment. One station in the market might, for example, focus on so-called "modern" rock, whereas another might tend toward more "classic" selections.

In any event, an AOR announcer must have a good working knowledge of the field because he or she will be expected to ad-lib at some length about the music and the artists.

Other suggestions are as follows:

1. Use an intimate and conversational style. This is virtually the hallmark of the AOR announcer.

2. Study the particular jargon and lifestyle of the listeners, their slang expressions, the concerts they attend, the clothes they wear.

3. Strengthen your ability to ad-lib effectively and at some length. Ad-libbing is important to most radio announcers, but this format, with its conversational approach, requires superior skills.

As with country music, interest in and knowledge of album-oriented rock is difficult to fake.

TALK RADIO   Talk radio has been around for many years but only recently has emerged into a widespread format. The entire rationale is to elicit responses from listeners who phone in and comment on various topics.

To function effectively in the talk radio format, follow these three rules:

1. Read as many newspapers and newsmagazines as you can. Knowledge in a wide variety of areas is essential. A talk-show host caught unaware of an important trend or news development can appear foolish.

2. Develop and practice the interview skills presented in Chapter 8. Many talk radio shows feature an interview segment. If there is no guest, the host must use the same skills to elicit responses from callers.

3. Pay particular attention to time and timing. The talk-radio host must know when and how to wrap up a discussion to hit the network news or other program element. Also, he or she cannot afford to be caught short, without material to finish a segment.

Talk radio requires the ultimate in one-to-one communication skills and a genuine interest in people and events. Glibness and superficiality are apparent immediately.

OTHER SPECIALIZED FORMATS   These include classical, all-jazz, urban contemporary, and foreign language formats. New formats evolve regularly, and existing formats split into narrower categories. At one time, "rock" was a reasonably accurate description of a station's format. Today there are narrower splintered variations of this format, ranging from new age to soft rock.

The narrower the format, the greater the knowledge required of the announcer. In classical music stations the announcer must be an expert. Besides knowing enough to program music, he or she must be able to discuss the pieces themselves and the life and times of each composer.

Daypart

A station's programming varies within the day, and programming elements in a particular **daypart** will differ from other time periods in the same station. A daypart is a segment of several hours, generally identified by the audience tuning in. In a typical adult contemporary station the morning period, usually from 6 A.M. to 10 A.M., is known as **drive time,** or *morning drive.* (In some commuter markets, drive time starts slightly earlier.) As you might guess, that term relates to the heavy listenership as people commute to work. Drive time also includes people in their homes, preparing for the day's activities. These listeners typically are assumed to be eager for news and information, and for a bright companion to get their day started.

As the daypart changes, so do the station's programming elements. The midday audience, listeners from 10 A.M. to 2 or 3 P.M., may not include a great many office or factory workers and is typically thought of at many stations as "housewife" time. The approach of a midday announcer therefore must be different and, at our hypothetical adult contemporary station, would be geared toward women. Delivery might be slower; there is not as much flow of news and information, and no traffic reports. Because the listeners have longer periods in which to listen, there may be longer features and interviews.

Later comes "afternoon drive." Here, the input of news and information is stepped up as listeners once again take to their autos. Afternoon drive is generally a bit lower keyed than morning drive.

In the evening, the station's listenership typically skews toward younger listeners. The announcer may gear his or her approach to high school or college students studying while listening to the radio.

Overnight segments have become more competitive for the advertiser's dollar. Once thought of as virtually a throwaway, the modern overnight shift often has substantial numbers of listeners, sometimes a very devoted audience. Listener composition typically changes throughout the overnight period. From midnight until 2 A.M. much of the audience may consist of people who have not yet gone to bed, whereas 2 A.M. to 4 A.M. often is the domain of night workers. Starting at 4 A.M., the emphasis may shift slightly to incorporate very early risers. Overnight on-air radio staff announcers often gear their approach and program content with these periods in mind. Overnight operations are frequently automated to some degree. Tech Talk provides a look at how computers can be used to assist a staff announcer.

Techniques of Radio Staff Announcing

To communicate effectively with the target audience, an air personality must combine natural talent and experience. Some elements can be taught, but skill as a staff announcer comes only with experience. Experimenting to determine what works and what doesn't is an invaluable part of the learning process.

Tech Talk

LIVE ASSIST AND AUTOMATION

Computer automation and partial automation are changing the way announcers do their business. And it's a safe bet you will encounter such high-tech equipment at one of your future job sites—perhaps the first one. You'll be expected to demonstrate at least some familiarity with the way live assist works.

Figure 5.13   *AudioVAULT's QuickStart toolbar permits the announcer to activate audio elements by touching the computer screen.*

Photo courtesy of Broadcast Electronics, Quincy, IL

Continues

Tech Talk Continued

The computer takes the place of more familiar playback devices, such as cart machines or minidiscs. Instead, the audio elements—such as commercials, jingles, sound effects, and music—are stored on a computer hard drive. The announcer/operator uses a mouse, or in some cases a touchscreen, to activate audio elements (see Figure 5.13).

In many cases, the events stored in the computer are "ganged" together so that several events fire in sequence. This practice is known as "live assist." Of course, the computer provides the option of ganging all program elements together and completely automating the station, which is an option some station owners elect to pursue. In this circumstance, the announcer may be called on to record all his or her commercials, narrations, record intros, and other program material in one sitting, and to program the computer to run music, commercials, and narration in the proper sequence.

Not all stations have converted to computer-driven programming, and some small stations probably will not for years to come. The fact is that old style equipment still works well and in some cases it is more cost effective to do things the old-fashioned way.

Audience feedback over the telephone plays a role, as do ratings. You can also learn a great deal by listening to other air people, selecting elements of their styles with which you can be comfortable. Of course direct imitation is not the goal, but most accomplished radio air personalities could name five or six other broadcasters who influenced their styles.

Finding Personality and Perspective

One guideline that almost never fails is this: be conservative when you first start out. An inexperienced announcer who tries to emulate another personality probably will produce a poor imitation at best and possibly a ludicrous flop. What seems like side-splitting humor to a novice announcer may simply sound inane to the listener.

Start slowly. Learn the station's equipment, program schedule, and format. Ad-lib with discretion. Experience and airtime will point up your strengths and weaknesses. You may find that you have a definite flair for humor. If so, expand on that base *slowly*. Here are two techniques for developing an on-air personality and a perspective from which to approach air work:

1. *Use imitation and trial and error.* Listen to other personalities and identify the elements in their deliveries that you can adapt to yourself and

your station. The key here is to listen critically, both to others and to yourself, to determine whether that joke, approach, or style really works.

2. *Polish your delivery with the audience in mind.* Put yourself in the place of a listener, a listener you believe to be typical of your station. Would you, the listener, find that remark funny, or tasteless? Is that 5-minute feature compelling or boring? Use this acid test before and after a program segment.

The artistic and technical aspects of delivering a commercial are evaluated in Chapter 10. See Box 5.2 for three techniques of commercial delivery that relate specifically to the radio staff announcer.

Entertaining with Humor and Taste

As stated, the development of a personality, as the term applies to on-air radio work, is largely a matter of trial and error and experimentation. Humor and entertainment value, which are important facets of that on-air personality, must be balanced by good taste.

When experimenting, consider that *humor* must be funny. That sounds tautological, but a scan of the radio spectrum suggests otherwise. Three points on humor during an airshift:

1. Avoid in-jokes.
2. Think before you say it. Is it really funny?
3. Don't keep repeating the same line. Listeners will notice.

Some radio air personalities subscribe to humor services that provide one-line jokes for a fee. These lines can be incorporated into the patter, and with practice they will sound original and topical. The danger with subscription humor is that you may not adequately make written material "your own." If a joke sounds as though it is being read off a sheet, it will fail.

Entertainment is really what the whole business is about. The overriding goal in the element of entertainment is to get and keep the attention of the audience. The audience must be interested in a commercial, a record, or a public service announcement. Therefore, you must be interested, and you must sound interested.

Good taste varies, to some extent, with the composition of the audience. A staff announcer is expected to avoid material and presentations that would offend the audience, unless the announcer's style is one of being offensive. There are, of course, some announcers whose style is built around bad taste, a provocative method of enticing listeners to tune in. But for most purposes good taste is still the name of the game.

In the demanding work of an air personality, there is considerable pressure to be funny and to come up with things to say. Often, this pressure may lead you to say things you shouldn't. When in doubt, especially at the beginning of your career, err on the conservative side.

Box 5.2

COMMERCIAL DELIVERY

1. *Avoid "going flat" on commercials.* One of the biggest problems encountered by an announcer pulling an airshift is a general flatness imparted to commercial copy. Often a radio staff announcer must read the same copy day after day for weeks. (One author of this book once worked at a radio station where a client's copy remained unchanged over a 15-year period. It became a badge of having earned your credentials as an announcer at the station to have the chance to read this classic, enduring copy on your airshift.) And with the increasingly heavy use of prerecorded commercials, only a few spots may be read live by the airshift announcer. The result: a mechanical, lackadaisical approach.

   Keep your energy level and enthusiasm high by reminding yourself that this is where you directly earn your paycheck. Remind yourself that the client has only you and your ability to interpret the copy as a means of persuading listeners of the value of his or her commercial message.

2. *Do not use the same rhythm, pattern, and inflections for every commercial.*

   Each commercial is an individual work and must be analyzed in terms of its own intent. What is the goal of the spot? To whom does it appeal? Why? To avoid mechanical reading, you must have an understanding of these points.

   Find the key words and use the techniques of marking copy described in Chapter 4. But vary your vocal delivery so that each commercial comes across to the listener as distinct and unique.

3. *Read what is written.* The quickest way to get into trouble as an on-air announcer is to take liberties with a client's commercial copy. The key guideline in 99 percent of the situations in which you are asked to read copy live is to *play it straight.* Don't change words, or rearrange the order of presentation. And avoid the temptation to make gratuitous remarks about the copy before, during, or after reading it. If you think you can do a better job of writing the copy, talk to the sales representative and make suggestions. Don't take it on yourself to punch up someone else's copy on the air. In most cases the copy has been cleared with the client, and most clients are quite specific about what they want said and what they don't want

Continues

Box 5.2   *Continued*

said in their radio commercials. The exceptions are commercials in which an announcer is asked to ad-lib a commercial from a fact sheet. When that situation occurs, it will be very clearly stated on the copy sheet.

Some radio announcers' careers are impeded by amateurish attempts to be outrageous or exceptionally funny. Understand that unless and until you attain the stature of a Don Imus, station managers will be far more concerned with complaints of sponsors and listeners than with your freedom of expression.

Analyzing Yourself and Others

How do you keep improving your skills? One major advantage of being in the broadcast business is the ease of making comparisons. Analyzing the strengths and weaknesses of others can significantly help your development.

Listening to yourself is important. Taping a show is an excellent tool. In some stations, monitoring airchecks (a recorded segment of an actual air-shift) is a requirement of the job.

Also, solicit the opinions of others. Friends and co-workers may sometimes tell you what they think you want to hear, but often they will be strikingly honest. Feedback may sometimes be tough on the ego, but it is worthwhile.

Sometimes announcers stop learning at a particular phase, perhaps in a small or medium market. Those announcers may never get any better because of a lack of talent or, more probably, because the situation does not force them to improve. If there are no expert programmers critiquing airshifts, and if competition does not force continual improvement, the announcer will not grow professionally.

Always remember that the very best announcers got that way by comparison and critique. At one major-market station, for example, the entire air staff receives a daily critique from the program director.

Careful analysis and self-critique are vitally important to honing on-air skills. Listen to yourself; then listen to others. A good-quality radio with a long antenna can bring in an astounding number of stations. You can immediately compare your performance with others all over the region. At night, when AM radio waves travel farther, your comparison can extend halfway across the nation.

When analyzing the deliveries of other announcers, refer to a copy of the *Broadcasting/Cablecasting Yearbook*. This annual publication, which is found in most major libraries, lists all the radio stations in the United States by call letters and by frequency along with much other information. Identifying the size of the station and market will help your analysis by showing exactly what format and market size you're listening to.

Airchecks

You will hear an amazing variety of material. On a major-market adult contemporary station, for example, a twist of the dial turns up a noted personality interviewing via telephone a public relations man trying to promote a product.

Announcer: Can I tell you something?

P.R. Man: Yes, of course.

Announcer: No offense, but you're kind of a jerk. Has anybody ever told you that?

This announcer makes a career out of being offensive.

Changing stations to a medium-market hit radio station, the listener encounters a robotic screamer who makes a living out of endless repetition.

> **(Jingle)**
> *Hey, that's Mariah Carey*
> **(Station ID)**
> *Everybody wins at _____! Nineteen after ten! Comin' at ya with . . .*

At a small-market country station, the announcer takes a more original approach:

> Well, howdy. C'mon in. Get set for some mighty fine country music. We've got Merle and Tanya Tucker and . . .

This air personality has developed a unique personality and plays the role well. Even his speech pattern, a virtual "country dialect," reinforces his image.

But on the neighboring adult contemporary station, the announcer is not doing so well.

> And that was Whitney Houston. And there's Bob coming in the studio . . . he's been over at Hank's office and we know what they've been talking about . . . heh, heh . . .

In-jokes just don't bolster communication between the air personality and the audience.

But in another state, an FM AOR personality plays personal communication to the hilt.

> How's it going? Wow, what a day, huh? The weather was just great . . . just great. Frank, who's working in the stockroom of the A&P, just called in and says he's depressed about having to work on such a beautiful day, and he thinks a double shot of R.E.M. might improve things . . .

She ad-libs a few remarks concerning that group's last concert in town.

In another city, an announcer at a large station that plays middle-of-the-road music, tending toward nostalgia, ad-libs beautifully.

> . . . When that song was recorded she was working as a vocalist with Tommy Dorsey. Nobody thought her style would make it, but after . . .

The announcer, one of the best in the business, gives an insightful and interesting background into the music. How did he get to that plateau? Presumably by doing his homework, listening to himself and to others, and always trying to improve. In the fast-changing world of the radio staff announcer, staying still is, in reality, moving backward.

Summary

Radio staff announcing is a complex job, involving entertaining, informing, and providing companionship. The duties and responsibilities of an air personality vary among particular stations and particular markets. Typical jobs involve performance duties, operational duties, and organizational duties. Performance is on-air work. Operations include operation of station equipment. Organizational duties include keeping logs and filing music.

In general, the larger the market, the greater the emphasis on performance duties. This means that the large-market performer must be a superior on-air performer and will generally have fewer operational or organizational duties.

Most announcers have operational duties, though, and even those who do not have operational duties certainly have to run the board at one point in their careers. The board is a mixing console allowing the operator to mix, route, and amplify signals from sound sources. Sound sources include computers, microphones, tape machines, compact discs, and cart machines.

Techniques of radio staff announcing include developing a personality and perspective, a task that involves trial and error, listening to and incorporating suggestions and feedback, and assessing one's performance from the point of view of the audience.

Delivery of commercials is an important part of the staff announcer's job. Two techniques that relate specifically to this task are maintaining energy and enthusiasm and varying delivery. These two techniques are particularly important because radio staff announcers often "go flat" when confronted with many commercials to be read in a shift.

Important to the staff announcer are humor, entertainment, and good taste. What is funny to the announcer may not be funny to the audience, so it is important to subject prospective humorous remarks to the acid test: is it really funny, and will it amuse a listener? The listener expects to be entertained by listening to a radio personality, and there is no surer way for an air personality to be entertaining than to enjoy what he or she is doing. But any humor and entertainment must be subject to the rules of good taste, and evaluating program elements and potential ad-libs with that in mind is worthwhile.

Radio staff announcers have a distinct professional advantage in that they can easily listen to others and compare their performance with that of announcers in local and distant areas. Use a copy of *Broadcasting/Cablecasting Yearbook* to find additional information on the markets to which you are listening.

Exercises

1. If you have access to a production facility, combo a 5-minute music show. Pot down the cut after the music has been established, and move into another piece of music. The timing is approximate, but the content must include

   a. an introduction to three discs
   b. a weather forecast
   c. a public service announcement (PSA)
   d. station identification
   e. one commercial
   f. two time announcements

   Do this with any style of music and style of delivery with which you feel comfortable.

   If at all possible, write your own commercial, PSA, and other material. If production facilities are not available, just read the copy into a tape recorder and pretend the records have played.

2. Repeat Exercise 1, but use music and delivery reflecting these formats:

   a. fast-paced hit radio, with a target audience of very young teens
   b. easy listening, with a very affluent, middle-aged target audience
   c. album-oriented rock, with a target audience of rock aficionados in their early twenties.

3. Select the largest and best radio station you can receive in your area and listen for 15 minutes at a time during three separate dayparts. Write down your impressions of the air personality, and describe that individual's

   a. timing
   b. pace
   c. general approach
   d. use of humor

   Do not undertake an extended discussion; just make brief notes. Also, note production values, such as how tightly recorded material is played together and integrated.

   If possible, listen during morning drive, midday, and afternoon drive. Compare and contrast the air personalities on the dayparts.

SIX

News Announcing Basics

*P*erhaps the most personally satisfying area of broadcast performance is news. News stands out among broadcast performance specialties because it is a distinct profession with its own professional standards, operating principles, and ethics. This chapter and the next one are devoted to broadcast news, and both chapters address the special qualities that comprise the news operations of radio and television.

Very few newspeople are employed simply to read news on the air. A major part of the day-to-day duties of broadcast newspeople is involved with preparing the news broadcast. The on-air newsperson must be able to gather, write, and produce some of the audio and visual elements that give form to broadcast news stories. Even those few individuals at the very top level of broadcast news have some involvement in assembling the elements of the on-air news product. And those people got to the top of that lofty pyramid because they were skilled journalists who advanced through the ranks. It is beyond the scope of this book to offer a full course in journalism, but Chapters 6 and 7 provide a broad view of the journalistic principles that relate most directly to on-air performance.

Broadcast journalism offers rewarding opportunities for talented and skilled broadcast performers. In television, news offers the greatest number of opportunities for entry into the medium. To succeed in this specialized area, we advise you to include some training in journalism, both broadcast and print, in your preparation. You should also become well grounded in other academic areas, such as economics, political science, English, foreign language, and sociology.

Broadcast News

In an overall sense, a journalist in a broadcast setting is under the same obligations and constraints as a print journalist is. The responsibility for accuracy and completeness is no less demanding in radio and television than in a newspaper. Broadcast news takes on some additional importance, however, because of its immediacy. Broadcast, especially radio, is the medium most capable of responding instantly to breaking news. Moreover, the impact of broadcast news is often considered to be greater than that of the print media. This impact was brought home vividly during the extensive coverage of the war in Iraq. The immediacy of live reports of events that were taking place as we saw them, and the ability of video to convey the effectiveness of high-tech weapons, were just two elements of coverage that print could not duplicate. Television, with the help of videophones and satellite hookups, allowed people at home to experience this war in ways that have never before been possible. In many ways, television viewers probably had a better concept of what was going on at any point in the war than did many of those who were actually on the ground in the war zone.

Often, broadcast news is looked on as something like show business, and many such criticisms have some justification. For example, the trend toward "happy talk" news programs of the 1970s produced, at the extremes, some inane results.

The power of the rating point in broadcast news is undisputed. No commercial station can afford to ignore audience considerations in news programming. But the charge that broadcast news is "pure show business" is false, and the source of much of this notion—namely, print critics—should be recognized. Print news sources are not exempt from the need to attract an audience, either. Newspapers, which have paid great attention to graphics, artwork, and readability, also show awareness of the "entertainment" function.

A commonsense look at the state of American broadcast news journalism shows that although show business plays an undeniable role, there is a great deal of quality, integrity, and inventiveness at every level of the profession.

Structures and Content

The structures of broadcast news fall into several broad categories that overlap. They are presented here to give an idea of the news functions, not to present a definitive listing.

NEWSCAST   In its simplest form, a newscast involves nothing more than reading aloud a string of news stories. In longer form, such as television news, the newscast is a mixture of breaking news and feature material. In essence, the newscast is a planned and structured assemblage of news, which encompasses some of the following forms.

REPORT   One element of a newscast, the report, deals with a single news item. It can take many forms, such as the *voice report* on radio, where the reporter delivers a minute or so on a news topic. The voice report, or voicer, is signed off with the reporter's name and affiliation, such as "This is Frank Lombardo reporting for WAAA News." The radio voicer can be expanded to include an actuality, or snippet of an interview or other relevant audio from a newsmaker or news event. Incorporating an actuality into the voice report produces what is known as a **voice-actuality.** This might consist of 10 seconds of the reporter delivering the first section of the voicer, an interview segment cut in for 20 seconds, then the reporter finishing up with a 10-second close and signing off. Actualities without a voice report wrapped around them are often used within the newscast. Sometimes actualities are simply introduced by the newscaster.

Television's version of the voicer is often referred to as a **stand-up.** The structure of the radio voice-actuality piece, when done with video, is usually called a **package.**

INTERVIEW   The exchange of information and ideas is often the crux of an entire news show, such as *Meet the Press.* The subject of interviewing is covered in detail in Chapter 8. When portions of an interview are used in a news report or newscast, they become actualities.

DOCUMENTARY   A documentary is a relatively long piece done in dramatic style. Generally, a documentary focuses on one issue and has a plot line. A documentary usually reaches a conclusion and makes a point. "Documentary" is clearly distinct from "docudrama," which is a dramatic reconstruction of an actual event in which actors representing real people work from scripts based on eyewitness accounts and the public record.

HARD VERSUS SOFT NEWS   **Hard news** generally deals with breaking stories and ongoing events that are newsworthy because of their immediate impact on listeners and viewers. **Soft news,** sometimes called *feature news,* is not necessarily linked to a time element or to a story of immediate impact. For example, the story of a fire in progress is hard news, whereas a follow-up report on the lives of the people thus made homeless crosses into the soft news category.

In many stories, soft and hard news overlap. An investigative report on the influence of organized crime in city government may uncover hard news, or material that becomes hard news.

Requirements and Duties of the Journalist

Broadcast journalism requires a number of specialized skills and talents. Aside from the standard requirements for other broadcast assignments, the following attributes are helpful and in many cases essential.

A BROAD EDUCATION   Knowing something about a wide variety of subjects is a great plus for a broadcast journalist. Proper pronunciation of words and names is largely a function of formal and informal education. It is also important to have an awareness of world events. After all, you can't report the news without understanding the context in which events occur.

WRITING SKILLS   Almost all broadcast news on-air people are required to write copy. Remember, too, that occupants of read-only positions generally got there through previous news positions in which they employed writing skills. You *must* develop the ability to write for the ear in broadcast style, a topic addressed later in this chapter.

AD-LIB SKILLS   The ability to ad-lib is especially important for the voice report, which in modern radio and television is frequently delivered live over the air. New remote gear means that more news pieces are done live from the field, and with improving broadcast technologies the ability to ad-lib will become increasingly important in broadcast journalism.

INTERPERSONAL SKILLS   Newsgathering personnel must sometimes prod, flatter, or browbeat news sources, depending on the situation. The ability to extract news requires finely honed interpersonal skills. Also, you are likely to encounter difficult situations in dealing with news sources, and often you must be particularly sensitive to the feelings of someone who is emotionally distraught.

NEWS SENSE   Few of us are born with news sense, but someone lacking it cannot determine what is news and what is not and cannot assess the relative importance of stories. A journalist develops this ability largely through experience and guidance from other professionals.

News Style and Impact

Style in broadcast news, in a general sense, concerns the way the news is presented. From a performer's standpoint, the desired result of a particular style is to draw attention to the news, not to the newscaster. Exceptional news personalities are usually highly regarded because they make the news coherent, exciting, and immediate for the listener or viewer, not because they are handsome or beautiful.

Yet popular folklore would have us believe that the typical news anchor is chosen exclusively because of his or her looks and voice. There is a kernel of truth in that, but journalistic know-how and the ability to communicate and convince are the deciding factors in hiring for most anchor jobs.

The factors that make any broadcast journalist able to communicate and convince include believability, energy, and authority.

- *Believability.* A newsperson with a believable style is able to communicate without artificiality, inspiring confidence in the truth of what he or she has to say. Believability is enhanced by forthright speech devoid of any artificial patterns and by knowledge of news and current events.

- *Energy.* Broadcast news performers are expected to inject energy into their delivery, to keep listeners and viewers interested. To succeed in this, the performer must be interested in the copy.

- *Authority.* The element of authority—a variant of believability—convinces the audience that the newsperson knows what he or she is talking about. Viewers and listeners almost always can tell the difference between a mere reader and a real reporter.

Broadcasters are required by the very nature of their jobs to have something distinctive about their on-air appearance and delivery, and style is important to newspeople as well as to other on-air personnel in broadcasting. Style—which includes the elements of believability, energy, authority, and miscellaneous personality traits and other elements discussed in Chapter 4—is a major factor in the success of many journalists. Box 6.1 gives some examples of newspeople who project various styles.

As the foregoing examples suggest, an effective communicator of news must develop beyond being a reader of copy. An important part of broadcast journalism is the interpretive role played by the newscaster, the energy, believability, and authority the newscaster imparts to the copy.

One caution: the development of your style must not affect content. Never let style distort facts.

Newswriting Basics

Newswriting is a complex field, and shelves full of books have been devoted to it. This introduction describes some basics of newswriting that are particularly useful for the on-air performer.

Why is newswriting important for on-air people? First, to succeed as a journalist, you must be able to write. Second, understanding how a news story evolves greatly enhances your ability to communicate facts and ideas.

Let's follow a radio news story from beginning to end. A radio news reporter hears from the police and fire scanner that there's a fire at a major furniture warehouse. She immediately calls the fire department, confirms that there is indeed a fire at that location, gets the name of her informant, receives permission to record the call, and gathers pertinent information.

Q: What's happening right now?

A: Two alarms have been called in. The call came in at 10:47 and we sent the first units. When the deputy chief arrived, he figured we needed another unit, so a second alarm was called in.

Q: Has anyone been hurt?

Box 6.1

EXAMPLES OF NEWS DELIVERY STYLES

- *George Stephanopoulis.* Host of ABC's Sunday morning news/politics program *This Week,* George Stephanopoulis projects an aura of calm believability. Stephanopoulis should sound like he knows about politics: Before coming to ABC News, Stephanopoulis served the Clinton White House as a senior advisor.

Figure 6.1   *George Stephanopoulis, host of ABC's* This Week, *interviews General Tommy Franks. With today's portable lights and camera equipment, reporters can conduct in-depth interviews from the field as well as from the studio.*

AP/Wide World Photos

- *Ted Koppel.* Authority and believability are strong points in Koppel's delivery. His apparent ability to stay completely in control regardless of the situation seems to have been a factor in his selection to act as host of *Nightline.* Although this program often deals with relatively abstract ideas, it also provides a forum for exploring ongoing news stories such as hijackings.

Continues

Box 6.1 *Continued*

- *Ed Bradley.* The no-nonsense approach of this veteran *Sixty Minutes* reporter conveys the image of someone who understands the essential elements of the story he is working on. His style is nonconfrontational, but he conveys to the audience that he is not going to be satisfied with the answers he receives until he gets the truth. Viewers get the impression that Bradley is carefully building his story bit by bit, filling in pieces that will eventually result in a complete picture.

- *Connie Chung.* A straightforward approach enhances Chung's authority and believability. She is a pleasant, serious journalist who does not hesitate to show her concern with the news.

A: Not that we know of, but rescue firefighters are searching the building right now.

Q: Do you have reason to believe that people are still inside?

A: No, the manager of the building says all employees are accounted for, but we have to check as a matter of routine.

Q: Could you describe the extent of the fire?

A: At last report, the building was about 50 percent engulfed. I just talked to the deputy chief on the scene and he thinks the roof might collapse, so the firefighters on the inside are going to have to get out pretty soon.

Q: Any danger to other buildings?

A: We don't think so. There's not much wind, and no buildings connect to the warehouse.

Q: Do you know what caused the fire?

A: Nope, no idea at this time. Listen, I gotta run because there's another call coming in. Call me back in 15 minutes or so and I'll know more.

From this information, the reporter can construct a story. Granted, it is far from complete, but that's what the reporter has, and she must go on the air with it in the next couple of minutes.

The first step is to write the lead, the first sentence of the story. The two primary categories of leads in broadcast writing are hard leads and soft leads, but there are many variations. A hard lead is a straight presentation of information, the major factors of the story. The soft lead is a more leisurely approach, designed to stir interest.

In the case of a fire story, an immediate piece of breaking news, a hard lead is called for:

> A two-alarm fire is racing through the Hoffman Furniture Warehouse at 511 Clinton Avenue West.

The lead sentence in broadcast newswriting is usually shorter than a lead in a newspaper article because broadcast news is written for a listener instead of a reader. If who, what, where, when, and why are all in the first sentence, a listener will have trouble comprehending it. A newspaper lead might look like this:

> A two-alarm fire raced through the Hoffman Furniture Warehouse at 511 Clinton Avenue West today, causing no injuries but heavily damaging the building, District Fire Chief Stanley J. Kusinski said.

That is a good newspaper lead, but even though considerations of "why" have been omitted, it would be difficult for a listener to digest.

The radio lead just given is more appropriate, and when followed by other important details, it forms the basis for a short, punchy story:

> A two-alarm fire is racing through the Hoffman Furniture Warehouse at 511 Clinton Avenue West. No injuries are reported. All employees are reportedly accounted for, but officials on the scene are conducting a room-by-room search. The building is 50 percent engulfed in flames, and firefighters worry that the roof may collapse.
>
> The initial report was called in at 10:47 this morning. When officials arrived on the scene, they called for additional apparatus.
>
> Fire officials say there's little danger of the fire spreading to nearby buildings. The cause has not yet been determined.

This story could also be written to include an actuality recorded from the telephone interview.

> A two-alarm fire is racing through the Hoffman Furniture Warehouse at 511 Clinton Avenue West. No injuries are reported. All employees are reportedly accounted for, but officials on the scene are conducting a room-by-room search.
>
> Here's how District Fire Chief Stanley Kusinski describes the scene:
> "The building is about 50 percent engulfed. I just talked to the deputy chief on the scene and he thinks the roof may collapse."
>
> The initial report was called in at 10:47 this morning. When fire officials arrived on the scene, they called for additional apparatus.
>
> Fire officials say there's little danger of the fire spreading to nearby buildings. The cause has not yet been determined.

The story will be updated throughout the day, and the lead will progress through several stages:

> Fire officials have finally left the scene of a stubborn, smoky fire at the Hoffman Furniture Warehouse . . .
>
> Investigation continues into the cause of this morning's fire at the Hoffman Furniture Warehouse . . .

When a story is no longer breaking news, the lead may change from a hard lead to a soft lead:

> It was an exhausting day for local firefighters, as 24 volunteers battled a stubborn blaze that burned for more than 7 hours . . .

In writing a television news script, the same general principles apply. The difference is that in television you will have the added element of pictures to deal with and your facts will be put together in a different way.

Using the same fire example, but in television scenario, we can illustrate the differences in approach. There may be less rush to get something together to put on the air. In radio, a regular newscast is usually scheduled a short time after the station's newsperson gets word of the story. As we have shown, the story can be developed over time as more and more details become available. In television, there are far fewer times when news can be broadcast. Usually there is an early evening and a late evening news block, and some stations have a news report at noon.

Because television has fewer newscasts and because it relies on pictures to tell much of the story, a very different approach is needed when a news story breaks. More work needs to be done to get the pictures that will tell much of the story, and more people are needed to do the work. Here is how the job will be set up:

1. Using the facts she has gathered, the reporter does an on-camera "bridge" as a transition between segments taped at the scene.
2. The reporter does an on-camera "stand-up," which will conclude the package when it is edited for air.
3. The reporter and cameraperson return to the studio.
4. The reporter writes copy to be read by the anchor in the studio as live "voice-over" audio while taped pictures of the fire appear on the screen.
5. The package is edited and prepared for use on the air.

The actual amount of writing involved in putting this package together is minimal. Much of the reporter's responsibility centers around quickly gathering essential information, selecting the items that best tell the story, and integrating the information with visual elements of the story.

A major consideration in writing the copy for a package like the one described here is how closely to follow the video. There is a fine line between ignoring what is on the screen and writing too directly about it. It would sound silly, on the one hand, to say, "This is a fire that erupted this morning." People can *see* there is a fire. To have the anchor say, "This is a fire," uses valuable time to provide information that the viewer already has. On the other hand, if you are showing firefighting action, this is the wrong time to talk about the progress of the investigation into the cause of the blaze.

When a television news director receives word of a breaking news story such as a major fire, a reporter and a news crew will likely be assigned to go to the scene and do the story. Several factors may influence how the story is handled at this point.

Let's assume that the story breaks a couple of hours before a scheduled newscast. If the news director feels the story is fairly important, a live remote may be set up to bring viewers the reports directly from the scene as the story develops. If the story is regarded as less important, the news director may tell the reporter to prepare a "package."

A package usually runs somewhere between 45 seconds and 2 minutes. It includes taped pictures of the news event, and interviews with key people connected to the event. The reporter also records on-camera reports at the scene.

Whether coverage is live or packaged, getting the story ready for the air requires the on-camera reporter to coordinate several different activities. We'll use the fire example to illustrate what a typical television reporter would have to do to get the story on the air.

1. Arriving at the scene of the fire, the reporter tells the cameraperson to get some shots of the fire and the firefighters battling the blaze.

2. The reporter locates the fire official in charge at the scene and does an on-camera interview.

3. The reporter locates workers who have evacuated the building and gets on-camera reactions from two or three of them.

The proper approach at this time might be to give an overview of the facts about the fire. The appropriate lead-in to the script might read:

> Fire officials are still not sure what touched off flames that engulfed this Clinton Avenue furniture warehouse this morning. The facility is owned by the Hoffman Furniture Company. No one was injured in the blaze, which caused an estimated 200 thousand dollars worth of damage to the facility.

Another consideration in writing the on-camera material from the scene is to avoid using material that may change later. For example, if you were to report in your stand-up that "officials are unsure if anyone was injured in the fire," your tape becomes useless if the question of injuries is answered before your report is aired. If you are in doubt about elements of the story, leave it out of your report from the scene and let the anchor fill in the information when the report airs.

As a final note, read your copy aloud as you write it. This is something most broadcast journalists do automatically. It helps you write in a style that is easy to read. For example, the phrase "sixty-six separate series of incidents" might look fine on paper, but when read aloud, problems quickly become evident. Reading your copy aloud is also necessary to determine how long it runs.

Television script writing makes unique demands of reporters. The major consideration is to be as brief as possible and yet to convey a lot of information. It takes a bit of practice to master the techniques of "tight" writing, but once mastered it becomes almost automatic.

Presenting Material

The goal of broadcast newswriting is to communicate facts quickly and accurately. There is little room for excess words. The same principles apply to ad-libbing live reports. In fact, because of the immediacy of broadcast news and the need to get a story on the air as quickly as possible, many reports from a news performer are half written, half ad-libbed. The roles of performer and journalist are inseparable.

To effectively present written or ad-libbed material, keep in mind the points highlighted in Box 6.2 and discussed in the text.

First, *use attribution correctly and when necessary.* Attribution is the association of material reported with the source of information. Failure to use correctly attributed information is a common mistake among beginning news reporters.

Controversial statements must always carry attribution. "Chemicals in the village water supply were responsible for the death of 5-year-old Heather Smith" is a statement that must be attributed to a qualified source. An appropriate attribution might be "according to County Director of Public Health Frank Johnson."

Statements of opinion must be attributed in news reporting. For example, "The mayor badly bungled the handling of the school bus strike" must be attributed to the source, such as "according to the Democratic members of the city council."

Legal charges must be attributed. If police arrest a suspect in a bank robbery, the phrases "police have charged" or "according to police" must be incorporated into the statement. It is wise to attribute all information on arrests or charges to the official source. One important reason is that streetwise criminals frequently give names and addresses of other real people when being booked. If you report, "John Jones of 211 Front St. held up the First National Bank" without attribution (such as, "according to Detective Frank Andrews of the city police physical crimes unit"), you are opening the door to legal problems if indeed the bank robber appropriated John Jones's name. This point is not purely academic; it's a troubling area for journalists. Several police officials have noted that use of false identities—someone else's name, address, and even place of employment and Social Security number—is occurring with great frequency today. By the time police sort out the arrestee's real identity, the damage may be done; so always attribute the charges to the legally constituted source.

Box 6.2

POINTERS FOR EFFECTIVE PRESENTATION

1. Use attribution correctly and when necessary.
2. Paraphrase quoted material.
3. Keep sentences short.
4. Use clear sentence construction and word choice.
5. Write for the ear.

Caution in handling crime stories is crucial because legal boundaries concerning lawsuits against news organizations are not always clear. Use "alleged" or "accused" when referring to someone charged with a crime. Even this caution is not always a blanket defense should the charges be proven false. Lawsuits concerning crime reporting are not very frequent in daily journalism, but the possibility always exists.

A commonsense guide to the problem is to use attribution when there is any doubt about the *factuality* and *verifiability* of the statement. For example,

- "The governor visited City Hall today" does not need attribution because it is a fact verifiable by photographs, TV footage, and eyewitness accounts. Viewers and listeners will not expect explicit attribution, nor will the governor's office demand it.

- "The governor will not run for reelection" demands attribution. The statement could, for example, be attributed to the governor: "Governor Masters made the surprise announcement during a press conference here at City Hall." Or, attribution could be made to "a statement from the governor's press secretary." A veteran reporter sure of his or her story and facts may link the statement to a "highly reliable source close to Governor Masters." In any case, the factuality and verifiability must be proven, to the largest extent possible, directly within the story.

Note that in broadcasting, the attribution is often given at the beginning of the sentence: "Police said that a human body has been found in Southtown Gorge," instead of the newspaper type of end-of-sentence attribution, "A human body has been found in Southtown Gorge, police report."

Second, *paraphrase quoted material.* For the most part, direct quotes are not used in broadcast writing. The quote is usually paraphrased. Continual reference to a direct quotation, such as "quoting now," is distracting, and is used only when necessary for absolute clarity in the case of controversial or sensitive material.

Third, *keep sentences short.* Usually 20 to 25 words is the top limit. Although a number of word formulas have been developed, common sense is the best guideline. Simply break up longer sentences in a natural place, and be aware that keeping sentences short is particularly important in ad-libbing. An occasional long sentence is all right, however, because continual short, choppy sentences become repetitive in rhythm and unappealing to the ear.

Fourth, *use clear sentence construction and word choice.* Listeners cannot go back and reread what you just said. Avoid using words easily confused by listeners, such as *can* and *can't.*

Fifth, *write for the ear.* The material is meant to be read aloud, so read it before putting it over the air. If it doesn't *sound* right, redo it.

Ethical Issues

A successful journalist must earn the trust and respect of the public. Certain canons of ethics apply to the job, and they are important to any performer who functions in news. Practices and policies vary from station to station, but two terms germane to any discussion of journalistic ethics are *right to privacy* and *libel.*

THE RIGHT TO PRIVACY   Possibly the reporter's first encounter with the right to privacy will involve the recording of a newsmaker's voice or image. In a few cases, you can record someone without his or her permission. Obviously, you do not need permission to record a press conference. In other cases, though, the line becomes blurred.

If you approach someone in a public place with microphone in hand and explain who you are and what you are doing, you're on solid ground to report or broadcast. Entering a private office or residence is another matter and should be considered case-by-case with your news executive.

Telephone interviews can cause problems because the interviewee may later claim to have been unaware of the recording. To protect yourself and your station, a mechanical beep tone is useful. Better yet, inform the person on the other end of the line that you are recording and get his or her consent *on tape.* Be sure to learn your station's individual policy governing recording phone calls before you air any portion of a recorded conversation.

In many cases the right to privacy is clear-cut, but in many cases it is not. Hidden-camera interviews and other investigative techniques should be used only under the supervision of an experienced news executive or attorney.

Sometimes the right to privacy is not so much a legal issue as a moral one. Does the grieving widow of a slain police officer have a right to privacy? Is she unnecessarily traumatized by having a microphone thrust in her face and being asked for comment? Common sense and good taste deny the right to invade her privacy just to get a story. By contrast, newspeople have swarmed over artificial heart recipients, and concern has been expressed that the patients' rights to privacy were being trampled. However, because these surgery patients consciously chose to participate in medical experiments of profound significance, the public's need to know seemed to legitimately take precedence over the individuals' rights of privacy.

The right to privacy also depends on whether the individual involved seeks notoriety. A person who is defined as a public figure, such as a politician or a performer, has sacrificed a considerable amount of right to privacy by entering the public spotlight. This has a bearing on the legal interpretations of damage to reputations, known as *libel.*

LIBEL   As recent court cases have demonstrated, there are very few clear-cut answers to the question of what constitutes libel.

Basically, libel is the act of issuing or publishing a statement that damages a person's reputation, defaming his or her character and exposing him or her to ridicule.

Simplistic definitions of libelous versus nonlibelous statements are worse than none at all because there are many gray areas within the law. The interpretation of libel laws is subject to change according to new court decisions.

To consider briefly the most basic points of libel as they apply to a news announcer, examine the contention that truth is a defense against libel. On close examination, you can see that this is a somewhat simplistic concept because truth is not always easily definable. If a reporter alleges that the subject of a story is an incompetent physician, can that charge be proven? If the word *incompetent* is used, can it be defined and verified? Has the physician been convicted of malpractice?

Yes, truth is a defense against libel, but often the question revolves around the recognized definitions of the words and terms used in the news item. As journalists Ted White, Adrian J. Meppen, and Steve Young put it,

> Proving the truth is not always easy, and the proving must be done by the writer or reporter. If you referred on the air to a labor leader as a racketeer, you had better be prepared to show that he was convicted of such a crime or that you have conclusive evidence of such activity that will stand up in a court of law. Otherwise, you and your station management could lose a lot of money.[1]

Another defense against libel is *privileged communication.* For example, you cannot be sued for repeating remarks made by members of Congress from the floor of the legislative chamber or judges in open court; those remarks are privileged communications. Certain other public statements and records are also privileged. In cases less clear-cut than judicial or legislative remarks, always check with a senior news executive if there is a possibility that the statements could be interpreted as libelous.

---

[1] *Broadcast News Writing, Reporting, and Production* (New York: Macmillan, 1984), p. 55.

A fair comment against a public official or public figure is not libel. Someone who runs for public office, by the very nature of that act, exposes himself or herself to public comment. The courts have ruled that people who seek publicity have, for all intents and purposes, less protection under libel laws. However, "fair" and "accurate" are subjective terms; a reporter does not have *carte blanche* when dealing with public figures. An irresponsible and unfounded statement against a celebrity can still be actionable (serve as the basis for a lawsuit).

Malice and reckless disregard of the truth are the primary factors a public official must prove to wage a successful libel suit. As was the case with William Westmoreland's 1983 suit against CBS, the issue was not only the truth of the allegations against him, but whether the allegations were made with the intent to harm and with prior knowledge that they were untrue. This can be a difficult case to make, as Westmoreland found; he eventually stopped pursuing the case in 1985.

Malice and reckless disregard continue to be criteria for cases involving public figures. But the scope of who, exactly, is a "public figure" appears to be shrinking.

Be aware that libel law interpretation changes as courts make decisions and set new precedents and that libel laws differ from state to state. It is very, very difficult to predict what the interpretation of libel laws will be if any gray area is entered. When in doubt, always check with a senior news executive or the station's legal counsel (see Box 6.3).

Radio News

Radio news can be the most immediate of all media. When people need to find out about a breaking news story, such as a weather emergency, they turn on the radio.

Radio news operates under the basic journalistic principles described earlier. This section deals with some of the specialized methods and equipment by which radio news is gathered and structured, and with the equipment used by radio reporters. Techniques and operations relating to delivery, formats, and news services are examined later.

Gathering Radio News

In radio, newsgathering consists of obtaining facts and sound sources. This can be done at a very basic level by one person working with a telephone and a telephone recording device, as demonstrated by the example of the reporter covering the furniture warehouse fire by phone. On a more sophisticated level, radio newsgathering can involve a staff of street reporters equipped with portable recording gear, covering specialized beats. Large radio news operations have people in charge of editing and production.

Box 6.3

A PRIMER ON PRIVACY AND LIBEL

First and foremost, remember that what follows is a brief summary of libel and privacy law—not specific legal advice. Laws differ from jurisdiction to jurisdiction. So when in doubt, consult with a senior news executive or your station's attorney.

Libel

Journalism professor Martin L. Gibson defines **libel** as published material that subjects a person to hatred, contempt, or ridicule. Beyond that, libel can be established if the person suffers loss of respect or if he or she is harmed in some way.

Certain things must happen for libel to be committed. Usually in case law these are called *elements of libel.* They are *publication, damage, identification,* and *fault. Publication* is self-explanatory, except that the word also applies to something disseminated over the airwaves. *Damage* can be emotional or monetary, but libel suits are often brought because a story causes loss of income to a business. Probably this is because balance sheets are easier to document than emotional suffering.

Identification, again, is relatively self-explanatory, but for the purpose of this discussion it's important to remember that identification usually means specific identification of an individual. Groups rarely sue for libel. Of particular importance to the broadcast journalist is avoiding accidental associations of people and events, such as using so-called wallpaper video showing a car repair establishment to illustrate a story about car repair scams. Someone whose shop is identified by the video may indeed have a viable libel action against you even if you chose that person's shop only as cover video. (*Cover video* simply refers to pictures used to illustrate a television news script.)

The fourth element is *fault.* It must be shown by the plaintiff that the information was incorrect and fulfilled the other elements. (Note that simply being incorrect does not expose you to a libel case. If you say someone is 6 feet tall when he is really 6 feet, 2 inches, there are very few instances where that would be construed as a mistake that caused damage.) Public people—that is, people who have thrust themselves into the public eye—must prove fault to a higher degree. They must show that the reporter disseminated the information knowing that it was false, and with the intent of causing damage. This is called the *actual malice rule.*

Continues

Box 6.3   *Continued*

There are a number of defenses against libel. For the purposes of our discussion, we will group these defenses into the categories of *provable truth, privilege, fair comment,* and *public figure exposure.*

Provable truth, as mentioned in the text, goes beyond simply knowing in your heart that the allegation is true. It must be documented and specifically proven in court. That is why newswriters frequently avoid words such as *incompetent.* This term is rather nebulous, difficult to prove, and you would be in a better position to simply list your documentation, rather than use the catchall term *incompetent.*

Privilege applies to statements made on the floor of a legislative body when that body is in session, or in court when court is in session. These statements are granted what is often called *absolute privilege,* and a reporter enjoys *qualified privilege,* meaning that he or she is protected from libel action as long as the remarks are repeated fairly and accurately.

Fair comment simply means the right to express an opinion. A journalist has every right, for example, to criticize a play, a restaurant, or a public performance. However, that criticism cannot include embellishments of the truth or unrelated and irrelevant personal attack. For example, a Supreme Court opinion handed down in 1990 held that an opinion column could be subject to libel action because it dealt with a serious issue—an implication that a local high school coach committed perjury.

Finally, **public figure.** Our concept of public figure exposure stems back to the 1964 Supreme Court case of *Times v. Sullivan.* In that ruling, the Supreme Court held that the American spirit of valuing free and robust debate causes a public official to expose himself or herself to public criticism. As a result, a public official—in this case a southern police commissioner—enjoys less protection.

Decisions following *Times v. Sullivan* broadened the definition of a public figure to include famous persons as well as elected or appointed officials. More recent cases, however, have moved the pendulum in the other direction, affording more protection for well-known people who are not public officials.

Privacy

Privacy actions are far less frequent than libel litigations. A good share of privacy case law, in fact, does not relate to news operations. For example, many privacy cases involve appropriation of someone's image for advertising without that person's consent.

The areas that should concern a news reporter are invasions of privacy, which in some way embarrass a person or portray that person in

Continues

> **Box 6.3** *Continued*
>
> false light. The issues are far from clear-cut. For example, successful privacy actions have been brought against news organizations that have carried "Where are they now?" stories that brought up true but embarrassing tales of what someone did decades ago.
>
> The defenses against privacy actions are as complex as the laws. However, as a general guideline you should remember that an item that embarrasses someone must be newsworthy—a difficult concept to determine. But judgments can and have been made against news organizations that pictured people in embarrassing situations simply for the sensational impact. Second, being a reporter does not give you the right to trespass. Third, you should be especially careful when dealing with minors or anyone who might be deemed to have diminished capacity to knowledgeably agree to be interviewed or appear on air. Finally, subjects of certain news stories do lose their right to privacy just because of their bad luck. However, be aware that laws do protect the privacy of victims of certain crimes—especially sex crimes. Remember that, even though there will always be exceptions, when someone seeks publicity, or is the subject of a current legitimate news story, you are probably on safe ground.

All radio news operations are under the command of a news director. In small stations, the news director may be the only newsperson on the payroll. In large radio stations, he or she is an executive in charge of large budgets and staffs. The radio news director usually reports to the station general manager or the program director.

The concept of actuality is very significant in radio news. Gathering actualities by phone or with a portable tape recorder has become one of the radio newsperson's primary responsibilities. Few stations are content simply to read stories over the air; somewhere in most newscasts there is actuality material.

Actualities can consist of an interview segment or a **wild sound bite,** that is, sound other than interview speech, recorded at the scene of a news event. The scream of sirens, for example, could be incorporated into a piece as a wild sound bite. Wild sounds might consist of the chanting of crowds on a picket line, or the roar of flames in a four-alarm fire. When an actuality consists of an interview segment, it is usually less than a minute long, more often less than 30 seconds. Longer actualities are used in documentary pieces.

The radio news reporter must choose a compelling piece of actuality rather than running an entire interview. When gathering and editing down an actuality, the reporter looks for responses that express opinion or give greater focus to the central issue of the story. A politician's description of

Figure 6.2   A portable cassette recorder used with a good-quality microphone is the workhorse of today's radio news reporter.

Photo by Philip Benoit

what he or she thinks a budget cut will do to the district is far more interesting than a recitation of budget figures.

In general, when choosing actuality, remember

1. Statements of fact made during the interview are best used in writing the script.

2. Statements that express emotion or opinion are best used as actualities within the news report.

Radio Reporting Equipment

The basic radio reporting tool is the portable recorder hooked to a good-quality microphone (see Figure 6.2). Because cassette tape is difficult to edit mechanically, it is frequently dubbed to a computer for editing. In some cases, the appropriate portions of the cassette material are dubbed onto a cart or minidisc.

Figure 6.3   A small production studio used for radio news production.

Photo by Fritz Messere

Often the newsperson uses a small production studio (see Figure 6.3) containing necessary equipment and an electronic link between the telephone and the recording gear.

Computers and cart machines are used extensively to hold voice reports, voice actualities, and actualities for use during a newscast. Practices vary among individual stations, but usually there is a standard method of labeling the segment with the name of the person being interviewed or the reporter filing the actuality, the length of the interview, and the **outcue.** The outcue is the final word or words spoken on the tape. Labeling an actuality with an outcue is a must because it indicates when the newscaster is to begin speaking again. Multiple actualities should be labeled sequentially or with a unique identifier (for example, Fire 1, Fire 2, and so forth). An interview used as the basis of a story that incorporates two actualities would look like this in script form:

CITING FAILING HEALTH, STATE SENATOR MARGARET BLANK TODAY ANNOUNCED HER WITHDRAWAL FROM THE UPCOMING RACE FOR REELECTION.

//BLANK #1//

. . . As I'm sure you're aware, I've had several operations within the past four years, and while my health is relatively good, I don't think I'm up to the strain of another term in office.

THE SURPRISE ANNOUNCEMENT HAS THROWN LOCAL REPUBLICANS INTO TURMOIL AS THEY JOCKEY FOR A SPOT ON THE PRIMARY TICKET. AS TO HER POSSIBLE SUCCESSOR, BLANK WON'T PLAY FAVORITES OTHER THAN TO SAY,

//BLANK #2//

At this point, I'm not endorsing anyone. I will pledge to oppose, though, anyone who plans to cut aid to education in our district.

THAT STATEMENT IS INTERPRETED BY SOME OBSERVERS AS A BACKHANDED ENDORSEMENT OF CITY SCHOOL SUPERINTENDENT PAUL WHITE, WHO HAS EXPRESSED AN INTEREST IN BLANK'S JOB.

The carts or computer files for this cut would be labeled

- Blank #1:09 (term in office)
- Blank #2.08 (in our district)

The format of capital letters for announcer copy and lowercase letters for actuality is used in many news operations, although practices vary. You should always have the actuality written down, though, in case the tape fails and you are obliged to paraphrase the statement.

Radio news reporters often feed cuts over the telephone with special wires leading from the tape recorder and sometimes feed taped material and live reports over two-way radios or specialized small transmitters. Stations in very large markets may have a series of these transmitters located throughout the city to boost the signal back to the station or to the station's antenna.

Today's sophisticated technology is helping the newsgathering in many ways. Focus on Technique discusses how audio edition software can be used to speed news preparation. Although a reporter can certainly do a decent job without sophisticated hardware, the new technologies give stations an edge. But as radio news becomes more highly competitive, the use of high-tech equipment will certainly increase.

Radio News Operations

Typically, a radio news anchor is responsible for gathering, editing, and reading news (see Figure 6.5). The operations involved include making calls to police and fire agencies and scanning newspapers and wire services for important stories. Working with wire service material is covered later in this chapter. Here we mention the practice, common in radio, of rewriting newspaper stories for broadcast. This practice should be pursued with caution,

Focus on Technique

The Computer Moves into the Newsroom

You've probably noticed that the computer is an integral part of today's radio station, and news production has recently undergone a rapid change.

The most visible aspect of the computer's advance is the digital audio workstation (DAW). It may be a specially configured computer (both Macs and PCs are popular) or it may be a stand-alone device. Radio production personnel commonly use DAWs in recording and mixing commercials and promotions; in those cases, the performer may not have any idea what's happening at the computer terminal.

But some radio personnel, particularly newspeople, must combine performance with some hands-on knowledge of DAW operation. In the last few years most stations have upgraded to digital when they needed new equipment. Oddly enough, DAWs are often cheaper than their analog counterparts.

Digital editing is surprisingly simple. In the most basic terms, it follows a standard cut and paste formula with which most people are already familiar. Editing is a three-step process:

- First information is digitized, meaning that audio sent to the computer is converted into a digital format. "Digital" simply means "made of numbers," and that's what happens to the sound signal. The computer sound card samples the sound thousands of times per second and constructs a numerical pattern that represents the recorded sound. A "waveform" (see Figure 6.4a) represents the sound. The peaks and valleys in the waveform represent the relative loudness.

- Using the computer mouse, you can highlight a portion of the audio that you want to edit. The block can easily be cut from the rest of the waveform (see Figure 6.4b), leaving you with an edited waveform that has joined the two parts of the actuality (Figure 6.4c). Most systems will allow you to undo a bad edit; if you make a mistake you can undo it and start over. Other systems create separate regions that are edited, preserving the original sound. Each system has its own unique features.

- Finally the information is stored on the computer's hard drive. It may then be called up for playback later or dubbed onto a cart or minidisc for playback during the next news segment.

Systems vary in operation and complexity, of course, but you'll find that this basic pattern is common to most systems you'll encounter.

Continues

Focus on Technique Continued

Figure 6.4   a. The waveform represents the sound recorded into the computer.

b. The highlighted area represents the sound portion to be cut
from the sound bite.

Continues

Focus on Technique Continued

Figure 6.4 *(Continued)*

c. *The edit is now complete.*

Used by permission of Syntrillium Software

Digital editing has other advantages beside simple precision, by the way. For one thing, you do not have to edit in a "linear" fashion—meaning in a line, from beginning to end. You can edit in any order that you want. Second, digital editing is nondestructive, meaning that you do not have to physically cut or erase any of your original material. Should you make an editing blunder, you can tell the computer to "undo" the edit.

because when a newspaper story is wrong and a radio reporter rewrites and uses it, the radio reporter is wrong, too. Many newspapers vigorously object to radio reporters' use of stories gathered by the newspaper staff. Nevertheless, the newspaper will always be an important source for the broadcast journalist, and once you have verified the story and done some additional checking and gathering, you are ethically entitled to use the story.

There will generally be pieces left over from the previous shift or the previous night, such as a report on a city council meeting. The morning news

Figure 6.5   A modern radio news operation. Reporters perform writing, editing, and recording functions from their desks as they prepare radio financial news reports from the headquarters of Bloomberg News in New York City.

Photo by Carl Hausman

anchor would certainly want to include such material in the early reports, but the council story may be rather stale by noon.

Stories must be written and rewritten throughout the morning. The reporter will follow up on tips from the public, items broadcast over police scanners, and story assignments set up in advance. Street reporters will cover stories in person, and often the morning anchor will take to the streets later in his or her shift.

These are the most basic operations. Now the journalist-performer must take the raw material and make it compelling.

Painting a Picture with Words

A radio journalist must make people visualize a story in the theater of the mind. The writer, who must choose the words and phrases, shoulders much of this responsibility. The performer, who may also have been the writer, has to read accurately with expression and meaning. This really becomes important to the journalist who has to ad-lib a report from hastily scrawled notes.

Box 6.4

TIPS FOR VIVID COMMUNICATION

1. Describe events with imagination.
2. Include sound in the story.
3. Make accurate mood changes.
4. Use and stress vivid words.
5. Pay attention to clarity in using actualities.
6. Develop a system for gauging time.

In that case, those words and phrases must paint a picture that is coherent as well as vivid.

The techniques for understanding the message (Chapter 3) and for communicating the message (Chapter 4) apply here. Some additional suggestions follow (highlighted in Box 6.4):

1. *Describe events with imagination.* Your words are virtually all the listener has to go on. Your ability to describe can be dramatically improved with practice, so practice as much as possible. One program director of a major market all-news station advises reporters to practice describing anything: ride along in the car and describe the countryside; look out the window and describe the neighbor's fence. In your descriptions, pay attention to details, such as the exact color of leaves or the shape of a yard.

2. *Include sound in the story.* Can you get the sound of a fire engine into your street report? By all means give it a try. Also, don't be afraid to incorporate the acoustics of the environment into your story, such as the sound of wind on a report concerning fast-moving brushfires. Do *not* manipulate sound elements in a way that will affect the content of the story. For example, do not use sounds of strikers chanting *recorded during the morning* as an element of a story covering the situation *in the afternoon,* when there were no strikers outside. Also, never use a sound effects record or other device to fake sound elements for a news story.

3. *Make accurate mood changes.* In radio, you have only your voice to communicate changes in moods, and this has to be done with precision because stories are typically short. One of the most common complaints about poor radio news announcers is the lack of mood change between and among stories.

Mark copy to reflect changes in moods. Do not use the same pitch, pace, and rhythm for a report on a double homicide and for a story on a senior citizens' outing.

4. *Use and stress vivid words.* A television shot of a smoky fire speaks for itself. In radio, you have to paint a word picture. Do not touch important words too lightly. If you are writing or ad-libbing, never be content with pedestrian phrasing. For example, which description is more vivid and compelling?

   • "There is a great deal of black smoke coming from the upper window."

   • "Greasy black smoke is *boiling* from the upper window."

   Simple words can paint vivid word pictures; there is no need to become flowery and lurid. Edward R. Murrow's historic word pictures of London during World War II were effective primarily because of the simplicity of the images and the straightforwardness of his delivery. Murrow used vivid small details to bring the picture to life in the theater of the listener's mind. He was not content, for example, simply to tell the listener that bombs were exploding. Instead, Murrow described the burn marks in pavement scorched by hot shrapnel. He was never content simply to describe the sight of people scurrying underground; he invoked other senses, too: "You cannot believe the stench of the air raid shelters."

5. *Pay attention to clarity in using actualities.* If you play an actuality during the delivery of a newscast, identify the speaker *before* and, if possible, *after* the actuality plays. It is best to do this by gracefully including the name of the speaker, such as "Professor Campbell of Georgetown went on to say . . ." If that is not possible, a simple declarative sentence will do: "That was Professor William Campbell of Georgetown University."

6. *Develop a system for gauging time.* Time yourself reading copy whenever possible so that you become able to look at a piece of copy and immediately gauge its length in airtime. Radio news often operates under extremely rigid time requirements, and it is important to be able to estimate how much copy can be read in an allotted time period.

   Your reading rate will probably be about 150 words per minute (wpm), although rapid news readers sometimes reach about 200 wpm. Rate of speech is much faster on a long-form announcement, such as a newscast, than on a 30-second commercial. You can determine your standard long-form reading rate simply by timing a minute's worth of reading and counting the words.

   Knowing the average number of words per line of copy will simplify word counting. Most standard word processors average about 12 words per line of copy, but that will vary with different script formats.

If you read 150 wpm, and your script averages 12 words a line, *you now know that 13 lines of copy will fill one minute.* Knowing how many lines of copy you read per minute is the most valuable method of time approximation.

Skilled announcers who must "stretch" copy often develop a method of prolonging vowels and gently slowing the reading rate so that the stretching is not noticeable. You would not want to use this method for stretching a 3-minute newscast to fill 5 minutes, but it is helpful when it appears that 5 lines of copy will fall 5 seconds short.

When news copy is running too long, it may be a simple matter to drop a line or two in the story. However, be sure you are thoroughly familiar with the story so that you don't drop vital elements, such as attribution or a punch line. With experience and a complete understanding of the story, you will be able to ad-lib a brief conclusion rather than just dropping some copy.

Fitting News to Station Format

There was a time when broadcast news was looked on as something of a burden, to fill FCC requirements. A pleasant development, especially for the journalist, was the discovery that news could make money. Audiences wanted well-done news, and advertisers were willing to pay for exposure on a newscast.

As a result, news has become just as much a part of a station's programming strategy as music and staff announcers. The news must reinforce and complement the sound of the station. This is accomplished in a variety of ways, using every kind of component, from the produced opening of the newscast to the style and pace of the newscaster to the selection of the news itself. A newscaster on an album-oriented rock station with a laid-back format should not use a delivery in the style of a teen-oriented all-hit station.

A modern radio journalist must be able to vary his or her delivery to fit the sound of the station. Unless you have the luxury of having an assured career with one particular format, it is highly advisable to practice flexibility in your delivery. Listen to what works at other stations, and practice communicating effectively within other formats.

The All-News Format in Radio

In 1965, New York's WINS became the first radio station to make a success of an all-news format. Many greeted the idea with skepticism. The nay-sayers felt that audiences wanted news only in small chunks. It seemed unlikely that anyone would stay tuned to one station for continuous news.

WINS proved that the format could succeed, and in the nearly three decades since its inception, the all-news format has become viable for stations in many markets. WCBS in New York, KYW in Philadelphia, and WPOP in Hartford, Connecticut, all have used the format to become some of the most successful stations in the country. In addition to those listeners who keep their radio dials tuned to all-news stations for the entire time they are listening to radio, many listeners tune in for brief updates on what is happening. This high turnover enables all-news stations to perform well in the category of ratings known as "cume" ratings—ratings that count the number of different people who tune in to a station during a certain segment of time. The hybrid format of news/talk combines news programming with listener call-in programming.

The all-news format is demanding for on-air news readers. The station's entire sound depends on the style in which the news is presented. That style is a function of (1) the length of news stories and news segments, (2) the selection and arrangements of news stories, and (3) the reading style of news readers.

The on-air performer must be able to maintain a presence over time that is sustained only by the sound of her or his voice. To do so requires considerable skill in several areas:

- *Rate.* The successful news reader at an all-news station must move along at a comfortable pace. If the rate is too fast, readers will miss important elements of the story. If readers are too slow, energy is lost, so the listener's attention is likely to wander. The most effective rate is one that strikes the reader as a comfortable conversational rate.

- *Inflection.* Inflection is probably the most crucial element of a news reader's delivery in the all-news format. A singsong rate or monotone delivery can be deadly. One is distracting but the second could literally lull listeners to sleep. (Incidentally, we have interviewed radio listeners who say that they use the all-news radio station in their vicinity to help them fall asleep at night. A news reader must guard against inflections that unduly emphasize this characteristic of the format.) Vary your inflection enough so that patterns do not repeat. If you tend to drop pitch every time you come to the end of a sentence, for example, the pattern quickly becomes noticeable. Be aware of your inflection and adjust it to avoid repetitive patterns, while guarding against inflections that do not fit the style of the copy.

- *Timing.* All-news radio is delivered in timed segments. A common promotional phrase used by one all-news station is "Give us 10 minutes, and we'll give you the world." Announcers must be precise enough in delivery to be able to read news scripts exactly to time, so that segments end on the dot at the right time. Very often news readers read copy that ends just before the station joins its network for its newscast. Networks begin their segments at the precise time scheduled. If a local news reader runs over or under the time allotted for the copy adjacent to the news, the cue will be missed.

- *Pitch.* Announcers who use a pitch that is too low or too high will stand out because of the length of time listeners have to discern the fault. A common fault among some inexperienced male announcers is to try to hit an unnaturally low pitch. This can be deadly to all-news performers because an inappropriate pitch stresses the voice. Eventually the constant voice strain on the all-news format will likely impair the announcer's ability to use his voice. Find the correct pitch for your voice, and the delivery will sound better and conserve your voice.

- *Error-free reading.* The most important hallmark of a good news reader in any circumstance is the ability to read copy without stumbling and with accurate pronunciation. Of course, everyone stumbles at some point, and in a format that demands that you continue reading without interruption for 15 minutes or so at a time, there is much more opportunity for stumbles to occur. Announcers who consistently have trouble reading copy smoothly, however, won't last long in an all-news format. There are no second takes in live on-air work. The performance must be as close to flawless as possible or it becomes distracting to listeners.

- *Proper pronunciation.* Words and names must not be mispronounced in all-news radio. Listeners associate the credibility of the station with the news reader on the air. If you mispronounce the name of a newsmaker or a place name, you can bet that someone listening knows you did it. Your credibility and that of the station is compromised. In the all-news format, credibility is everything. If listeners don't think you are knowledgeable about the news you're reading, they won't continue to listen.

In general, the key to giving a good performance in an all-news format is to be very solid in the principles that apply to all news reading. Credibility is crucial. In the all-news format, the elements of effective performance are emphasized by the long periods when your talents will be on display. Flaws are magnified many times over, whereas the absence of flaws won't be noticed much. That is as it should be. Remember that the important element of the format is the news. Your job as news reader is to showcase the news. The most effective performers are noted by average listeners, not because of their outstanding voice and delivery, but because they communicate. The trick is to make the listener think it is easy to do that.

Radio News Services

News services are an important cog in radio news operations; they provide a link to news sources not available at the local level. From the standpoint of news operations and technique, a local reporter does well to gain a thorough understanding of these services because they are effective tools for making the station's entire news effort more effective and professional.

One familiar news service available to radio stations is the hourly newscast provided by radio networks through a landline or satellite link. Because of the increasing importance of formatting, network newscasts are sometimes provided in different forms for various stations, with one feed tailored for rock stations and another for stations serving an easy listening audience. Networks also provide features that can be broadcast live or recorded for later airplay; in some cases, they furnish voicers and actualities for use in local newscasts.

Another important tool for the radio news professional is the wire service. Wire services such as the Associated Press typically provide information via satellite feeds in the form of ready-to-broadcast copy. This includes newscasts, feature material, weather, and state news. A variety of wire service copy is included in Appendixes A and B.

Wire services offer localized feeds known as "state splits," which can be quite useful to newspeople on slow days. You can further localize a state report on aid to education, for instance, by calling city or town officials and asking for comment.

Wire services do such a capable job that some local operations become overly dependent on the wire, which results in what is commonly termed a "rip-and-read" operation. The best use of a wire service is as a supplement to an active news operation.

For stations that assemble national newscasts at the local level, audio services provide actualities, voicers, and voice-actualities for integration with wire copy. The wire service feeds a copy describing the cuts, known as a **billboard,** which lists the cuts by number, time, content, and structure. These cuts are fed according to a regular time schedule. A tone precedes each cut so that newspeople can cart the cuts, starting the cart machine at the end of the tone.

Many private organizations provide news feeds in return for the exposure. Colleges and some professional associations offer material free to stations in return for exposure.

Summary

Radio news is a sophisticated business, requiring much more than an ability to read aloud. In addition, radio is *not* television without the picture. The radio medium offers a unique blend of immediacy, intimacy, and drama. The broadcast news field is dominated by journalists; therefore, a radio or TV newsperson is bound by the responsibilities and ethics applied to all journalists. Although it undeniably has elements of show business, broadcast news is a serious and formidable type of journalism.

The general structures of broadcast news include the newscast, the report, and the interview. The documentary is a long form of broadcast news containing dramatic elements. Broadcast news content generally can be categorized as hard news or soft news. Hard news deals with breaking stories. Soft news presents feature material.

The basic requirements of a broadcast journalist include a broad-based education, the ability to write, the ability to ad-lib, the ability to interact with people, and the possession of a news sense. Style is an important element for an on-air broadcast journalist. The journalist must project believability, energy, and authority.

Anyone who aspires to a news anchor position must know how to write. Most newspeople do their own writing, and even those who no longer write the material they broadcast achieved their positions by being skilled writers and journalists. Broadcast news consists of a short but informative lead, followed by a succinct and compelling recitation of the facts. Among the skills to be mastered in writing or ad-libbing a news story are correct use of attribution and the ability to paraphrase quoted material accurately. Using short sentences, using clear sentence construction and appropriate word choice, and writing for the ear are also important.

Ethical issues affect the broadcast journalist, who must have a basic understanding of when and how someone's image or remarks can be recorded. Because the issues of right to privacy and libel are complex, and the related rulings are subject to change, you must ask for guidance by your news executives when dealing with sensitive issues. Think About It (at the end of this chapter) tells about a famous reporter, Edward R. Murrow, and his clash with Senator Joe McCarthy. This box poses questions aspiring journalists should ask.

The foregoing principles apply to both radio and television news. For radio news specifically, you need to have an understanding of how radio news is gathered and structured. A basic component of radio news is the actuality, the recorded sound of a newsmaker or event. Radio actualities can be inserted into a story in a number of ways.

Radio news anchors and reporters are generally responsible for gathering, editing, and reading news. Sources include news services such as the radio networks, wire services, and news services offered by private organizations.

Radio journalists must be able to paint a picture with words. This process involves describing with imagination, including sound in the story, making accurate mood changes, and using and stressing vivid words. To preserve clarity and flow in the word picture, the announcer must pay attention to clarity of stories and actualities, and be able to gauge time effectively.

News is a component of the station's overall format, and the news effort and news announcers' deliveries must be compatible with the station's overall sound.

Exercises

1. Take five local stories from the newspaper and rewrite them into broadcast style for a 3-minute newscast. Record the newscast, making sure it runs *exactly* 3 minutes.

2. Write brief, descriptive phrases for the following circumstances. Feel free to take some liberties because you are not operating from a strict factual base, but keep within the bounds of reason. The goal is to use

descriptive, colorful adjectives and punchy verbs. Use the active, rather than the passive, voice. For example,

- *Circumstance:* A tractor trailer carrying chemicals tipped over on the expressway and broke open. The payload of chemicals went onto the highway.

- *Description:* A tractor trailer ruptured, spewing chemicals onto the expressway.

Get the idea? Take out those flat-sounding words, and make the sentence paint a picture. Try these circumstances:

- *Circumstance:* An escaped convict was shot and killed while running away from the police.

- *Circumstance:* A tree was blown over by the wind. The roots were pulled out of the ground and stuck up in the air. The falling tree broke through the roof of a house.

- *Circumstance:* An angry Senator Jacobs called his opponent a liar. Jacobs said his opponent should withdraw from the race. Said his opponent was lacking in morals. *Hint:* Come up with variations for "said" and "called."

- *Circumstance:* Tractors were driven by farmers into the grounds of the state capitol. Onlookers were frightened by the onslaught of tractors. *Hint:* Use the active voice.

- *Circumstance:* People at a funeral walked past a casket, walking slowly. The wife of the slain policeman began to cry loudly as she passed the casket. She leaned on top of the casket.

3. Select one of the newscasts created in Exercise 1 and critique it. Rate from excellent, fair, to poor on the following categories:

   a. Were ideas presented clearly?

   b. Was energy level sufficient?

   c. Was there an adequate change of mood between stories?

   d. Were all pronunciations correct?

   e. Was delivery natural sounding?

   f. Did the reader sound interested in the material?

Compare your evaluations. If there is disagreement among critics, play back the recording and examine the specific instances. Be prepared to defend your criticisms.

Think About It

DO YOU DROP YOUR "OBJECTIVITY" WHEN YOU'RE SURE YOU ARE RIGHT AND THERE IS A CRISIS?

The man who set the standard for a modern broadcast announcer and journalist—in fact, the man who pretty much invented the persona of the on-air reporter—was Edward R. Murrow.

Murrow was trained in public speaking, not journalism, and he went to work for CBS as an administrator. But when World War II began to brew in Europe, Murrow put himself behind the microphone. Later, beginning in the 1950s, he appeared on television and became the nation's most recognizable broadcast journalist.

It was probably inevitable that Murrow would clash with another key figure of the 1950s, Joseph McCarthy.

Joseph McCarthy (Figure 6.6) rose to political fame on his credentials as a war hero. He called himself "Tail Gunner Joe," referring to the position of the soldier who defended a bomber from a position near the tail of the airplane.

But McCarthy was never a war hero nor a tail gunner. His habit of making up details for personal benefit would stick with him through his political career.

McCarthy rose to national prominence by exposing "The Red Menace," the threat to U.S. security posed by alleged communist sympathizers and infiltrators. McCarthy again did not let facts get in the way of his career. He recklessly accused hundreds of people of having communist leanings, ruining lives and careers. Almost all of these accusations were made without proof or even anything that remotely resembled evidence: McCarthy would claim to have a "list" that never materialized, a list from high government "sources" who were never named.

Edward R. Murrow and his partner Fred Friendly wanted to produce a program that exposed McCarthy. Murrow had sterling credentials from his years as an on-air correspondent. Friendly, who worked behind the scenes, was a respected producer. For a series of programs called "See It Now," they gathered film showing McCarthy at his worst: bullying, waving sheets of paper that contained the "lists" that never materialized, spewing "facts" that were simply untrue.

McCarthy's political career was doomed after that, and though he tried to counter-attack, Americans had experienced a big dose of the real Tail Gunner Joe and did not like the taste it left in their mouths.

Continues

Think About It   Continued

Figure 6.6   *Senator Joseph McCarthy's reckless tactics—during hearings to expose what he termed "The Red Menace"—were the focus of a series of CBS television broadcasts produced by Fred Friendly and Edward R. Murrow that helped to discredit the man who called himself "Tail Gunner Joe."*

© Bettmann/CORBIS

That, anyway, is the skeleton of the story, most of which you probably know because "McCarthyism" has become a common phrase that lives on today, meaning guilt by association and blind bigotry against assumed "enemies."

But here is the rest of the story, followed by some rather difficult questions.

McCarthy was a clever schemer, but the news media were responsible for making him so brutally powerful. Reporters, both from print and the newly emerging broadcast organizations, often repeated his patently

Continues

Think About It   *Continued*

bogus claims without checking them out. McCarthy staged events that had no real meaning; he would often call a press conference to announce that he was calling another press conference tomorrow. (Historian Daniel Boorstin calls this a "pseudo-event.") And it is not inconceivable that many of the news media were themselves terrified of McCarthy, who leveled charges of communism against his political enemies—meaning anyone who dared challenge him.

Also, viewers watching the final program in the series are struck by the fact that it is not so much an objective news report as an editorial. Murrow took a stand and went after McCarthy. According to CBS News Anchor and Managing Editor Dan Rather, "he knew it and felt uncomfortable about it . . . The question is still relevant. When do we go from telling the story into interpretive reporting?"

The famous closing Murrow delivered also seems somewhat over the top by today's standards:

> We will not walk in fear . . . we will not be driven by fear into an age of unreason, if we dig deep into our history and our doctrine, and remember that we are not descended from fearful men. Cassius was right. "The fault, dear Brutus, is not in our stars, but in ourselves," Good night, and good luck.

Put yourself in the place of a reporter covering modern stories that have similar parallels.

- Suppose, for example, a senator levels a scandalous charge of financial impropriety against another politician. Would you, as a reporter, repeat the remark, attributing it to the senator, or would you hold off until you personally had checked it out? What would happen if other reporters simply repeated the charge (as they probably would); would you risk being hopelessly behind on the story? And suppose the senator making the charge was way off base. Would you stop quoting him in the future? At what point?

- What would you do if you concluded that the senator was just a bald-faced liar? How far would you feel compelled to go to prove this? Would you allow him equal time on a show you produced to show him for what he is? Would you try to *balance* the program? What, exactly, constitutes "balance?" Are you obligated to give balance to a crook?

Also, would you call your viewers to action at the end, telling them, "We will not walk in fear?"

SEVEN

Television News Announcing

*M*uch more is involved in on-air work in television news than sitting before a studio camera and mouthing words convincingly. Television newspeople function as a part of a team that must work closely together to get the news on the air. Television news reporters and anchors are expected to know how to put together a story from start to finish in a short period of time. So they must be able to write clearly and quickly and be familiar with the basics of video production. The performer must have a firm grasp on how television news is gathered, structured, and produced. You simply cannot do the job without understanding the basics.

Television News Basics

A tremendous amount of advance planning and thinking about content is necessary for TV news coverage. Getting each report on the air involves a technical crew and a reporter. So personnel must be scheduled with care so that all important stories during the day can be covered, with flexibility for breaking stories.

After the story has been photographed, the pieces are assembled and a script is written. The finished report must pass the scrutiny of the station's news executive(s), who decides whether it will be used. Sometimes news reports do not pan out, and they are pulled. In many cases, news items are bumped to make room for more timely stories. The entire process is often harrowing, always exciting. This section examines the basics of the business, including gathering the material, structuring it in a form useful for telecast, and putting it over the air within a newscast.

How TV News Is Gathered and Structured

Television news operations vary quite a bit in scope, depending on market size and other factors. A small-market newsroom might house only four or five full-time employees, but a major-market operation may have close to a hundred participants.

Although the particulars of staffing differ from station to station, the basic functions of the TV newsroom are roughly similar in all markets and operations. In larger markets, with bigger staffs, the operations are more specialized. Basic functions include administration, production, gathering, and reporting.

NEWS ADMINISTRATION   This function, headed by a news director, involves decision making on news coverage and responsibility for staffing and budgeting. News directors in major-market stations often find themselves rather removed from actual newsgathering, having to focus instead on fighting for budgetary allotments, new equipment, and additional personnel. The news director of a small station may supervise only two or three other reporters and will cover stories and perhaps anchor the evening newscasts, as well.

The number of administrative layers in a news department varies according to the size of the department. Most medium-market stations employ an assignment editor, whose responsibilities include scheduling crews and reporters and assigning and developing stories.

In summary, the functions of news administration are

- Personnel and budgetary management
- Decision making and editorial policy
- Planning coverage of news

NEWS PRODUCTION   News production was radically transformed by development of lighter, more easily portable video equipment and transmission facilities. Today news has moved toward digital production as more and more stations adopt nonlinear editing. The result is that news is produced faster and more easily than in the past.

Production duties range from the basic technical jobs of such staffers as audio specialists (see Figure 7.1), to the producer, who is in overall charge of assembling the production elements of a newscast and often some editorial elements. The producer reports to the news director.

Within the production function are such specialists as camera operators in studio and in-field producers who put breaking news on live from satellite links (see Figure 7.2), studio assistants, control room operators, and field producers. A field producer, as the name implies, supervises the production function outside the studio. The job description varies in different markets,

Figure 7.1   Audio specialists are an integral part of news production work. Running an audio console requires concentration in order to properly maintain the proper "levels."

Photo by Philip Benoit

Figure 7.2   News is frequently broadcast "live" from the field using state-of-the-art remote satellite trucks like this one.

Photo by Philip Benoit

however. In very large markets and networks, associate producers and assistant producers work under the field producer's supervision in gathering news from the field.

In larger markets all duties become more specialized. A major-market operation may have one or more people responsible for electronic graphics, and the graphics designer may be an executive who supervises the entire "look" of the newscast. Some people specialize in editing, the process of arranging and rearranging the raw materials of news into a final product.

Although not strictly a part of the production function, broadcast engineers keep equipment maintained and operating, as well as supervising ongoing technical functions. A particular requirement for production engineering concerns live remotes, where a microwave unit is used to transmit directly from the news scene.

In summary, duties of news production people include

- Operating equipment needed to record or air the news
- Presenting visual elements, such as graphics and sets
- Editing and assembling raw materials

NEWSGATHERING AND REPORTING   Once news administration has assigned stories, journalists must gather the facts, outline the story elements, write copy, and deliver the copy to the camera either in a field report or as an anchor segment during a newscast. In larger markets, full-time writers compose copy, do research, and to some extent edit and revise copy. In some large markets, writers are assigned to work with a reporter in the field, a function bordering on field production. Today as news coverage has expanded in many markets, more and more field segments air live within the newscast. This requires the field reporter to provide a lucid news segment using a combination of field notes and ad-libbing.

The primary duties of the newsgathering and reporting arm of the television news effort include

- Assembling facts and writing stories or presenting stories live
- Working with the production function to get visual and aural elements such as interviews and cover shots
- Delivering the news copy

The various functions interact a great deal. An on-air member of the newsgathering and reporting arm cannot operate without understanding the other functions and working closely with staffers in the other areas of television news.

How the TV Newscast Developed

In the early development of television, a newscast was radio with pictures, and very few pictures at that. Typically, newscasts were no longer than

15 minutes and featured a camera focused unblinkingly on a news **anchor,** a personality who virtually carried the show.

The evolution of the modern newscast came about through experimentation. At the local level, stations expanded coverage of sports and weather into separate segments. But even through the late 1960s, the local news was often done halfheartedly; it might feature only one or two short film pieces juxtaposed with the anchor reading.

At the same time, broadcast executives began to realize that the newscast could produce revenue for the station. That revelation brought about gradual but tremendous change. For one thing, the increased competition for audience shares sparked innovation and creativity as news and station executives sought new ways to attract viewers. The many developments that have changed the news picture since the 1960s include the supplanting of film cameras with portable video gear, vivid graphics, fast-moving and evocative formats, and *the increasing focus on the newscaster as an informer, performer, and personality.*

Personality did, indeed, become important in the content of most TV news shows. Packaging became and remains a prime issue, as demonstrated by the increase in news consultants. These specialists advise on the impact and acceptability of elements within the newscasts, from newscasters to news writing, from selection of stories to the color schemes of sets.

A formidable amount of criticism has been aimed at the consultant trend. That criticism has been balanced by the vigorous pursuit of ratings by station management. Many seasoned journalists and critics feel that accepting consultants' recommendations was selling out to show business and that news judgments were being subjugated to non-news considerations designed solely to increase revenues.

Station executives are motivated by a desire to survive. Rating points translate into salaries and jobs, including the salaries and jobs of the news staff. So ratings are important for the health of the station and the very existence of the news operation.

In reality, the pendulum swings both ways. In the early 1970s it became apparent, especially in light of the ubiquitous "happy talk" formats, that gimmickry and audience hunting were being carried to extremes. Today the newscast has a reasonable balance between journalism and show business. It is important to realize that the on-air reporter must meet a variety of requirements, for both journalism and entertainment.

The Typical Process

On-air news work is generally done under extreme time pressure. Here is how a television news operation might handle a typical day's developments:

9 A.M.   The news director arrives at work, scans the files of upcoming events, and discusses stories with the assignment editor. The assignment editor looks over scripts done by the two early-morning newspeople and arranges for news crews to be sent out.

Among the major preplanned stories today are a news conference on police sting operations, a meeting of the mayor's task force concerning whether a new municipal building will be constructed downtown, and the arrival in town of a famous rock singer. The celebrity's imminent arrival is causing great excitement, and the news department's live transmission facility, the "Live Eye," will be stationed at the airport. Breaking stories include a brush fire threatening to spread in the far western region of the county and a state police manhunt for an escaped convict.

Some of the feature stories, known around the news department as "back of the book" material, were photographed yesterday but are being edited together today. The feature piece is a three-part series on adoption, running tonight and the following two nights.

10 A.M.   The producer begins putting together a rundown of the stories that are being considered for the newscast. This rundown will change many, many times before the 6 o'clock news. The producer and the assignment editor discuss some of the visual elements of the stories, too.

Throughout the morning, the assignment editor is in telephone contact with reporters covering assignments in the field.

1 P.M.   There are now several other breaking stories. A tractor trailer has overturned on the expressway, and a photographer is dispatched to the scene to take footage of the accident. A writer will gather facts over the telephone and write a script for a voice-over. Tonight, the anchor will read the story off camera while the video of the accident rolls.

3 P.M.   The newscast is beginning to take shape. Writers are composing some of the script material that will hold up throughout the day, "timeless" stories that won't change by 6 P.M. Some reporters have returned from field assignments, have written up their scripts, and are working with production people in editing together the package.

The manhunt for the escaped prisoner continues, so a script will not be written until shortly before airtime. If the situation does not change, some cover video that was shot early in the day will suffice for the voice-over.

Production people are looking at and editing videotape, making decisions on the amount of time to allocate to each story.

4 P.M.   The producer and the news director find themselves with several files of video that have been edited on nonlinear systems. These segments include the following:

- Four packages (stories filed by reporters), including the reporter's introduction and closing, along with an interview segment and other material.
- Seven pieces of cover video, to be used while an anchor reads over the footage. In the case of the truck accident, for example, there will be a shot panning the scene of the accident, and the anchor will read the story over the video. Total time for the voice-over is 15 seconds.

- A segment of the three-part piece on adoption. Editing was finished late in the afternoon.

Each time a story is added or subtracted from the storyline up the station's news computer system automatically updates the running order. Video segments and graphics are placed in the rundown.

4:40 P.M.   Here is what the producer and news director do not have:

- Any idea when the rock star will arrive. Her plane was supposed to land shortly before news time, but it is going to be late.

(The assignment editor is given the responsibility of coordinating with the airline to figure out when the plane will arrive.)

- Any footage of a serious house fire that broke out minutes ago. One person is believed dead. A crew is on its way.
- Anything new on the manhunt.

5:05 P.M.   The list of stories is firming up. The production staff is choosing the artwork, which will be projected behind the anchors; the sports and weather people are preparing their segments (details on this in Chapter 9); and the assignment editor is beginning to think about the 11 o'clock newscast. He has to cover several meetings and schedule the crews for their dinner breaks.

5:35 P.M.   A voice on the police scanner indicates that shots have been fired at the site of the police manhunt. No further information is available by phone from the state police. There's no time to get a crew out and back, and no one knows for sure what the shots mean.

Meanwhile, the control tower at the airport says the plane will be only five minutes late, allowing plenty of time for coverage by the Live Eye. The arrival of one of the country's most famous rock stars certainly is a major story, but the shots fired at the manhunt site indicate the potential for an even larger story. Was the convict shot? Was a policeman shot? No one knows, and there is no time to find out, for if the Live Eye is to reach the remote site by airtime, it must leave the airport now.

"Go to the search site," the news director orders. His reasoning: any deaths or injuries occurring in the manhunt would amount to a major story. Also, the manhunt is in the third day with no end in sight, and the other two local stations have backed off coverage; thus there is potential for a scoop. No one here knows where the competitors' remote vans are, of course, but it's worth a gamble to be the only station in town to have coverage of the capture—if, indeed, there is a capture.

One other point influences the news director's decision. Tape of interviews with the rock star's fans waiting at the airport has already been fed back to the station.

6 P.M.   Airtime: the anchors introduce themselves and tease (read a short piece of copy that tells viewers about top stories coming up) the top stories of the evening. One anchor must ad-lib, from hastily assembled notes, the introduction to the live manhunt coverage, the signal for which is just coming over the air.

The reporter covering the manhunt has just arrived and has absolutely nothing to go on other than the sound of shots, heard a half-hour ago. She ad-libs a brief stand-up from the scene, giving some background on the search and the convict, who is believed to be hiding in the woods. Then she indicates that the story will be followed up shortly.

Back at the studio, anchors read through their scripts, several copies of which have been distributed to the producer, the director, and the audio director. The news computer has automatically updated all changes and the finished script is displayed on the station's teleprompter. Anchors will read some stories straight to camera, do voice-overs for taped footage, and introduce reporters' packages.

During a commercial, the director cues the anchors: "We're going to the Live Eye right after the commercial." The anchor again must ad-lib an intro. This time, there's dramatic live footage of a wounded prisoner being led to an ambulance. Also played back is video made moments ago showing the actual capture. The reporter on the scene must, of course, make sense of all this and communicate the excitement of the situation to the viewer.

This action is produced by a corps of on-air performers who, as we have seen, must not only speak to the camera but must also work within the technical constraints imposed by television. Part of their job is to create material under intense time pressure and to be able to communicate with accuracy and completeness.

This extended examination of a "typical" day shows the primary difficulty, and appeal, of the challenging field of TV news. It takes a great deal of stamina just to cope with the pressures and physical activities of the job. And, of course, considerable skill and experience are necessary to be able to deliver a story coherently to a camera. The work of a television reporter may look easy, but this is only because of many reporters' competence and ability to work under pressure and because these on-air journalists have acquired a grasp of techniques and operations.

Television News Techniques and Operations

Until now, our exploration of TV news has centered on the structure and elements of the operations. This section examines the considerations of newspeople who actually go before the camera, the techniques of effective delivery and working on the air with the tools of the TV news trade.

TV News Delivery

TV news delivery incorporates the general principles described in Chapters 3 and 4. The following areas are specific to the on-air newsperson.

Focus on Technique

OVERCOMING THE EDITING OBSTACLE

Many who aspire to television news on-air jobs quickly find that there are plenty of requirements for the work other than a good delivery and appearance. We've spoken about writing skills and news judgement, abilities that are (or should be) obvious.

But on-air reporters need to be able to understand the editing process. Often, they must "cut" their own material; at the very least, they must be able to give coherent instructions to the person operating the editing equipment.

It is surprising how often on-air candidates fail to learn how to edit. Perhaps it is fear of the equipment or the reluctance to admit ignorance of the process. *But every television journalist must know the rudiments, at a minimum.*

If at all possible, take as many courses as you can in broadcast journalism and TV production. But get hands-on experience in editing as soon as possible.

Here is a basic introductory "crash course" that will familiarize you with the process and how it's done. Remember that despite variations in editing equipment and software packages, the technique is the same.

Editing Basics

The process of editing can be confusing, especially to those without a background in television production. If you are going to be manipulating a computer workstation that is used to edit video you do not need extensive familiarity of the controls. (Software packages can be very complex but your news editing is less complex than commercial editing.) This box is meant to show you the basics of how video would be manipulated, but you will need to get some instruction in the specific system that you are going to use.

Let's start by stating exactly what editing is and what we're going to do. Editing is the process of manipulating video and audio so that the shots are arranged into a specific order. It may mean that not all the material shot on camera will be used and that some of the material may be used out of the order that it was shot. For example, a news crew may arrive on the scene of a fire that's already well in progress. The cameraperson may immediately start shooting footage of the firemen's progress in battling the blaze while the reporter begins gathering details and facts that will be used in his story stand-up. After the cameraperson has shot footage of the blaze, the reporter does an interview with the chief. The

Continues

Focus on Technique *Continued*

Figure 7.3

Raw Footage

a. House fire in progress
Shot 1

b. Reporter interviews fire chief
Shot 2

c. Reporter does stand up—
both open and close are
shot at the same time
Shot 3

d. Edited Package

Opening shot
Shot 1

Interview with
fire chief
Shot 2

Insert fire video
over voice of chief
Shot 3

Back to fire chief
Shot 4

Reporter's closing
Shot 5

cameraperson may then shoot the reporter detailing the events on the scene of the fire (with the fire in the background over the reporter's shoulder). The order of the shooting looks like this in block form. We have three separate segments and they were shot in the order shown in Figure 7.3a, b, and c.

Through the editing process, the order of our final package will be different. We'll start first with the reporter's stand-up detailing the event, edit in the interview with the chief, insert some of the fire footage over the audio of the chief's comments, go back to a shot of the chief ending the interview and then finish with a shot of the reporter for a closing wrap up. The final order of shots will look like that shown in Figure 7.3d.

Continues

Focus on Technique Continued

Figure 7.4   *a. Editing window for Final Cut Pro.*

This edited arrangement is fairly typical for a news package at the scene of a fire. Note that because of the editing process it will not matter which shots were recorded first or second or last. We will edit the segment in such a way to tell the viewers the story in a logical way.

In news, you'll generally be doing "cuts-only" editing, meaning that your story will be done with one video segment edited right next to another in a logical order. There will be no dissolves or special effects because these effects are generally not used in hard news package segments. To make the package described in Figure 7.3d, we will have to choose the appropriate video footage, note the appropriate beginning and ending points, and then place these segments together to form the seamless package.

The process of shooting, selecting, and ordering shots is not difficult, and with some practice, you and your cameraperson will get into a routine that will help it become second nature. However, that doesn't mean that gathering the news and shooting the news footage is easy.

Continues

Focus on Technique   Continued

Figure 7.4   b. *Video segment one now appears in both the video timeline and editing window.*

Field reporters and camera crews frequently work under extremely adverse conditions.

To give you a better feel for the actual process of assembling a news package, we'll assemble a short video piece about a student arriving on campus. In this illustration we'll be using Final Cut Pro, a popular video-editing package (shown in Figure 7.4a). You can see the screen is divided into four segment areas. Dominating the top portion of the screen, two video windows provide viewing capabilities for segments that will be brought into the editing program. Each screen section has buttons for play, forward, and so on. In the lower-left corner we have the names of video files, and the lower-right corner of the screen represents video and audio timelines. Figure 7.4b shows a segment that has been moved to the video timeline. The editor accomplished this by simply clicking on the highlighted file in the lower-left corner. The computer automatically moved the file into the timeline and by using the mouse the video editor

Continues

Focus on Technique *Continued*

Figure 7.4   c. *Segment two has been added to video timeline. Video in and out points are selected in editing windows.*

aligned this segment to the beginning of the timeline, making this segment one. In the upper-right corner, you see the video from segment one. Figure 7.4c shows a second video segment that has been brought into the timeline. The editor used the mouse pointer to butt segment one and two together and then using pointers in the left video screen, he picked "in" and "out" points for segment two. Note that the in point for segment two is seen on one video screen while the second video screen shows the out point for segment two.

The editor located the in and out points on segment two by scrolling through (playing) the video segment with the mouse pointer. If you look at the upper left video screen in Figure 7.4d you will see pointer brackets that show the video in and out points for segment two. Now, a third video segment is added to the package as shown in Figure 7.4e. Notice how the timeline shows the video and audio segments. The timeline also shows the total video time.

Continues

Focus on Technique Continued

Figure 7.4   *d. Markers show in and out points on video segment.*

Here we see the markers used to locate the in and out points for segment two.

An audio track is added in Figure 7.4f. This could be a voice over or music or any other audio that the editor chooses. Again, the editor aligned the audio track by dragging the mouse pointer over the track and aligning it to match the video segments.

Using this example, you can see how various shots can be assembled along the timeline to create story packages. Whether you work in a small station, where you'll need to manipulate editing equipment yourself or a large station where video editors work with you to build the news packages, understanding the process will help you to assemble your stories quickly and efficiently.

Figure 7.4 screen shots provided by Fritz Messere.

Continues

Focus on Technique Continued

Figure 7.4   *e. Segment three has been added to the video timeline.*

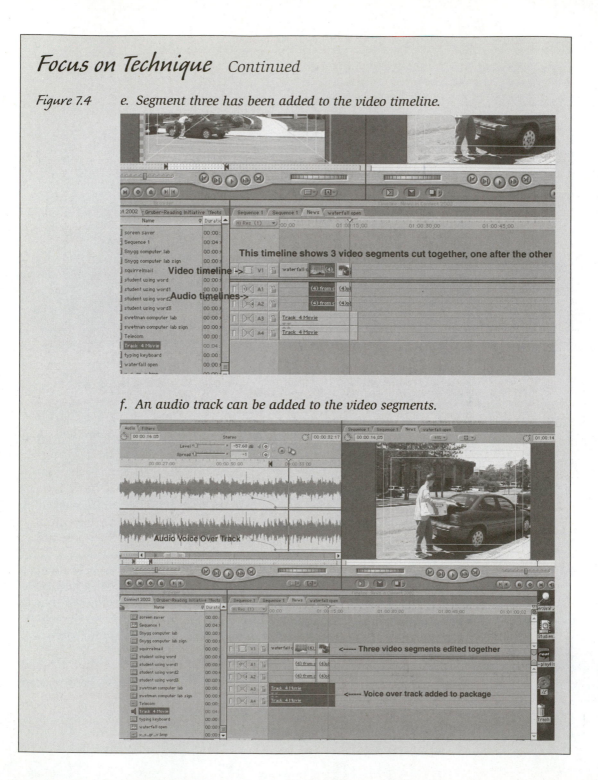

f. An audio track can be added to the video segments.

PHRASING   Giving the impression that you understand what you say is extremely important. As phrasing relates to TV news, the important element is to group words together in natural-sounding patterns and to communicate thoughts, rather than words. It is crucial to be "on top of" the copy, reading a sentence or phrase ahead. Getting lost in the copy, or hesitating in your delivery, can seriously impair credibility.

PACE   You can improve your chances of success in television news by developing a proper pace, a pace that is not rushed yet conveys energy. Equally important to an anchor is development of a *steady* pace. Production people have to roll taped segments (which may be on tape or hard drive) according to the news anchor's reading of a script, and constant speeding up and slowing down plays havoc with this process. In your drill and on-air work, strive for a consistent pace.

EMOTION   A newscaster must be able to communicate feelings as well as facts. The expression of feelings, however, should not be maudlin or phony. A mechanical "sad face" on a newscaster who is narrating a story that truly *is* tragic, borders on being offensive (see Figure 7.5). Although it is natural for people's facial expressions to reflect emotion, television is not a natural medium. Some practice is necessary to acquire a serviceable technique.

Review tapes of yourself to judge your expression. The most common mistake is the adoption of robotic expressions obviously called up to match the story. Scan tapes for the "sad face" or "happy face," and modify these expressions in further air efforts.

The next most common problem in expressing emotion is giving mixed signals: for example, maintaining a stern and rigid posture when reading a light story. The practical reason for mixed signals or improper expression may simply be that the on-air person is thinking about the next camera change or trying to remember when the next package will be introduced. Focusing on the thoughts and ideas of the story can eliminate mixed signals caused by lapses in concentration.

INTEREST   A news reporter in any situation must *show* interest in the subject at hand. Practice is essential because it is possible to be extremely interested in the copy and still appear indifferent because of poor delivery technique. Ideally, you should practice on camera. If that is not possible, audiotape will do. Get any airtime possible to develop your skill of projecting interest in the story.

Projecting interest involves enthusiasm for the task at hand and involvement in the material. Remember that you cannot evince genuine interest in a subject of which you have no understanding, so a wide-ranging knowledge of current events will help.

Finally, determine as much as possible *why* each story is of interest to you and your viewers. Does the city council's action translate into higher

Figure 7.5   News anchors get ready for newscast. The anchor on the right will lose his expression of bored disdain once the tally lights come on.

Photo by Carl Hausman

taxes? If so, stress that connection. If you grasp the essential points, your manner and communicative abilities will get the message across.

CREDIBILITY   Related to the need to understand the material and for the viewers to understand you is the viewer's faith in what you say. Polls regularly show that the most trusted people in the United States are television network and local newscasters. Trusted newscasters are perceived as honest and impartial and as experienced and intelligent enough to understand the news and give a fair rendering.

This concept affects the American tradition of using journalists as on-camera performers. A news director could hire much better and better-looking readers from the ranks of actors than from the world of journalism. This has in fact been tried—but without much success. The actors, people without news backgrounds, do not project credibility. Some successful news anchors do not have backgrounds in journalism, but they are the exceptions, not the rule. With the increasing focus on journalistic background for anchors, aspirants are well advised to develop a strong background in journalism.

There is no magic formula for developing credibility. It may largely be a function of avoiding negatives: do not mispronounce local names, do not use poor grammar, do not be uninformed or appear to be uninformed of local news and newsmakers, and do not look sloppy.

CONTACT   On a tangible level, contact means eye contact. On an intangible level, the concept of contact is defined by how well an on-air performer seems to move off the screen into the living room. Many of the subtleties can be developed after a good grounding in the proper techniques of eye contact, particularly in news reading and interviewing.

One trademark of on-air professionals is knowing what to do with their eyes. For example, note how interviews often portray the questioner as being calm, forthright, and direct, while the guest (or victim) appears nervous and shifty. This often has to do with eye movements, natural movements that the TV performer has learned to override. Many of us, during conversation, shift our eyes downward or to the side. While quite normal during conversation, shifting of eyes, especially from side to side, is both apparent and distracting on television. It inevitably creates a poor impression.

The only way to correct eye contact problems is by viewing and critiquing tapes. Remember, you must maintain steady and unwavering, but not glassy-eyed, contact with the lens. Even being slightly off in gazing at the lens is perceptible.

Field Reporting in Television News

The job of the field reporter is crucial to the success of any station's news programming. Taped news packages are the building blocks of television news programs. Without them, even the most talented, credible news anchor would be useless. The days are long gone when a news program could be carried by a "talking head" reading copy. Television news today depends on pictures. And those pictures are gathered and explained by field reporters and news crews.

The job of a television field reporter requires resourceful men and women who can quickly grasp the news value in a variety of situations and make solid news judgments in a short period of time. They must be able to shape the story, plan the sequence of events, gather the visual elements of the story, write a script, and do on-camera work—all very quickly and often several times a day. Several specialized skills and techniques are used by effective field reporters that must be mastered by anyone who aspires to this kind of work. Bear in mind that the immediacy of on-camera fieldwork requires that reporters be guided by a strong sense of ethics (see Box 7.1).

GETTING THE INFORMATION   The first thing you must do at the scene of a news event is find out what's going on. Generally you will get some information about the event when the story is assigned. Usually, though, the information is very sketchy, and sometimes it is wrong. Moreover, in fast-breaking stories things may change rapidly. So you must catch up on the facts as soon as possible after arriving on the scene.

The best way to start is to try to find someone in a position of authority. If the event involves breaking news, getting information may mean just walking up to someone who looks as if he or she should know something. At a fire, you need only ask any firefighter who is in charge. When it is not immediately obvious who is in charge, just start asking questions of people in the vicinity. It usually won't take you long to get to the right person. There is

Box 7.1

THE ETHICS OF FIELD REPORTING

Television field reporters need to be keenly aware of the standards of excellence and fairness that govern their role as journalists. Many news departments and several national associations have codes of ethics. Many of those codes, including the code of the Radio Television News Directors Association (RTNDA), insist that video be used in such a way as not to alter its context. You should not use a cutaway shot, for example, that makes someone appear furtive or nervous when that might not really be the case, or if a subject's nervousness is simply normal stage fright and not an indicator of guilt.

Suffice it to say that television news reporters have powerful tools in their hands. Misrepresentation for the sake of sensationalizing a story or to introduce drama simply cannot be tolerated. The cardinal principle of television news reporting is to tell the story accurately. Don't embellish or distort. Never manipulate information to prove a preconceived idea of how the story should go together. Hard work and persistence pay handsome dividends for those fortunate enough to work in this exciting profession. Those who engage in shady practices and clever manipulation seldom last long.

usually only a limited amount of time that a news crew can spend at the scene. Other stories may need to be covered, and the report still must be edited for broadcast, so there is always a need to work quickly.

While the reporter is looking for information, the camera operator can be getting tape of the general activities at the scene. When it is time to edit the story, there will be a need for video that shows generally what is going on at the scene. Shots of firefighters at work, or striking workers picketing a work site, or crowds gathered at the scene of a homicide are some examples of video that can be shot while the reporter gets information.

ON-CAMERA INTERVIEWS Lining up the interviews is the next priority for the reporter. First you need to decide who should be interviewed on camera. Some events require bystander reactions. At other times you'll want a spokesperson who can respond to questions about an organization's activities or a police investigation, for example.

The neighbors of a gun-wielding homeowner who has taken a hostage might provide insight into the person's recent behavior that can shed light on the reasons for his or her actions. A homicide victim's relatives and friends might provide comments that set the story in context. An official spokesperson for a college can talk about the institution's response to community complaints about a noisy fraternity.

Interviews fill out the news story factually and help convey its human dimensions. Field reporters must develop a good sense of which subjects will best add the necessary impact to the story. Once you have decided whom you want to interview, sometimes you must persuade them to appear on camera. People at the scene are often shy about going on camera, or may simply not want to get involved. Officials of organizations are often fearful about their comments being "taken out of context." Or they may fear looking foolish when a difficult question is posed.

In such circumstances, be persistent without being annoying. Coax, rather than browbeat. If you can reassure subjects that they are talking to you as a reporter and not to the camera, they are more likely to relax. You can reassure them that serious mistakes can be edited out, and that they can stop and try again if they make a mistake or say something that they suddenly realize they shouldn't have said. Use this technique only when necessary, to reassure particularly nervous subjects. If you make such an offer routinely, you may encounter subjects who ask for endless retakes to improve their performances. Others may feel that they have the prerogative to ask you to edit out any comments that, on reflection, they decide may be misinterpreted.

When conducting the interview, follow the techniques of effective interviewing described in Chapter 8 of this text. Avoid long interviews. This will help in editing, and minimize the uneasiness of the subject. Don't be afraid to keep questioning the subject, though, if you don't immediately get the answers you need. Keep in mind that you are looking for those few seconds that provide a key element of information or add insight to the story.

Usually the reporter stands near the camera and slightly off to one side. Have the interview subject look at you, not at the camera lens. It is generally not good to have a lot of background activity when you're interviewing someone. The viewer's attention should be focused on the subject of the interview and on what is being said. If your video shows a lot of activity in the background, the viewer's attention is likely to wander away from the subject. Often reporters use tight closeups for interviews. This technique eliminates background distractions and lets the person's facial expressions be seen more easily.

Cutaways and Reverses.   When you have completed the interview, you will usually have your camera operator shoot cutaways and reverses. A **cutaway** is any shot that can be edited into your interview segments to make smooth transitions when you want to edit out some of the interviewee's comments without breaking continuity.

If you butt together two segments of tape showing the interview subject at two different times of the interview, you most likely will get a sudden change in facial expression or bodily position. This jump looks unnatural and is distracting to the viewer. To avoid this, a different video element, the cutaway, is inserted at the point where the edit occurs. This eliminates the jump cut and establishes smooth continuity.

Some news organizations, though, now prefer using jump cuts rather than covering the cut with video. The reason is that a jump cut emphatically demonstrates to the viewer that something has been taken out of the tape, and the time frame of the statements compressed.

One reason for the increased use of jump cuts is that technology is now available that creates a dissolve effect. This technique is often used in CBS news reports, for example.

Some shots that are commonly used as cutaways are a group of reporters at a news conference, firefighters at work, an emergency vehicle with flashing lights, a cover shot of a building, crowds at the scene, or even a street sign (a street sign achieves the added function of locating the news event visually).

Reverse shots are those of the reporter doing the interview. They are shot from behind the interview subject—a reverse of the shot featuring the interview subject. Reverses are commonly used as cutaways. Reverses can also be used however, to re-ask a question. This is usually done only when it is deemed useful to show viewers how the reporter asked a particular question. If a question draws a dramatic response, featuring hitherto unknown information, it may be desirable to show viewers how the question was asked.

Be careful when you do such a reverse shot. It is important to try to duplicate the original question word for word. Inflections should be the same, as should the facial expressions of the reporter. Of course, this can be done without the interview subject in the shot, but usually you'll want to have the subject visible when the "re-ask" is shot. Never use this technique just to convey the impression that you can ask tough questions. It is considered a serious breach of professional ethics to create a false impression through editing techniques.

When your camera operator is shooting reverses, to be used as cutaways, the mic is usually off. The reporter needs to appear to be listening to the subject of the interview, so that the reverse appears to have been taken during the interview. Good reporters try to keep the subject talking. They use this informal conversation with the interview subject to get further information that may help put the story together. The subject is usually more relaxed at this time than when the mic is live. This may be the time that a subject gives you something that he or she didn't feel comfortable saying while the mic was on. Such information will often make your story just a bit better than the one done by the competition. It can also provide information useful for your stand-up or in writing copy to be read in the studio by the anchor.

Stand-ups. The **stand-up** gets its name from the fact that it is shot with the reporter standing up in front of the camera at the scene of the news story. When the story is edited into a package back at the studio, the stand-up can open and close the report. Stand-ups are almost always done as the last segment recorded at the scene. (As we pointed out earlier, it is increasingly common for reporters to do their opens and closes live from the scene during the newscast.)

You'll write short pieces of copy for delivery during your stand-up. This copy usually must be memorized before you go on camera. There are no prompting devices in the field, and you don't want to read word for word from your notes.

Memorizing your open and close should not be too difficult. You wrote it, so you probably have played with several versions of the copy before you got it the way you want it. By the time you've written it to your satisfaction, it will be well established in your mind.

When the camera is running, though, many things can keep you from concentrating on memorized copy. There are usually bystanders watching. You have to think about your cue from the camera operator, your facial expression, and the inflection and rate of your delivery. Most of the time you don't need to be concerned to get each word exactly the way you have written it. As long as your delivery is smooth and natural, altered phrases won't matter much.

Occasionally, though, the situation is such that you must stick to exact wording. If each word is vital, be sure to take the precaution of overmemorizing your copy. One technique that helps you memorize copy verbatim is to build the piece in your mind sentence by sentence. Repeat the first sentence over several times until you have it fixed in your mind. Then repeat the first two sentences over and over. Next repeat the first three sentences, and so on. In this way you'll be reinforcing your memorization of the earlier parts each time you add a sentence.

Another technique is to focus attention on the words at the beginning and end of each sentence. Most people who get lost trying to deliver memorized copy segments, do so at the end of a sentence. They get through one or two sentences fine, but they can't recall the next sentence. To avoid this, memorize the words that form the transitions between sentences. For example, memorize the last word in the first sentence in conjunction with the first word in the second sentence, and so on.

If the stand-up is complex, remember that there is no shame in glancing at your notes. Key words, on a notebook that is held just out of the camera shot, can help you move from point to point. Even the top pros sometimes use their notes in stand-ups. If you do use a notebook that you want to keep out of the shot, by the way, be sure to tell your camera operator to keep the shot tight enough so the notebook does not show. When you use a notebook with key words, write in large letters with a black felt-tip marker.

Some reporters have opted not to worry at all about memorization. They rely instead on electronics. It is a relatively simple matter for a script to be read into a small, portable audiocassette recorder. The reporter can then play back the recorded piece through an earpiece while speaking into the camera. This method takes some practice to master, but it can provide for impressive eye contact during delivery of a long or involved story in the field.

A device called The Ear Talk System™ is specifically designed for use in such circumstances. Ear Talk improves on the cassette recorder by eliminating the wire that leads to the earpiece. The earpiece receives a signal from an induction loop connected to a small tape recorder. The loop is worn under the shirt, blouse, or sweater. A small switch, worn elsewhere on the body, lets the reporter pause the audiotape at any point. The earpiece is completely undetectable to the viewer. The device is particularly useful for long stand-ups with few intervening taped segments. It is also helpful for on-camera narrations.

The device has an in-studio setup that allows on-air talent to stay in communication with the control room. The loop is simply mounted under the anchor desk. Separate loops can be provided for each member of the news team and at various locations in the news studio, for example in the weather map area.

Dealing with Crowds. When you show up at a news scene with a camera crew, you automatically become a "moron magnet," to use a phrase coined by one frustrated field reporter. People often want to get behind you and perform, while you're on camera trying to do a stand-up or when you're conducting an interview. Several things can be done to cope with this kind of situation.

If you have trouble with crowds in the background, try doing your on-camera work against the wall of a building or, if you happen to be near a body of water, next to the waterline with the water in the background. Sometimes you can get permission to use private property where public access is restricted. If police are on the scene (at a demonstration, for example), crowd interference can sometimes be minimized by setting up near a concentration of uniformed officers.

Sometimes you can get rowdy crowds out of the shot, but their noise interferes. In that case, try holding the mic close to your chin. That usually minimizes background noise. Sometimes you must deal directly with the crowd and try to reduce the incentive for interference. Veteran television reporters have developed several techniques that sometimes help in this kind of situation. One technique used occasionally by one author of this book as a field reporter was to co-opt one member of the group. In a group of rowdy kids, for example, he would seek out the biggest, toughest-looking member of the crowd and persuade or pay him to act as an enforcer (encouraging the use of intimidation rather than physical violence).

If you have a television monitor in the field, have the camera operator take a tight head-and-shoulders shot of you. Place the monitor where the would-be troublemakers can see it. They'll note the fact that their background activity is not in the shot, and sometimes that will discourage further antics.

Another reporter tries to wear down the crowd by doing an endless number of takes of the same script. Eventually the crowd gets bored and leaves.

Tape doesn't roll until the crowd departs. Then the reporter does his real take. He says the phony takes help him smooth his delivery and memorize his copy.

Sometimes there is no alternative but to appeal to a sense of decency. It sometimes helps to point out to disruptive kids that immature, idiotic behavior may prove embarrassing when they actually see it on the air. Worse yet, their friends, parents, and teachers will also see it.

A final point about dealing with crowds: it is important that the reporter realize his or her responsibility to protect the camera operator, who is extremely vulnerable. When the camera is running, the operator is looking straight ahead. He or she can't see trouble coming. The recent appearance of trade journal ads for body armor for camera operators is a disturbing indication of the increasing number of dangerous news assignments crews are covering these days.

WORKING TO THE CAMERA   One factor that complicates good contact is the multicamera setup unique to the TV news studio. An anchor must shift his or her attention from one camera to another without interrupting content and flow. An audience does not notice when a performer does camera changes well (see Figure 7.6). But those who make camera changes poorly do call attention to the process.

If you find camera changes difficult (and some performers do), pay attention to the sort of movement by which you naturally change glances, during a party, perhaps. Use the same natural motion you use to address another person.

Often the transition can be made easier by a brief glance at the script; that is, down. In fact, brief downward glances are a good idea even if you are reading from a prompting device. An unblinking stare is rather unnerving to the viewers. When changing from one camera to another, you may choose to take a short downward glance at the script and then raise your gaze to the other camera.

Here are three additional points on working to the camera. First, TV cameras are equipped with tally lights to indicate which camera is on air. If you look to what you think is the proper camera but there's no tally light, you must make a decision. Do you hunt for the right camera or wait for the director to follow you and punch up the camera to which you are looking? Generally, a floor director's cues and gestures can help sort the situation out. Discuss this matter with the director in advance, and always follow the floor director's instructions.

Because the floor director cannot speak to you, he or she must rely on gestures, and you must understand these gestures. Figure 7.7 shows some of the more common cues used by floor directors. Television news and interviewing are the most common areas in which you will encounter floor directors.

Figure 7.6   Knowing which camera is in use is an important skill for news anchors.

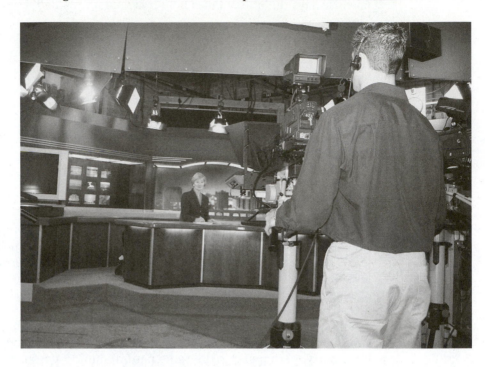

Photo by Fritz Messere

Second, in many news systems the teleprompter script is automatically generated from the news story filed. The output image from the news computer is displayed on the prompter screen. That image, projected on a mirror directly in front of the performer's camera lens (the script is visible to the performer but not to the viewer), produces a "roll" in which there are only several words per line. Precisely timing the roll—the job of the crew member who operates the prompting device—is demanding. See Box 7.2 for some tips on using the prompting device.

Third, remember that changing cameras will also result in a closer or wider shot. Because of the visual requirement of the medium, transitions between identically framed shots are almost never used. Close-ups call for caution in movement. Move too much, and you will be out of the frame. Wide shots allow for more expressive gestures to make up for the increased perceived distance between the performer and the viewer.

In news, a medium shot includes part of the desk and the newscaster. A closeup includes the head and shoulders, while an extreme close-up generally shows the face from the chin to the hairline.

Figure 7.7   Some of the cues frequently used by floor directors in a television studio. Signals in common usage vary among stations, so always go over the signals with your floor director before air or taping time. A pointed finger (a) means "You're on!" A sweeping and pointing motion (b) indicates a camera change. One finger twirled (c) is often used to mean "speed up." A motion imitating stretching a rubber band (d) means "stretch" or "slow down." Two-handed twirling motion (e) means "wrap up." Finger drawn across throat (f) means "cut." When hand signals indicate time (sometimes printed cards are used), minute cues are generally given with the fingers of one hand: (g) means 2 minutes, (h) means 1. In many stations, a clenched fist (i) means 30 seconds remaining, and crossed arms (j) mean 15 seconds, but these two signals are often used to indicate exactly the opposite timings, so check the custom in your station. Counting down on fingers (k) is often used to help you keep an exact time: 8 seconds as indicated.

Continues

Figure 7.7   *(Continued)*

Robotics

Many television news studios today are equipped with automated cameras—sometimes referred to as robot-operated cameras, or simply robotics. The distinguishing characteristic of studios using these camera systems is that there are no camera operators in the studio. The cameras are programmed to respond to commands conveyed electronically from the control room.

Robotics are generally used in situations in which camera shots are fairly simple and there is not much need for cameras to move around. The most commonly found robotics studios are news sets. NBC television has used automated cameras on its evening news broadcasts and in other news-type programs since 1988. NBC is reportedly satisfied with its system, and local news studios have been equipping studios with robotics systems for many years.

Box 7.2

Some Tips on Using the Prompting Device

It is often difficult for announcers to pick up the tricks of the trade when reading from a prompting device (see Figure 7.8). Some hints:

- Read the prompter at a steady pace. That way, the operator of the device will have a better handle on your reading rate.

- Although it is tempting to try to compensate for variations in the crawl speed, remember that it is the newscaster's job to set the pace and the prompter operator's job to follow. Don't get involved in a game of catch-up. Dictate your own speed—but be sure you read at that speed steadily.

- Some performers find it a great help to read a specific line of the prompter crawl. Try reading the third line down. This usually gives you some cushion above and below. Once the operator perceives that you are consistently reading the third line, he or she will be able to develop a steadier hand in operating the device.

Figure 7.8   *This anchorwoman is reading from a prompting device on the camera. The script is "scrolled" through the equipment in the foreground.*

Photo by Philip Benoit

Continues

Box 7.2   *Continued*

- Remember to look down from time to time. The audience can be unnerved by an unwavering stare. Also, remember that you must keep your place in the written script that you hold in your hand. If the prompter breaks down—and it often does—you'll need to go immediately to the written script.

Early systems tended to have control problems now and then. It could be quite disconcerting for both talent and viewer to notice the automated camera panning away from the news reader while she was still in the middle of a story, to say nothing of the distress felt by the control room people. Today's systems, however, have eliminated most such problems. When they do occur, they are usually the result of an incorrectly entered command, and a manual override can usually rectify the problem before it becomes noticeable.

Nevertheless, it can be somewhat disconcerting to on-air talent to work in a studio with no human operators at the camera positions. In many robotics studios, there is still a floor director to cue talent to the proper camera and to alert the announcer to impending shot changes. In these studios, air people need to learn to concentrate on the floor directors and trust the cues they give. You need to disregard other camera movement in the studio and work to the camera that is currently operating. Although this is also true of cameras operated by people, the potential for distraction increases when unmanned cameras start to move around, seemingly on their own.

In cases where there is no floor director, you need to pay attention to control room directions received through your earpiece. This can be distracting while you are reading, but with practice you will be able to take in the comments of the director in the control room while seeming to be fully engaged with your viewers. If you become confused, ask questions during commercial breaks or prerecorded segments.

If automated cameras start to move improperly during a shot, the on-air talent should try to adapt as much as possible. There isn't much you can do if a camera starts to pan or tilt away from you as you are reading. You can't move with it, so you'll just have to play it straight and hope that control room people quickly fix the problem. In such a situation, you might lose sight of the prompting device on the camera you're working to. If that happens, use your script. It may be possible to shift to another camera's prompter, but that may distract viewers even more than the errant camera shot. Probably it is best simply to read from your script. It is wise to practice doing that from time to time anyway, in case a prompting device develops problems at some point.

The automated studio is becoming more and more commonplace in news studios, and in other applications where camera shots are relatively uncomplicated. Learn to be comfortable in such situations, and gain an understanding of how these systems can affect the operation of studios so equipped. A little bit of knowledge about the attributes of automated studios can go a long way to help you maintain your composure should something go wrong.

Ad-Libbing for News

Even the finest readers stand little chance of success in news if they cannot **ad-lib.** From the standpoint of the field reporter, ad-libbing is the name of the game. Anchors must be able to speak extemporaneously in introductions to breaking stories or for coverage of special events such as elections.

Some special considerations apply to ad-libbing in news situations. First, you are doing news and will be held accountable for what you say. Liberties with the truth cannot be taken. A storm of controversy can erupt over an ill-chosen phrase used in relation to a sensitive story. Always ad-lib in phrases

1. *That you know to be factual.* If you are repeating a statement of opinion or conjecture, be sure to qualify it as such.

2. *That are not subject to misinterpretation.* Using shorter sentences and phrases can help keep meanings clear.

Time is limited for newspeople ad-libbing stories. You may not have the luxury of doing five or ten takes. During live coverage, of course, there is no second chance.

The process of compartmentalizing and encapsulating thoughts outlined in Chapter 4 is applicable to news ad-libs and helps both in ensuring accuracy of facts and in producing mistake-free takes. To apply the principles of Chapter 4 to a news ad-lib, consider the following framework:

1. *Be well informed about the issue.* You must be able to call up names, facts, and figures.

2. *Do a quick encapsulation of thoughts and rehearse, mentally or out loud, what you are going to say.* Break up the ad-lib into complete thoughts. List those thoughts, either mentally or in a notebook, before speaking.

3. *Deliver the ad-lib briefly.* Do not be concerned with stretching for time, and never try to expand without adequate information. Strive for a definite ending of the ad-lib, a brief conclusion or summary.

Production Equipment

A performer does not always have to be an expert on production, but knowledge never hurts. Such expertise enhances ability to work creatively and within technical constraints and also will help you earn the respect of production people on the news team. In many cases, especially in small markets,

Figure 7.9   A studio camera focused on a single performer.

Photo by Philip Benoit

the on-air person will have to do editing and other production work. Here, of course, a good grounding in production is essential. Reporters in the field often call their own shots and must be aware of the visual rules of assembling TV news. Our discussion of working with equipment is only the briefest of introductions to the tools of the trade of modern television.

The studio camera, as shown in Figure 7.9, is a large camera equipped for smooth movement across the floor. It has a zoom lens. Attached to certain studio cameras is a prompting device (see Figure 7.8).

Camera and on-air people work in the studio. As Figure 7.10 indicates, the studio is brightly lighted for the sake of the cameras, which need more light to produce a sharp image than the human eye does. The studio is connected electronically to the control room (see Figure 7.11). In the control room, production specialists such as the director, the audio operator, and videotape operators physically put program elements over the air.

Portable electronic newsgathering (ENG) cameras produce a signal that is often recorded on videotape (such as Beta–SP and DV cam), which is housed in a cassette. Tape output is dumped into an editing computer in a

Figure 7.10 The nightly telecast of CBS News requires a huge studio and host of personnel in addition to on-air performers.

Photo by Carl Hausman

system such as the one pictured in Figure 7.12. The process of editing involves cutting together various video segments to tell the story in a compelling way. The software used in editing allows the operator to assemble the raw stock in virtually any sequence wanted.

Audio can be dubbed separately from video, so a voice can be recorded separately and added over cover shots.

Integrating Technical Tasks

A performer needs to understand how the technical aspects of TV affect him or her. As shown throughout this chapter, an on-air journalist must have a base of technical knowledge, if only for decoding the typical TV script. An example of a script is presented in Appendix A of this book.

As performers become more comfortable with technology, they frequently invent shortcuts and adopt laborsaving devices. Here are two examples.

1. *"Slating" takes in a field report.* Many journalists find that identifying the cuts on the tape makes the editing process much smoother. A slated cut is easier to find and easier to edit: "This is the introduction to the bank robbery story, take two, rolling in five, four, three, two. . . ." This cut would not be hard to extricate from a reel of material. The countdown would also aid in cueing up the tape for the editing process.

Figure 7.11   A television control room.

Photo by Philip Benoit

Figure 7.12   A video-editing suite.

Photo by Fritz Messere

It is best, incidentally, to avoid saying the number "one," since there's a chance of that part of the countdown winding up on the air. Skip over the number, but give a silent segment in the same rhythm. Start the report where you would ordinarily say "zero."

2. *Carrying and using a small audiotape recorder.* This allows you to capture the interviews and stand-up material that also have been recorded on the video. On the way back to the station, the street journalist can play back the audiotape, using it as a guide to choosing sound bites. When time is tight, virtually the entire script can be written in the notebook during the trip back to the studio.

These are just two examples of how an understanding of the technical function can make work simpler for the performer. There are others, and after some trial and error you will certainly invent your own.

Recent Trends in TV News

Television news has undergone a gradual but significant change. The widespread, sophisticated use of technologies such as remote trucks and improved microwave transmission technology let TV news producers air remote broadcasts live from almost anywhere and almost anytime. Add to this a host of new syndication services that focus on the "news you can use" variety of feature material, and even stations in the smallest markets in the country can offer their viewers a level of professionalism undreamed of even 15 years ago. A wider variety of news stories and features can be presented on a regular basis, and production quality is maintained at the highest levels.

When it comes to actually putting the newscast together, many stations today have installed computerized news automation systems that streamline the process of developing and delivering newscasts. Modern computer editing systems by Avid and Apple provide a high level of sophistication in moderately priced workstations. Stations that have invested in such systems have increased flexibility in organizing and arranging stories for broadcast, and producers can update material right up to the time that a story is actually aired.

With this increased capability, stations can more readily attract and hold the attention of their audiences. And the trend in many markets toward devoting more airtime to local newscasts means that the increase in numbers of news features and expanded coverage through live remotes need not necessarily displace harder news stories.

Stations that once received feeds only from the network with which they were affiliated can now look at several sources and choose the feeds that best fit their style and time requirements. Stations can do a better job of reporting on important national stories and can present feature material that would otherwise cost so much to produce that it would not be profitable. Sports reporting is also greatly improved by the availability of a better selection of taped highlights from major games and sporting events from all over the country.

It is important for those who want to enter the field of television news to be familiar with these services and to develop the skills needed to work effectively with them. Let's look at some of these developments a bit more closely.

Live Remote Coverage

Just a few years ago, live broadcasting from a remote location was a novelty for most TV journalists. As stations began to explore the capabilities offered by live remotes, they often seemed to be straining to find uses for the technology. Live reports from the scene of news events implied that the event was very important and that it was necessary to be at the scene live to provide coverage that included the very latest information. Unfortunately, events that received such coverage very often just happened to be going on while the news block was on the air. Viewers were often left wondering why a reporter had to be on the scene to report immediately on the latest developments, when the news event was relatively unimportant in comparison with other happenings in the area.

Today, with live coverage becoming more common, stations have learned how to better integrate this immediacy into the rest of the newscast. Live reports often serve only as an expanded stand-up in a news package that features segments taped earlier. Brief on-camera interviews are sometimes included as a part of live remote coverage, but fewer attempts are made to convey the impression that the live presence is necessary to bring viewers the latest developments. Live reporting is used in such situations to add interest and variety.

The concept of using live remotes to provide viewers with the latest developments in an ongoing story can still be important, however, when breaking news is unfolding moment by moment as when news organizations report on natural disasters like hurricanes (see Figure 7.13).

Sportscasts also benefit from live coverage (see Figure 7.14). The sports anchor can increase audience interest in the sports segment by reporting from the spring training camp of the local baseball team or from the scene of a major golf tournament in the area. Nothing much changes about the arrangement and variety of stories covered. The lineup is usually pretty much the same as it would have been anyway. The station shows its interest in the event and its capability of keeping up with developments through the live presence at the event. As in news, live interviews from the scene often add a dimension of interest as well.

If reporters are allowed to move off the news set and out into the community, the feeling is conveyed that the station is interested and involved in the community. (One medium-market television station used its live remote capability to move the entire news set out to various community locations for several days while their studio set was rebuilt.) Stations can use this capability to increase audience interest and attract viewers in a particular community. Although some view this as a questionable compromise, when the practice is used judiciously, little harm is done to the integrity of the news.

Figure 7.13   Live news coverage of natural disasters keeps viewers informed of the event as it unfolds.

© AFP/CORBIS

Figure 7.14

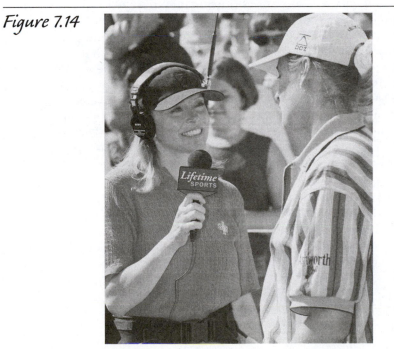

Cheryl Ladd, announcer for "Lifetime For Women," interviews Kelly Robbins after Round 3 of the AFLAC Tournament of Champions at the Grand National Golf Course in Opelika, Alabama, in 1998.

AP/Wide World Photos

Think About It

TV SUICIDE

Daniel V. Jones spread his scrawled banner skyward before he blew most of his head off on live TV April 30, 1998. The message, "HMOs are in it for the money!! Live free, love safe, or die," didn't make much more sense than his entire strange odyssey. He had already caused a massive traffic jam on a Los Angeles freeway. Later, pulled over on an interchange, he set fire to his truck, his dog, and himself, walked from the truck with his clothes smoldering, unfurled his banner, and returned to the truck to get his shotgun.

But even in his final mindless moments of dementia Jones had the uncanny presence of mind to face the message to the sky—where the TV helicopters hovered.

Jones's suicide was carried live by seven local stations in Los Angeles and by MS-NBC, a national cable news channel. In the final seconds of the drama, two local stations stayed on a relatively tight shot that showed the shotgun blast ripping away his skull. Other stations moved to wide shots in the 11 seconds or so from the time Jones retrieved his gun to when he pulled the trigger.

In the immediate aftermath of the suicide, there was a banquet of self-conscious reassessment. Anchorpeople for many of the stations in L.A. apologized on air for showing the graphic details in mid-afternoon. KTLA anchor Hal Fishman went on the air to say, "KTLA shares with its viewers their distress." Several station managers and news directors promised to reevaluate their policies regarding live coverage, and MS-NBC considered implementing a several-second delay for live shots.

Some found the apologies disingenuous. Media critic Howard Rosenberg, writing in the *Los Angeles Times*, put it this way: " They'll never admit it, perhaps not even to themselves, but Thursday was the day Los Angeles television stations finally got what they wanted. In their heart of hearts, this was it. Oh mama, was it ever. Not just another routine pursuit across freeways and a meek surrender. Not just some bumps and sideswipes. . . . This time it was the full payoff, the big public splatter. . . ."

As we have noted throughout *Announcing: Broadcast Communicating Today,* there is increasing pressure for on-air people to be able to handle live, breaking events. The live shot has become part and parcel of news coverage.

But as we've seen, live shots can go terribly wrong.

Continues

Think About It   Continued

Some questions for discussion: Would you have gone along with the close-up right until the final shot? What would you have said to your viewing audience immediately after if your station had pictured the final moment? Think about your response, but don't think too much—if you were on-air, you'd have ten seconds, tops, to think about it.

In general, on-air talent must be more flexible when dealing with live coverage. The stand-up you deliver live on camera from city hall will be done in one take. If you usually flub the first two takes of your stand-up, you will want to practice getting through your material with no mistakes. Your announcing style on a live report can be more relaxed than is usually the case in a package. The whole idea of the live report is to convey immediacy. If your live report looks well rehearsed and tightly scripted, you won't come across appropriately.

This doesn't mean you don't need to prepare. If anything, you generally need more preparation for live reports than you otherwise would. You may need to fill additional time or to respond to questions from the anchor in the studio. There is always some uncertainty about how the live segment will unfold. The better you have prepared by becoming completely informed about the situation, the better able you'll be to respond to any unexpected circumstances that may arise while you're on the air.

Syndicated Feature Services

Not too many years ago, most TV news directors depended solely on the network they were affiliated with to provide feeds of news events that took place outside their coverage area. The same was true for sports highlights needed for local sports reports. Today, though, stations have available to them several news feeds that can be picked up and used by anyone who has a couple of satellite dishes to receive them. Services like CNN's Newsource provide more stories each day than some stations can even look at. These services provide affiliates and independents a wide variety of news feeds supplied by stations from virtually everywhere in the country.

CNN offers its two hundred affiliates 24-hour service. Its sole product is news, so it need not interrupt other programming to provide live coverage of breaking news. Affiliates may broadcast news-breaking special reports as they occur. Thus CNN affiliates were able to tap into live reports during student demonstrations at Tiananmen Square in Beijing, for example. During the war in Iraq, stations carried live reports from CNN reporters in the Persian

Gulf. Affiliate stations are allowed to excerpt package features from *Headline News* to carry in local news programs. And they may elect to carry up to four *Headline News* half-hours on local air per day.

CNN Newsource provides a daily series of news feeds that includes national and international breaking stories, features on topics such as medical and science news, nutrition and women's issues, for example, and sports highlights. This allows local news directors to integrate this material into local newscasts, using local announcers for voice-overs and intros.

TV news directors also have available to them a large selection of syndicated feature material that can be integrated into newscasts in ways that give viewers the impression that the segments were produced locally. Products such as *Consumer Reports TV News,* produced using the resources of the Consumers' Union (which puts out *Consumer Reports* magazine) provide stations with short features several times a week.

Typical syndicated packages run about 90 seconds, and stations receive three features a week. Depending on market size, features might cost a station anywhere from $3,000 a year to $40,000. The packages usually feature a split-track audio, which allows the station to use its own talent to narrate the piece rather than using talent of the original producers. This conveys the impression that the reports are produced locally.

Many stations find that using syndicated feature material lets them cover specialized news beats, such as business reports and medical news, without the considerable expense of producing the material themselves. According to Walter Gilbride, a syndicator of news features, many news directors find that using such material frees up their own reporters and resources to do a better job of reporting local features.

Some stations use the syndicated material as the foundation for five-day-a-week segments on a particular topic. The voice of the reporter is used in the syndicated material and the station's own reports (usually featuring a local angle on the general topic) are produced by the same reporter. Often, by the way, that local reporter is a member of the profession most closely related to the topic area covered in the reports. A local doctor is often used as the reporter on feature segments about medical topics, for example. If the syndicated material is integrated smoothly, and local production quality is matched to that of the syndicated material, the audience will have the impression that the station produces all five reports each week.

The increased use of syndicated feature material and satellite news feeds requires reporters to be able to mesh effectively with the styles of those who produce the syndicated packages. In hiring, this may mean that news directors will be looking for more generic styles for some slots than they might look for in others. The announcer whose style seems generally reminiscent of news reporters may be more useful in some circumstances than a reporter with a distinctly individual style. In contrast, some openings in television news may require reporters with specialized knowledge and with expertise in specific areas. Rather than emphasizing on-air talent, for example, a station may want to fill a slot that covers a distinctive beat such as crime reporting or consumer affairs.

Another consideration for on-air talent when working with syndicated feature material is that the appeal of the feature material is its usefulness to viewers. The material itself is of paramount importance. The role of talent in such circumstances is to localize and smooth out the presentation of the material but not necessarily to draw attention to the reporter.

To prepare for the changing requirements for on-air talent in television news, try to become adept at a variety of styles. Take the time to watch the news reporters on as many different stations as you can. Take note of both the differences and similarities. See if you can categorize various newspeople by the styles they use. Do styles change for various types of reporting—a feature on how high school students choose a college, for example, compared with a news report about citizens who oppose the construction of a landfill near their housing development? Can you tell what elements of rate, inflection, energy, and facial expression are responsible for defining the style? Through close observation of many different newspeople and styles of presentation, you'll begin to know how to adapt your own delivery to create different styles.

The next step is to practice the different styles. Write scripts of your own that are representative of different assignments you have noticed in your analyses of various TV news operations. Practice the scripts using various styles of delivery. Notice how inappropriate some scripts sound when they don't fit the news story. Work on nuances of inflection and rate that make the delivery particularly effective.

Beware of overdoing it, though. Remember you are trying to draw the viewer's attention to the story, not to you. Get feedback on your performances from others. Don't just go to professors or other broadcasting students—try to find people who are *not* familiar with the devices you're using. They will be in a better position to tell you how you might be coming across to the average viewer.

In Chapter 12, when we talk about ways to prepare for your first broadcasting job, we stress the importance of broadening your academic background beyond the field of communications or journalism. Syndicator Walter Gilbride, who has studied television news operations all over the country, recommends that students get a solid educational background in areas that might be helpful in reporting on specialized areas. Gilbride says that news reporters trying to report on complex topics such as AIDS or personal finance, often make fundamental mistakes that could have been avoided if the reporter had some formal education in the area. For those interested in crime reporting, for example, one approach might be to major in communications or journalism as an undergraduate and go on for a master's degree in criminology. Other experts recommend a double major as an undergraduate.

Figure 7.15   News automation software screen.

Screen shot of E-Z News courtesy of Automated Data Systems

Newsroom Automation

One of the most dramatic advances in television news in recent years is the development of computerized newsroom systems. With sophisticated computer hardware, running specially designed software programs, modern television newsrooms can streamline all their news functions in ways that add speed and quality to news coverage.

Automated Data Systems EZ News, for example (see Figure 7.15), provides word processing, sorting and filing of wire service material, a script-writing format program, a rundown program that will automatically sequence and update the order of stories, and an archiving capability for keeping stories that have already aired. The latest version developed by EZ News lets a system operator control the way the show goes on the air. It can drive the prompting device and provide the timing of all stories, both as the newscast is assembled and when it airs.

Such software has many advantages. Breaking news can be updated instantly without the need to laboriously refigure how the update affects the timing. The software automatically calculates new in-times, out-times, and back-times (the point in a script where a video insert must roll so it can reach the proper playing speed, if it is on tape, when aired) of new material so that the necessary adjustments can be made. Producers can instantly check on the status of any story and find out if it is ready to go on the air. With some software programs, tapes can be controlled automatically. Automation systems can be configured to meet the individual needs of any station. Various options are available for inputting wire service material and information from remote news bureaus, for example. Costs to stations vary depending on the types of hardware and software options selected.

The impact of computerized newsrooms on on-air talent is great. The modern television newsroom requires a familiarity with computers. Basic operations are not difficult to master. If you can operate word processing systems and understand how computers control systems, you will be in the best position to make the latest technology function to enhance the station's competitive standing.

On-air talent must be adaptable and ready to make changes in stories right up to the last possible moment before air. Reporters have to follow developments on breaking stories more closely and be prepared to update them when new information becomes available. It may be necessary to rewrite copy many times before the story actually hits the air. Anchors must be ready for last-minute changes to the story rundown. They must be able to cope with last-minute script changes while maintaining their professional manner on camera.

For producers and news directors, computer automation means that it is easier to assemble the newscast. It is simple to determine the status of the newscast at any point in time, and to monitor the progress of individual stories as they are being written. With this technology, people responsible for putting the newscast together will be expected to provide more timely stories than in the past. To do so, they will need to closely monitor reporters and news crews and follow the progress of breaking stories that are subject to change. In simplifying the physical assembly of the newscast, computer automation also demands more minute-to-the-minute decision making on the part of news executives.

The skills you will need to cope with automation include good journalistic judgment and computer literacy. A pleasant appearance and the ability to read copy smoothly will not take anyone far in television news. People who want an on-the-air news position increasingly need to provide a certain degree of technical capability in addition to a solid on-air presence.

Appearance

It goes without saying that good appearance helps a television news performer. In fact, news requires exact attention to certain aspects of appearance because the credibility of the performer is involved. The following brief guidelines are particularly helpful for newspeople.

Clothing and Hair

For men, the choice of clothing is really not an issue. Newscasters wear a virtual uniform of suit or sports jacket and tie. Women have a wider choice, but most newswomen stick to simple clothes with basic lines. For field reporters, simple and durable clothes are an advantage because the afternoon's story may involve slogging through a potato field. Box 7.3 gives some basic tips for achieving a good appearance.

Beware of a tendency to dress inappropriately for the role of a newsperson. Steven Osborne, former news director of WOR-TV in New York (now WWOR-TV in New Jersey), says that he's noticed a trend among some television newspeople to present themselves as fashion plates. "They should remember that they are newspeople, not aristocracy," he says. High salaries and their position as celebrities in the community often provide an affluent lifestyle for newspeople, but on the air they should not draw attention to their socioeconomic status through their appearance, says Osborne. "Clothes shouldn't say 'Look at me—I can afford nice clothes.'"

He notes that too many of today's television newspeople drip heavy jewelry or wear expensive clothes when covering stories on location. He recommends simplicity when it comes to clothing. Men should avoid heavy plaids in coats. Ties should have relatively simple patterns. Women should watch out for loud patterns and outlandish colors. Hairstyles on women should be conservative, not flashy. Elizabeth Vargas (see Figure 7.16) is an example of a stylish news anchor.

Another crucial tip is to *get a good haircut!* Find a barber or stylist who will work with you to get the style you want, and request the same person for every visit. Frequently, television stations will trade out advertising for haircuts at a particular salon.

Men often do not pay much attention to their hair, and it shows. To improve the neatness of your hair dramatically, get it cut every 2 to 4 weeks. One warning: tell your regular barber that you will be getting frequent cuts and that you want a relatively *small* amount of hair taken off each time.

Men also usually do not experiment with styles as much as women, and do not receive as much guidance from stylists. Experiment with different lengths and partings to show off your best features and to camouflage poor features. Box 7.4 provides some hair tips for both men and women.

Makeup

Professional makeup kits are available at many television facilities. These provide talcum-based makeup in stick or cake form. Makeup experts also use a variety of special effects to add wrinkles, paste on facial hair, or make a character appear threatening. For most television applications, you won't

Box 7.3

GUIDELINES FOR DRESSING WELL ON THE AIR

1. *Avoid complex patterns.* Herringbones can cause a wavy effect, especially when photographed by older cameras.

2. *Check with your station engineer regarding the chroma key color.* A chroma key is one device used to remove a background from a TV scene and insert a new image, usually a slide behind the newscaster. In modern facilities, the clothes versus chroma-key problem is not serious, but older gear may be insufficiently selective as to which shade of blue, for instance, it chooses to eliminate. If your clothes are too close to the chroma key color, they may be replaced with the keyed image.

3. *Avoid stiff clothing.* Men seated at news desks have a particular problem with stiff-woven jackets bunching up behind the neck. A tailor can take out the "roll" in the upper back and keep the collar down.

4. *Make sure clothing is not restrictive.* Tight European-fit double-breasted jackets are not a good choice for a weather reporter who has to move and gesture.

5. *Avoid too masculine a look in women's clothes.* There was a time when women entering the field felt it necessary to wear man-tailored clothes. Those times are pretty well past, but simple women's clothes are still advisable. Frills and bows have a habit of coming out of place and can also be distracting to the viewer.

6. *Be conscious of what your clothing looks like from the rear or side.* The camera may occasionally catch a view of you from an off-angle. Men, be sure your jacket covers your middle when you sit.

7. *Avoid extreme cuts of any clothes.* Although bizarre or unusual clothes may build an image for an actor, newscasters have never gained recognition for their style of dress, except for the very low-key style represented by Peter Jennings. Jennings dresses conservatively and with a European flair, a very subtle differentiation from other newscasters.

8. *Avoid gaudy jewelry.* The camera has a tendency to emphasize and, in both a literal and a figurative way, to magnify. A large pair of earrings may look grotesque on the air.

9. *Remember that cameras also magnify girth.* If you need to lose weight, lose it now, before cutting audition tapes. If you have a blocky appearance, concentrate on clothes that lessen that impression. Women can do especially well with V-necks. Stocky men must avoid checks, blocks, or any lateral design element. Stick to plain colors or vertical pinstripes.

Figure 7.16

Elizabeth Vargas of ABC News.

Copyright © 2003 ABC Photography Archive

need the type of theatrical makeup used to create characters in acted presentations. You'll probably be content with

1. *A compact containing an oil-absorbing makeup.* The makeup should be a shade darker than your normal skin tone. For most work, you don't need special theatrical makeup; the stuff available from the drugstore will do just fine. Make sure to apply it in short, downward strokes. Don't smear it when applying. The advantage of a compact, by the way, is that it can easily be used in the field and carried in your pocket or bag.

2. *Eyebrow pencil.* Eyebrows are expressive features, but some people have wispy or very light eyebrows. An eyebrow pencil or mascara brush is a useful tool for both men and women.

Don't be afraid to experiment. Try different types of makeup and see what works best for you. Remember, though, the final criterion in judging how well it works is not how you look in the mirror, but on the monitor.

Skin, Teeth, and Eyes

Developing a skin care regimen is a healthy idea for both men and women. In lieu of experimenting with various preparations to clear up skin problems, visit a professional. Dermatologists can frequently clear up long-standing problems that have not responded to inexpert trial and error.

Teeth deserve the same special attention. As you will notice from a quick scan of local channels, TV newspeople hardly ever have bad teeth. A cosmetic tooth problem could cripple your on-air career, so attend to those con-

Box 7.4

Style Your Hair to Enhance Your Appearance

- Short hair makes weak facial features seem stronger.
- Long hair camouflages too-strong features.
- Long hair in back emphasizes the jawline and can make up for a weak jaw area.
- Attention can be drawn away from a large nose by hair that projects higher on the head and farther out from the forehead.
- Parting the hair higher (closer to the center of the head) visually narrows the face. Parting hair closer to the temples widens the face.
- A lock of hair down on the forehead breaks up a too-wide or too-high forehead appearance.
- People with very round faces should avoid very short hair.

ditions now. New developments such as invisible braces and bonding can correct a variety of problems.

Eyeglasses may become part of a newsperson's style, but in general they are distractions, another barrier to contact between the news reader and the viewer. That is why many on-air people opt for contact lenses. Modern lenses are easy to adapt to and even people with moderate astigmatism can be fitted with contacts. In addition, soft and gas-permeable lenses are more comfortable than the old-style hard contact lenses.

The major drawback to contact lenses is the difficulty many people encounter in adjusting to them. Yes, it is difficult to adjust to foreign objects in your eye, and it may take months or a year to become comfortable with the idea of wearing contacts and *not wearing glasses*. If you cannot see well without glasses, it would be worthwhile to investigate this option.

Image

All these appearance factors add up to that semitangible concept of an image. Although there is no prescription for a proper image, do weigh various appearance factors and make sure they don't work against you. A good appearance is important. You need not be strikingly beautiful, nor particularly good looking, but you must be well groomed and have a generally attractive appearance as a news performer.

Remember, too, that image and credibility are much more than simple matters of cosmetics. Physical impressiveness will never compensate for a lack of professional or intellectual depth.

Summary

Television reporters are journalists as well as performers. TV news is a team effort, and many people are involved in coverage of news events. The basic components of a TV news organization are news administration, news production, and the gathering and reporting of news.

The typical television newscast has evolved over the years. In the early days of television, the newscast was little more than an audio newscast with a picture of the reader. Today, many different program elements are integrated into the newscast. Gathering and assembling news events for a TV newscast involves teamwork, quick decisions, and hustling by reporters and crews. In addition, news and production people must be flexible because the typical television newscast is often being put together seconds before airtime.

Television field reporting requires good judgment and the ability to work quickly. The field reporter must be able to interview with skill and write, memorize, and record copy on camera. Other duties of the field reporter may include directing the activities of the camera operator and dealing with crowds.

Television news delivery involves proper use of phrasing and pace, as well as the expression of emotion and interest. News reporters must project an aura of credibility. Contact with the viewer is enhanced by smooth use of prompting devices and good physical eye contact with the camera. Working to the camera is an important part of TV news delivery, and it involves making frequent transitions from camera to camera and following the orders of a floor director. The news reporter must be aware of tally lights and must realize that the relative closeness of the shot will change when the director changes cameras.

Ad-libbing is an extremely important skill for the newsperson. A reporter must be certain to ad-lib in words and phrases that are factual and are not subject to misinterpretation. The same techniques used in basic announcing are applied to news ad-libbing.

Television news involves working within technical constraints and working with equipment. Equipment includes studio cameras, prompting devices, and the studio and control room in general. Modern digital technology has enhanced newsgathering.

Many TV stations use live reports from the scene of news events. There is also increased use of syndicated feature material, some of which is localized by using a local announcer as the reporter. Most newsrooms are automated with computers that make it possible to update stories right up to the moment they are aired.

The TV news announcer should understand the technical aspects of the field well enough to take advantage of them in preparing for his or her performance. Slating cuts to keep track of edit points and using a portable audio recorder are two examples of integrating technology into one's work habits.

Television news requires particular standards of appearance. Part of being a successful news reporter is paying attention to clothing, hair, skin, and teeth. Contact lenses are often useful. All the factors of appearance and performance add up to the newsperson's image. However, success in TV news is not a matter of cosmetics. You must be a first-rate journalist and a competent performer.

Exercises

1. Design and execute a mock-up newscast. This is an ambitious three-day project, but worthwhile if you have the time and facilities.

   Day 1: Elect or ask your instructor to appoint a news director, who will appoint
   a. The head of production for the class news department
   b. The head writer
   c. The assignment editor

   Those three people will then choose classmates to work under their direction. You will need approximately 25 percent of the class working in production, 50 percent in writing, and 25 percent as on-air people. The assignment editor will choose on-air people. The duties are as follows:

   - *Production people* will design the newscast with whatever equipment they have available. If there is no video equipment, the newscast will be presented to an audience. Production people will determine the construction of the set, placement of cameras, and so on.
   - *Writers* will each decide on one story, preferably an easily done local story. The stories will be assembled in the next class session. Each story must be no longer than one minute when read.
   - *On-air people* will file some of these stories as taped reports, if equipment is available, and the two anchors will coordinate the newscast.

   Day 2: The news director and all three department heads will meet to decide story assignments and other production details. If remote gear is not available, reports will be delivered directly to the camera or audience during the newscast.

   Day 3: Now prepare the final lineup and assemble the script; this must be done in less than 15 minutes. The newscast itself is to be 20 minutes long, and must start *exactly* 15 minutes after the start of class.

   This set of guidelines is intentionally open-ended. The duties and time frames must be adapted to circumstances in class. Also, particular sequences and responsibilities are not specified because in an actual TV news situation, getting organized and figuring out who will do what, and when and how it will be done, is half the battle.

In this exercise, *teams* will have to decide what can be done and what resources can be allocated, all within a time limit. If you are selected to work on the air, you will certainly find that the backup and cooperation you receive go a long way in determining how good you look on air.

2. Do the following exercise, strictly to time. It is a good one to do during class and in front of other class members.

   Your instructor will clip a daily newspaper and assign stories to class members. You will have 10 minutes, no more and no less, to study the story and take as many notes as you can fit on one side of a 3-by-5 index card. Your goal is to ad-lib a 1-minute report before the class, with each class member giving a report according to random selection. If facilities allow, tape the reports.

   Maintain as much eye contact as possible. *Hint:* Copious notes crammed on the 3-by-5 card will not necessarily be as helpful as a concise outline.

3. Choose a network or well-known local news reporter for each of the following hypothetical assignments. Pick the person you believe could do the best possible job and explain why in one or two paragraphs. Specify what qualities of this reporter would make him or her the best choice for the job.

   a. A host for an hour-long documentary on the stock market. Technical information must be made interesting to a wide audience.

   b. A host for a morning news/entertainment program in an industrial city where audience research shows that many of the workers arise at 5 A.M. and want a show and host to brighten their day.

   c. A reporter for a 10-minute segment on the plight of the homeless in New York City.

   d. A reporter to do a 5-minute feature on inflatable furniture.

   e. A host for a 15-minute feature on fine wines.

   f. A reporter to confront a tough big-city mayor on charges of corruption in municipal government.

   g. An anchor to handle the first reports of possible outbreak of a war involving the United States. You would likely want someone adept at presenting breaking information, someone who inspires confidence and remains calm under pressure.

   h. An interviewer to talk to the mother of a servicewoman killed in one of the initial skirmishes of the war.

The Craft of Interviewing

*A*sk a simple question and get an answer. It seems simple enough to do. But when you're a journalist, getting the right answer is more complicated than it might seem.

Whether you're talking about print journalism or radio or television, the interviewer's skill can spell the difference between a news report that actually contains news and one that merely fills space or time. Interviews can be tough. Some interview subjects are extremely nervous on camera. Some are unresponsive or evasive. Others talk only about their own specific interests no matter what question is asked. To add to the pressure, the broadcast newsperson often works under rigid time and technical constraints. Regardless of the obstacles, though, you as a reporter are charged with the task of coming up with an interview that is logical, informative, and interesting.

The focus of this chapter is to explore and demonstrate the principles and techniques that will help you conduct an effective interview. Whether the interview forms the basis for television news, a radio talk format, or an entire program in which a single guest is the subject of an extended interview on a variety of subjects, a succession of pat, bland questions will not provide much useful and lively information. Successful interviewing involves three steps:

1. Determining the type of interview and adjusting the approach accordingly.

2. Preparing for the interview, which involves selecting questions and topics, narrowing the topic for a logical discussion, prescreening guests, and doing a good deal of homework.

3. Executing the interview, which entails proper attention to the logistics of an interview, making it flow logically, and avoiding major pitfalls.

Types of Interviews

A broadcast interview is not always conducted in a comfortable chair in an air-conditioned studio. With the advent of modern television gear, television on-air personnel find themselves in a wide variety of situations, which boil down to two basic types: the **actuality interview** and the **studio interview.** The actuality interview is generally a straightforward attempt at obtaining information. The studio interview can be of several varieties, ranging from brief personality interviews to in-depth discussions of serious and complex topics.

Actuality Interview

An **actuality** is a response or statement from a newsmaker, which is typically edited and used in another format, such as the "package" described previously, or used in a newscast after an anchor's introduction. The key to successful actuality interviewing is obtaining a response in a form that *can* be edited out and used, perhaps, in a 90-second report. You're looking for short, succinct answers, so the way you phrase each question is important. Ways to devise questions are suggested throughout this chapter.

Studio Interview

Although parts of an interview conducted in the studio may be used as actuality, most studio interviews are meant to be broadcast in full, with a definite beginning, middle, and end.

Generally a specific amount of time is allotted for a studio interview, but usually there is more latitude in time and content than is the case for the actuality interview.

Dealing gracefully with time restrictions is one of the most difficult aspects of interviewing. An interview to be edited can run to virtually any length, but a talk show type of interview must make its point and wrap up when the clock (and the director) says so. This means that pacing within the interview must conform to the time frame. A half-hour interview should not reach an emotional peak in the first 5 minutes and coast downhill from there. Likewise, important questions should not be left unanswered at 28 minutes into the program.

The broadest categories of studio interviews are the personality type and the issue type.

The *personality interview* explores the life or career of an important or well-known individual. Entertainment value comes into consideration here. In most cases, the interviewer is expected to keep the session reasonably light and engaging.

In the *issue interview,* the personalities of the guest and host are less in focus than is the topic at hand. The interviewer, generally a program host, is expected to highlight various points of view and present them fairly. In-depth analysis and discussion are frequently used in the issue interview.

Think About It

BAD ADVICE

One recent permutation of the television talk program is the "confrontational" interview where essentially dysfunctional people air their problems and occasionally come to blows with others in their families or social groups they see as part of the problem.

After a wave of criticism stemming from a murder related to an appearance on the *Jenny Jones Show,* and various chair-throwing encounters on the *Jerry Springer Show,* the programs set out to reform themselves. (It may not have been the criticism but the threat of governmental regulation that sparked the reform.) The confrontational aspects of the programs were toned down, but as an apparent result, ratings dipped.

Programs such as *Jenny Jones, Jerry Springer,* and the *Montel Williams Show* also instituted other changes in the wake of public criticism. As Vicki Abt and Mel Seesholtz, authors of a book about the talk show circuit titled *The Shameless World,* write,

> Since *The Shameless World* and the ensuing wave of negative media attention, most talk shows have made cosmetic, self-legitimizing "improvements," such as . . . Jerry Springer's "final thoughts," and the *Montel Williams Show*'s offers to transport "addicted" guests straight from the stage to "therapy" or recovery programs. The shows' framework of "helpfulness" and "altruistic interest" in the psychological well-being of their guests . . . is clearly disingenuous in that it omits any reference to the real reasons for the show—revenues and ratings. It further presumes to know and oversimplify the motivation of both the studio audience (who usually do not know in advance what the show is about and, indeed, might have preferred a show on male strippers) and the home viewing audience (who may have the television on as background noise or be watching it solely for entertainment).[1]

What is your opinion? Do these shows offer legitimate catharsis for disturbed people, or are they exploitative? Aren't these guests adults, and can't they make their own decisions?

Moreover, what would you do if you were the host of such a program, on a national or local level? Would you dispense advice? Would you worry that your standing as a public personality would cause a disturbed person to take your advice more seriously than perhaps that person should?

---

[1] Vicki Abt and Mel Seesholtz, "'The Shameless World' Revisited," *Journal of Popular Film and Television,* Summer, 1998, pp. 43.

How the Type of Interview Affects Style

Keep the foregoing distinctions in mind because style and execution of the interview differ for each type. The elements are not mutually exclusive, of course, for there certainly can be entertainment in a talk-show presentation of an in-depth analysis of a serious topic. But if discussion of a serious topic is too flip, the results can be offensive.

Likewise, the interviewer will not want to adopt for an issue interview the same style that would be used in an actuality interview. Have you ever watched a half-hour talk show that seemed to consist of nothing more than an endless, hypnotic interrogation? What you were seeing was a host who asked for specific fact or reaction but neglected to ask the guest to *discuss* the issue and *analyze its meaning.* The chance to discuss and analyze is the main strength of the studio interview, and failing to take advantage of it can lead to an awkward and boring product. Listening carefully to responses can help you develop relevant follow-up questions.

Regardless of the type of interview, the goal is the same: to obtain interesting, relevant, and provocative responses. Some factors will be out of your control, but the most important aspect is your responsibility: you must adequately prepare for the interview.

Preparing for the Interview

Much of the interviewing you will do is off-camera/off-mic interviewing. Although at times the interviewer barges in with lights burning and cameras rolling, most interviews are set up well in advance, and information has been gathered before the videotapes or audiotapes roll. The information-gathering process might involve calling the interviewee and putting together some basic facts before inviting him or her to the station for a studio interview.

Preparing Questions

How much information to gather before turning on the cameras or mics is a judgment call. On one hand, too little preparation before the tape rolls can result in a clumsy session, and it will be obvious to the audience that it was thrown together at the last minute. At the other extreme, too much advance preparation can result in a "flat" interview over the air. The interviewee who is responding to the same set of questions for the second or third time may sound as if he or she is being very patient with a slightly stupid interviewer. Also, too-extensive preparation can put guests on guard, giving them a chance to prepare evasive responses to questions they'd rather not answer.

There is one other important point. Many people will be reluctant to give you the most mundane information when you start the conversation with microphone in hand. Some subtle, low-pressure questioning in a conversational tone, done off-mic or off-camera, often elicits a much better response for the air. One additional advantage of preparatory information gathering is that guests are very hard put to omit or refuse to comment on information they have already given to you or confirmed before the tapes rolled.

Importance of Research

Research is an important factor in interview preparation. An interviewer's lack of knowledge is usually very apparent once the conversation starts. Never let cockiness and overconfidence seduce you into walking into an interview unprepared. Preparation should always be a priority for two major reasons, one obvious and one not so obvious:

1. You can conduct a much more intelligent interview by being well informed.
2. You can fulfill your responsibilities to management, your audience, and yourself by not letting outrageous statements slip by unchallenged.

For example, let's say you are a talk-show host and your guest, the leader of a neighborhood group, assails the city for not providing enough low-income housing. After the program airs, you receive an angry call from a city official who informs you that there have been low-income units sitting vacant for months. This situation was highlighted at the city council meeting last week. It made all the papers. Where were you?

Some basic research would have allowed you to question your guest more closely, challenging the assertion by citing the recent council discussion. Lack of preparation in the following areas can also lead to on-air gaffes or unnecessarily dull interviews:

1. *Not knowing the political opinions of your guest.* Politics color responses, and if you do not know a guest's politics you will have trouble filtering out the party line. Or you might fail to follow up on an important statement by not realizing when a politician has opposed the party line.
2. *Not knowing or not completely understanding the vested interests of your guest.* For example, if your guest is employed by an organization or lobbying group to promote a particular product or belief, it is your obligation to know this and point it out to the audience. It is also important to find out if a politician has any personal interest in a particular piece of legislation, or what boards of directors a banker serves on. Knowing the background of, and reasons for, a guest's position on a subject is vital to an open, complete interview. Only careful questioning and research in advance will determine whether the guest is an impartial observer or a paid spokesperson. Having incomplete information in this respect is, in effect, a distortion in itself.

Research Material and Resources

One good way to prepare for an interview is to check through newspaper or magazine clippings on the topic, and the best place to start is with a newspaper database. Lexus/Nexus is a good electronic database to consider because it updates regional and national editions of newspapers on a weekly basis. As a result, you can retrieve very current information about people and subjects. These databases may have limited value if you are looking for a local issue and do not live in a major metropolitan area.

If you are doing an interview with a local figure or about a local subject, you'll want to visit the local public library. Libraries will usually have back issues of the local newspaper. Many colleges develop microfilm files of the local newspaper, but those files may not be in a form that can be easily searchable by subject or date. In some cases you may be able to gain access to the files of the local newspaper. Usually the newspaper's morgue is indexed in some way.

The World Wide Web is another excellent source of information, both for regional/national and local issues. There are several approaches to conducting a thorough Web-based search. Starting with a meta search engine may present you with a dilemma. On one hand, you will get many "hits" but some search engines will provide you with many duplicate sites. However, a new generation of meta search engines provides some relief from the problems of earlier search engines. According to *Business and Management Practices,* some of the best search engines are these:

- *Metor.com* (www.metor.com) will provide keyword searches based on the results of seven other powerful search engines including Google, AltaVista, and HotBot. It is possible to search for a string of keywords or for exact phrases.

- *Surfwax* (www.surfwax.com) looks at traditional Web sites as well as newsfeeds and intranets. It will display results along with the various search engines that it used to gain information. Overall, it is a useful search tool.

- *Query Server* (www.queryserver.com) allows you to search from the following categories: Web pages, news sources, government, health and money. The search engines used in the search are displayed as well.

Try the following general search tools:

- *Google* (www.google.com) is one of the best general search engines. Google's advanced search feature allows you to customize your query, allowing you to target information available on the World Wide Web.

- *Yahoo!* (www.yahoo.com) is the granddaddy of hierarchical search engines. Yahoo can provide a guided search, which can be useful when you are starting research on a topic where you have little or no previous knowledge.

Another avenue for a local search is simply to ask questions from co-workers, friends, and neighbors. You cannot accept everything they tell you as a fact, but the leads you gather can be useful in opening other areas of research. Writers of nonfiction, who use this technique extensively, gather a great deal of material just by continually broaching a subject among various groups, even at cocktail parties. It is often surprising how a casual conversation can steer you to an appropriate resource or helpful individual.

Selecting a Guest and Topic

One final note concerning research and preparation: the success of an interview, especially a studio interview, depends on selecting a guest and a reasonable narrowing of the topic.

By prescreening guests, you can sometimes avoid having to deal on the air with someone who is too nervous or obstinate to give a productive interview. Unfortunately, there are no foolproof predictors of a guest's performance. Oddly, the guests who initially, off-camera or off-mic, appear to be the most blasé about the prospects of being interviewed are often the ones who "freeze up." Your initial dealings with a prospective guest may lead you to believe that he or she either is not interested enough to give an enthusiastic interview, or is covering fright by adopting an uncaring attitude. If this happens, you will have to work harder at making the guest feel comfortable. You might boost the guest's ego by explaining how pleased you are that someone of his or her stature or knowledge of the subject has agreed to be interviewed. Try to make the reticent guest more self-confident.

One way to avoid trouble is to put the guest at ease and explain what is going to happen during the interview. This is especially appropriate for TV talk shows, where there is a great deal of motion on the set, and some noise also. The setting probably is unfamiliar to your guest and is likely to be perceived as threatening. Remember, the guest who has not been briefed may not understand what's going on. It's not unusual for a guest to turn and stare at the wild gesticulations of a floor manager who's trying to get your attention. Guests have been known to freeze in panic as a camera ominously slides toward them.

Think about it from your guests' standpoint. Explain, while you are preparing to go on the air (see Figure 8.1), that there is a great deal of activity in a television studio, but none of it need concern them. Let guests know that they should not look at the monitor, and warn them specifically that cameras may move. Remember that radio can be intimidating to guests, too, and a pre-air orientation can be calming to an interviewee.

A good time to reinforce the importance of the interview is when you meet with the guest just before the actual taping or airing of the program. Creating a personal relationship is useful in allowing the guest to understand that you value her or his time. Make it known that you will respect her or his point of view, even though you may disagree with that viewpoint. These discussions should also serve as a vehicle for you to narrow the topic. Usually,

Figure 8.1 Pre-air preparation is essential. Here, on *AM/Philadelphia*, a long-running television talk show aired on WPVI-TV in Philadelphia, guests are prepped just before airtime.

Photo by Philip Benoit

a guest will press you for a specific list of the questions you plan to ask. As suggested earlier, giving out a list of questions before airtime is not a good idea. First, the guest may respond with rehearsed, flat answers. Second, if the guest assumes that these are the *only* questions to be covered, he or she may balk at any question that was not on the list.

To lay the groundwork for the interview, however, a definition of the areas to be discussed is necessary. For example, your initial off-camera/off-mic discussion with a state economic development official may prompt you to narrow the topic to explore the revitalization of your city's downtown area, rather than a shotgun-type discussion of the official's office and what it does.

One of the more difficult aspects of interviewing is dealing with callers on a telephone call-in program. Some suggestions are given in Box 8.1.

Doing the Interview

A successfully executed interview is usually the result of a three-pronged effort to

1. Get an interview that is appropriate for the format or intended use, also making sure that the topic is of interest to the target audience.

Box 8.1

DEALING WITH TELEPHONE CALL-INS

- *In the radio talk interview, never allow your attention to wander.* A call can go sour very quickly and degenerate into obscene or libelous invective. Although most stations have a delay system, those systems are not always infallible; many things slip by. By keeping ahead of the caller, you may avoid the necessity of cleaning up an embarrassing mess.

- *Be especially careful not to misidentify the caller.* Most stations have some sort of monitor arrangement with which the host is shown the name, and sometimes the hometown, of the caller. (In small markets, there are still cases where the engineer writes the name and town on a piece of paper and holds it up to the glass.) An occasional mistake is unavoidable, but continually saying hello to "Marjorie from Trenton" when it's really "Bob from Brooklyn" ruins your credibility in a hurry.

- *Keep callers to time limits.* Timing is always difficult. Many talk show hosts—such as Bruce Williams, who moderates an exceptionally popular finance-oriented program—make a diligent effort to wrap up segments before a commercial break. Williams can't always manage to finish each discussion on schedule, but he usually does. Listening to him is instructive. Note that he's not shy about prompting callers to condense their story. Also note that he speeds up his responses and questions as time grows short, thus cueing the caller to pick up the pace of the conversation.

2. Work effectively within technical limitations (such as time limits) and performance considerations (such as opening and closing the show, keeping the interview flowing, and making the program run smoothly).

3. Elicit responsive answers from the interviewee.

   Let's examine these principles of interview execution in detail.

Appropriateness of the Interview

News interviewers are frequently sent out to obtain a specific fact ("What will next year's tax rate be?") or reaction ("What is your opinion about the sentence given to the defendant?"). Often the fact or reaction is edited down into a short piece that can be inserted into a newscast. Thus, an interviewer looking for a response from which 30 seconds can be edited might ask,

"What will be the most immediate impact of the rise in the prime rate on an average-income American?"

A reporter at a press conference is also seeking specific answers. Even if the segment is to be shown in its entirety, the goal is still to elicit facts or reactions about a specific subject. An awkward way to phrase the same question under this circumstance would be "Mr. Smith, what is the long-range impact of the increase in the prime rate, and how will it affect the various segments of the economy, such as manufacturing, services, and eventually, the consumer?" This question is likely to provoke a full-blown lecture, not a succinct reply.

Technical and Performance Considerations

An interview is not a natural situation, although a skilled broadcaster can make it appear so. If an excellent interview has the character of a conversation in the host's living room, it is because the host is skilled in working within the technical limitations of the TV or radio facility and equipment. The graceful wrap-up that appears so simple and easy is probably a product of preparation, experience, and instinct.

Following are some suggestions on ways to work within the confines of broadcast structure and format and to deliver a professional-appearing performance. Specific techniques of the question-and-answer aspects of the interview itself are discussed later in this chapter.

PREPARING INTRODUCTIONS AND CLOSINGS Do not put too much faith in your ad-libbing abilities; you can ruin an otherwise good talk show by flubbing the beginning or the end. On a talk show, the host is responsible for setting the scene properly. Four elements should be part of an opening:

1. What the topic is

2. Who the guest is

3. Why the guest is worth listening to

4. *Why the audience should care about the topic*

The final factor is vital. A show on economics might be of little interest to viewers or listeners unless you explain that the prime rate will determine whether they can buy new houses. A show on food additives won't have much appeal unless you specify that certain additives, which may be harmful, may be in the food your audience and your audience's family will eat for dinner. It is generally good practice to write notes on the openings and closings and use them for reference.

PREPARING QUESTIONS AND FOLLOW UP Prepare questions, but don't be a slave to your list. Preparing questions helps to focus your own thinking about the thrust of the interview. A prepared list can be a lifesaver when an unresponsive guest fails to give answers that lead into other questions. A list of prepared questions is useful, but it should not be the end-all of the interview. Here is an excerpt from an actual interview.

Interviewer: Mr. _____, what do you think of the majority leader's actions?

State Representative: To be honest, it makes me feel ashamed of the whole system. This sort of thing just takes the heart out of you, and I don't feel right associating with the system. I don't think I'm going to run for reelection.

Interviewer: Now, what do you think of the chances for a tax hike next year?

This interviewer stuck to a prepared list to the point of ignoring an unexpected answer and managed to miss a major story. Always listen to the answers to your questions and follow up when appropriate.

KEEPING AUDIENCE ATTENTION   A major responsibility of an interviewer, of course, is to keep the audience from tuning out. Lack of interesting material is a major culprit, but distractions also steal the audience's interest from the subject at hand. See Box 8.2 for some suggestions for avoiding distractions and keeping the viewers' and listeners' interest levels high.

DEALING WITH TIME RESTRICTIONS   One of the most awkward aspects of a talk show format is dealing with the clock. A good segment can be spoiled by having to cut off a guest in midsentence with a frantic closing.

One of the most frequent questions guests ask before going on the air is how they will know when to stop talking. Try telling your guest, "Just watch me. You'll know when it's time to wrap up."

You usually don't have to do anything special; having the guest tuned into your body language cues is often enough. After all, can't you tell when someone is in a hurry, regardless of whether that person states it verbally? If you find that the subliminal approach doesn't work, and you are having trouble getting out of the show in time for commercials or the program end, you may elect to set up some sort of cue with guests.

USING YOUR GUEST'S TALENTS   Although the principle of taking advantage of a guest's talent sounds obvious, many interviewers have become infatuated with the technique of asking comedians about the tragic aspects of their lives. A little of this is all right, but a little also goes a long way. Be sure to give your funny guest an opportunity to be funny. The audience expects this and will, by and large, be disappointed if it doesn't happen.

Likewise, if you are interviewing a wise analyst of current affairs, be certain to give the guest the latitude to do what he or she does best. Along

Box 8.2

SUGGESTIONS FOR HOLDING YOUR AUDIENCE

1. *Don't make meaningless noises.* You might say "uh-huh" 30 times in a normal conversation, but it appears downright silly on the air. "I see," "yes," "right," and "you know" are other verbal tics to be avoided.

2. *Fill in your listeners and viewers from time to time.* The first piece of advice usually offered to play-by-play sports announcers is "Give the score, because if the listener doesn't know the score, you're not doing your job." The same advice, to a lesser degree, goes for talk show hosts. The audience won't always know exactly what the interview is about if they tuned in late or weren't paying attention, and it is up to you to fill them in, perhaps after a commercial: "We're back with Dr. Frank Adams, who is telling us how to get in shape for spring sports. . . ." That's all it takes.

3. *Stick to the subject.* If you are talking to a fire chief about ways to prevent house fires, you do not want to get into an extended dialogue about the social problems that cause arson. Some examination of that issue is important, and probably necessary, but it should not take over the show. Be particularly wary of guests who wander into controversial areas that are not within the boundaries of their expertise.

4. *Establish the guest's qualifications, and reaffirm them from time to time.* The audience wants to know why they should bother listening to your guest: "We're talking about poison prevention with Dr. Janice Jones, who is a toxicologist, a specialist in the study of poisons, and is head of University Hospital's Poison Control Center. . . ."

5. *Don't assume too much knowledge by the audience.* If you are conducting an interview about vacation travel, remember that a good share of your audience may never have been on an airplane. Likewise, don't assume that every viewer or listener has an up-to-date knowledge of current events.

    If the discussion starts at a level beyond the knowledge of a good share of your audience, you will lose the attention of many listeners and viewers. Set the groundwork simply and completely, giving information that will be obvious to some members of your audience but not to others.

the same lines, don't try to steal the show from your guest. Remember, the audience is listening and watching because of the guest, not because of you. If you were the star, the station wouldn't bother cluttering up the set with interviewees.

Eliciting Responsive Answers

Despite the considerable overlap between the performance considerations just discussed and the specific techniques of questioning discussed next, it is productive to concentrate on some of the methods used by interviewers to obtain logical, reasonable, and useful responses. Here are some principles and their applications.

AVOIDING "DEAD-END" QUESTIONS   Sometimes an interview can grind to a halt because the questions just don't lend themselves to lively conversation. There are two main methods of preventing this from happening.

1. *Avoid asking questions that can result in yes or no answers.* Instead of saying, "I gather you don't think this is fair?" try asking, "What do you think is unfair about the situation?" A yes-or-no question may be very useful, however, if you are trying to pin down a guest who is being evasive.

2. *Avoid obvious questions, and avoid obscure questions.* Do not ask a politician who has lost an election if he or she is disappointed. On the other end of the scale, do not start off an interview by quizzing a scientist on the molecular structure of a high-performance ceramic, unless you are doing an in-house presentation geared for people who have a technical understanding of the subject.

GETTING A COMPLETE ANSWER   Often, through accident or intent, an interviewee fails to provide an entire answer, or leaves an issue hanging. The hallmark of a skilled interviewer, however, is the ability to elicit complete answers to his or her questions. This often involves waiting for an answer to be completed or, at the end of a response, stating that the question hasn't been answered completely. To get a complete answer, use the following techniques, which are highlighted in Box 8.3.

1. *Wait out a noncommunicative interviewee.* Some people might not be willing to give complete answers, but some are simply terse and short-spoken. When you need a more complete answer, just keep looking at the interviewee. He or she will get the message that more is expected.

   If the interviewee is trying to evade giving a full answer, he or she may just stare back at you—but that is an answer in itself. Usually, though, interviewees will give in before you will.

> ## Box 8.3
>
> ### GET A COMPLETE ANSWER
>
> 1. Wait out a noncommunicative interviewee.
> 2. Point out that you are not getting an answer, and repeat the question.
> 3. Take your responsibilities seriously when looking for an answer.

2. *Point out that you are not getting an answer, and repeat the question.* Never be afraid to say, "Excuse me, Senator, but that's not what I was asking. My question is . . . "

   Many public figures are experts at avoiding unpleasant questions and at giving the answer they want to give regardless of what is asked. It's up to you to get the interview back on track and not let the evasive answer go unchallenged. For example,

   Interviewer: Do you expect another round of layoffs?

   Corporate Vice President: We anticipate a very healthy turnaround of the economic situation, especially when our new division opens in 18 months, when we actually expect to add jobs to the payroll.

   Interviewer: I'm glad to know the long-range job situation looks good but what about the immediate future? Do you expect another round of layoffs before the new division opens?

3. *Take your responsibilities seriously when looking for an answer.* Do not become pontifical on the subject, but remember that a broadcast interviewer is, in effect, a representative of the public. You have a right to ask questions and a right to a reasonable answer.

   Always be polite, but never let yourself be cowed by a high-ranking official who is 30 years your senior. Never mind how well the interviewee says he or she knows the station manager. Do your job, and remember that you are not doing your job if you let yourself be intimidated.

DEVELOPING A STYLE   The key to developing a successful interviewing style lies in finding the approach that works best and polishing it. The boyish appearance and demeanor of one excellent interviewer gain him a stunning amount of cooperation and information. His approach is usually something along the lines of "Gosh, I really don't understand this, and I'm sort of

Figure 8.2   Studios for XM Radio's USA Today Channel. Note the studio is set up to interview as many as five guests.

Photo courtesy of XM Satellite Radio

in a jam to get a story so I'd really appreciate any help you can give me." He uses his style very well, and invariably comes away with more information than do overbearing, bullying competitors.

Perhaps an aggressive attitude is best for you, however. Style is a matter of experience, so experiment and cultivate methods that work well on an individual basis.

UNDERSTANDING WHY QUESTIONS BACKFIRE   In an interview situation, the host can inadvertently create negative impressions of himself or herself and of the guests by falling into the traps of mincing around unpleasant questions and being a cheerleader.

1. *Don't be hesitant about asking unpleasant questions.* Suppose you are interviewing a former convict who now works with a children's group. Questions about why the guest was in prison and what he or she learned from that experience are unavoidable, so ask them straight out and don't hedge.

   Your inclination to preserve the dignity of your guest is perfectly natural. Remember, though, that a direct question will be far less damaging to your guest's dignity than will a mincing, indirect approach, which leads the audience to believe that the subject is distasteful to you.

2. *Avoid being a cheerleader for a guest.* You may be interviewing a celebrity whom you greatly admire, but your audience won't be well served by having you gush all over him or her for 30 minutes. Maintain your perspective.

FOCUSING THE ISSUE   Perhaps the clearest distinction between a poor interviewer and a good one is that the good interviewer keeps the discussion focused on a central theme, whittling away verbiage to keep answers understandable and to the point. Two valuable techniques for focusing the issue are *using transitions* and *paraphrasing.*

First, *focus the issue with transitions.* People being interviewed for talk shows or for newscasts may wander from the point, either by accident or because they want to avoid the topic under discussion.

The interviewer can politely steer the conversation back on track by using a smooth transition. For example, assume that you are interviewing a home economist on the subject of budget-saving meals. The economist has mentioned the inexpensiveness of Chinese cooking, but has gotten off on a tangent about the benefits of Mandarin versus Cantonese spices. You can gently return the conversation to the subject by saying, "Yes, Chinese food is very good and very inexpensive. Are there other ethnic foods that represent good bargains?" This gets you back to the topic of budget-saving meals tactfully, without making an abrupt jump, and the conversation can continue naturally. You may, of course, want to be abrupt when an interviewee is obviously trying to duck a question.

In some cases, the guest might stray from the point because he or she has an ax to grind. For example, the head of a police union, asked if a strike by uniformed officers would endanger residents of high-crime neighborhoods, might overlook the question and begin a discourse on how the city failed to bargain in good faith. If you want to preserve the ambience of the interview without taking a blunt approach at that particular time, you can use a gentle transition: "Well, the collective bargaining has been going on for months, with no solution in sight. But it seems that the situation in high-crime areas during a police strike could be an immediate problem, and I wonder if you could tell me . . . "

If the transition fails, you may elect to resort to the more direct principle of stating flatly that the question hasn't been answered. This heavy-handed technique, though, is generally more useful in an interview that will be edited than in a talk show. The reason? If you start pressing a guest 5 minutes into a half-hour talk show, you may have 25 tough, uncommunicative minutes ahead.

Second, *focus the issue through a paraphrase.* In many cases the answer you receive from a guest simply won't make much sense, either because the guest cannot express it better or because he or she does not want to say it more clearly. For example, a politician being quizzed on government finance might say, "Well, as the people of this great state know, budgets are tight in this day and age, and some form of revenue enhancement may be in order to preserve the programs that have made this great state a leader in . . ." One way to make sense of such a response is to paraphrase what you think the interviewee just said and see if he or she agrees with it: "Governor, do I understand that you are saying there may be a tax increase next year?"

Now you are forcing an answer and focusing the issue. The governor can agree with what you said, back off from what he said, refuse to make a specific statement at this time, or blandly offer another waffling answer. A more detailed response is necessary, and you may have finessed him into predicting a tax increase in plain English.

KEEPING STATEMENTS FAIR   Interviewers are not required to judge the validity of every statement made by every guest, but they are responsible for challenging what appear to be unfair attacks and illogical or unsupported statements. As a representative of the public, you have a duty to call attention to unfair or misleading statements.

Specifically, you must balance both sides of the issue and keep the discussion logical.

1. *Balance the issue.* A trend in talk shows is to invite several guests with opposing views and let them battle it out before mics and cameras. Guests on the same show may differ widely in their eloquence and communication abilities, so it is up to you to see that an aggressive guest does not trample a less-skilled interviewee. You may have to play devil's advocate, just to ensure that all sides of a matter are fairly represented.

   Your most important responsibility as a pseudo-referee is to make sure that if charges are made, they are supported or are clearly identified as unsupported allegations or personal opinions. Potentially damaging allegations should not be left hanging. Try to resolve such matters before moving on to the next point. The next technique may be quite useful in this regard.

2. *Keep the discussion logical.* A discussion of formal logic is beyond the scope of this book, but if you have the opportunity for further instruction in logic, take advantage of it. Essentially, it is your responsibility to ensure that the statements presented by your guests are factual, and that the conclusions and inferences drawn make sense. Here are some examples of lapses in logic that should make your antennae tingle:

   • An interviewee says that all homosexuals are dangerous deviates and that "Dr. Smith" has proven it. Don't let something like this go unchallenged. Who, exactly, is Smith? What is he or she a doctor of? Exactly what does the proof that is claimed consist of?

   • A guest says, "ten people died in yesterday's fire because there were no smoke detectors." This is a dangerous type of statement because

Focus on Technique
WORKING IN TALK RADIO

Talk radio is not a new phenomenon, but it has undergone a noticeable transformation in recent years. Where talk programs were once "filler" for many stations, they now provide a generous share of the station's bread-and-butter.

Acting as a talk-radio host, where you interview callers or guests over the phone, or in studio, or play master of ceremonies to guests who are interviewed by callers, is more difficult than you might suspect.

The interview techniques described in this chapter can be adapted to talk radio. But aside from the pure performance aspects we have discussed, you must be able to handle an array of operational tasks. Here are some of the duties you will encounter if you host a call-in talk radio program:

- You will have to keep the program on time. Usually you'll be hitting network news or the legal ID at the top of the hour, and you may have many other milestones that must be reached at a precise moment. Techniques described in this chapter to help interviewees wrap up will prove handy, but in talk radio you often have no choice but to say, "Jim, you've got 30 seconds . . . what's your point?" You often will not have the option of keeping callers on the line through breaks; radio program directors generally dislike that tactic because it makes the show seem disconnected.

- You must work with a delay system. Callers can (and do) say things they shouldn't, such as obscenities and libelous remarks. Delay systems used to be more complex than they are today. Just a decade or so ago, most call-in programs used a loop of tape that fed back on itself seven seconds later. Today the majority of stations use digital technology that allows for various delay intervals and makes the process of getting back on the air after editing out an obscenity or libel less complex. But you, as the host, must still work out a protocol with the engineer for how you will handle slipping back into "delay time" after the offensive remark is excised.

- You must use what will seem, at first, to be an awkward system of communication with the control room. Most modern facilities have computer terminal displays that present the name of the next caller, where he or she is calling from, and the subject of the call.[2] (A

---

[2] One of the authors was a radio talk show host 10 years ago and used a decidedly low-tech device: the producer wrote the name, location, and topic for each caller on a 3-by-5 index card and taped it to the window. While it does not allow for much flexibility, this system *does* work in a pinch.

Continues

Focus on Technique   Continued

"screener" gets all this information in advance and weeds out the more obvious problems.) In some cases, you will have a choice whom to pick next; if that's the case, you usually will be responsible for opening the right switch on your console.

- What's really tricky is the communication between guests, host, and control room. You will often have an interruptible foldback (IFB) line in your headphones that allows you to hear the control room operator or producer or both in addition to the program output. This may not seem so difficult until you try it and realize that in some circumstances you may be carrying the threads of on-air conversation between an in-studio guest, an out-of-studio guest, a stream of callers, and your producer, who is insisting that you get into the commercial now, because you're 15 seconds late!

it may be true, though unprovable, and even if it's not true at all (seven victims were in a narcotic stupor, two were unattended infants, and the guy who set the fire left a suicide note in a metal safe), there's an element of validity that tempts the broadcaster to violate the rules of logic.

- A politician running for reelection contends that the fears of the elderly in a certain rundown neighborhood are groundless. He cites statistics indicating that an elderly person has less chance of falling victim to street crime in that neighborhood than a young person does.

Statistics are very difficult to sort out, but a broadcast communicator should always be prepared to challenge them. In the case of the politician and home for the elderly, the interviewer remembered that the neighborhood in question contained a very large nursing home.

Interviewer: But Mayor _____, don't these figures include residents of the _____ Nursing Home?

Mayor: Well, yes.

Interviewer: There are hundreds of elderly people in that nursing home, and many of them are bedridden. They couldn't be victims of street crime if they wanted to. *Doesn't this cast some doubt on your statistics?*

You will not always be able to score this type of coup, of course. But a healthy understanding that statistics can be extremely misleading if used with self-serving intent may shed light on many illogical contentions put forth by interviewees.

DRAWING OUT RELUCTANT GUESTS   Fear is a strong element in the performance of a guest. Being on the air *can* be frightening, even to experienced performers. Remember, too, that some people simply are not verbally oriented. A "man of few words" can be admirable in many respects, but he may not make an ideal interviewee.

Two ways of getting a guest to open up include *personalizing the questions* and, if the situation really deteriorates, using your list of *disaster questions.*

Personalizing questions is a useful technique because guests who are afraid of repercussions often are reluctant to give complete and responsive answers. A lower-level manager of a social program, for example, may be very edgy about providing specifics because he or she "can't set policy." If you are confronted with such a situation, avoid questions that make the guest seem to be a policymaker. Instead of asking, "What is your agency's position on . . . ," try the following approach: "What sorts of things is your agency doing to overcome . . . " This approach is *very useful* when dealing with workers in a highly structured bureaucracy.

Some people do not fear repercussions; they just don't like to talk, aren't very interesting, or don't care very much about getting their messages across. For some reason these people can and do appear on talk shows, so you need to know some techniques for opening them up.

A good way to elicit a response from an untalkative guest is to ask, more or less, "What does your program (service, etc.) mean to our audience? How could it affect them?" Even the most uncommunicative guests will be reluctant to admit that what they do with their lives has no impact on other people. This is what makes personalized questions good "disaster questions," as discussed later. Such questions also lend themselves to follow-ups.

Sometimes, however, interviews just go badly, and you must be prepared for that rare guest who "clams up." The reasons may be varied, but often they are seated in people's ignorance of the impression they make on television or radio. Thus a guest may sit as tight-lipped as a murder defendant for 30 minutes to keep from appearing "too gabby," or "undignified." But at the conclusion of the program, he or she will turn to the host with a worried look and ask, "I didn't run off at the mouth too much, did I?"

In such situations, when a guest only mumbles monosyllabic answers, you may need some of the following *disaster questions.*

1. "What are some of the personal success stories you've had in your experience with the program (agency, organization, etc.)?" It is a rare guest indeed who doesn't have something he or she is proud of and willing to talk about at greater length.

2. "Why did you get into this line of work (support this cause, etc.)?" This is an intensely personal question, and even the most uncommunicative guest will not let it slide.

3. "What advice would you give to someone starting off in this line of work (interested in supporting a similar cause, facing this problem,

etc.)?" Likewise, personal questions, which give an opportunity for the guest to draw on his or her experience, are very difficult to slough off.

This is not the definitive list of disaster questions, and you might want to develop some of your own. The key, of course, is the personal angle, an angle that just might help in all your interviewing tasks. Why? Because the prime factor in any type of interview, with any purpose, is *what the subject means to people.* People and their lives, not facts and theories, are what interests an audience.

Summary

Interviewing can be made difficult by a number of factors, including rigid time restrictions, nervous guests, and interviewees who want to use your program as a soapbox. Overcoming these obstacles and conducting a successful interview involves determining the type of interview (that is, studio or actuality), preparing for the interview, and doing the interview.

Preparing for the interview involves drawing up a list of questions and doing research. Selecting the guest and topic is often the interviewer's responsibility, also. Doing the interview entails effectively working within technical restrictions and performance considerations, and eliciting valid responses that are appropriate for the format or intended use of the interview.

The technical restrictions and performance considerations just mentioned involve openings and closings of interview segments, proper use of prepared questions and following up on questions, and keeping listeners' and viewers' attention. Time restrictions must be dealt with effectively, and the interviewer must grasp the techniques of closing an interview segment gracefully.

An interviewer must be concerned with getting a *response,* not simply an answer. Techniques to spur continued conversation and get complete, relevant answers are essential.

Some questions backfire for reasons not immediately apparent. Reasons may include interviewer hesitancy toward asking unpleasant questions or, conversely, an obvious "cheerleading" attitude toward the guest.

Skilled interviewers know how to focus an issue. They do this through use of devices such as transitions and paraphrases.

The interviewer is responsible for keeping statements and allegations fair. Inherent in this responsibility are the tasks of balancing issues during an interview and keeping the discussion and contentions within the bounds of logic.

Some guests are very frightened or simply uncommunicative. Talk shows with such guests can be disastrous, but the technique of personalizing the question can often elicit good responses. Every interviewer should be prepared with a list of "disaster questions"—material that can be used at any time and almost always will resurrect the interview. Such questions involve explorations of the individual's personal success stories or lifelong goals, and usually are not sloughed off by even the most uncommunicative guest.

Exercises

1. Ask a classmate or co-worker to read a newspaper article on a particular subject and to take notes. Your job is to interview him or her for five minutes on that topic.

   This is a realistic type of interview situation, because many of your interviewees will have a limited knowledge about the topic, and the interviewer will have to stay within certain boundaries. Admittedly, you and your guest will be operating from a small data base, but this exercise will prove helpful if you try to maintain a rhythm and a level of interest, regardless of the rough spots.

2. Prepare a list of the five most immediate and pressing questions you would want to ask in the following circumstances. Assume that you will have a limited amount of time, so make the questions brief and to the point. List them in descending order of importance.

   a. You have arrived at the scene of an explosion and have cornered the police chief. Your questions, for example, might be "Is anyone hurt or dead? Are people still in danger? How did the explosion happen? How will the investigation proceed? Is this incident related to a similar explosion last week?"

   b. You are interviewing an actress who will open tonight in a play she also wrote and directed.

   c. You are asking a person who has just been acquitted of a crime for his reaction.

   d. You are speaking with the head of a suicide hotline agency about how teenage suicide can be prevented.

   e. You are interviewing a college professor who says that the elderly in the United States are treated very shoddily and do not get the respect they deserve from the younger generations.

   Discuss your list of questions with classmates or co-workers.

3. Watch a television interview program and keep track of the questions asked by the host. Grade those questions on how interesting they were *to you*. In other words, how badly did you want to ask that question yourself?

   Keep track of issues you feel were left hanging, or weren't dealt with adequately. Also, write down questions you feel the guest evaded or did not answer completely.

   By taking careful notes, you will wind up with a virtual flow sheet of the interview program, and you should have a much better idea of how such programs progress when they are done well, and even when they are not.

Connections

LOGIC

In this chapter we have referred to the obligation of an interviewer, especially a talk show host, to keep the discussion logical—that is, to keep it within the bounds of reason.

A skilled interviewer can gain insight from the study of logic, the academic field dealing with the validity of arguments.

The most simple application of logic is that an argument is valid if the premises on which the argument is based are true and if they relate to the conclusion in such a way that the conclusion must follow from the premises.

For example, consider the classic syllogism, which is a three-part way of coming to a reasoned conclusion:

1. All Greeks are mortal.

2. Socrates is a Greek.

---

3. Therefore, Socrates is mortal.

Note that logical deduction does not "prove" that the assumptions are true, only that there is a valid relationship among them.

The "valid relationship" is what matters. For example, you can see that this syllogism does not carry a valid relationship:

1. All Greeks are mortal.

2. Socrates is mortal.

---

3. Therefore, Socrates is a Greek.

Suppose Socrates were Swiss. Could he still be mortal? Statement #1 does not rule that out. The Swiss can be mortal, too. Premise #1 doesn't say that *only* Greeks are mortal. And therefore the validity of the argument is ruined.

Several classic logical fallacies relate directly to the broadcast interviewer. We will list and describe them briefly here, but you can explore these and other fallacies more fully in a course on logic; such courses are offered at most colleges and universities.

Cause and Effect

Because something happened before another incident does not *necessarily* mean that it caused the incident. For example: There were no smoke

Continues

Connections   *Continued*

detectors in the building, the building burned down, and five people died. Are you being logical if you broadcast, "five people died because there were no smoke detectors in the building?" No; you cannot prove the argument from that premise. Suppose one of the dead was an unattended infant? Suppose one of the dead set the fire to commit suicide? Without further evidence, you cannot jump to such a conclusion. Remember: Just because there is a consistent relationship among actions, there is not necessarily a cause and effect relationship. After the rooster crows in the morning, the sun comes up. Does the rooster cause the sun to rise?

Ignoring the Exposure Base

If you don't know the field from which the evidence was drawn, you cannot ascertain the validity of the conclusion. If, for example, a poll indicates that nine out of ten respondents favor a particular measure, you must ask how the respondents were drawn. Did they phone in their responses voluntarily? Are they members of a specific group?

Fallacies of Vacuity

Empty arguments can be persuasive if you don't recognize the empty (vacuous) premises. Often, fallacies of vacuity involve simply re-stating the argument in different words and pretending that a valid deduction has been made. For example, a talk-show guest says: "The draft is morally wrong, because it is wrong to force someone to join the armed services."

Regardless of whether the premises are correct (and remember, in logic we do not judge the premises, only the relationship between and among them) the "conclusion" is flawed because it is simply a restatement of the premise. Forcing someone to join the armed services *is* the draft. Simply re-stating the premise does not make it valid.

Here is another example:

1. It is always wrong to murder human beings.
2. Capital punishment involves murdering human beings.
3. Therefore, capital punishment is wrong.

Restating the premise in different words and using it as another premise is illogical, and in this case, we have simply called capital punishment "murder" and in a circular fashion used that as an improper premise to "prove" the argument.[3]

[3] Example from R. J. Fogelin, *Understanding Arguments,* 3rd. ed., Orlando, FL: Harcourt-Brace, 1987.

NINE

Television and Radio Specialties

*Y*ou can explore a number of specialty areas as a professional on-air broadcast performer. Sports reporting and play-by-play announcing, weather reporting, hosting radio talk shows, and narration are some common examples. Some broadcasters move into one of these areas by chance. For others, a career as a sportscaster or weather reporter is a lifelong goal, attained after years of preparation for that big break that brings success.

Every area of on-air endeavor has its own special requirements. The special talents and skills needed for success in any given area are developed with experience. No one can prepare to be a great play-by-play announcer without on-air experience. Certainly practice off the air can help, but the actual pressure of being live and on the air provides the special incentive that lets you exceed even your own expectations.

Despite the fact that you can only hone your skills and develop the specialized knowledge you need through practice, the main requirement for proficiency in any specialty assignment is the same as for any on-air assignment. You need to start out as an effective broadcast communicator.

This chapter discusses some specialty assignments in broadcasting and gives a broad overview of the techniques used. The basic principles are refinements of the broader elements of good communication presented throughout this text. And broadcasting specialists use many of the specific techniques covered here:

- A sportscaster often must conduct an extensive interview (Chapter 8) and, during play-by-play, must do a good job on commercials (Chapter 10).

- A weathercaster, especially in times of weather emergency, must gather and present facts lucidly and responsibly in the news function (Chapters 6 and 7).

- A narrator must have an effective voice (Chapter 2) and must be able to grasp the essentials of the copy (Chapter 3).

There is really no way to explain how to become a sportscaster or a weather reporter. A few lessons and drills will never come close to providing the specialized knowledge required. That's why this chapter is brief and primarily introductory, touching on sports, weather, narration, and acting as host of special types of programming such as children's shows and movie presentations.

Sports

Knowledge of sports cannot be faked. Sports fans are often experts themselves, and this means that an aspiring sportscaster must have a strong interest in, and knowledge of, the games to be reported. A sports anchor must be well informed about all sports, even activities he or she may not find personally appealing. In many cities, for example, competitive bowling is extremely popular. Hence, the sports reporter must project knowledge and enthusiasm, qualities that come about only by painstaking homework, in a sport that may be unfamiliar.

In addition, a wide personal database is important because opportunities for sports coverage open very quickly. Should a major fight be booked for your city, someone will have to handle the story, and if you work in the sports department, that someone is likely to be you. It is worthwhile to be aware of and interested in all the various types of sports work.

Types of Sports Assignments

Sports work generally falls into four categories: anchor work, sports reporting, play-by-play, and color. Anchor work in sports parallels that of news. Sports reporting also translates the role of radio or TV reporter from news to sports.

Play-by-play is unique and requires a specialized set of abilities, discussed later in this section. Color work, dealt with in the section on play-by-play, provides commentary and insight.

Personality in Sports

It has been said that the sports reporter provides as much entertainment as the sport being covered. Personality and entertainment value play a much stronger role in sports than in news. In one market, for example, a popular feature of the top-rated sports reporter is a weekly recap of all the blunders that occurred in various sporting events, complete with musical background. Such an approach obviously could not be used with news. Neither would the remark of a reporter that he had egg on his face (after an inaccurate prediction) be followed by the cracking of an egg on the reporter's forehead, as once happened in sports. Although this example is extreme, be aware that sports does allow for more expression of personality and entertainment values and, therefore, places an additional demand on the sports announcer.

Issues in Sports Coverage

Sports certainly is not all fun and games. Recent scandals in Division I basketball and Olympic judging show that sports have a far-too-serious side. So although an element of entertainment is part of the sports broadcaster's repertoire, he or she must also function as a reporter, sometimes asking hard questions. Sensitive information must be dealt with responsibly. Also, anyone who has ever mixed up a score on the air knows that there is no room for error in the recital of who beat whom. Fans find such mistakes virtually unforgivable.

Sports Anchor Work

Typically, many games are still running or just ending as the TV sportscaster is about to go on the air. Network sports feeds, showing highlights of games and events, are fed at 5:10 P.M., 7:35 P.M., and 11:10 P.M. EST. In many cases, this means that some segments for the 11 o'clock news are recorded and put on air by a production person. The sports anchor, who has not seen the material, knows, from a printed rundown fed in advance, only that there is a 20-second piece on the Boston–New York game.

To further complicate matters, the sports anchor must keep track of games in progress. Some stations have courtesy arrangements with broadcast and cable networks that televise certain teams. These arrangements allow sportscasters to air clips of the contests, but in many cases *after each game has ended.* Imagine the rush to get a clip on the air when a home run in the bottom of the ninth inning breaks a tie game at 11:15!

The sports reporter, who often is an alternate anchor on weekends, helps out with production in stations large enough to support more than one sports person and also files local packages to be integrated into the sports segment.

Sports anchoring, then, requires the on-air enthusiasm of a die-hard sports fan combined with the pressure-handling ability of a wire service news editor. Sports reporting calls for the ability to assemble a news package and an eye and ear for stories that will interest fans. Some suggestions for effective anchoring and reporting are given in Box 9.1.

Sports Play-by-Play

A talented play-by-play announcer can generally find abundant work in local markets, although this work will usually be on a part-time basis. In small and medium markets, newspeople, staff announcers, and even sales personnel add to their income by broadcasting local sports. This is a difficult

Box 9.1

TIPS FOR SPORTS ANCHORS AND REPORTERS

1. *Stress stories that interest your local audience.* Remember, taking a new job and moving to a new area involves learning what makes headlines in local sports. In parts of Texas, for example, high school football often creates more excitement than the pro sport does. Other cities in various parts of the nation have strong passions for greyhound racing, candlepin bowling, or lacrosse.

2. *Prewrite as much as possible, and overplan for the sports segment.* Because of the last-minute nature of TV sports, expected segments do not always materialize and you must have material to fill.

3. *Write your copy as close to the visual as possible.* Unlike news, where it is considered undesirable to point copy to the video, in sports you must do so. Copy has to coordinate precisely with what appears on the screen at any given moment: "and he whacked this pitch . . ."

4. *Pay particular attention to variety in reading scores.* In radio especially, the sportscaster must invent many verbs to take the place of "defeated" or "beat." A long list of scores requires some imagination. A phrase such as "Boston overpowered New York, 9–3," adds color. Other useful verbs include, "squeaked past," "downed," and "hammered." Avoid stretching too far, though. "Obliterated" and "decimated" get a bit tedious. In fact, some local sportscasters can become rather comic in their attempts to hype the delivery of scores. If you do not feel comfortable using this type of device, it is better to avoid it. If possible, write the verbs right into the copy.

5. *Always keep your energy level high. Speak with intensity.* Enjoy what you are doing, and let it show.

6. *Remember that the personalities of the athletes are as important as the outcome of the games.* Listeners and viewers are interested in personal items relating to the players, too.

assignment, however, requiring good on-air skills and an extensive knowledge of the sport.

One important aspect of play-by-play is the differing nature of individual events. Think of the different approaches and knowledge bases required for hockey and for football. To illustrate, we contrast the attributes of play-by-play announcers for baseball, football, basketball, hockey, and boxing.

Baseball games have many periods of little or no activity, so the play-by-play person must be able to fill with talk of interest to the audience. This ability will become particularly apparent in rain-delay situations.

Baseball play-by-play also entails the ability to follow action quite a distance away. Good vision, or the ability to compensate for poor vision by an in-depth knowledge of the game, is essential.

Football is a technically oriented game, and the play-by-play announcer has to be up on the plays and able to follow them. A color commentator often provides in-depth analysis. Many statistics must be followed, including downs, yardage on previous carries, and so on. Things happen fast in football, and it takes great skill by the announcer to convey the action accurately and add an element of excitement.

Basketball, from the announcer's standpoint, can become almost nightmarish in its complexity. Listeners want the announcer to keep track of how many fouls a player has, how many rebounds, and how many points each player has scored in the game so far. There are fewer players than in football, however, and the announcer usually is stationed in a press box close to the action or on the floor next to the playing area.

Hockey is challenging. By the time the announcer has told the audience who is in possession of the puck, the game has moved to the other end of the rink. Hockey play-by-play announcers must be able to paint vivid word pictures on radio and keep up with the action on television.

Boxing entails the ability to speculate and analyze. Almost all boxing broadcast today is televised, so the play-by-play commentator must be able to do much more than relay reports of who hit whom. The broadcaster must analyze the bout to determine why one fighter's style makes him vulnerable to the punches of the other or whether one fighter is being tired by body blows. It is also necessary to speculate, for example, whether a contestant's jabs are piling up points with the judges.

There are occasional opportunities to cover sports such as golf, where an announcer must constantly fill time, and track and field, where the play-by-play person must keep close track of the shifting positions of runners.

Although the requirements for individual sports differ widely, some of the basic skills and procedures remain constant. No game coverage procedure is more important than preparation. Rosters must be obtained, along with as much factual information about the team and its players as possible. In most colleges and all professional organizations, sports information directors prepare kits of information especially for the play-by-play and color commentators. Pay close attention to special rules, such as a three-knockdown rule in boxing or a sudden-death playoff in football. Learn the positions of the players, and check for hard-to-pronounce names.

Circumstances will dictate how much help you will have in preparation and actual coverage of the game. In football, spotters may be provided. For baseball, you will want access to the official scorer, who can inform you of rulings. Baseball fans have a particular interest in rulings, wanting to know,

John Madden, seen here with former broadcast partner Pat Summerall, is one of the top personalities in sports broadcasting.

Photo by Aaron Rappaport/FOX

for example, if the player will be credited with an RBI (run batted in) or if the run resulted from a fielder's error.

John Madden (see Figure 9.1), whose play-by-play announcing of NFL football broadcasts for ABC has made him one of the most popular personalities in sports broadcasting, spends many hours preparing for every broadcast. As former coach of the Oakland Raiders, Madden brings an in-depth knowledge of the game to his telecasts, but colleagues say he still spends hours talking and reading, trying to stay current.[1]

The popular combination of play-by-play announcer and color commentator allows for a logical division of duties and enables each sportscaster to concentrate more fully on the game. Although in many cases the color and play-by-play roles are integrated into one announcer's duties, when a separate color announcer is employed, he or she is expected to provide highly informative insights into the sport, including

1. Details the casual fan might miss.

2. Anecdotes about the game and the players.

3. A personalized "feel" for what it is like to play the game—for example, how it feels to be checked into the boards or caught for a safety in the end zone.

---

[1] "The Sportscasters," by Charles Siebert, *The New York Times Magazine,* August 19, 1990, p. 37.

The chemistry that makes certain announcing teams successful is an elusive concept. Among the more easily spelled out play-by-play and color principles are the following:

1. Let yourself become excited by the sport. Many former players are successful sportscasters because they love the game and are thrilled by a fine play, not merely because of their technical knowledge.

   Phil Rizzuto's famous exclamation, "HOLY COW!" is more than just a trademark. He loves baseball and is not afraid to show it.

2. Don't repeat yourself. Listeners do not need to be told "It's a beautiful day here in Cleveland" more than once or twice. Reacting to the pressure of the need to fill time, announcers often become repetitious, and the only cure is awareness of this pitfall and an adequate supply of material to fill time.

   However, audience members do appreciate frequent repetition of the score. When in doubt and desperate for something to say, the score is as good as anything. Time can also be filled by reading scores of other games.

3. When in doubt about a play, wait until you know for sure to make the call. Identifying football players can become difficult, especially on a muddy field when uniform numbers become obscured. However, a delay in calling a play sounds much better than having to backtrack and figure out who really did take the handoff.

4. When using statistics, communicate with those numbers rather than repeating them. The audience may or may not be interested to learn that the man at the plate is a .310 hitter. To be compelling, the announcer might say, "The pitcher is left-handed and the batter is a .400 hitter against lefties. He's also known as a good man in the clutch, and this is really one of the clutch situations of the season, with the Sox down by one run in the bottom of the ninth with a runner on second . . ."

5. Never let up on energy or enthusiasm during the commercials. Play-by-play announcers are often called on to do commercials and should keep in mind that those commercials help pay their salaries.

6. Be sure to keep up with rule changes and ground rules. Getting acquainted with an official who can fill you in on changes is an excellent idea. Similarly, learn officials' hand signals.

7. It is better to give the score and time remaining too often than not often enough.

8. Practice and develop your own methods of quickly spotting players and plays. Many knowledgeable sportscasters maintain that a sportscaster who lags behind the public address announcer is not doing his or her job.

9. Pronunciation of names is often a problem. In college and high school games, one of the best ways to check on pronunciation is to ask the

cheerleaders, who often know the athletes personally. Use this option if you don't have time to track down coaches, players, or sports information people.

10. In play-by-play, avoid using numbers to designate people. Each player has a name, and it should be used.

In Focus on Technique, we outline some strategies for improving your presentation.

Weather

Today's weather forecast has evolved into a high-tech, graphically stunning presentation. In addition, weather forecasters are called on to make highly localized predictions that will affect hundreds or thousands of audience members in a particular region.

The Weathercaster's Role

The modern weather reporter is often both a meteorologist and an entertainer. The American Meteorological Society has established qualifications for meteorologists, and this professional organization issues a seal that is displayed on approved weather forecasters' programs.

For all practical purposes, a meteorologist entering today's world of broadcasting needs a four-year degree in that field. Although it is perfectly legal to be employed as a weather forecaster without a degree, meteorologist John Flanders notes that the competition for jobs is stiff and a degree in meteorology may be a decided advantage.

Why is it advantageous for a local weathercaster to be a trained meteorologist? Advancing technology has made weather forecasting a more exact science, and the process of giving a detailed weather forecast now involves much more than ripping a paragraph or two off the news wire and drawing warm and cold fronts on a map.

Listeners and viewers now expect more specific and more localized forecasts, and a forecaster with training is better able to predict such events as the likely path of a snowfall or a thunderstorm. Remember, a small variation in the path of a snow storm can make an enormous difference to the city that is either hit or missed.

Note, too, that all forecasts are not the same. In periods of good weather, forecasts are similar, bad weather introduces the factors subject to analysis and interpretation. The modern meteorologist-entertainer provides this type of information, and does so in a way that holds the interest of the audience.

The image of the TV weathercaster has gradually changed over the years. At one time it was common for the weather segment to be treated as comic relief for the local news block. The weathercaster was often cast in the role

Focus on Technique

IMPROVING PLAY-BY-PLAY AND COLOR

Sportscasting is highly competitive but appears to be a growing field. The proliferation of super-segmented sports cable channels has opened new opportunities for broadcast communicators conversant with the nuances of describing a game.

Almost anyone who has some knowledge of how a game is played can do play-by-play or color; unfortunately, very few of these people can do it well.

Many sports announcers note that practice is the key element in separating lackluster and incompetent sports calling from quality work. By and large they contend that if you work on *better preparation, on-air organization,* and *verbal skills,* you will consistently improve.

Here are some suggestions for improving in those three categories.

Preparation

- When you know you are going to be calling a game, work closely with the sports information director (usually called an SID) for both teams. The SID is the person who will be providing you with rosters and statistics. Call the SID early. Hone a good working relationship with the SID: a thank-you note is unexpected but quite welcome. If you want to thank the visiting team's SID in person, do so before the game because he or she will be too busy after.

- Make up detailed charts. Most sports announcers have their own system for their charts (which are often called "boards"). For football, as an example, many draw rectangular blocks to represent the various positions and fill in the starter and the backup. Whatever system you use, it is important that you can look down and perceive the names and numbers at a glance.

- Drill yourself on names and numbers. When you get the starting lineup from the other team's SID, make up a set of flashcards with the numbers. Pretty soon, you'll be able to recall all the names. (For example, shuffle the cards and pull out 22: it will be Rodriguez. 43 will be Martin. You may have to check the first few times, but you'll get it soon. It goes without saying that you will have learned all your team's numbers and names early in the season.)

Don't bother learning first names unless there are two or more players on the team with the same last name.

Continues

Focus on Technique   Continued

- On your charts, or on index cards, or in whatever system you favor, keep lists of factors such as:

  —Personal anecdotes. ("LaRue's father was a halfback for the Cleveland Browns in the 1960s.")

  —Any records that might be broken during game day.

  —Stats from last year.

- As part of your preparation, listen to a tape of your previous week's show. If you're working on radio, get the game videotape and run it at the same time to see how well your play-by-play and color matched up.

- As you near show time, let the color commentator do the pregame show, if possible, and allow the play-by-play announcer time to go over the names and numbers. This is particularly important in hockey; hockey personnel change so quickly and the game is so fluid that the play-by-play announcer must be completely conversant with the names. (Note how much better a third period often is in terms of play calling than the first period; you can guess the reason.)

- When the opposing team takes the field or court, take note of any physical characteristics that stand out and write them down on your boards:

  Number 22 = Mike Cowphin RED HAIR AND GLASSES

  You'll find this particularly useful in basketball because in basketball it is difficult or impossible to see numbers during much of the play.

On-Air Organization

- Make sure that the play-by-play, color, and statistician/spotter stay in rhythm. One of the problems you are going to encounter is listening to directions from the control room (usually in a remote truck). A good technique is for only the play-by-play to listen to the truck when color is talking and vice-versa. Have the statistician/spotter take care of reminding the on-air people of duties they might forget, such as giving the legal ID at the top of the hour.

- Use some consistent method to remind yourself to give the score. Research shows that failure to give the score is the most frequently cited irritant among listeners and viewers. Some announcers use an

Continues

Focus on Technique Continued

egg timer. Others always give the score during a line change in hockey (which averages perhaps 70 seconds between changes) or after two outs in baseball.

- Make sure your statistician and everybody else who is going to be on air has a consistent formula for giving statistics. The hallmark of a novice is to give every statistic on the boards before the end of the first inning. Know in advance when the stats are going to be parceled out. Do not, for example, say, "Willis has stolen 30 bases this season" when he steps up to bat. Wait until and if he is on base. "That's Morris's third three-pointer in the game . . . he averages five per game this season!" is an example of how to work in statistics.

Verbal Skills

- When calling a game, be sure to rid your verbiage of clichés. Don't ape the routines of famous announcers. No one is going to be impressed by your impression of Marv Albert—"Yes!"

- Try never to use the word "we." Once you start saying, "We need to stop them on this drive," people will start asking, "What number are you?" Don't become what's known in the industry as a "homer"—someone who roots for the home team. It is increasingly considered unprofessional.

- Remember that many color commentators are noted players and, as WBSU-FM General Manager Warren Kosierski notes, if you are not a noted player you cannot speak with the same authority as they can. So, instead of saying, "I predict they're going to run to the right," say, "They've run to the right in eight of their last ten running plays . . . let's see if they do it again."

- Keep in mind that verbal skills for radio and TV are different. With radio, you must carry more of the action. This becomes a problem when someone brought up on watching TV sportscasts gets on radio and doesn't describe the action properly. ("Yes!" will not help a radio listener much.) Remember, too, that play-by-play will dominate radio coverage while color will dominate TV.

- Use different approaches to giving the score. Although listeners and viewers complain that the score is not given often enough, they will also complain if it becomes repetitive. So instead of always saying, "Bulldogs 14, Pirates 7," try: "The Bulldogs are up by a touchdown. . . ."

Continues

Focus on Technique Continued

A final note: remember that sports coverage, like the sporting event itself, is a team event. Big egos are seldom if ever appreciated. On-air people should take note that dozens of dedicated folks are working as hard as they are. Theresa Schindler, head of the Big East Sports Network, requires announcers to sit in the production truck before the game. "We want them to realize," she says, "how many people work hard to make the program a success."[2]

[2] Remarks made November 12, 1994, at National Association of College Broadcasters panel "Sports Production," presented with Len Clark, general manager of WJEV-FM, and Warren Kozierski, WBSU-FM; several of the suggestions provided here were discussed at that panel.

of buffoon. He or she always got the forecast wrong, but went on day after day oblivious to this incredible ineptitude. The weathercaster stood in front of a crude map on which he or she drew crude lines with a marker. If the weather person was a woman, she was often chosen for her good looks and treated as a bubblehead.

Most local weather people today are cast in an image that is the complete opposite of the insulting image of the incompetent buffoon or the empty-headed blonde. Weathercasting in general is given the status of a scientific endeavor that can affect the safety and well-being of viewers as well as their lifestyles. The weather person, as a result, is treated with the respect appropriate for a knowledgeable expert in a complex field.

Computerized Weather Graphic Systems

The image of competence in weather people is enhanced by the high-tech surroundings that now make up the typical weather segment. Sophisticated computerized graphic systems, like the one in Figure 9.2, make complex weather patterns and principles easy to understand for even the most unscientific of viewers.

Accu-Weather's Joel Myers, whose Pennsylvania-based weather service is used by CNN, MSNBC, and some two hundred television stations in the United States and Canada, says that the sophisticated weather graphics came into their own during the 1980s. It was a time of "dramatic transition from hand-drawn weather maps and magnetic boards to sophisticated, attractive graphics prepared on microcomputer graphic systems," says Myers.

Among the graphics offered by Accu-Weather are regional maps, temperature band and thunderstorm graphics, and jet stream graphics that show

Figure 9.2   This surface map by Accu-Weather is one of several varieties of weather graphics available to its clients. Maps are updated throughout the day and delivered to clients via phone line or satellite.

Photo courtesy of Accu-Weather, Inc.

movement. A staff of 100 meteorologists and artists create the graphics and are available to speak with on-air talent, according to Myers.

The NOAA Weather Service (www.NOAA.gov) is another source available to weather forecasters. Both radio and television stations use it to get the latest Weather Service data quickly so that listeners and viewers can be apprised regularly of changes in weather conditions in the listening and viewing area. Television stations use the service to create the severe weather advisories that are broadcast using a crawl across the television screen while regular programming continues.

The extensive use of TV weather graphics means that weather people often work closely with station art departments to create tailor-made computer graphics that combine the capabilities of more than one system. Computer "graphics" systems combine with the general weather data systems to allow for specialized maps that focus on specific weather features of particular interest on a given day.

For the aspiring weather person, all this technology means that to prepare for a job in TV weather, you need enough computer literacy to let you learn how to operate computerized graphic systems that use the latest innovations in software. Systems vary widely from station to station and they change continually. Your best bet is to become generally knowledgeable with computer graphics, so you'll be able to apply your skills to whatever system you may encounter.

In small-market operations, the weather person often prepares the graphics that form the centerpiece of weather segments. In some markets art departments may provide assistance, but the weather person still does much of the hands-on work of preparing the graphics. Most veteran weather reporters say that the best way to get this experience is by interning at a local TV station. Although difficult to come by, weather internships will give you a substantial advantage in learning what's currently available in weather graphics and how they can be used to create an authoritative on-air weather segment.

In radio, weather is seldom a specialty for on-air talent, although some stations use reports by area meteorologists to lend authority to forecasts and to tailor them specifically to the listening area. For most stations, weather information is supplied by the same wire service that provides news and feature material to the station. The sheer volume of weather information on the AP wire service seems out of proportion to its presence on the air. Figure 9.3, for example, shows the kinds of data supplied by the AP wire. The reason for the high volume of weather information, of course, is that stations have little need for old weather information. Timely forecasts are essential, as are accurate data on current conditions. All wire service clients receive forecasts for a number of regions. They then select the data that fit their particular needs at the time.

The use of radar systems in radio allows stations to track weather systems over time and alert listeners to changes in conditions in specific localities. This information is available to stations via the Internet. And computerized systems—such as Meteorlogix's MxWeatherSpan—supply stations with real-time data fed into a computer to produce forecasts, road conditions, and wind conditions.

Weather, then, has become a broadcast specialty that requires some highly specific skills by the on-air talent. In television and to an extent in radio, those reporting weather need more than an ability to perform well on the air. They also need a good basic knowledge of meteorology, and the computer skills necessary to effectively use the sophisticated computerized graphic and information systems that have become major components of modern broadcast weather reporting.

Meteorologists working exclusively in radio often are employed by one of a number of forecasting firms that provide local feeds to radio stations.

A Typical Workday for a Weathercaster

In television, the weathercaster for the 6 and 11 o'clock news might arrive at the station at 3:30 and begin to extract weather information from a computerized database. Several different weather maps are fed via the Web, and the information on those maps must be studied and digested. Such information

---

Figure 9.3   Weather information from the Associated Press wire.

```
AP-PA-HTEMPS     V0000 07-30 0217

AP-PA-HTEMPS<

12PM EST PENNSYLVANIA THIS HOUR
```

TOWN	WEATHER	TEMP	WIND	FLSLK	VIS	HUM	BRMTR	HI	LOW	PCPN
ERIE	HAZE	83	S 14	92	6	57%	29.88F	83	69	
FRANKLIN	HIGH CLDS	79	S 12	87	7	64%	29.96F			
PITTSBURG INTL	HIGH CLDS	83	S 9	96	7	65%	29.95F	83	66	
PITTSBURG ALGY	HIGH CLDS	79	S 6	90	7	64%	29.95F	79	67	
LATROBE	PTLY CLDY	84	SW 6		8		30.00F	84	63	
DU BOIS	MSTLY CDY	78	S 7	87	10	64%	30.00F	78	62	
BRADFORD	MSTLY CDY	78	S 12	84	10	60%	30.01F	78	60	
ALTOONA	HIGH CLDS	77	SW 5	88	10	69%	30.00S	78	63	
WILLIAMSPORT	MSTLY CLDY	81	SE 3	94	15	65%	29.98F	81	67	
HARRISBURG	HAZE	79	NE 6	91	6	69%	29.97F	79	69	
MIDDLETOWN	MSTLY CDY	78	E 6	92	7	76%	29.96F	79	70	
WLKS BRE SCRTN	PTLY CLDY	81	N 5	90	12	54%	29.98F	81	64	
ALLENTOWN	HAZE	80	S 6	90	5	60%	29.98F	80	69	
READING	MSTLY CDY	82	SE 7	99	7	77%	29.95F	82	74	
WILLOW GROVE	HAZE	81	E 6	91	6	58%	30.01S	81	68	
PHILDLPHIA INT	MSTLY CDY	80	E 8	90	7	62%	29.98S	80	69	
PHILDLPHIA NE	MSTLY CDY	81	NE 9	91	7	60%	29.98S	81	68	

```
AP-NP-07-30-90   1204EDT<+
```

---

includes patterns of upper air movement, temperature, and wind direction. The weathercaster then begins to prepare his or her maps. The maps are computer generated, like the one pictured in Figure 9.4.

Preparation for the Show

For some weathercasts, as many as 15 or 20 different maps will be prepared. Data are updated constantly and stored on computer disk for recall during

Figure 9.4   A detail of a TV weathercaster's weather map, which is fed to the station by special printing machines.

airing of the weather. Before the weather segment airs, the forecaster will have prepared the maps and determined their order. He or she does a quick rehearsal of the patter that accompanies each graphic.

Graphic	Audio
Large satellite projection	A nice day in the Northeast today, with only a bit of light cloud cover from Pennsylvania . . .
Closer projection	The only trouble spot is this warm front, which will move . . .
Fronts illustrated on colored map	. . . into our area by tomorrow morning.

Good weathercasting requires poise before the camera, a confident delivery, ability to ad-lib, and careful attention to posture and gestures. Many beginning weathercasters have a tendency to speak too quickly. Slowing down and delivering the forecast with greater interest and intensity can almost always improve the effort.

Remember that during most weather presentations you'll be standing in front of a blank wall. Although actual physical maps are sometimes used in weather forecasting, computer images electronically projected behind the announcer are the norm.

The first rule is to keep a close eye on the camera that shows the map (and you) on the prompting device. Ask the camera operator to move as close to you as he or she can so you can clearly perceive the relationship of you to the map, which is electronically keyed in behind you.

Second, don't be too quick to point to a particular area on the map. Pointing in an imaginary dimension (at a blank wall while you are coordinating your hand motion with the image you see on the prompter) takes practice. While you're picking up the skill, try to confine your gestures to general regions—or else you may wind up talking about tornadoes in Kansas when you are pointing to Illinois.

Weather Emergencies

In times of potentially unpleasant or violent weather, the weather forecaster's job becomes pressured. Weather reporting is particularly intense during the thunderstorm season in midsummer and in periods of heavy winter snowfall. Probably the most white-knuckled of all forecasting is done in the Midwest, where tornadoes are a major threat, or along the East Coast and Gulf Coast during hurricane season. Weather forecasters may be called on to do extensive explanations of weather phenomena and must be prepared to respond to audience questions during weather emergencies.

If you plan a career in weather, be aware that there is more involved than designing maps and developing an on-air style. In times of weather emergency, you will have the heaviest responsibilities in the news report.

Narration

The art and science of reading audio to juxtapose with video is rapidly developing into a distinct specialty. One reason for this is that firms and organizations increasingly use videotapes and PowerPoint presentations.

Documentaries also frequently use an off-camera narrator. Some narration is done on camera, but most is done voice over video. However, the term *voice-over* has acquired a separate meaning in relation to commercials and news, so the word *narration* more accurately describes the process of reading a script off the camera.

Purpose of a Narration

A narration must reinforce the program, providing an ebb and flow that matches with the video image on the screen. The voice must communicate

Box 9.2

EFFECTIVE NARRATION TECHNIQUES

Industrial narrations, news narrations, and documentary work require some specialized skills. The vocal approach to a narration is not the same as for commercials or news. Among the techniques useful for this task are the following:

1. Strive to develop an open easiness, a personality behind the voice that communicates but does not dominate.

2. If working to a picture, position the screen and your script where both can be seen easily, so that you don't have to strain and adopt an unnatural posture. The problem of awkward posture, with its negative effects on voice and delivery, is common in narration situations but not often recognized.

3. Pay close attention to the projection of mood, a major requirement in narration. Project what you feel is the appropriate mood, along with the appropriate measure of personal involvement with the copy.

4. Avoid a hard-sell delivery. Narration, for the most part, requires more subtlety than do other assignments.

5. If long segments must be delivered strictly to time, use the mark-ups shown in Chapter 3 to indicate time cues. The right reading, for example, might have the second paragraph begin 2.5 seconds into the manufacturing scene. A note of this on your copy can indicate whether an adjustment is in order to hit the next scene properly.

effectively without being intrusive. Box 9.2 highlights some effective narration techniques.

Synchronizing Narration with Video or Slides

Narration can be recorded with the performer looking at a monitor, or simply taped and edited in later. Many producers favor narration working to picture because it saves them additional work in the editing process. Many announcers, though, favor recording the narration straight, without the distraction of a monitor. Some narrators will choose to work one way or the other, depending on the situation. Will Lyman (Figure 9.5), narrator of the PBS series *Frontline* and *Vietnam: A Television History*, notes that his technique varies.

Figure 9.5

Will Lyman, narrator of the PBS *Frontline* **series and** *Vietnam: A Television History.*

Photo courtesy of Will Lyman.

"*Frontline* is occasionally done without seeing the video. But for the Vietnam series, I requested to work to picture so I would know what kind of scene I was speaking over. I didn't want to blast through some shocking picture."

Hosting Special Programming

Many of the more interesting assignments in broadcast work, such as acting as host of a children's show, are mostly extinct on the local level. Others, including being host of a radio call-in program, are increasing. The role of host in any presentation, though, can be an interesting one. Many of the specialty assignments described in this chapter are good part-time options for a broadcaster. Play-by-play, for instance, is an interesting way to supplement your income in a small market. Rare assignments such as game shows or movie programs will be part time by their very natures.

If you have an opportunity to try a specialty assignment, take the job if at all possible and if the job will not sidetrack you from your ultimate career goal. Exposure to the demands of these jobs will help you improve as an all-around broadcast professional.

Master of Ceremonies

An infrequent but challenging assignment involves MCing such events as telethons or on-air fund-raisers. Here, the performer must have the ability to ad-lib virtually indefinitely. Also, he or she has to keep track of various and sundry schedules and activities.

Think About It

RACIAL STEREOTYPES FROM A DIFFERENT ERA

During the Golden Age of Radio—the time when radio, not television, was the mass entertainer—situation comedies flourished over the airwaves. One extraordinarily popular comedy was called *Amos 'n' Andy* and featured a white cast playing blacks. The program was so popular in the 1920s and 1930s that people planned their evenings around it, and some stores would simply close down during an *Amos 'n' Andy* show because they knew that most people would be home, by their radios.

The comedians spoke in a broad, absurdly exaggerated dialect, and many of the characters were portrayed as shiftless and lazy, keenly interested only in gambling and drinking.

Amos 'n' Andy was frequently revived for retrospective radio programs, but beginning in the 1960s some listeners began to object to the program because it perpetuated a stereotype and ridiculed blacks. Some stations refused to play *Amos 'n' Andy*, but others did, maintaining that the program was a reflection of the past, and history is history.

What would you do? If you were a specialty host of a program that featured clips from old-time radio, would you play *Amos 'n' Andy*? What about World War II–era radio dramas that referred to the Japanese, with whom we were at war, as "Japs"? Would you play these?

The MC job, as those who have tried it know, entails a huge amount of physical and mental strain. Humor, intelligence, and good interviewing skills are essential. The primary responsibility is the ability to inject excitement into what may be intrinsically dull. Being an MC requires you to weigh the needs of the program against the sensibilities of your audience. In Think About It, you'll see that this job requires poise and good, sound judgment.

Radio Talk Show Host

As discussed earlier, the role of talk show host is demanding. It primarily demands interviewing skills but also requires good to excellent ad-libbing ability and strong projection of a personality.

Because radio talk is an entertainment medium, a host's career will be short-lived if he or she cannot captivate an audience. Another useful attribute is a sense of humor because callers can be rude or abusive. Helpful, too, is a good sense of when the talk is bordering on the slanderous.

A broad base of knowledge is essential to the talk show host's job. You simply cannot do without it.

Movie Host

The "sprocket jockey" still flourishes in some markets. The setting is usually a simulated screening room, but some presentations involve the host in costume, particularly the shows that feature horror movies. Specialized movie channels such as American Movie Classics have brought a resurgence of this job.

Few announcers make their entire living from hosting movie presentations, but it is an interesting assignment. The prime requirement is the ability to act relaxed and natural in an unnatural situation. Knowledge is important, too. Movie buffs can be more fanatical about trivia than even sports fans.

Children's Show Host

It is probably impossible to manufacture an on-screen liking for children if you prefer to avoid them in real life. Hosting a children's show involves understanding youngsters and being able to talk with them, not at them or down to them. Many elementary school teachers have become successful hosts in this sort of programming.

On the local level, children's shows are largely a thing of the past. A well-intentioned FCC regulation prohibiting the show host from delivering commercials or introducing the product has resulted in a decline of local advertisers, which has all but eliminated this important source of funding.

Game Show Host

Although rare, local game shows still exist, often in the form of quiz programs that pit one school against another. On the national level, only a handful of personalities make a living at game shows.

The requirements for hosting programming of this type include the ability to handle figures easily because almost any game requires tallying points. You'll have to think quickly if something goes wrong, and above all you must be able to instill excitement and enthusiasm in each contestant's performance.

Health and Medicine Reporting

An increasing number of local television stations employ on-air talent who cover, either as their entire beat or as parts of their jobs, issues related to health. In some areas, especially large markets, those reporters are often physicians. General-assignment reporters, though, can and do take on these assignments.

Often the health and medicine report is mated with material fed from various satellite news services. The national reporter, who may be a physician, will feed material that can be localized and integrated with material gathered locally.

Although physicians and other health professionals have a natural "in" for such coverage, it's probably safe to say that any reporter can cover the medical beat as long as he or she knows how to talk with medical professionals, gather information, and relate it to viewers' and listeners' everyday lives. In fact, an experienced journalist has an advantage over the health professional in some respects, in that the journalist generally has few preconceived notions or biases and is likely to have a keen insight into what topics interest the average citizen.

Consumer Reporting

Just as physicians have worked their way onto the air as health reporters, many attorneys find themselves employed as consumer reporters. But being a lawyer is certainly not a requirement for this job; tenacity is. You generally cover stories of long duration; investigating a complaint may take weeks or months of waiting for responses by mail or telephone.

The role of the consumer reporter is sometimes broadened to that of something like a freewheeling social critic. For example, a very successful series that ran in the New York area recently dealt with drivers' increasing propensity not to yield the right of way to ambulances and fire trucks. This is an example of "consumer" reporting, because taxpayers are paying for services slowed down by inconsiderate drivers, and it also touches on some deep and important social issues.

Summary

Specialty assignments in broadcasting can be challenging. Although they call for special skills, the basic requirements of broadcast communication still form the underpinning of the announcer's abilities. To specialize successfully, one often needs a specific academic or practical background.

Sports requires a great deal of knowledge and a willingness by the announcer to learn about sports new to him or her. Many sportscasters make their reputations as "personalities," but there are serious issues in sports coverage, and journalistic skills are necessary.

Sports anchoring is stressful because it involves a great deal of last-minute checking before going on the air. Sports anchors must appeal to local audience interests, and they must be energetic and versatile in their on-air approach. Play-by-play announcers must have an in-depth knowledge of the sport. Each sport presents its own particular set of problems. Football, for example, is hard to follow because it involves so many players, rules, and technically oriented plays.

Play-by-play announcers must be excited by the games they cover. They must avoid repetition, and they must not call plays before they have verified the information. Also, announcers must do a good job on commercials.

Weather reporters are often certified meteorologists. They work with computerized databases and, for television, create attractive graphic presentations. In addition, the weather anchor must present the information succinctly and with poise. The job of a weather forecaster can become very tense during weather emergencies.

Narration is a specialized skill. Good narrators do not intrude on program content. Narration must be relatively low key, and the projection of the proper mood is imperative.

Broadcasters occasionally have the opportunity to act as hosts of special types of programming. Except for radio talk show hosts, most of these assignments, such as telethon MC and host of movie presentations or children's shows, are not full-time jobs but, rather, offer supplemental income and interesting opportunities to expand skills.

Exercises

1. Use a portable cassette machine to record a play-by-play segment for a televised basketball, football, baseball, or hockey game. Do your preparation by compiling information from prewrites in the newspaper. If there is not enough information in the local paper, pick up a relevant copy of a sporting magazine. With the TV audio down, of course, record your own version of the play-by-play, and review the tape.

2. Record the narration from the script in the drill section, Appendix A, of this book. You can get a fair idea of the video components from the shot descriptions immediately above the copy to be read by the narrator. Pay particular attention to mood and pace.

3. Watch three weather forecasters on the three major network affiliates in your area. Take comprehensive notes on program elements. In a few paragraphs, compare and contrast the weathercasters for the following:

   a. Level of interest they show

   b. Level of interest they instill in you

   c. Energy conveyed

   d. Credibility

   e. Use of graphics

TEN

Commercials and Acting

*C*ombining commercials and acting in one chapter may seem odd at first glance. Acting is usually considered to be an artistic endeavor. And critics of broadcasting often give us the impression that commercials could never be an art form.

In fact, however, broadcast commercials are done with the highest production standards, using the best talent available. The people you see and hear in broadcast commercials have usually had years of classical training and considerable experience in drama. The competition is fierce, the rewards great, and the work exacting.

This chapter discusses the basics of commercials and the performer's role in them. The techniques of acting are presented and discussed, with a focus on how they apply to radio and television commercials. The chapter closes with an exploration of freelance commercial roles.

Basics of Commercial Announcing

During the past 20 years, broadcast advertising has come into its own as a separate discipline. Production capabilities are part of the reason. In the early days of television, for example, a standard commercial might involve nothing more than one camera pointing at an announcer pouring a glass of beer and giving his pitch. Only occasionally did any sort of drama come into play.

Modern commercials, though, run the gamut from 30-second mini-dramas, to collages of action scenes, to the mundane hidden-camera testimonial.

Radio commercials have evolved, too. In the early days of radio, many advertisements featured grand-sounding speeches describing the high quality of a particular product. Today the emphasis has shifted to shorter phrases that usually do not so much describe the attributes of the product as portray its benefits (how it will make you feel better, look better, and so on). Radio advertising now also makes much greater use of the dramatic scene, the mini-drama.

The biggest difference in modern radio advertising is the focus on communicating with a *particular* audience. Commercial producers often fashion several versions of an ad: one for hit radio, one for country, one for easy listening, and one for adult contemporary formats. Hitting a specific target audience is what modern radio is all about. A really good performer can gear his or her reading to a specific audience.

Types of Commercials

Commercials come in several shapes and sizes, and a familiarity with them is helpful to a performer. Although there is some overlap, we discuss radio and television commercials separately.

RADIO COMMERCIALS   Most ads fall into these categories: a straight reading of a *script,* a *donut,* an *ad-lib,* an *acted scene,* a *man-in-the-street,* or a heavily produced *montage.* Many spots contain elements from several of these categories. The following descriptions summarize the particular demands the respective categories place on a performer.

Straight reading: All you have to work with are the words in the copy. A straight reading demands careful attention to variations of pitch and pace. The performer must also be aware of the need for proper emphasis on words. Vocal quality is important, as is a good level of energy in the voice. The straight reading sometimes has music underneath the voice, called a music "bed."

Donut: Usually furnished by an advertising agency, a donut has copy already recorded on the beginning and end. The commercial is called a donut because it has a "hole" in the middle, which a local performer is called on to fill. For example, a typical donut may open with 10 seconds of a jingle for shock absorbers, then 10 seconds of musical bed, followed by another 10 seconds of jingle and copy. The 10 seconds of musical bed in the middle—the hole—allows the local franchiser of the shock absorbers to give his (or her) message. From the performer's standpoint, a donut requires particular attention to timing; the copy must be read in the time allotted. Also, the performer needs to match the style projected by the prerecorded elements. Reading over a bed requires timing and attention to the flow of the music.

Ad-lib: "Ad-lib" means improvised, done extemporaneously. An ad-lib commercial is usually done from a fact sheet, like the one on page 301. Sometimes, skilled broadcast performers can construct a convincing ad-lib by playing around with the wording of a set script. Ad-lib spots are quite popular at radio stations that employ one particularly good, well-known announcer. The ad-lib commercial is usually done live, although sometimes it is recorded for later airplay. Some buyers of airtime are fond of the ad-lib commercial because they feel that their product or service will benefit from identification with the air personality. In fact, the ad-lib commercial gives the appearance of a personal endorsement of the product.

The ad-lib is probably the most difficult type of radio commercial to do well. Rather than simply reading a phrase, you have to think of that phrase at the exact second you need it and deliver that line convincingly. The only way to train for this skill is constant practice. Bill St. James, one of the top freelance announcers in New York, recalls that he developed ad-lib ability by inventing descriptive copy for magazine photos. This is a good practice, and one of the exercises in this chapter focuses on it.

Incidentally, an announcer who can ad-lib convincingly has an eye and ear for detail, which also is developed only by practice. Keep alert for the inspiration you can draw from the sleek lines of a car or the condensation on a bottle of beer. Good ad-lib skills are extremely valuable to an air personality.

Acted scene: Normally, two voices are used in this kind of commercial, often a male and female. Because radio spots are short and lacking visual cues, every effort is made to avoid distraction, hence the variation between voices and the limited number.

The dialogue is usually informal, uncomplicated, and often humorous. At best it is the beautifully timed exchanges of the legendary Bob and Ray or Dick and Bert. At worst, an acted scene is a local "husband and wife" enactment, something to the effect of "My, dear, have you seen the prices at . . ."

The acted scene demands a skill often overlooked in typical broadcast training: the ability to assume a character and sound natural while doing it. Remember, the husband who complains about scratchy collars is not supposed to sound like Don Pardo announcing a game show contestant, and the wife is not convincing if she delivers a line about spray starch like Dame Judith Anderson playing Lady Macbeth.

Acting skills are essential for performers who want to pursue commercial work, and we address those skills later in this chapter.

Man-in-the-street: The man (or woman) interviewed about a product or caught unaware in the act of choosing the sponsor's detergent is not always a professional performer, although professionals do appear in such ads. Aspiring actors and actresses have been known to write companies praising a product in hopes of securing a man-in-the-street role. When a professional performer does assume such a role, a natural and unaffected manner is an absolute must.

Heavily produced montage: In the fast-moving genre of hit radio, some commercials contain many production elements and brief snippets of copy.

This category can entail a combination of almost all the others: a sound effect, a quick dramatic scene, several pieces of music, and so forth.

This type of commercial requires the ability to put a great deal of meaning and excitement into a few words. You do not have time to develop thoughts or characterizations, so those words must be precisely right. "Stock car racing at the fairground—the time of your life!" is an example. That one line has to convey all the excitement and allure of the event.

During production of these montage commercials, a good sense of timing is also required because a phrase might have to fit precisely between two sound effects or other production elements.

TELEVISION COMMERCIALS   Many of the structures common in radio are adapted to television, although the TV ads have their own particular set of nuances. The basic categories of TV commercials are *mini-dramas, spokesperson presentations, pitch presentations,* and *voice-overs.*

Mini-drama: In TV, this kind of commercial is usually more than just an acted scene. It is a full-range 30- or 60-second drama that presents characters, conflict, and resolution at breakneck speed. When done for national agencies, these commercials are at the very top level of production lavishness and can be incredibly expensive. They involve the top competitive actors and actresses in the field, often chosen because they have the right smiles or interesting, arresting faces.

Although some of these mini-dramas appear downright hokey, keep in mind that they generally do the job they're constructed to do. Do you remember a series of Sprint commercials where there is an interpersonal problem created in each situation as a result of cellular static? Even though these commercials are attempts to make us laugh at a ridiculous situation, they do deliver the message that analog cellular service is not as good as digital service. If you think about it, you'll be able to recall dozens of mini-dramas where some soap, food or household product has helped resolve conflict in a situation. Effective performance in a mini-drama requires excellent acting skills and a high level of energy.

Spokesperson presentation: This type of commercial often involves a celebrity using his or her actual identity, or it can be an *implied identity,* using someone who is recognizable as a character, but not necessarily as himself or herself. Jerry Seinfeld, for example, has done a series of commercials as a comedian in a variety of comedic situations for a credit card company.

A spokesperson does not have to be a celebrity, but he or she must have some sort of implied identity. In other words, an unknown but distinguished-looking performer can give a very convincing spokesperson presentation for a product or service. In this case, the performer's implied identity as a distinguished and intelligent person, rather than celebrity status, lends authority to the commercial.

What does this require of a performer? Basically, an authoritative presence and an honest, convincing delivery.

Pitch presentation: This harkens back to the old days of television, when the "pitchman" would deliver a sales message about a product. The difference between a pitchman and a spokesperson is that the former is identified neither as a celebrity nor as a particular kind of individual. The product is of prime importance; the pitchman purely a conduit of information.

For example, consider a well-known celebrity who sells life insurance and dog food (not at the same time, of course). When he sells life insurance, he acts as a trusted spokesperson, implying that he, as an intelligent and trustworthy person, endorses the insurance. When he gives a stand-up dog food commercial on the set of a variety show, he is not claiming any expertise but only touting the product's benefits, acting as a conveyor of information. The dog food is the star, rather than the performer.

A performer in a pitch presentation must have a very high energy level and must move well and handle props with ease.

Voice-over: The performer who reads the copy is not seen in a voice-over commercial. Rather, the performer's voice is heard as a major component of the sound track.

The voice-over format is an extremely popular way of constructing commercials. It has the advantage of giving top billing to the product, not to an on-camera performer. A variant of voice-over work is dubbing in the voice of an actor who looks but does not sound the part in a commercial.

What we usually refer to as voice-over requires an excellent sense of timing, the ability to read voice to picture, and the skill to communicate vocally without distracting from the visual elements of the presentation. In many cases, the voice-over announcer is virtually anonymous, in the sense that a trumpet player is anonymous in an orchestral setting. After all, no one listening to a musical bed in a commercial stands up and says, "Listen to that trumpet!" If that were the case, the trumpet player, regardless of his or her skill, would have detracted from the message. This is a rather roundabout way of making the point that the viewer is not supposed to be astounded by the voice-over announcer's fine delivery. In fact, much of the general public probably is not aware that there is such a category as voice-over announcers. Voice-over work is quite challenging and, under the right set of circumstances, very profitable.

Radio and television commercials take a variety of incarnations. Keep in mind that many hybrid forms use several elements of the foregoing categories.

Now that we've defined the *whats,* let's examine some of the *whys.*

Goals of a Commercial

It is often assumed that the goal of a commercial is simply "to sell a product." In the long run that may be true, but there are many intermediate steps in the process. Is the purpose of a line to "sell" a bank or to make the listener believe that the bank is staffed by knowledgeable and helpful people who take an individual interest in their clients? More often, the latter statement is the immediate goal, with selling the bank a broader objective.

A performer really has to understand the goal of a commercial before he or she can come up with a decent delivery. Dig a little deeper into the copy. Find out what the copywriter is trying to get across in each word and phrase. For example, do not assume that the only goal of a travel agent's commercial is to sell vacations. In the long run, that may be true, but the immediate goals for a broadcast communicator might be to

- Make the listener aware of how absolutely miserable this winter weather is
- Convey a sense of excitement concerning the possibility of visiting a Caribbean resort
- Communicate the idea that this vacation is a real possibility, an affordable option

Being fully aware of the goals of a commercial will give you valuable cues to the points that ought to be stressed and to the proper inflections and rate of reading. This applies to any line you're delivering as an "announcer" or to any copy being delivered in the character of someone else, an "acted" part.

Straight versus Acted Delivery

One common fault of commercial performers is the inability to assume a role, the tendency to take the guise of an announcer when the performer should be donning the persona of a character in a play. There is a very fine line between a **straight delivery,** as in the delivery used by a radio personality reading a script, and an **acted delivery.** The importance of understanding acted deliveries lies not in differentiating but in being able to play a role convincingly.

For example, the producer of a college promotional film looking for a narrator auditioned a number of announcers who made their livings in broadcasting, and actors who made their livings on stage and in film. An actor won hands down. "I wanted someone who could convince the audience that he was an alumnus of our college," the producer said, "and who could assume that role. The fellow we chose had only an average voice, but he really slipped into that identity. Most of the announcers would have been inappropriate."

Do not assume, however, that a broadcast communicator is always required to take on an identity. Whereas an identity was indicated for the college film, the narrator of a *National Geographic* documentary would appropriately use a straight delivery, almost a news style. The narrator, in that case, is not taking on a role.

In most cases, the producer of a commercial or other work will give you guidance about which type of delivery to give. The crucial thing from your standpoint is the ability to summon acting skills when you are called on to play a part.

Acting

Although this book cannot present an acting course per se, acting skills are essential to a performer and are often overlooked in broadcast curricula. Many professionals in the commercial field recommend that students take as many drama courses as possible, and that's good advice. You cannot be trained as an actor in one chapter, but some exposure to the principles of acting is valuable, both for picking up practical skills and as a jumping-off point to further instruction.

In this overview we discuss the methods of *assuming a role, giving a natural delivery,* and using actors' *techniques.*

Assuming a Role

Many jokes have been made about the actor who stops in midscene and asks the director, "But what's my motivation?" That is often a legitimate question because motivation is the key to assuming a role and carrying it through a situation described in a plot.

Why does a character say a line? Why does he or she say it in a particular manner? Why does the character look, talk, walk a certain way? All those aspects should reflect motivation, and being able to convey motivation is what spells the difference between an actor and a mere reader of lines.

An actor playing a southern gentleman type will have to do more than work up a drawl. If the character is indeed a southern gentleman, he will undoubtedly have a certain way of moving: courtly and gentle gestures, perhaps. A southern gentleman is likely to have a proud bearing. If he is older, he will undoubtedly move differently from another southerner, 20 years younger.

A wide array of physical traits make up a character. As the great acting teacher Konstantin Stanislavski noted, small physical actions "and the moments of belief in them" acquire a great deal of significance on stage.

Other traits will play a role in the actor's rendition of a character. Do highly educated people speak differently than people with little education do? In most cases, they do, of course. And these traits must be *consistent* within the portrayal of a character. That is why television and screen writers often work up a complete biography of a character, including education, military service, political affiliations, and family history. Most of this information is never used directly, but it is important to the actors for the sake of character development and consistency. Novelists often undertake much the same process, drawing up an extensive biography of each character before the book is started.

You must do the same as an actor in a commercial. If background information is not presented to you, invent some. Make the character a *real* person. Assume you have been assigned to do the voice of a banker in a commercial. What kind of neighborhood does she live in? What does her family

---

Box 10.1

TRAITS OF A CHARACTER

- Voice quality
- Posture and movement
- Facial expression
- General character traits

---

mean to her? What political party does she belong to? How much education has she had? Many of the questions may seem irrelevant. Indeed, for the immediate needs of the role, they very well may be, but filling in the details that make a character human can help you bring that character to life.

Let's look at another example. You have been cast in the role of a tough cop in a TV commercial for cold medicine. The advertiser, who wants to overcome the "macho" male's disdain for taking medicine for the sniffles, has constructed a commercial featuring a big-city patrol officer walking down the street, saying, "You know, when people are depending on me, I have to be at my best. I can't let a cold get me down. So when I feel the first signs of a cold coming on, I take Coldex. It's tougher than even *my* cold."

The lines have all been written, the camera angles all blocked out, but it is your job to do the most important part. You must bring this character to life. How do you do it? By creating a personality sketch and relating those traits to your character's traits. Here is a possible—but not definitive—point-by-point analysis (highlighted in Box 10.1).

- *Voice quality.* Do big-city cops talk softly? Hardly. A gritty, rough voice is a possibility, as is a faint hint of an Irish brogue.

- *Posture and movement.* Most likely this character would have a purposeful stride, with a great deal of confidence in his step. One realistic gesture quite in keeping with this character is to point to the camera (the viewer) when he says, "You know, when people. . . ." When he finishes the line ". . . tougher than even *my* cold," this character just might point to himself with his thumb. Gestures would typically be heavy and broad.

  Assuming this manner of posture and movement would be helpful even if the characterization were for radio. Many radio performers use posture, gestures, and facial expression as a way of reinforcing the character.

- *Facial expression.* In the movies, police officers run the gamut from social smiles to angry insolence. Perhaps the image of a concerned but tough Irish cop would be in order here, assuming you physically look the part of an Irish cop.

Talking slightly out of the corner of the mouth would be appropriate for this character. (Remember, *appropriateness* is the key. Talking from the side of the mouth would not be appropriate for the character of a librarian.) Another appropriate trait would be a squinty expression, common among patrol officers who walk dusty, windy city streets. Other facial expressions? Try a knitted brow for the line ". . . when people are depending on me" and a slight jut of the jaw for the line ". . . tougher than even *my* cold."

Note that the goal is not to assemble a mechanical grab-bag of expressions, but rather to decide what expressions and mannerisms would be believable in this character and would accentuate the message.

- *General character traits.* We want the character to be likable, so let's invent some likable points. He is easygoing but tough. Our cop has a lot of street smarts, but probably not an extensive formal education. He likes making small talk with the merchants on his route and has a real fondness for kids, but he won't take any guff from them.

  A little personal history: he is the father of six, his brother is a priest, and he gets misty-eyed at Irish ballads.

  Obviously, all these details will not be reflected point by point in the commercial, but the traits will build a persona for the character you invent. The personality traits add up to a satisfying whole, rather than a cardboard cutout.

Think of those four categories—voice quality, posture and movement, facial expression, and character traits—for any character you portray in a radio or television commercial. And although acting in a dramatic series is beyond the scope of this book, keep in mind that the process of defining characters applies to all types of drama.

Now let's apply those four categories to two different characters.

PERSONALITY SKETCH

Character: A young male homeowner telling us why he got his mortgage at a particular bank.

Voice Quality: You would not expect a gravelly voice or a deep bass from a younger man. However, the voice should transmit the qualities of confidence and responsibility. After all, he is trying to convince you of the right way to make an important decision.

Posture and Movement: Youth is important here, to show that young people can get mortgages, so the character's posture and movement must reflect health and vigor. He probably exercises regularly, perhaps playing racquetball. His body language would surely be open and direct. He would not sit hunched over with hands crossed over his chest. And although his posture reflects confidence, he doesn't have a cocky swagger, and he projects a certain vulnerability.

Facial Expressions: Smiles easily, but definitely is not the giggly type. Sincere, he has a level, but not challenging, gaze. By contrast, our policeman friend probably had eyes that drilled right through you.

Character Traits: Probably well educated, an engineer perhaps. He is organized, neat, owns an SUV, and is a member of his local church group.

PERSONALITY SKETCH

Character: A 25-year-old career woman searching for a new car. The commercial copy is intended to show that she knows what she wants, and knows that the people at Smith Dodge can give it to her with a minimum of fuss.

Voice Quality: Bright and energetic, but certainly not sultry and definitely not dumb-blonde breathless. There's no aggressive quality in her voice, just a confident assertiveness.

Posture and Movement: She walks purposefully, and her posture is straight. She does not make unnecessary movements.

Facial Expressions: Intelligent expression, level gaze, smiles easily but is not a jovial type.

Character traits: Well-educated person with strongly shaped goals. She probably works very hard at her job. She is physically active and has a variety of hobbies and interests, such as skiing and jogging.

Employing character sketches has the advantage of helping you determine whether an action will be in character or out of character. Basing the personality on character sketches allows the actor to assume a role and deliver the lines with naturalness.

A "Natural" Delivery

Aim at giving a "natural" delivery. The word "natural" is somewhat deceptive because a radio or TV commercial is not a natural situation. Instead, the important element is the *appearance* of naturalness. In real life, people mumble, have speech impediments, and exhibit other characteristics we generally do not want to reproduce in a performance. "Naturalness" boils down to an unaffected performance, a projection of a recognizable character to the audience. When assuming a role, the broadcast communicator must make every effort to avoid a cloud of artificiality.

Here is where *motivation* comes into play once again. There's nothing more to motivation than understanding something about the character and understanding why he or she is delivering the line. Is the character surprised? Angry? Patiently trying to convince us of something? For instance, expand on the character of the career woman looking for a car. To give some additional insight into the character, here are some invented lines of dialogue: "I want a car that fits my lifestyle—practical, but not *too* practical. After all, what's life without a little excitement?"

These lines reveal a little more of the character's personality. She is a bit adventuresome and wants a car that does something besides transport her from place to place. However, she's a hard-working career woman, not an heiress, and probably would not opt for an exotic, expensive auto. So the lines assume a new meaning, and the actress would be wise to add just a touch of mischief to her voice and expression, some hint of the thirst for excitement that dwells beneath a staid exterior.

Another example concerns a different motivation. It is a scene in a shabby auto repair shop where the mechanic tells a young man he needs a new exhaust system.

"A whole new exhaust system?" the young man replies. "But you put in a new system just a month ago!" What is the motivation for this line? Frustration, anger, disgust with the whole operation. The character will, of course, go to the sponsor's shop next time. His reaction is pretty obvious. Other reactions and motivations might require more thought, especially in a voice-over, where there are no visual cues to reinforce the message. In most cases, the voice-over calls for a straight delivery, not assuming a role, but there is no reason not to assume certain personality traits if they are appropriate. Here are some possible ways to analyze the motivation behind voice-over copy:

Copy: Voice-over for special airline fare to California.

What the performer wants to communicate: A sense of excitement, almost incredulity, at these extremely low fares. The voice-over performer is a bearer of good news.

Copy: Voice-over to convince small investors to deal with a certain brokerage house.

What the performer wants to communicate: The voice-over performer's vocal qualities and delivery must imply that he or she is a sincere person who really wants to tell others about the good service at this particular brokerage house. The voice-over announcer might think in terms of playing the role of an intelligent neighbor.

The point is that unless these lines are delivered with motivation in mind, some artificiality will be projected into the delivery, regardless of whether

Box 10.2

CAUSES OF ARTIFICIAL DELIVERY

- Undeveloped character
- Lack of character motivation
- Unnatural pronunciation
- Stilted dialogue
- Overacting
- Inappropriate movement

the performer assumes a character. The voice-over for the airline fares, as a case in point, would not be very effective if the delivery were somber. The investment brokerage spot would be very ineffective with a singsong, top-40 disc jockey delivery. Would you invest with a brokerage house represented by an announcer who sounds as if he or she is about to say, "Hey there, girls and guys"?

One other point: it is entirely possible to assume a character and understand the meaning and motivation of the copy and still appear artificial. If character and motivation are in order, the causes of artificiality (highlighted in Box 10.2) can include the following:

1. *Unnatural pronunciation.* Be wary of saying "thee" for *the* or "ay" as in *skate* for the article *a,* which is usually pronounced "uh." Don't overenunciate.

   If the script calls for a dialect, make sure you can speak it convincingly. Critical listening with a tape recorder is the only reliable guide. Most acting textbooks contain phoneticized dialect guides, and it would be very helpful to study them. Dialect work is extraordinarily difficult, so there's no disgrace in not being able to master it. Many broadcasters don't; just turn on your radio anywhere in the country on St. Patrick's Day.

2. *Stilted dialogue.* Sometimes artificiality is the copywriter's fault. However, the performer usually can't change dialogue. If you are having trouble with a line such as "My, this certainly is a wonderful product, Joyce; we must order it right away," walk away from the line for a few minutes. Try to say the line in your own words, paying attention to believable phrasing. Now, give the stilted line with the same type of delivery you used when in your own paraphrase. Some pieces of dialogue will never sound right, but this method can sometimes help.

3. *Overacting.* Putting too much into a performance is just as bad as inject-ing too little. The most effective way to catch overacting, or "a stench of ham," as it is sometimes called, is to have a knowledgeable teacher or colleague critique your performance. Videotaping and audiotaping help, too, of course.

4. *Inappropriate movement.* A gesture that is completely in character with the part you're playing may appear totally inappropriate on television. On TV, you are working in a confined space and must often create the illusion of movement rather than executing the movement itself.

   For example, a commercial that calls for you to walk across a used car lot requires compact and controlled movement because the distor-tion of the TV lens would make a normal gait appear as though you were bounding across a basketball court. Walking and moving on televi-sion is a skill in itself, which can be developed only by practice and viewing tapes.

Factors that add artificiality to an otherwise well-constructed perfor-mance can be eliminated only by awareness and constant practice. There are very few "naturals" who can stroll onto a site and walk and talk well because appearing on television is, as mentioned, an "unnatural" situation. The same principle applies to radio, perhaps more strongly because a performance re-lying entirely on voice can be difficult to pull off well.

Techniques

In addition to the abilities required to assume a role and to bring about a nat-ural delivery, television and radio commercials, whether acted or with a straight delivery, require mastery of certain specialized techniques. A tech-nique is loosely defined as a method whereby a performer treats certain de-tails of his or her craft. Techniques unique to television and radio are consid-ered in the sections on those topics, but we'll close this acting session by discussing techniques for improving any type of broadcast performance.

Of primary importance is the ability to *animate your delivery.* Animation literally means "putting life into," and that's exactly what you'll be called on to do when reading copy. Veteran New York voice-over commercial actor Nick Schatzki (see Figure 10.1), who has voiced commercials for clients such as Eastman Kodak Company and *Newsday,* notes that one way to bring copy to life is to visualize someone to whom you are speaking. Picture a single in-dividual, he advises, and talk directly to that person. If necessary, form a mental image of that person sitting, in miniature, on top of your microphone.

Breathing life into copy is not accomplished purely by voice quality. When talent agent Lester Lewis judges the ability of a performer, he listens for the ability to animate copy. "Don't assume that just because you have a good voice you can do commercials," Lewis says. "It's not the voice, but what you do with the voice, that's important. Also, don't think that reading 30 seconds of copy is going to be a cinch. You have to bring that copy to life. Look closely at the

Figure 10.1

Nick Schatzki, an actor who frequently does voice-over work, brings copy to life for accounts like *Newsday*, Olympia Beer, and Eastman Kodak.

Photo courtesy of Nick Schatzki

copy: What is the copywriter trying to say? What are the important points in the copy? Without understanding that, you can't give a good reading."

Understanding copy is largely a function of the methods of analysis discussed in Chapter 3. If you combine that analysis with the techniques of identifying motivation and determining the goals of a particular commercial, you can attack the job with a thorough comprehension. The following pointers are important to developing commercial technique:

1. Good acting skills will always increase your ability to communicate and animate copy. Acting training usually focuses heavily on methods of infusing life into a character. Many pros, including Lester Lewis, recommend that you take a variety of drama courses and get some stage experience, if you can.

2. Working before a live audience is a helpful experience for any broadcast communicator because it gives a sense of how things play. Broadcasters trained only in broadcasting sometimes lack a sense of comedic timing, for example, a skill best honed in front of living, laughing people.

The ability to animate copy is a technique useful in both radio and television commercials, and for all practical purposes, in any other form of broadcasting, too. Techniques specific to each medium are discussed next in the sections summarizing radio commercials and television commercials.

Radio Commercials

Earlier, the basic types and structures of radio commercials were described. Radio spots rely entirely on sound, so the broadcast communicator must be particularly sensitive to what sound can do and must be adept at maximizing the impact of the sound elements. This means that you will be concerned with more than just the vocal delivery. Also important is the ability to play off other elements, such as music and sound effects. In addition, special talents are required of a radio commercial performer, talents unique to the field.

Unique Aspects of Radio Commercials

In a sense, the producer of a radio commercial has a more difficult task than does someone constructing an ad for television. Why? Because the radio copy must be aimed with pinpoint precision at a target audience. In another sense, this factor can be regarded as making the job easier because the TV producer is in the position of having to please almost everyone.

The essence of the discussion is that radio is a one-to-one medium. The successful performer on radio is the performer who can put across a message on a personal basis. You will be called on to do some tasks unique to the medium. Of primary importance is ad-libbing from a **fact sheet.**

FACT SHEET   The ability to do a credible job ad-libbing from a fact sheet, and the related ability to please sponsors, can take you very far in modern radio. The effectiveness of an ad-lib commercial lies in the injection of the performer's personality into the spot. In radio, personality is still very much alive. In earlier times, personalities such as Dick Clark could maintain that kind of role on television. Clark was the acknowledged master of the ad-lib commercial, both on radio and television. His absolutely natural delivery was stunningly effective in pleasing sponsors and motivating buyers.

There are many differences between radio and TV commercials, but the injection of personality, as shown in Box 10.3, is one thing that makes radio such a unique and compelling medium.

Production Basics

In radio, the performer often does the production work as well. This requires basic skills such as using an audio console, mixing sources, and operating a variety of equipment. The skills are essentially the same as those outlined in Chapter 5. In a commercial, the goal is to use these skills to enhance the commercial message.

The performer must be sensitive to production details, such as relative levels of sound from different sources. For example, reading over a music bed requires a delicate balance. The music can't be loud enough to drown out the voice, but the music must not be so soft as to be imperceptible.

Extensive instruction in production is beyond the scope of this text. Note that knowledge of production can always be helpful to a performer, so even if your ambitions lie in on-air work, taking as many production courses as possible will be extremely worthwhile. Why? Notice how a good grounding

Box 10.3

Ad-Libbing from a Fact Sheet: An Example

Build an effective ad-lib around this fact sheet.

- The Charter House Restaurant, 411 Grand Avenue, serves the widest array of seafood dishes in the city.
- Seafood is caught fresh every day and brought right from the boat to the kitchen.
- Specialties include lobster for two, a complete dinner with wine, Caesar salad prepared at the table, and baked potato. All for $27.95.
- Colorful atmosphere, including the Clipper Ship Lounge where fishnets line the walls. There are brass nautical decorations. One-ton anchor outside entrance.
- Owners Joey and Paul Italiano provide first-class hospitality at bargain prices.

Here is one way, but not the only way, a radio air personality might do the ad-lib:

> When you dine at the Charter House Restaurant, you get a great bargain, and you can choose from the widest array of fine seafood dishes served anywhere in the city. Do you know where the Charter House is? Well, it's up on 411 Grand Avenue, right off the Seashore Expressway, and that's important because if you know that section of the city you also know that the Charter House sits right on the water, next to where the fishing boats dock. The seafood comes right off the boats and into the Charter House kitchen, so whenever you eat at the Charter House you're getting today's catch.
>
> Right now you can enjoy the "Lobster for Two" special, a complete dinner that comes with a Caesar salad prepared at your table—hey, that's a show in itself—and you also get wine and baked potato. All for $27.95. . . remember, that's for two people, $27.95 for a complete dinner.
>
> By the way, the food at the Charter House is only part of the experience. If you've never been there, make it a point to stop in and have a drink at the Clipper Ship Lounge. . . that's the place where they have fishnets on the walls and all those brass nautical gizmos. And you'll know you're in the right place when you see the one-ton anchor outside the door.
>
> We were there last week and had a great meal and great service, too. The owners, Joey and Paul Italiano, make sure you get first-class hospitality at bargain prices. That's the Charter House Restaurant, 411 Grand Avenue.

Continues

Box 10.3 *Continued*

This announcer gave the sponsors a good deal for their advertising dollar, both in terms of content and time. And this type of commercial provides for variety: a good performer could ad-lib it four or five different ways during the day or week, giving a different emphasis each time.

---

in production techniques can help you enhance a message in a radio commercial in these examples:

- You are reading a piece that is set outdoors, but you're in the studio and picking up a lot of echo and reverberation from the walls. A basic knowledge of acoustics would let you make your spot more believable by setting up a simple baffle to block sound reflection and eliminate the echo and reverberation.

- Knowing the characteristics of different mics can enable you to choose a mic with a great deal of "presence" for an intimate feel in a perfume commercial.

- A knowledge of special effects and how to produce them can add to the message. Use of filters, for example, can cut down on the frequencies passed through the console and can produce a weird, unearthly effect, useful for attracting attention if used appropriately.

Delivery Techniques

Two more specialized techniques are indispensable in radio and also have some specific applications in television, especially in voice-over work. The techniques are *reading to time* and **compressing copy**. They are two of the most useful skills you can develop, and frequently are the talents that separate a good description from one recognized as being top drawer.

READING TO TIME   Some professionals maintain that reading to time calls for an ability you are, or are not, born with. Others contend that constant practice can develop this skill, and we're inclined to agree with the latter view. The bottom line in this dispute is that no one can teach you how to read copy in exactly 30 seconds. It is a talent that can be achieved only by experience. The goal is to develop an internal clock that lets you know when the pace has to be picked up or slowed down.

Why read to time? Well, many commercials have a certain time slot allotted for copy, and if it is 19 seconds the copy *has* to be 19 seconds, no more and no less. In most radio stations, 30-second spots must last precisely

30 seconds because they may be used in a "hole" provided in a network newscast and therefore can't fall short or run long.

Although there is no magic formula for developing this skill, incorporating the following suggestions into your practice can help speed the process of learning.

1. *Develop a familiarity with music and music phrasing.* Listen critically to music and learn to identify key changes, or the distinction between a trumpet solo and a clarinet solo. This is helpful because music beds can be used as cues. If, after a couple of rehearsals, you find that you should be giving the prices of the products when the musical key changes from C to G, you can use the key change as a landmark from which to adjust the rate at which you read the rest of your copy. In the long run, this will be easier and less distracting than trying to keep one eye glued to a timer or stopwatch. Knowing the background music also helps you to match your delivery more naturally to the music bed.

2. *When you start practicing development of a time sense, shoot for hitting 10 seconds, not 30, on the dot.* Once you have mastered 10 seconds, try reading 30-second spots exactly to time, thinking in terms of three 10-second segments. Another way to practice is to read a 30-second spot and then cut it down to 25 seconds. Do it again, aiming for 35 seconds.

3. *Mark your copy with time cues, as shown in Chapter 3.*

Compressing Copy

Successful performers frequently point out that one of the most valuable skills in their arsenals is the ability to put a lot of words into a short time. The reason is simple. Time is money, and the more commercial words a sponsor gets for his or her time allotment, the happier the sponsor will be. As a result, copy is often written very tightly, and frequently there are more words in a 30-second spot than could normally be read comfortably in 30 seconds.

This requirement may get out of hand. A merchant once presented one of the authors with a page and a half of single-spaced typewritten copy and requested that it be "squeezed into" a 60-second spot.

Compressing copy, reading rapidly without a rushed, chatterbox delivery, is a valuable skill that can be enhanced by practice and the following specialized techniques.

First, *use a musical analogy.* When an orchestra speeds up a piece of music, the relationship among the notes and rests remains the same: a quarter-note is still one-fourth as long in duration as a whole note, but both will be shorter in duration when the tempo is picked up. The same is true of rests between notes. They remain proportional.

The biggest fault of the performer who produces a rushed, hurry-up sound is reading the elements of the copy out of proportion. The result is a change in the phrasing, sometimes eliminating all natural pauses between words or phrases. Another symptom of the hurry-up syndrome is a monotone, where the "melody" of the copy is altered.

When you have to speed up your delivery, remember not to change the *relative* rate of delivery, and don't alter the melody of your voice. Speed up everything, but do not change the relationship among words.

Second, *read ahead in your script.* Reading ahead allows you to speed up the copy and retain its naturalness. Typically, in a hurry-up delivery, the performer forms a direct connection between eye and mouth, becoming less a communicator and more a reading machine, concentrating on speed and losing meaning and flow. Stay a sentence ahead in the copy, and you will phrase the words in a more natural way because you will be saying a sentence, not reading words.

Television Commercials

Earlier, we examined some types of television commercials and discussed what they demand of a performer, as well as how to create a character for television or radio. This section explores some specific techniques of making television commercials.

It is important to understand that the television commercial industry is, in most cases, not a part of the television broadcast industry. Many commercials are produced by independent production houses, and the performers generally are trained as actors, not as broadcasters. Television voice-over work has a greater percentage of broadcasters.

Local TV stations do produce commercials, but the broadcaster in these markets usually doesn't do a lot of on-camerawork. Voice-over work is, however, typically assigned to the broadcaster in local markets.

On the national level, commercial production is a highly specialized business, with spots written by ad agencies and produced by independent houses. In this environment, performers typically work on a freelance basis.

Regardless of whether the assignment is on a local or on a nationally syndicated TV spot, the importance of properly creating a character and giving a genuine delivery cannot be overstated. In addition, TV has some very stringent technical requirements that, if not adhered to, can put performers out of the running before they get a chance to show their talents. These techniques are unique to on-camera acting.

On-Camera Acting

A television camera is a merciless instrument, capable of picking up every detail of a performance, good and bad. An actor or performer must constantly be aware of the power of this unblinking eye and must develop the following specialized skills.

ABILITY TO CONTROL MOVEMENT   Turning to face someone, a simple act in everyday life, can be horrendously complicated in a television studio. The performer must be able to turn without causing the studio lighting to cast uncomplimentary shadows. Too large a movement will pull the performer from his or her mark, usually a piece of tape on the floor, thus throwing off all the camera angles.

Performers frequently must be able to talk with another on-air person without looking directly at him or her. In the theater, actors typically direct their gazes downstage, toward the audience, so that more of their faces are visible to the audience. In some circumstances, you must do the same on TV: look in an unnatural direction during dialogue so that the camera sees more of your face.

Television, like football, is a game of inches. The performer must develop the necessary skills to stay on a mark, move the same way in subsequent takes, and remember his or her body positions at the end of a take so that they can be matched up with the beginning of the next take.

ABILITY TO CONTROL MANNERISMS   "You wouldn't believe some of the faces people make when they're on camera," says Vangie Hayes, casting director for the J. Walter Thompson advertising agency in New York. She notes, "Some performers feel that they have a talent for punctuating everything they say with a raised eyebrow. But that mannerism becomes very distracting."

ABILITY TO PROJECT A TYPE   Time in a television commercial is limited, so there is little opportunity to build a character by dialogue or exposition. Much of the character's personality must be readily apparent, which is why the woman who plays a young mother has to be a young mother "type." Her identity must virtually leap from the screen.

Types in commercial acting include the young mother, the young father, the distinguished spokesperson, the sexy leading-lady type, the macho male, and the "character" part. Cultivating your particular type, whether you are destined to play college professors or cab drivers, is important. Obviously, you must be believable within your type, meeting age and physical requirements. A strong Brooklyn accent may work to your advantage in seeking cab driver parts, although you would be well advised to lose it for any other type of mass media work.

Type casting is very important in commercial work, and specialists often put "young father" or "character type" right on their résumés. Identify your strengths, especially your ability to play a type, and exploit them.

Handling Props

The days of the stand-up commercial with prop in hand are pretty well past, although some local stations still use this structure and on occasion a national spot will do it for novelty. When a product is held, the close-up often features a professional hand model.

For simply handling a prop, the rule of thumb is not to let it glare on the camera lens. A book, for example, must be tipped at the proper angle to keep the reflection from the lights from making the cover glare badly. A second, but just as important, rule is never cover the product with hand or fingers.

Props in modern commercials are more likely to serve as items to be consumed. Commercial performers frequently are called on to ingest a product, and they must do so with as much satisfied, ecstatic zeal as can be summoned within the bounds of common sense. If you are eating a slice of pizza, the director will expect you to be capable of reacting to the taste of the pizza. If you are drinking milk, be prepared to communicate enjoyment.

You will be expected to portray an enormous amount of delight in the consumption of a product. Remember, if you ever are lucky enough to secure a part in a commercial such as this, you will be operating in a big business and will be expected to perform on cue, as a professional.

Freelance Assignments

National commercial work is mostly done on a freelance basis. Many of the performers are actors, and some, especially in voice-over work, are broadcasters. On a local level, more professional broadcasters participate.

Freelance assignments are available on the national and local levels, although an employee of a particular station may frequently find restrictions placed on the types of outside work in which he or she may engage. Parts in commercials are obtained through

- Ad agencies, which handle advertising accounts for clients and often do the scripting and casting for the commercial
- Model and talent agencies, which supply talent and take a cut of the talent's compensation
- Production houses, the firms that actually film or tape the commercial
- Broadcast stations, which assign commercials to in-house talent and sometimes hire freelancers

The competition for parts in commercials, especially TV commercials on the national level, is intense. Before you even enter the ring, you should have tapes (audio, video, or both, depending on your interest) of your best work to present to the casting director of the organization you approach, or to an agent. You will also need a résumé summarizing your previous commercial experience, if any, along with your training. An 8-by-10 black-and-white portrait photo is also required.

In some cases, a commercial performer must belong to a union, such as the Screen Actors Guild (SAG) or the American Federation of Television and Radio Artists (**AFTRA**). Unions are examined more closely in Chapter 12.

What are the qualifications for picking up a commercial role? The principal quality casting director Vangie Hayes looks for is "the ability to talk to someone. There was a time when most announcers were the 'deep, disembodied voice,' but today the emphasis is on communication."

One attribute of a performer's voice, Hayes notes, is the level of interest it carries. "I think a good voice is a voice that you would hear on a TV in another room, and walk into that room just to see what's going on. A good voice is also an interesting voice . . . perhaps even a voice with a little rasp in it."

Hayes agrees with those who advise that practice is the only way to improve. Hear yourself on audiotape, she says, and see yourself on video. Compare your performance to those of professionals, and always be aware of areas in which you can polish your skills.

A Final Note

Commercial performance can be extremely lucrative, a comforting thought when you consider that broadcasting on-air work as a whole does not pay very well. Yes, top performers do make a great deal of money. But at the local level, especially in small markets, on-air talent generally makes less than salespeople or management and in very small stations, than secretarial help. Remember that those at the top *are* at the top, the very top, of a fiercely competitive pyramid. The top news anchor jobs, for example, are not easily obtained.

Securing commercial roles is never easy, but the field does offer quite a bit of opportunity. And for staff radio personalities and certain television staff on-air performers, the ability to deliver a commercial convincingly is a sure step to career advancement. *Never* underestimate the role of commercials and the value of developing the talent to do them well. As long as there is broadcast advertising, the performer who can convince us to use a product or service will be in demand.

Summary

Broadcast advertising has emerged as a separate discipline. Modern commercials take many forms. Among those forms in radio are straight reading, donut, ad-lib from a fact sheet, acted scene, man-in-the-street, and heavily produced montage. Forms in television include mini-drama, spokesperson presentation, pitch presentation, and voice-over.

The long-range goal of a commercial is to sell a product or service, but there are many intermediate steps. The commercial, for example, might seek to create a sense of excitement in the listener and then communicate that the product or service offered is affordable and a realistic option. This is much more sophisticated than simply saying, "Buy this product."

A commercial performer must be able to do a straight delivery (announcing) and an acted delivery (assuming a role).

Acting is a discipline within itself, and proficiency can require years of study. However, familiarity with some basic principles is helpful for any broadcaster interested in commercial performance. The primary consideration in acting a role is determining the motivation, the complex of factors that cause a character to say a line in a particular manner.

The actor must do an analysis of a character and determine that character's physical traits, level of education, voice quality, posture and movement, facial expression, and other traits. It is vital that the actor's delivery be consistent with the overall personality sketch of the character.

Commercial actors must particularly avoid unnatural-sounding speech, stilted dialogue, overacting, and inappropriate movement.

The way a performer treats his or her craft is often defined as technique. In very basic terms, applying to both television and radio, technique is the means of animating copy, bringing it to life.

Radio and television commercials have unique aspects to which special techniques must be applied. Radio commercials involve polishing the technique of reading from a fact sheet, being able to integrate production basics into the overall effort, and such specialized delivery techniques as reading to time and compressing copy. Television commercials call for the specialized techniques of on-camera acting and handling props.

Most performers in commercials that are broadcast nationwide work on a freelance basis. Parts for commercials are subject to stiff competition, but the financial rewards are great. In fact, the entire broadcast commercial industry offers handsome rewards to performers at many levels.

Exercises

1. Write a 30-second television commercial for a raincoat. The commercial must contain a dramatic scene, with one actor talking about why his or her raincoat is a great piece of apparel. Here's an example.

Video	Audio
Salesman gets off airplane, coat slung over his shoulder	My St. Cloud raincoat has put up with a lot . . . downpours in New Orleans, snow in Buffalo, wind in Chicago.
Puts coat on	It's even been stuffed in a travel case and used as a pillow. But it always looks good . . . and I look good in it.
Salesman sees distinguished-looking client, walks up to him, shakes hand, turns to camera	And in my business, you can't afford to look sloppy. I've got to look sharp and be sharp.

In addition to writing a commercial, prepare a personality sketch of the main figure. Decide on voice quality, posture and movement, facial expressions, and general character traits. For example, traits for our sales-man would probably include a hard-driving personality and a lack of tolerance for poor products. Because he is demanding, he picks a good coat, which is the point of the commercial.

Do this for the following four characters. The characters can be male or female, and you can vary the characteristics of the coat (it does not have to be a dress topcoat). Write a script and a personality sketch for

a.   A fisherman

b.   A rich, dashing man or woman about town

c.   An international reporter

d.   A detective on a long outdoor stakeout

After you have written the commercials and character sketches, perform the scene. Do it from the standpoint of each of your four characters.

2.   Record three versions of a standard 30-second radio script, using copy from the drill section (Appendix B) or copy provided by your instructor. Do one version in exactly 25 seconds, one version in exactly 30 seconds, and another in exactly 35 seconds.

3.   Ad-lib a 60-second (approximately) commercial from a magazine ad. Use as little of the ad's direct wording as possible. Try to draw inspiration from the photo, rather than the text.

ELEVEN

Polishing Your Skills

*W*hat separates those few broadcast performers who reach the top from those who seem to get stalled down below? The answer is complicated; it has to do partly with native skill, luck, and ambition. But beyond those factors, what most characterizes people who get to the top and stay there is the ability and the determination to improve. Those are the people who learn from their mistakes and benefit from self-critiques and critiques by others.

This chapter, though brief, is very important. It tells you how to use self-evaluation to improve your skills. These are the methods used by top professionals. If you regard self-improvement as a lifelong discipline, you'll be less likely to stagnate in your career and more likely to rise to the heights of this very competitive field.

Evaluation

You can improve on-air delivery in three ways:

1. Listening to or viewing a tape of yourself and doing a self-critique
2. Having a teacher, supervisor, or co-worker critique your performance
3. Ask a local professional to review your tape

The third option is often more productive, but sometimes more difficult to come by. In small markets, for example, few people may be willing or able to offer a worthwhile critique and suggestions for improvement.

When an external critique is available, it frequently comes as part of the process of grading in an educational setting or standard performance evaluation in an employment situation. Such advice is valuable, and although it may not always be correct, it is wise to listen, file the information away mentally, and use it for reference whenever you engage in self-criticism.

Evaluating your own performance may lack objectivity, but it can provide an irreplaceable insight into performance. Viewing or listening to your own tapes, at regular intervals, during all stages of your professional advancement, is invaluable.

What to Look for in Tapes

Be as objective as you can, and don't make excuses. Don't think, "Well, I really meant to say something else, but I understood what came out." Evaluation must be done from outside your own head, so to speak, from the standpoint of the listener or viewer. *Evaluate in terms of pure communication.*

Be sure that ideas and moods are communicated in such a way that the audience will perceive them immediately. Ask yourself if the communication elements are clear.

Next, break down the *whys*. Why was a commercial not as good as it could have been? Where were the mistakes, and how could weak areas be improved? Do not settle for a general overall negative feeling: *break down problem areas into specifics.*

Be vigilant in hunting for mistakes in pace, a lack of variety in the reading. Is the pitch right? Does the delivery sound phony? Isolating any and all of these factors can help in your quest for self-improvement. If the pace is inappropriate, for example, experiment until you arrive at a pace that reinforces the message, rather than detracting from it.

As noted in Chapter 3, any interference in communication detracts from the impact. In addition to the problem areas just specified, distractions such as poor diction, regionalism, unusual voice patterns, or oddities in appearance divert the audience's attention from the message. When viewing or listening to tapes, *identify distractions.*

For example, do you constantly raise one eyebrow during a newscast? Make a consistent effort to keep that eyebrow down from now on. If your pitch drops repeatedly at the end of each and every sentence, work on vocal variety.

You can evaluate pure communication, breaking down problems into specifics and identifying distractions for airchecks or in practice sessions. Practice sessions are a must for improving on-air ability and provide a low-pressure environment for ironing out the problems uncovered during self-critique. Additional applications for practice sessions are listed in the following section on improvement.

Self-evaluation can be painful but extraordinarily productive. Use tapes as much as possible; at the very least, practice before a mirror. Look and listen objectively. One excellent prescription for self-evaluation is to have someone tape you when you are not aware it is being done. This way, you will be natural and won't be *trying* to do an exceptional job.

This strategy works well with critiquing sports play-by-play. Have your play-by-play recorded and set the tape aside for a few days. Then listen to your description; if you can follow the game by what you've said, you probably did a good job. It is important not to play the tape for two or three days because if you listen right after the game, you will be filling in from memory many details that should be clear from your description alone.

Remember that self-evaluation can be positive as well as negative. Note what you do well, in addition to finding fault. This will identify strengths and head off discouragement. *Do not give up. Keep working.*

A Complete Self-Evaluation

When listening to or viewing a tape, keep the checklist shown in Box 11.1 before you. The section titled "Voice and Diction" applies to both television and radio; "Visual Presentation" contains items specific to television.

As you evaluate your performance, jot down the "no's" on a separate sheet of paper and, if possible, the counter numbers of the audio- or videotape machine at the point where you noticed the particular problem. This will give you the opportunity to go back and review the negative aspects of your performance. You should note the positive aspects of your work, too. Also write down some coherent notes (notes you will understand next week or next year) to yourself on your separate sheet of paper.

Performance can be evaluated many ways. Sometimes you may want only a quick review, at other times an in-depth study. This list is kept flexible so that you can tailor it to your individual needs. Exercise 1 at the end of this chapter provides a possible framework for complete self-evaluation. Keep your notes and your tapes *forever*. This way, you can establish a lifelong baseline from which to judge your improvement. A checklist for long-term plans is shown in Box 11.2.

Improvement

Once problems have been identified, you can practice to eliminate the distracting or inappropriate elements. You need a low-pressure environment in which to practice the following skills:

1. *Hone your ability to read a sentence or more ahead in copy.* This is valuable for radio as well as television. To repeat an important point made earlier, radio announcers must be able to glance up from copy to read clocks, find carts, or look for other pieces of copy. Reading ahead helps you think in terms of communicating phrases and thoughts, rather than just reading words.

   When you are practicing, force yourself to keep your eyes moving ahead in the copy. Aim for staying a full sentence ahead, but experiment by going as far ahead as possible.

Box 11.1

SELF-EVALUATION CHECKLIST

Voice and Diction

Pitch	Does my voice rise and fall naturally, without any artificial patterns?	Yes ___	No ___
Voice quality	Is there resonance in my voice?	Yes ___	No ___
	Is it free of a tight, pinched quality?	Yes ___	No ___
	Is it free from hoarseness or a guttural quality?	Yes ___	No ___
Diction	Do I clearly separate words? Do I say "it was," rather than "ih twas"?	Yes ___	No ___
	Is my delivery free from regionalism?	Yes ___	No ___
	Is my diction free of clipped, too-precise quality?	Yes ___	No ___
	Is my diction free of other distractions? Do I say "bottle," rather than "bah-ull"?	Yes ___	No ___
Breath control	Is my voice free from breathiness?	Yes ___	No ___
	Do I sound as though I have an adequate air support and supply?	Yes ___	No ___
	Do I avoid running low on breath during reading?	Yes ___	No ___
	Do I have adequate diaphragmatic support during the reading (check this during the on-air session)?	Yes ___	No ___
Interpretation	Do I understand the basic ideas of the copy?	Yes ___	No ___
	Do I *appear* to understand the basic ideas of the copy?	Yes ___	No ___
	Can I now, after listening to the tape, immediately repeat the flow of ideas in the copy?	Yes ___	No ___
	If the piece is a commercial or public service announcement, can I now summarize the thrust of the copy in a single sentence?	Yes ___	No ___
	Checking the reading against the script, do the key words I had marked still appear to be the correct words?	Yes ___	No ___

Continues

Box 11.1 *Continued*

Expression	Did I give proper stress to the key words?	Yes ___ No ___
	Does the reading make sense and lead to a compelling point?	Yes ___ No ___
Mood	Do I project a proper and appropriate mood for the copy?	Yes ___ No ___
	Is the reading devoid of overplaying, overacting, or a maudlin quality?	Yes ___ No ___
	Are transitions clear? Is it perfectly evident where one piece of copy stops and another begins?	Yes ___ No ___
	Does mood change during transitions?	Yes ___ No ___
Pace	Is the pace appropriate to the piece? Does it reinforce the message?	Yes ___ No ___
	Does the pace sound natural?	Yes ___ No ___
	Does the pace vary within copy? Are the variations appropriate?	Yes ___ No ___
Naturalness	Does delivery sound conversational?	Yes ___ No ___
	Does it sound like speech, and not like reading?	Yes ___ No ___
	Is my reading believable?	Yes ___ No ___
	Is my reading sincere?	Yes ___ No ___
	Is my reading free of elements of obvious and outright imitation?	Yes ___ No ___
Phrasing	Are words naturally delivered in phrases?	Yes ___ No ___
	Is the reading free of any unclear phrasing (an adjective that "dangles," for example, leaving the listener unsure of exactly what is being described)?	Yes ___ No ___
	Are pauses used properly and effectively?	Yes ___ No ___
	Are unnecessary pauses added to the copy? (such as *ums, ahs, ers*)?	Yes ___ No ___
Energy and interest level	Does the delivery interest you, and would it interest members of the audience?	Yes ___ No ___

Continues

Box 11.1 Continued

	Is energy level appropriate to the copy, not too hyper or too laid-back?	Yes ___	No ___
	Do I appear to care about what I am reading?	Yes ___	No ___

Visual Presentation

Appearance	Is my on-camera presentation free of visual distractions such as unruly hair or poorly fitting clothes?	Yes ___	No ___
Gestures and movement	Are gestures natural, instead of seeming stiff or forced?	Yes ___	No ___
	Is eye contact direct and level, while still seeming natural and comfortable to the viewer?	Yes ___	No ___
Facial expression	Is my expression appropriate for the copy?	Yes ___	No ___
	Do my expressions change during reading?	Yes ___	No ___
	Is head movement natural and not distracting, free of bobbing, and always within the frame?	Yes ___	No ___
Posture and body language	Does my posture express interest and energy?	Yes ___	No ___
	Is my body position natural and not rigid or stiff?	Yes ___	No ___

Take your self-evaluation seriously, and be critical. If you are fortunate enough to have a colleague willing to provide an honest critique, share this checklist with him or her.

2. *Ad-lib.* You can't be embarrassed by clumsy ad-libs made during practice, and practicing extemporaneous skills can prevent those ad-libs from being clumsy in the future. Ad-lib anything during practice: humorous patter, record intros, news reports based on notes. Ad-libbing is largely an acquired skill.

3. *Fine-tune your sense of timing.* Practice condensing 30 seconds worth of copy into 15 seconds. This skill will be a lifesaver when you are trying to hit a network newscast "on the money." Also practice reading copy strictly to time, developing the accuracy of your internal clock.

Box 11.2

A CHECKLIST FOR LONG-TERM PLANS

Evaluation does not end with an examination of the mechanics of an aircheck. There is also a strong need for lifelong, career-wide checks and plans. Ask yourself the following questions.

Do I have a daily regimen of vocal and breathing exercises, such as those described in Chapter 2?	Yes ___	No ___
Do I have a target body weight, and do I maintain that weight?	Yes ___	No ___
Do I take advantage of any opportunity to ad-lib (sports coverage, acting as host of telethon, etc.)?	Yes ___	No ___
Do I constantly develop my vocabulary by reading widely and looking up unfamiliar words?	Yes ___	No ___
Do I read a variety of material, including news magazines, trade journals, and literature?	Yes ___	No ___
Do I observe and learn from others?	Yes ___	No ___
Do I have long-term goals?	Yes ___	No ___

Accenting Your Strengths

Improvement is more than eliminating the negative. The positive points in your delivery, and your particular strengths and abilities, deserve to be accentuated, too.

The first goal of a broadcast communicator should be to correct deficiencies. But once those problem areas are uncovered and corrective work is under way, start thinking about exploiting those strong points.

- Do you have a strong sense of logic and analytical thinking? You may be able to develop world-class interview skills.

- Do you have an engaging personality? Perhaps a career as a radio personality, specializing in strong personality identification, is for you.

- Do you have a strong interest in people and their ideas? Then you may have a valuable advantage in the radio or television talk-show field.

- Do you have an interest in, and understanding of, business and finance? Try your hand at some business-related news reporting, and you may find yourself in demand.

- Are you a good writer? Think about strengthening that skill and applying it to radio or television news. Good writing, to a newsperson, is *always* an asset.

- Are you a hustler and self-promoter, always making calls, meeting people, and making deals? Think about possibilities in freelance commercial or voice-over work, where talent and the ability to promote yourself can lead to high financial rewards.

The list is just about endless. Look within yourself and your background for special qualities that can be polished and strengthened. Adapting your special talents to meet specific broadcast requirements can be vital for getting that specific job. Focus on Technique discusses how important it is to be able to assess which aspects of reporting news fit within the stylistic requirements of public radio.

A Word About Health and Fitness

Physical vigor, a key to success in broadcasting, is often overlooked as a factor in skill building and career advancement. Realistically, you need not be a bodybuilder or marathon runner to compete in on-air broadcasting. You must, however, have the stamina to work long hours and still appear bright and energetic on mic or camera. Remember, too, that taking time off from work due to illness is very much frowned on in the broadcast industry.

Although broadcasting is a demanding job, both physically and mentally, those demands won't contribute to your level of physical fitness. A mail carrier benefits from walking and a warehouse worker from lifting, but you'll spend most of your working hours sitting in a studio or driving from appointment to appointment. That is why a personal fitness program is beneficial and just as important as any skill-building program. There is no shortage of good physical fitness advice today, so take the responsibility for researching the issue and finding what's right for you.

A special note for TV performers: weight will always be a concern to you, so consider diet strongly when planning a fitness program. Face facts. Few fat people stay on the air, and gaining weight can hinder your career advancement.

Case Histories

The material presented in this chapter is not isolated theory passed down from an ivory tower. Almost any successful professional has a history of career experimentation and broadening professional horizons, combined with a calculated plan of personal improvement. Various career paths might be taken. Consider, for example, the case of a salesman for a large manufacturing firm. This man was extremely successful but not very happy. He had a background in amateur theatricals and decided to audition for some part-time television and radio work.

His audition showed promise, and he was signed on to do some television booth announcing. Booth announcers were rapidly becoming an endangered

Focus on Technique

DEVELOPING A DELIVERY STYLE: PRACTICAL EXAMPLES FROM PUBLIC VERSUS COMMERCIAL RADIO

A valuable skill in today's increasingly segmented broadcast market is the ability to adapt your style to the medium in which you work or plan to work.

Look and listen for the nuances in the type of delivery used at the station you would like to work for. Incorporate that into your practice routine.

You will have to analyze what those nuances are. Here is an excellent example of how Jay Sapir, a radio bureau chief, analyzes the difference between delivery style and substance in public and commercial radio.

Delivery Differences

By Jay Sapir

Public radio trains their reporters and anchors not to sound "too commercial." What sorts of stories and styles survive in the rarefied air of public broadcasting?

The public radio reporters huddled in an intense NPR workshop. The focus was on delivery. How not to sound "too commercial" on the air. One reporter volunteered to impersonate the pompous, overwrought, stentorian tones of an imaginary commercial network newscaster. He boomed his newscast into the room from a microphone behind a wall. Laughter filled the room with every strained nuance. The lesson was clear. Commercial radio style was a joke. It was a "how not to" sound for serious public radio journalists.

What makes some stories and styles sound "too commercial" for the rarefied air of public broadcasting? Do public radio people have an attitude about news heard on the made-for-money frequencies on the dial? Are old commercial news hands jealous of their brethren across the band who have infinitely more time and talent to tell their stories? Does anybody really *want* to work inside the straitjacket of 38-second wraps tucked into four-minute newscasts?

More questions than answers were blowing in the Wisconsin wind as it fanned pungent fumes from the Ambrosia Chocolate factory in Milwaukee. More puzzling was the putrid odor drifting from the kitchen of

Continues

Focus on Technique   *Continued*

a factory worker named Jeffrey Dahmer. A thousand miles away in Washington, the editors of NPR's *Morning Edition* had gone to bed, not knowing they would awake to one of the most bizarre stories of the century.

Morning Edition host Renee Montagne wanted at least one more day before going with the Dahmer story. "It was 3 A.M., all we had at that point was a head in the refrigerator. . . . I'm the culprit. I made that choice." Her editors suggested a "Q & A" with a Milwaukee reporter, but Montagne found it "too disgusting" for her breakfast listeners. "That kind of stuff is even more powerful when you eat it with your morning cereal."

NPR will go with lurid, even sensational news so long as it speaks to larger issues. In the Dahmer case, larger issues emerged—police response, minority victims, homophobia—but as the story was breaking, NPR listeners were spared the demented details the rest of the nation digested with breakfast.

Morning Edition and *All Things Considered* at first also saved their listeners from news of the Menendez Brothers trial and the Bobbitt case. Long-form stories exploring the deeper issues were aired toward the end of both trials. But you won't hear coverage of Zsa Zsa's police problems or the Heidi Fleiss call-girl case. Montagne says, "NPR likes to take a step back, take a deep breath and count to ten when bizarre, titillating news breaks."

Indeed, Montagne herself, now NPR's L.A. correspondent, took a four-day deep breath before reporting anything on the O.J. Simpson saga.

The line NPR editors drew was O.J.'s arrest. That was when they would do long-form reporting for *Morning Edition* and *ATC*. The story was merely mentioned on the brief top-of-the-hour news roundups. But Montagne admits that by the night of the slow-speed pursuit even if O.J. had not been arrested she was ready to go with a story and have it out with Washington. "NPR has a problem resolving how soon to cover (these kinds of stories). There are a lot of different voices on when to jump in and how much."

The O.J. story, of course, is "a thing unto itself." Montagne blames much of the inaccurate reporting of leaks on the competitive deadline pressures of commercial media. Pressure to file every hour. Pressures she is not pushed by.

Still, she allows, "there's always a lot of internal tension and argument" over when and how deep to cover sensational news.

No one knows this better than Shari Hemesath. She covered the Dahmer story for NPR while a reporter for a Milwaukee public radio station. "NPR called and wasn't sure what they wanted to do. There was a lot of

Continues

Focus on Technique   *Continued*

hemming and hawing, and by the end of the day all they wanted was one (sound bite) for the newscast."

Hemesath's own NPR affiliate station also "sat on its hands for a long time" trying to decide when and how to cover the story in their backyard that was screaming in headlines worldwide. Hemesath says it was days before the network did any long-form reports on Dahmer, and when it did, graphic details would be cut from her stories. "They didn't want me to use stuff about Dahmer's staring at the 'iridescent innards of a fish.'" By the end of the Dahmer trial, Hemesath's nerves were strained by editorial demands that seemed to change day to day.

NPR's "internal tensions and arguments" pay off with millions of loyal listeners, who are called upon for financial support. Chicagoan Jennifer O'Hara wouldn't think of getting her news anywhere but public radio. "I want to know a little bit more about a story, . . . NPR gets to the humanity of it all, it explains why things happen."

NBC Mutual's Frank Gentry speaks with the authoritative pipes of the radio network anchor he is. Gentry squeezes 10 to 12 stories into his 2-minute, 45-second newscasts. "At times it's frustrating. You can't compete with NPR or the newspapers." He makes no apologies for news that must be tightly written. Or sensational stories that get play every hour. He does allow that "we *were* dangerously close to overkill on O.J."

Gentry is not one of those commercial radio types that takes shots at public broadcasting. He sees it as a different medium. Gentry recalls a long *Monitor* report on Christian Science Monitor Radio that started out, "It's been eight months since Mount Penatubo blew its top. How has life changed for Filipino farmers?"

Gentry's amazed that "someone actually pitched that and someone bought it." He stresses that many other pieces he hears on *Monitor* are "quite good."

Monitor Radio editors have been known to tell stringers who work in commercial radio to try and sound more intelligent. Avoid clichés and slang. Don't sound too happy or upbeat. Actualities can't be cut so tight that they're too fast on the ear. Delivery should be softer, more laid-back than the frantic-paced, ratings-driven networks.

Public Radio International's *Market Place* manages to talk about money without sounding "too commercial." The half-hour report may be radio's most popular business show. It's heard on 260 stations. The audience has quadrupled in five years. The style is bold and breezy. As producer Jim Russell humorously puts it: "We like to sound hip. You don't go to the school to sound hip. You *either* is or isn't."

Continues

Focus on Technique   *Continued*

Russell is well aware that some public broadcasters feel "smug and hostile" toward the commercial wave-length. "They spend their time thinking they're better and different." Not Russell.

He even takes a swipe at public radio reports for going on "ad nauseam" in some cases. "We used to say NPR tells you everything you ever wanted to know about a subject—and more."

Market Place production focuses on pacing, music and tone. "No data without context" makes numbers easier to swallow. For on-air style, "There are some obvious no-no's: The rock-jock announcer with the DJ mentality." Russell thinks those bawdy ones are offensive to commercial and noncommercial news listeners.

NPR editor Jude Doherty would agree. She hears public broadcasting's delivery as more conversational and toned down than that of the commercial networks. Doherty says she has a lot of respect for the major networks. But on lurid stories like rape trials or the New York jogger attack, she seeks news angles that are "emblematic of bigger trends." Safety clearly was an issue in the jogger case. So NPR's reports, she says, didn't "bang away at the gory details of the attack . . . the truncated ten-second blood and guts stuff."

"If it bleeds, it leads," the old network anchors quip, with more than a trace of irony. Indeed, death and destruction are the daily grist of network news mills. Reporter and anchor deliveries sometimes seem melodramatic.

UPI Radio's Pye Chamberlayne has been the voice of authority from Capitol Hill for a quarter century. When Chamberlayne sinks his teeth into a story, you can almost sense the blood dripping from his gums. But his cogent writing and keen analytical style have made him popular on public radio airwaves, too. He's often heard on NPR's and Monitor Radio's top and bottom of the hour news roundups.

Pye himself is undaunted by those who might find his style too hard-hitting. "I only know one way to do what I do. And when I'm done doing it (if I'm not hungover or sick that day) no human being alive has ever done it any better than me." Pye says he has considered working in public radio but warns with a grin in his voice: "If you're a man, rather, a 'male person,' you have to get an operation to work there and it's too goddammed painful. . . . When you're dealing with a 'vaginocracy' they require you to get your testicles removed so there isn't all this threatening testosterone around."

The NPR workshop broke down into focus groups. Some guy from Alaska joked that if he wanted to be sure to get his stuff on NPR, he need only fade in the natural sound of seagulls under any piece. Reporters

Continues

Focus on Technique   *Continued*

listened to each other's stories, then savagely tore them apart. NPR stars were assigned to each group. The guy from Alaska played a self-serving report on how his station "had learned" that McDonalds planned to plant its golden arches on a pristine patch of earth. "Sources tell KCAW news that . . . ," it started.

"Stop right there," the workshop leader said. "The story is not about you or your station, it's about McDonalds coming to Alaska."

"But Cokie," the aspiring NPR reporter implored, "Everybody, from Peter Jennings to Dan Rather to the *New York Times,* they all mention their news organization's name when they get a scoop."

"Yeah," she replied, "and they all sound like assholes, too."

Jay Sapir toiled in the vineyards of commercial radio before becoming a news director at an NPR affiliate in Alaska. He's now Midwest bureau chief for the UPI Radio Network in Chicago.

From the November 1994 *RTDNA Communicator.* Reprinted with permission.

species, however, so he began to supplement his income with commercials. What a natural career extension for a salesman! His contacts and knowledge of advertising helped him to become highly successful.

Success in commercials brought him to New York City, where a role in a soap opera was added to his résumé. Quality of life in New York was not up to his expectations though, so he applied for, and got, a weathercaster job in his hometown, a smaller market. The weather job evolved into a host position on a magazine-type show.

The career path did not stop there, however. His knowledge of advertising eventually led him to establish an advertising and public relations agency, which provides artistic and financial rewards, combined with the challenge of running a small business.

Although this broadcaster tried a number of career paths, none were false starts and none of the effort was wasted. All this experience and all the skills acquired add up to a whole in his present job.

Persistence and a constant drive for self-improvement pay off. Take the case of an announcer who worked weekends while in college. He was a DJ at a CHR station, but that job soon became unsatisfying and the pay was poor. He was offered work at a station doing album-oriented rock, and it proved to be an excellent slot. But the station's format was changed to nostalgia, which he did not particularly like. He did a competent job, though, studying the music and making a tremendous effort to fit within the format.

Eventually, a sales position opened at a country station, and he took it, wanting to discover whether sales was really the part of broadcasting that would make him happy. That did not turn out to be the case. Air work was his goal, and he started sending out tapes and extending feelers through friends in the business. He did not regret having tried sales, because the question of whether sales was his natural spot always would have been a haunting one if the effort had not been made.

The result of his career search? The morning drive job in an AOR station in one of the nation's largest markets. The program director who hired him was impressed not only with his radio background but also with his demonstrated willingness to work hard and adapt.

The ability to recognize and correct deficiencies is crucial. Note the case of a young woman, a recent college graduate. Rather stocky and having a coarse-sounding voice, she lacked at first some of the physical attributes expected of a news reporter.

Her main attribute was her skill as an on-air newsperson, cultivated by endless, backbreaking experience. Eventually, she also made some improvements in appearance and vocal ability.

After college, she returned to her hometown and became a volunteer at the cable station, doing anything and everything she was asked. On-air work didn't come until a year later, when she convinced the cable system director to let her produce and host a 15-minute weekly feature. The feature enjoyed moderate success, and after another year she asked the director of the cable station to help her find a job in news. The director made some calls and secured an interview for her at a small station.

The woman advanced to a larger station. It happened to be in the same market as her college, so she could ask her former performance professor to watch her newscasts and critique them. Eventually, she moved on to a good job in one of the larger medium markets.

Although she did not have a large amount of natural talent, her constant efforts to improve, and her willingness to seek and accept criticism, *made* her a good on-the-air communicator.

Roadblocks

Some people stall at roadblocks, but others look around them, try to decide what's wrong, and make changes. Al Roker (see Figure 11.1) is the weatherman for NBC's *Today* show. He attributes much of his success to being at the right place at the right time, but also points out that he made conscious efforts to improve his on-air skills and appearance.

Figure 11.1

NBC's Al Roker rose to the top as a major broadcasting personality through a combination of being in the right place at the right time and working on aspects of performance and personal appearance that improved his odds of being hired for television work.

© Janaette Beckman/CORBIS Outline

"When I was in Syracuse I wanted to move on, but something was holding me back," he says. "I had been up for a job in Washington, D.C., but was turned down. Word got back to me that my weight had been part of the problem."

Roker lost weight and was again seen by an executive of the station in Washington. This time, he got the job. The next stop was in Cleveland. "After five years in Cleveland I felt that I had grown professionally as much as I could there," Roker says. "I was stalled and had to figure out what was going wrong. What I did was to concentrate on other parts of my career, such as reporting and interviewing." (Quotes reprinted with permission.)

Roker took on additional duties as host of a talk show, for which he won an Emmy. He also began focusing on field reporting and won an Emmy and a UPI award in that category, also.

Roker says he is not sure whether those additional skills were directly responsible for landing the job at WNBC but notes that versatility never hurts. "In New York, those skills may not necessarily open the door, but once you're through that door they'll help you stay in the room."

Other broadcasters can point to similar efforts to pass a roadblock in their careers. Anne Montgomery felt she was encountering a credibility problem as a female sportscaster, so she immersed herself in sports as a referee.

Skeptical station managers could hardly doubt the sports knowledge of someone who had officiated in so many different events.

Persistence pays. Will Lyman, now one of the best-known voice talents in the country, worked for years without much recognition until the break into the *Frontline* program. Then things began to take off.

Not all of you will achieve national fame, or a regular job in a major or medium market. But each of you can and should make the most of your talent, constantly working to improve. Otherwise, you are cheating yourself.

Summary

The ability and determination to improve is as important to the on-air broadcaster as raw talent. Evaluation is vital to improvement; you can listen to or view a tape of yourself, or have an instructor or colleague monitor the tape and offer criticism. When reviewing your own tapes, be as objective as possible. Evaluate in terms of pure communication. Break down problem areas into specifics. Identify distracting elements, such as poor speech habits. Use the self-evaluation checklist presented in this chapter, as well as the checklist for long-term planning.

Once problems have been identified, you can begin the process of improvement. In addition to working on problems uncovered in critique, an improvement program centers on enhancing strong points. Discover your special abilities and capitalize on them.

Many pros project the image of smooth success. Often, however, it took struggle, failure, and more struggle to get where they are today. And it took determination, careful attention to make improvements, and the willingness to adapt and to sample opportunities.

Exercises

1. Evaluate one of your tapes, using the checklist provided in this chapter. Prepare a tape in a field you particularly enjoy and hold as a career goal, such as rock music air personality work or television news.

   Make an effort to check yes or no in every category. If the answer to a question is yes, grade your performance on that particular attribute—excellent, good, or fair. For example, after answering this question

   Does the pace sound natural? Yes ___ No ___

   try to quantify the naturalness of the sound on a scale of 1 to 5. Was the level of naturalness good (4) or excellent (5)? In the margin of the checklist, make notes on these and other items.

2. Use the same method for evaluating the performance of an on-air professional in your selected field. Choose someone whose work you particularly admire.

3. Design a series of five exercises to deal with the particular problems you encounter in your on-air delivery.

One announcer who had problems with ending patterns, for example, read 10 minutes' worth of copy and played back the tape, carefully scrutinizing the ending patterns. The tape confirmed that every sentence ending went down in pitch, over and over and over. Then the announcer wrote notes in her copy to help overcome the problem. Her notes represented changes in pitch and looked like this:

would ^still^ be _unavailable to_ the ^public.^

These notations, and constant repetition, were able to help the situation significantly.

Remember that the point of self-evaluation and self-improvement is that no standard set of exercises will help everyone in every situation. As a professional, you must take responsibility for isolating problem areas and working toward their resolution. The five exercises you develop can be a good start toward this goal.

TWELVE

Career Advancement

*T*alent, skill, hard work, and a desire to improve are useless if you can't get a job. On-air broadcast work is difficult to break into. Competition is tough even for low-paying, entry-level jobs. And if your career pattern is typical, once you have broken into broadcasting, you will change jobs several times.

Your first job will probably be the toughest to get. The pay will be low and the work demanding. But you'll probably learn more about the business of broadcasting in your first job than in any course you take. Professionalism in on-air work comes only through experience. Broadcasting is a business you learn in the business.

In this chapter, we focus on what you need to do to get and hold a job. We discuss opportunities available to broadcasters and pass on hints from broadcast managers and talent agents about what techniques are most likely to help you get started in the field. We also discuss the tools of getting hired—résumés, audition tapes, and developing contacts. And finally we look at salaries and contracts.

On-Air Opportunities for Broadcasters

With the understanding that a beginner will be paid as a beginner, even with a college degree, you are ready to start your search for a broadcast on-air position. That first job will almost certainly involve duties you will not like or want to do, but versatility is essential. Although your goal may be TV news anchoring, you may have to pull many radio music show shifts. Aspiring radio personalities must do news. Sportscasters may have to produce commercials. All duties you will be asked to perform must be done with a smile, for realists understand that there are dozens of applicants for even the most humble positions, and hundreds for the desirable jobs.

You must be in good physical condition because your career will frequently involve terrible hours. A shift may start at 5 A.M., continue until 2 P.M., and then begin again with the evening newscast at 5 P.M. In radio, shifts of six days per week are common. And don't expect holidays off. The show, so to speak, must go on. Colds and the flu won't automatically qualify you for a day off, either. If you are expected to sign on the station at 6 A.M., you *must* be there unless you can rouse the manager out of bed to take over your shift.

After a year or so of successful and dedicated work in a small market, you might, repeat *might,* be able to move on to a better small market or a medium market. Never take such advancement for granted because the competition is stiff. A modest broadcast job, which does not pay more than that of a kitchen helper in a good restaurant, can easily attract dozens of applicants.

If these prospects do not discourage you, if you are so set on on-air work that you can ignore the odds, and if you realistically think you possess the talent to overcome the challenge of hundreds of other applicants, you may have a future as on-air talent.

On-Air Jobs

An important consideration in the life of an on-air performer, in news or radio personality work or any other part of the industry, is that your career path is likely to resemble that of a gypsy. Your résumé will look like it was written by Rand-McNally, as some broadcasters say.

There is no reason why a broadcaster must move from market to market if he or she is content to work in a small town. Broadcasting from small towns often is of high quality, and the small-market environment offers safety and ease of existence unknown in major cities. Small-market broadcasters do not become rich and famous, but they enjoy a fine quality of life and a great deal of influence.

Medium-market on-air people also can enjoy good-quality lifestyle, and cities considered to be medium markets—such as Syracuse, New York, or Austin, Texas—offer, in smaller doses, every advantage of a major city. Medium markets frequently have professional sports teams, symphony orchestras, and major universities. They also are more likely to have affordable housing than major markets do.

The big money, however, comes in the major markets, like Boston and Philadelphia. Radio personalities make generous salaries, and the salaries of TV news anchors are in the six-figure range. The majors are difficult to crack, however, and there is no accompanying rise in job security.

Sometimes newcomers to broadcasting elect to settle in major markets and work their way up through low-level jobs, such as mailroom or even janitorial duties. This approach has pluses and minuses, which we discuss shortly.

As we mentioned, the beginner will have to do many jobs not directly related to what he or she perceives as an ultimate career goal. Such exposure is beneficial for two reasons:

1. Trying a wide variety of jobs gives you exposure that will be valuable later on in your career. The value might not be apparent immediately, but any experience in the business usually is an asset regardless of your career path. If, for example, you wind up in some form of management, that period in sales or production will certainly enhance your knowledge of the business overall and make you a better manager.

2. You may not have enough ability to pursue the career path you think you want to follow. Or, you may want to do well as a disc jockey but find that you hate the job. Many an aspiring disc jockey has found more satisfaction in news, and vice versa.

People in a position to hire you will appreciate—even demand—versatility and a willingness to work in a variety of assignments. Virtually without exception, they will place a higher premium on demonstrable professional experience than on a professor's statement that you were a fine student. And you may be required to start in an off-air job and earn the chance to go before the camera or microphone.

Humility is important, not so much as a rite of initiation but as a realistic approach to the task of finding a broadcast job. Your realistic self-assessment and willingness to work will translate into what broadcast executives think of as a good attitude.

Jeff Rosser (see Figure 12.1), former news director of WNEV Television, Boston, who is now a top-level broadcast executive, discusses the advantage of a good attitude for an applicant. Sitting in his office in the station's modern headquarters, he gestures toward a table stacked twelve-deep with videotapes. "All those tapes," he says, "are from professionals with years of experience in small and medium markets. Yet I still receive applications from recent graduates who want to start on-air." (Quotes reprinted with permission.)

Rosser and other broadcast executives echo the contention that the chances of a newcomer, slim to begin with, are often made worse by a somewhat arrogant approach to the application process. Many neophytes refuse to hear of anything other than on-air work, even though production or writing or other duties might be the only available avenue toward their goals. Other applicants destroy their credibility by overstating their résumé qualifications, for example, by listing "extensive experience in documentaries" to describe participation in two college projects.

In essence, Rosser advises that Boston is not the place to start looking for a job. "Start at a smaller station. You'll be allowed to try a wide variety of

Figure 12.1

Jeff Rosser, broadcast news executive.

Photo courtesy Raycom Media, AL

jobs, and will get to make some mistakes and learn from them. The only way to learn a job is by doing it."

"Some people do start as copy-rippers in major markets, but a lot of them, after a couple of years, are asking themselves, 'Why am I still ripping copy?' Wouldn't it have been better for that person to have gone to Vermont and learned how to write, or how to run a camera?"

Even though Rosser's advice is aimed at aspiring newspeople, it also applies to graduates in any broadcast field. And his final point perfectly sums up the goal of the applicant in the broadcast industry: "When I hire someone, I tell that person, 'All right, you're good, and I'm going to grant your wish. I'm going to put you on air, and provide you with a staff of more than a hundred people to help. We're also going to provide you with millions of dollars' worth of equipment for you to use in preparing your work. Then, we're going to take your piece and present it to hundreds of thousands of people. And we're going to pay you very well in the process.' Now, who could hear that and not be enthusiastic about the job?"

Moving into Management or Related Duties

A realistic assessment of on-air work shows that it is difficult to obtain, and advancement involves tooth-and-nail competition among a veritable army of dedicated, talented people. But even though on-air work does not become a lifelong career for many, it does provide an excellent springboard into other occupations. Some on-air talent moves into management, especially in radio. Program directors often started as announcers. Today's radio program director has a job that is often a cross between chief announcer and executive in charge of the music, programming legalities, and overall station sound. News on-air people can move into news management. Most news directors have some on-air background, which contributes to their understanding of the overall news effort. The top levels of station management are generally drawn from the ranks of sales. But there is nothing to prevent a radio staff announcer from combining his or her early career with experience in time sales. In some markets, selling is part of the job. In most radio markets, good salespeople outearn on-air talent.

The entire chain of human communication is interrelated at almost all levels. On-air performers frequently elect to move into positions in advertising and public relations. Contacts made during and after working hours facilitate this kind of change, and the insights picked up during years of on-air work will help in this or any other career.

Preparing for Your First Job

Your first job in broadcasting will probably be the most difficult to get. There is intense competition. If you have talent, though, and are willing to take a job that may be less than ideal, eventually you will get hired. Once your foot is in the door, you have a chance to compile a record of performance. Then you will be better able to select the kinds of situations that let you advance in the career direction that suits you best.

Preparation for a career in broadcasting involves two major components: academics and practical experience. For on-air work, a third ingredient is a certain amount of native talent. You can't do much about your degree of innate talent, so let's look at the things you can do something about.

Academics

It is difficult to recommend a precise academic program without knowing exactly what career path you will follow. You will probably explore several areas before settling into your major career focus. Let's look at some academic preparation that can be helpful in on-air work.

You're reading this textbook, so you are probably taking at least one academic course in broadcasting or communications. Preparation in this area can be a focused program given in professional training schools, a slightly longer preparation in two-year schools, or a four-year program that adds other courses and awards a bachelor's degree. More advanced work at the master's degree level and beyond is usually designed to prepare people for broader professional responsibilities in the communications field.

Whether you're aiming for on-air work in radio or TV, in news or entertainment, one overall guideline applies: *Learn as much as you can about as many things as you can.* You're looking for depth *and* breadth.

If you're a communications major in a four-year program, take as many courses outside that major as you can. Try for a good mixture of such areas as political science, history, economics, and literature. Earlier we recommended that you consider a double major. If you do, select your second major in one of the areas just mentioned.

In Focus on Technique, Dan Rather reinforces the notion that good writing skills and hard work are essential if you aspire to succeed in this field.

If you aspire to a career in television news, you might want to consider journalism as a possible major or second major. According to talent representative Sherlee Barish, an increasing number of people being hired for TV news jobs have had experience in print journalism. They know how to write, and they know how a news story goes together. Barish says that being knowledgeable in political science and economics can be very helpful to TV news reporters as well.

In modern "personality" radio formats, on-air DJs need to be extremely creative. They need to know how to write and produce material quickly and professionally. To prepare for that kind of work, courses in creative writing and drama are very helpful.

Courses that help you with technical aspects of broadcasting will be an asset. Particularly at the entry level, knowledge of camera operation and editing in television news, and of audio production in radio, is usually necessary. Formal training in performance skills is also valuable, of course.

Preparing yourself academically is easier to do *before* you get a job. If you find out later that you should have taken more history courses while you were in college or that advanced TV production would have been helpful, it can be difficult to correct the deficiencies. Get as much academic preparation as you can while you are still in school and you'll improve your immediate employment prospects as well as your ability to advance.

Practical Experience

In broadcasting, a vital ingredient in preparing for a career is getting practical experience. Get all the practical experience you can while you're in school. People who do the hiring in broadcasting will invariably ask you what you did as a student to develop your skills in a practical setting.

You can get a certain amount of useful practical experience by working at the campus radio station. If you're interested in broadcast journalism, you can also gain useful experience by writing for the student newspaper or literary publications. If you're fortunate enough to have radio or television facilities on your campus, take advantage of any opportunities to work on production crews or in other assignments related to the media. Remember that these experiences will look good on your résumé, so you'll want to keep track

Focus on Technique

THE MOST VALUABLE ATTRIBUTES IN A BROADCAST CAREER

Those who have successfully navigated the career path that puts them in front of cameras and microphones are almost unanimous in identifying two off-camera attributes that propelled them in their careers.

1. The ability to write well
2. The willingness to work very, very hard

A connection between writing well and working in news is reasonably apparent to even the most casual observer, but many students enter the field expecting to survive solely on their presentation skills. Even though a small number do, most find that the ability to put thoughts on paper is critical.

Dan Rather (see Figure 12.2), who offered his thoughts during an interview relating to the points presented in this chapter, notes that writing

Figure 12.2   *CBS News anchor Dan Rather prepares to go on the air.*

Photo by Carl Hausman

Continues

Focus on Technique   Continued

skills are among the first attributes looked for in the arduous process of getting and keeping a job at CBS News.

But the value of writing extends beyond news jobs. Radio staff announcers often write and read their own copy. Sportscasters must be lucid writers, and even sports personnel who do play-by-play and color must compose clear descriptive copy for such program parts as the pregame show.

Don't forget that the *process of job hunting* requires extensive written communication. Broadcast executives are virtually unanimous in their contention that a well-written cover letter is the essential part of the application package. And once you get a job, you must *keep* it.

Hard work and long hours are the coin of the realm in broadcasting. Students often harbor the misconception that once you've made it on-air, the ride is downhill. Actually, though, the path becomes steeper. As Rather puts it: "Some people think this is a glamorous business. And in a way, it is. But don't be seduced by that. It doesn't come without a price . . . this line of work requires extraordinary commitment." Those who succeed, he notes, are the people "who burn with a bright flame."

of exactly what you did for these productions. Don't overstate what you did, but give yourself credit where appropriate.

Give yourself an advantage when you get involved in these on-campus "laboratory"-type experiences: take them seriously. The more disciplined you are in such situations, the better you will be prepared to work in a professional setting.

This is the place to make mistakes. And, like everyone else, you'll make plenty of them. The difference between your on-campus job and the professional setting is that in the campus setting there usually is life after mistakes. Try not to write off mistakes by assuming they don't matter because "it is just the college station." Instead, find out what you need to do to correct the problems. Don't let yourself develop a careless attitude about your performance. Strive to be as good as a paid professional broadcaster.

All the campus media experience you can get will not take the place of work in an actual professional setting. Internships and summer work offer you the best chances to get real professional experience while you are still a student.

Landing an entry-level position in broadcasting is tough enough. If you have not had an internship, it's even tougher. Most people who hire broadcasters say they consider internships more valuable than a heavy concentration of academic work in broadcasting.

Learn as much as you can early in your college career about how to get the internships that will give you the kinds of experience you need. Most internship programs have good and bad jobs. Try to find out which internships provide solid experience. Don't be afraid to branch out from on-air work. The fact is that there simply aren't many opportunities for on-air work in most internship programs. Do try, however, to aim for the general area you want to work in. If you're interested in radio, don't jump at the first internship that comes along in a TV promotions department.

And when it comes to internships, you don't necessarily gain an advantage by looking for the biggest market. According to Sandy Moore, in an article written titled "Tips for Scaling the Job Hunt Wall" (in *The Quill,* published by the Society of Professional Journalists), most professionals recommend smaller markets for internships rather than large operations.

The pros with whom Moore spoke noted that in large media operations interns often get stuck running for coffee. In addition, large operations often have too many levels of staff people who do the kinds of work that you're trying to learn. So you are less likely to actually perform hands-on tasks.

Shoot for something smaller. There are usually plenty of opportunities to get into the thick of things in medium-market stations. You'll also have a better chance to get feedback from supervisors. One broadcaster Moore consulted said that, in his experience, large operations often tend to give some students an unrealistic view of the broadcasting profession. In most broadcast settings, fewer staff people do more things. The large operations, with several people assigned to most areas, are the exception rather than the rule.

If the market is too small, you may find it difficult to get any feedback. Often in such operations interns get shunted into an area that is not covered by other staff people. In such situations, you can get tied down to performing a single task throughout your internship. As a result, you have less chance to gain experience and knowledge outside of that single area.

Regardless of operation size, it is of primary importance to get at least one internship. If you have the opportunity to do more than one internship, take it. The experience you get from internships is worth sacrifice and hard work. Remember there are many more applicants than entry-level jobs in the broadcasting profession, and the vast majority of those you'll be competing with will have either professional experience or internships on their résumés. To compete effectively, you'll need the edge that internships can provide.

Job Hunting

Once you have finished your academic and practical preparation, you begin making your bid to enter the broadcasting field. Getting your first job is extremely difficult. Many more people are looking for on-air work than there are good jobs. People with talent who really want a job badly will find opportunities, and eventually there may even be well-paying, prestigious positions. The key is to persevere long enough to get your foot in the door.

Television

You will find it particularly difficult to start out in TV on the air. You will be competing for jobs with experienced people with tapes that show actual news-reporting assignments. Those who manage to land on-air TV jobs usually start out as news reporters.

In a small market, the job of reporter can include camera operation and tape editing. The hours can be long and the work exhausting. When your contemporaries work 9 to 5 and earn much better money, it can be difficult to hang on long enough to turn the corner in your career.

Sherlee Barish, who represents on-air talent in television news, weather, and sports, says that people who want entry-level positions in television should be willing to start in small markets and relocate every couple of years as they try to move to larger and larger markets. "It's a glamour industry and it's overpopulated," says Barish.

Barish says that the current economics of television have reduced the size of news staffs at many stations. Huge debts incurred in purchasing TV stations at enormous prices have led to efforts to economize. "A station that once had seven or eight news crews may have had to cut back to three or four," says Barish. Economics have also caused shrinkage in the level of salary increases as well. "Stations that used to give 10 to 15 percent pay increases are now giving 3, 4, and 5 percent increases," she says. In some cases, anchors have even taken salary cuts, according to Barish.

Radio

Brad Murray, former general manager of WQSR-FM in Baltimore, says that getting started in an on-air career in radio is a matter, for most, of learning the ropes in small markets and shooting for the larger markets when you have made your mistakes and learned how to handle yourself in a variety of situations. Murray says that there are virtually no opportunities on the air for entry-level on-air people in the large markets.

Hiring in major markets is very precise. WQSR-FM tries to hire on-air people who fit the demographics of the listeners. The station appeals primarily to people ages 35 to 44. On-air people in that age range are far more likely to understand what the music means to listeners than is someone who doesn't have the same associations between life experiences and particular record cuts.

Breaking into radio at the small-market level is a matter of being willing to take jobs that may not offer much pay and benefits. Be willing to take almost any on-air opening you can get as a first job. Your objectives are to start building a résumé, get as much experience as possible, and perfect your skills as an on-air performer. Once you've gotten some practical experience, you can begin to look at opportunities that more precisely fit your requirements for salary and career advancement.

Whether you're looking for your first job or shooting for that major-market anchor position, though, you need to develop some specific tools and techniques to present yourself effectively to whoever is doing the hiring.

Self-Marketing Techniques

Now that the groundwork has been established, let's consider the nuts-and-bolts business of getting hired and, once you're hired, furthering your career. Your college experience and academic preparation will serve as a good foundation. To properly showcase your academic preparation and practical experience, you'll need to put together an effective résumé and a showcase tape, two of the tools commonly used in self-marketing.

Résumés and Tapes

Although a good **résumé** and tape are important for a beginning broadcaster, they are not the be-all and end-all of a job search. A beginner's résumé rarely if ever contains elements evocative enough to urge a program director, news director, or station manager to hire that person based on the résumé alone. A tape is obviously important, and must demonstrate raw talent, but in the absence of good, solid, professional on-air work, a tape is not in itself a very powerful marketing tool for the beginner.

Experienced broadcasters can send a tape and résumé and expect results. The tapes and résumés of beginners will commonly be in direct competition with those of experienced professionals, and experience is usually the deciding factor.

Résumés and tapes are only tools in the marketing effort. By themselves, they will not get you hired. Being hired requires interviewing, following up on leads, and making contacts. With the understanding that a tape and résumé are the first steps in job hunting and career development, let's examine each tool.

RÉSUMÉS   A good résumé will stress experience. Recognizing that experience for a recent graduate will be sparse, stress whatever coursework or internships you have had that are particularly relevant.

Richard Labunski, a faculty member in the School of Communications of the University of Kentucky, noted in a primer prepared for conferees and interns of the International Radio and Television Society, "Generally speaking, a résumé of a new college graduate with internships and work at the campus radio station should only take one page." In a seminar on job seeking, Labunski advised, "If you need to, you can run your résumé to two pages, but under no circumstances should it be longer than that." The résumé shown in Figure 12.3 is an example of a good résumé format.

Activities or work experience unrelated to your field are superfluous on a résumé unless an entry for a civic or voluntary activity reflects favorably on you. Labunski advocates two other points.

1. Avoid putting in your résumé an "objective" or "position sought" category. You can always discuss in your cover letter why you are seeking and are qualified for a certain job. Keep your résumé as generic as possible so you can use it for many different positions.

2. You do not need to list references in your résumé if the space would be better allocated to something else. An employer will almost always ask you for references anyway, before you start in the job. If the résumé looks too short, references can be used to fill space. (Courtesy of Professor Richard E. Labunski, University of Washington.)

It goes without saying that your résumé must be clearly typed and free of any mistakes. Have the résumé typed on an excellent-quality computer printer, and shop around for a good printing job. Be sure that the reproductions are crisp and clear. One worthwhile option that is not especially expensive is to have your résumé reproduced on stiff, good-quality paper. Ask for a bond paper with 25 percent rag content.

AUDIOTAPES AND CDS   Your audiotape or CD should reflect experience with the kinds of duty available at the station to which you are applying or needed for the particular job you seek. If the job involves afternoon drive at a radio station featuring a hard-rock format, you will be well served by a tape featuring a similar approach.

For audio, cassettes are acceptable but CDs are better and are connected to better-quality speakers, and you can gain a subtle advantage by presenting yourself in this manner. The best way to present a tape is at an interview.

For audiotapes, you can probably do some individual tailoring because radio production equipment is more readily available than video. But in many cases you will have to produce a general tape showing basic skills. For a basic audiotape, consider assembling a brief—5 minutes or less—collection of pieces that includes the items shown in Box 12.1.

If you feel confident that you will specialize in radio news, your tape can emphasize that area. But do not rule out airshift work because that may be all that is available.

VIDEOTAPES   This, of course, is the ideal situation. Tapes are difficult and expensive to produce, especially for television. Realistically, you must make do with what is available at your school or campus station. A job for a general-assignment reporter at a TV station requires a tape with one or more pack-

Figure 12.3   A sample résumé.

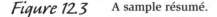

Deborah Smith-Jones
422 Spruce Street
Highspire, PA 17034-1526

Phone: 717 – 555- 2356   Email: djsmith2@hometown.com

Qualifications Summary: Experienced radio/ television reporter and anchor. Strong writing and verbal skills. Skilled at making complex issues understandable. Knowledge of non-linear editing and production techniques.

Experience:
- 9/03 – 12/03 Weekend and replacement anchor – WWWW-TV, Grand Isle, Iowa. Served as weekend anchor over four-month period as intern in television news. Received commendation from news director for report on Grand Isle's homeless population
- 11/01 – 12/03 Writer/ Producer/ Talent – WNNN-FM, Grand Isle, Iowa. Wrote, produced, and voiced a regular feature series called "Fun and Finance" for university radio station. The series on personal finance for teenagers ran for two years.
- 3/00 – 2/04 News Anchor – WNNN-FM, Grand Isle, Iowa. Wrote and delivered news broadcasts over three-year period. Served as News Director during senior year. Produced award winning series on student/community relations, which was credited with improving community understanding of student life in the community.

Accomplishments and Honors:
- Selected to represent university at meeting of student leaders in Washington, DC.
- Recipient of the Alpha Chi Rho – "Broadcaster of the Year Award" for District 7.

Education: B.A. Broadcast Journalism, University of Iowa, Grand Isle, Iowa (May, 2004)

References: Available on request.

Audition Materials: Talent samples on video and audio CD available on request.

---

ages, perhaps a minute or 1:30 in length. If you have the ability to produce a videotape in school, by all means do so, because hiring a professional studio is very expensive. One method of putting together a tape is to showcase a broad range of skills in television performance. A tape that does this (on VHS cassette) might include the items shown in Box 12.2.

Box 12.1

An Audiotape or CD Collection for Job Hunting

1. *A few record intros.* Do not, of course, play the records all the way through. Fade down the cuts after a few seconds. Demonstrate your enthusiasm in this very brief time, as well as your ability to match vocal style to the music and to handle the console.

2. *A brief newscast.* Pay particular attention to showing contrast between and among stories and to reading with meaning.

3. *One or two commercials.* Show your naturalness and acting ability.

4. *An ad-lib.* The ad-lib can be part of your music intros. Have it show humor, have it show knowledge of music, but above all make it demonstrate *your ability to be conversational.*

If you're shooting for a job as an on-camera news reporter, showcase your various talents in that area. According to Lou Fox, a talent agent with many years of experience in placing people in broadcast news positions, such a tape can make you or break you.

Fox says that too few students coming right out of college submit audition tapes that truly represent their talents in news reporting. Fox lists the following guidelines in preparing a new audition tape.

1. *Begin with the piece that does the best job of showing you and your talents.* Saving the best piece for last is not a good idea. If a news director doesn't see something good right away, chances are he or she will stop the tape and never see that great piece you used as the grand finale. So although you may have looked like a budding Connie Chung, no one will know it. Remember that the story is not the important thing. It's better to have a school board story that features you than a tornado story with your only appearance being a brief stand-up at the end.

2. *Include samples from a variety of different types of reporting assignments.* Include stand-ups, live interview segments, voice-overs, and feature pieces that you put together. Don't assume that a lengthy segment at the anchor desk is going to do it. Most first-time jobs will be in general-assignment reporting, not anchoring. So focus on the category that counts.

3. *If possible, include something that shows how well you edit and handle a camera.* The small-market news reporter will need to have those skills.

Box 12.2

A VIDEOTAPE COLLECTION FOR JOB HUNTING

1. *A news anchor segment.* Show eye contact. Use a teleprompter if one is available. Demonstrate as much as possible your ability to convey information and show your interest in the news.

2. *A stand-up commercial delivered straight to the camera.* Write a commercial yourself, and deliver it. If possible, use props.

3. *A short interview* (no longer than two minutes). Put an opening and closing on the interview to demonstrate that you can manage time restrictions. Show that you can handle yourself and others in an on-air situation and that you can get right to the heart of a topic.

4. *A news package, if available.* If not, deliver a stand-up news report to the camera.

Don't overdo this part, but try to include it somewhere, possibly as the last thing on the tape.

4. *Don't put a lot of leader on the tape.* Busy news directors who must scan 150 to 200 tapes don't want to sit through 30 seconds of color bars and 10 seconds of black before they get to what they want to see.

5. *Make sure the first thing anyone sees on the tape is you.* Don't lead off with 50 seconds of a fire chief's long-winded comments and end with 15 seconds of your stand-up. By the same token, take the time to compress the actuality segments. The news director is not interested in 90 seconds of the fire chief after you've asked him a 5-second question. Edit out the extra material and keep the focus on you. Total length of your tape shouldn't be more than about five or six minutes.

6. *Spend the necessary time and effort to produce the best tape you can.* When the news director is getting down to the final two or three tapes and all are pretty good, he or she is looking for reasons to eliminate one or more of them. Don't give him or her a reason to dump you simply because you didn't correct something minor that you thought would be overlooked. You'll seldom know why you didn't get the job or how close you came. Don't take the chance of missing out just because you didn't want to be bothered to do another take or because your production was sloppy.

It can of course be difficult, when you don't report news every day, to come up with a tape that does everything. Fox advises candidates to be creative. Ask for help from local news directors. They probably won't put a camera crew and studio time at your disposal to produce your tape, but they might spend a few minutes telling you what they look for in a good tape. That will help you avoid the considerable expense of commercially producing a tape that is useless because it contains the wrong material.

In rare cases, you might be allowed to tag along with a news crew for a day or two. If things work just right, the crew may let you reinterview a news subject and use the tape in your audition. One of the authors of this book, who had just appeared as a guest on a live segment of a local newscast, was asked if he would mind being reinterviewed on tape by a candidate for a reporting position at that station. As it turned out, the candidate did the reinterview more professionally than the reporter did the on-air interview.

The point is that if you want to beat the odds and land that first job in TV news, you must be creative and aggressive. If one approach doesn't work, try another. Persistence may well pay off in a tape you can be proud of.

It is unlikely that you'll get your tape returned. With videotape, this can get expensive. You can improve your chances by enclosing a stamped, self-addressed envelope. You may be able to present your tape at an interview if the hiring station has only requested résumés and letters as the first step in the search for candidates. But given the large number of candidates who desperately want the jobs that become available, most stations can skip that first step and simply request tapes in the initial ad. In that case there's no point in telling them you'll be happy to supply a tape if and when you're interviewed. Go ahead and duplicate your master tape, and write off the cost as an expense of your job search.

Job Leads and Sources of Leads

One of your best tools for uncovering job leads is an effective letter. It may be the cover letter for your résumé, or simply a letter addressed to the program director, manager, or news director of a station in which you are interested. Such a letter to a station executive should do three things:

1. *Tell the program director that you are going to be in town on a particular date.* Broadcast executives are more likely to agree to talk to you if you will be in the area anyway because they are very reluctant to invite anyone to travel a long distance to discuss a job that may not exist.

2. *Let you meet the executive and discuss the station and the broadcasting business in general, not a particular job or future employment at that station.* Again, giving the impression that you are courting an immediate job will often draw the response "We don't have any jobs." A more general request can often be more productive.

3. *Introduce you, the writer, tell something about your background and qualifications, and show that you have undertaken to research that par-*

ticular station. Never send out a form letter, either as a cover letter or in scattergun applications.

Be sure to send letters to a person, not a title. This shows that you have made some effort to find out the identity of your prospective boss. To confirm his or her name, you can call the station's news department (in the evening, to save telephone tolls). Also, if you can show that you understand the community and its needs, so much the better. If you secure an interview, you may have a chance to play your tape and to discuss career goals and opportunities at this particular station.

Volumes have been written on the technique for a successful interview, and little can be added to this body of knowledge other than to emphasize the most important points of all:

- Express enthusiasm and a willingness to work in any capacity.
- Know something about the station, its format, and its audience.

Information about stations and station personnel and information on cable operations can be gleaned from the same source that yielded the name and address to which you sent the letter: *Broadcasting/Cablecasting Yearbook.* This expensive volume (about $80 at the time of this writing) is available at the reference desk in larger libraries and furnishes the call letters, addresses, telephone numbers, and names of management personnel for all radio and television stations in the United States. Other information concerning technical specifications, format, and special programming is also supplied. Remember that broadcast employees change jobs frequently, so if your budget permits, call to confirm that an executive listed in the *Yearbook* still works at the station.

Other sources of job leads include the classified sections in *Broadcasting and Cable,* a weekly periodical also found in many large libraries. You may want to subscribe to this magazine, and the address is provided in the Suggested Readings at the end of this book. Do not rely too heavily on the classifieds in *Broadcasting;* very few employers will pay for an ad in a nationwide trade to recruit beginners. Several online resources have jobs listed. Try Broadcast Net's job related page (www.broadcast.net/mailman/listinfo /broadcast-jobs) and Radio TV Jobs.com (www.radiotvjobs.com).

Your first job may be turned up by a job search, or may surface from word of mouth. That is why contacts are so important.

Developing Contacts

Friends, friends of friends, and even their friends can be valuable to you in the search for employment. Broadcasting is a tightly knit club, and many jobs are never advertised. They open, are heard about on the grapevine, and are filled by someone who knows someone.

This is a business where an announcer might quit on the same day you walk in, tape and résumé in hand. By virtue of being in the right place at the right time, you may land the position. Or a friend in the station may let you know about the opening. Sometimes the executive with whom you have had a "getting to know you" interview will remember you, like you, and retrieve your telephone number from the top of the résumé.

Every contact you make, every interview you arrange, is a factor in your favor. Do not look on "contacts" as a dirty word because in the business of broadcasting it is not. Broadcasting is a business of contacts. Here are suggestions for developing your own set of contacts:

1. *Stay in touch with your college communications department and with the alumni association.*

2. *Keep in touch with alumni.* Write down the names and addresses of alums and keep track of their progress. College and university "old boy" networks can be extremely valuable.

3. *If you are turned down for a job, try to keep the person who turned you down as a contact.* Never, never burn your bridges with an executive who does not hire you. You may have been a close second choice, but if you express anger and outrage at not getting the job, you'll never be in contention again. Instead, contact the person who did not hire you and find out, in a nonconfrontational way, why you didn't get the job. Say that you are concerned with self-improvement and would like to know how to better yourself. Perhaps it was a simple matter of needing more experience, and the job could be yours next time.

The Business End

Broadcasting is a business run by businesspeople. Some of these people may have been performers at one time, but they are not generally motivated by artistic goals. Quite properly, they are concerned with turning a profit. The fact that broadcasting is a business means that we must discuss pay and general working conditions.

Salaries

Salaries in the broadcast field, particularly for on-air performers, are generally far lower than most members of the general public might expect. This is particularly true in small markets, where even well-known local broadcasters may be making close to minimum wage.

At the entry level in broadcasting, pay is very low. Along with print journalism, broadcasting ranks among the lowest professions in salaries paid to beginners.

Until you have established a track record, there isn't really much to be done about the poor pay level. This situation holds generally true whether you're looking at television or radio. Expect to be offered between $15,000 and $23,000 per year in most small- and medium-market stations if you're looking at news jobs.

Talent agent Lou Fox points out that many entry-level TV news reporters with no commercial experience start out in the $18,000 range. On that salary, he notes, they not only have to pay the same living expenses as everyone else, such as food and place to live, but they also need to have a very good wardrobe. Their on-camera appearance must not reflect the poverty-level wages they're making.

The Radio Television News Directors Association (RTNDA) compiles detailed statistics each year for broadcast salaries. Figures from the survey conducted in 2001 show entry-level salaries continuing to be abysmal, with reporters in small markets sometimes earning about $20,000 per year. If you do manage to make it to a reporting job in a medium market, 2001 figures show you might still be earning about $28,000 per year.[1] These salaries have remained constant for more than three years.

In radio, entry-level salaries can still begin at about $16,000. At the top levels, radio personalities in the major markets working in drive time can make as much as $250,000, although $100,000 is much closer to the average. In the Baltimore market, the highest salaries for radio personalities were around $175,000 in 1999. More commonly in a market the size of Baltimore, salaries for staff announcers with a morning, afternoon, or evening airshift range from a low of about $28,000 up to $75,000. That's because salaries in radio have been stagnating during the last few years. Group-owned radio stations frequently hire announcers to record voice tracks for shows on many stations. One announcer, who works in a large California market, records his local show and tracks for two other markets every morning, for example.

Large-market radio personalities often supplement their income by making personal appearances. They can often add $20,000 or so to their annual salaries through these extras. However, there are fewer good announcing jobs. The U.S. Bureau of Labor Statistics estimates that there will be an 8 percent reduction in the number of radio and television announcers as a result of media consolidation.

TV newspeople in mid-career outpace their news counterparts in radio, though large-market radio news directors are currently averaging around $40,000.

In general, as has been discussed, salary is pegged to market size. Market size is described by the ratings of *areas of dominant influence,* commonly known as ADIs. There are slightly more than 200 ADIs in the United States, with New York being the largest and Los Angeles the second largest. The smaller the ADI number, the larger the market. Thus, New York is ADI 1 and Los Angeles is ADI 2.

---

[1] For a discussion of salaries for various broadcast jobs, see the discussion at the Radio Television News Directors Association Web site: www.rtnda.org/research /salaries02.shtml.

A beginner generally does not have a good chance of cracking the top 60 or so markets. That means, for a while at least, working in a smaller market and accepting a small salary. Your starting salary will reflect the size of the market, the health of the station, and the worth of your position. Every station manager has a good idea of the maximum value of a particular job. The morning drive announcer at a local radio station, for example, will never be paid more than the position generates in advertising revenue. The station owner and/or manager, obviously, will also have to deduct overhead and allow for a fair profit. Therefore, the person controlling the purse strings will know that no morning announcer, no matter how good, is worth more than $400 a week for this particular position. The market reaches a point of diminishing returns.

The particular economic conditions in a market, such as the popularity of the station and the amount of competing signals from major stations, will determine the maximum value of that position. There is so much variety among markets that quoting salaries based on market size is misleading. One profitable radio station in Watertown, New York, for example, will pay a morning drive announcer in the neighborhood of $35,000 per year, even though the market size is in the 160 category. Other markets deep in the hundreds might pay a fraction above minimum wage. One television reporter in the 60th market makes about $25,000 per year, despite almost two decades of experience. He works at a station with poor profits in a market dominated by competing TV news operations.

Yes, major-market air professionals make a great deal of money, but that is a long trip down a difficult road. And even a moderate salary in a larger market can leave you devastatingly poor because the cost of living in a big city is so high. When considering jobs, check the cost of apartment rentals before committing yourself.

Contracts

You may be asked to sign a one- to three-year contract after being hired by a broadcast station. This is not likely for a beginner, however, because most small markets do not have contracts.

Contracts specify many different things but always put salary figures in black and white, often with built-in escalator clauses. Sometimes the salary is renegotiated yearly.

A contract entails an obligation on your part and on the station's part. It will state a specific period of time in which you agree to stay in the station's employ, but in *most* cases stations will not hold you strictly to this clause. You can typically escape a contract as long as you are not going to a directly competitive station within the market. If you want to move to a competitor before your contract has expired, however, you may have a fight on your hands.

Contracts also work for you, specifying some of your working conditions and hours. Most contracts say that you can be discharged only for "good cause." That vague term is not ironclad protection, but it is better than none at all.

Agents

For top performers, an agent is a necessity. For beginners, an agent is out of the question. Agents act as middlemen between a performer and management. In return, they take a percentage of a broadcaster's salary.

As a beginner, your salary will be too low to attract any agent who works on a percentage basis. As you progress, you might engage an agent, or, when the time is right, an agent will contact you.

Many big-time performers find that an agent not only attracts and screens assignments and negotiates the best possible financial package but also serves as a buffer between management and the performer. A performer will not have to haggle directly with his or her boss.

Unions

The primary union for on-air talent is the American Federation of Television and Radio Artists, known as AFTRA (www.AFTRA.org). Other unions that may have some involvement in a performer's career are the National Association of Broadcast Engineers and Technicians (**NABET**) (www.nabetcwa.org) and the Screen Actors Guild (SAG) (www.sag.org). Unions set minimum salaries for employees at covered stations, along with guidelines for working conditions, hours, duties, recording fees, and residuals.

You do not have to be a union member to be considered for a job at a union station. Because unionized stations are generally, but not always, those in the larger markets, most beginners will not have to join a union. As you progress, you may be hired at a unionized station. Then, after a certain grace period, you will be required to join the union.

Union shops may restrict your activity to the duties described in a rigidly drawn contract, which is why large markets with tightly specified union restrictions are not the place to experiment with various aspects of the job.

The Impact of Ratings

Broadcasting is a simple business, really. If programs on the air do not deliver a sufficient audience, the station gets rid of the programs—and with them, the talent. The business of broadcasting must have a bottom line, and the rating system determines much of that bottom line. Although everyone involved in broadcasting agrees that current rating systems are far from perfect, they are the only way broadcasters can quantify success or failure.

A **rating** is a percentage of all possible listeners or viewers in an area who are watching or listening to you. A share is the percentage of listeners who are watching or listening at a particular time who are tuned into a particular station. Thus, a 2 rating and a 20 share on a radio program means that the program had 2 percent of people with radios tuned in, and 20 percent of all the people tuned in were listening to that particular show.

The A. C. Nielsen Company conducts the primary ratings for television. In radio, Arbitron is the primary service, although there are a few others. Ratings are done by electronic monitoring, by the filing of written logs, and by other methods including telephone polling. In all but the smallest markets, ratings are vitally important to a station and to a performer. Ratings are published at different intervals, depending on the size of the market, ranging from monthly to semiannually. These published figures are commonly referred to as "the book."

Jobs are lost when ratings fall. If you are a news anchor, and your newscast is last in two consecutive books, your job may be in serious jeopardy.

Station executives will make a variety of program and personnel decisions based on the book. From a performer's standpoint, remember that ratings are nothing more than information. Station management may recommend changes and policy based on analysis of those ratings, and those changes may directly affect you. Perhaps the ratings indicate a need to appeal to a more youthful market in a morning drive program. The music and overall approach of the program may be changed, and the announcer is expected to adapt his or her delivery to reflect those changes. Similar situations may be encountered in news, or in any portion of the broadcast schedule.

Conclusion

Your study of broadcasting in college and your early work experiences do not lock you into an announcing career. If your career does not develop as you want, your broad education and communication skills will serve you well in any type of job.

Many interesting alternatives are related to announcing. The authors of this book, for example, have intertwined years of work as air talent with jobs in teaching, journalism, advertising, writing, public relations, civilian and military broadcast management, and acting.

Yes, it is a tough business. But do not be unnecessarily discouraged, because although many who study broadcast announcing do not make it, *thousands DO!* If you honestly believe you have the talent, motivation, and drive, *go for it.*

Drill Material: News, Sports, Weather, and Miscellaneous Wire Service Copy

The material in this section is copy that has been provided by several radio and television broadcasters. There is a selection of news, sports, and weather copy, and some items of information that stations might use as general, miscellaneous information in DJ shows or other formats.

Some of the material is wire service information from the Associated Press. Other material has been written by local newspeople at the station level. Both radio and television news copy are included. We have selected copy that is broadly representative of copy you are likely to encounter in day-to-day broadcast operations.

To make most effective use of this copy, take the time to analyze the material. When you've completed your analysis, identify the techniques you as the performer can use to breathe life into the written message and to help viewers or listeners understand the information.

Keep in mind that nearly anyone can render an understandable reading of this copy. But of those who try, very few succeed in the competitive arena that leads to the top of the broadcasting professions. To succeed, you must combine your innate talent with careful attention to the techniques described in this book and a determination to bring something unique to each piece of copy you encounter. The process takes time, hard work, and persistence in addition to a fair amount of good, old-fashioned luck.

Wire Service Copy

Wire service copy provides broadcast stations with continuous current information about ongoing events. Everything from the latest sports scores to the most recent developments in foreign and domestic news is available at any time of the day for subscribers to these services. What follows in this section includes a representative sample from a single day's feed from the Associated Press Radio Wire.

Use the information to practice reading and ad-libbing skills discussed in this book. A variety of copy types have been included.

Wire Service News Feeds

Through each day and night AP feeds subscribers news copy ready for reading on the air. "Newswatch" is a compilation of the latest news stories, presented in a format that can be used as copy for regularly scheduled newscasts. There is more than enough material for a five-minute newscast, but many stations select stories from the feed and combine them with local stories to build their own newscasts.

A shorter summary of the latest news is presented in the "Newsminute." It takes about 60 seconds for the average announcer to read the material in this feature. It is used for quick updates on current stories.

In addition to news presented in a format, some stories are simply fed as stand-alone items. These can be substituted for stories in the newscast format or simply integrated in the station's own newscast format.

We have included in this section a sampling of typical wire service copy that will give practice in reading news, sports, weather, and feature material that you are likely to encounter in many on-air situations.

Also in this section is local news copy written by news staff at a single station.

```
^AP-1st Morning Drive NewsWatch
^<
            - - - - - - - - - - - - - - - - - -
                  !  AP NEWSWATCH  !
- - - - - - - - - - - - - - - - - - - - - - - - - - - - - - - - - -
North Korea compromise plan...Al-Qaida on the move...Gephardt
running
- - - - - - - - - - - - - - - - - - - - - - - - - - - - - - - - - -
^
    (Seoul, South Korea-AP) -- South Korea's incoming president
wants to broker a compromise to defuse the standoff over North
Korea's nuclear program. Roh Moon-hyun's (noh moo-hyuhnz) plan would
require concessions by North Korea and the U-S. Roh doesn't think
the North will bow to economic pressure.
^
    (New York-AP) -- N-B-C news says al-Qaida operatives are
shuttling between Yemen and Saudi Arabia in cars, pickups and
S-U-V's. The network's Web site reports U-S officials think 30 to
```

50 al-Qaida members are in Saudi Arabia at any given time. A Saudi
spokesman calls the report "total nonsense."
^

(Washington-AP) -- Departing House Democratic leader Dick
Gephardt may be the latest Democratic candidate for the White House.
The A-P has learned Gephardt is forming an exploratory committee.
Gephardt sought the presidency in 1988. He won the Iowa caucus and
finished second in New Hampshire.
^

(Crawford, Texas-AP) -- President Bush today rallies troops who
could be sent to the Persian Gulf to fight Iraq. Bush addresses
troops at Fort Hood, Texas, the country's biggest military base.
About 25-thousand Fort Hood troops fought in the Gulf War.
^

(White House-AP) -- President bush is readying an economic
stimulus package he plans to release next Tuesday at a speech in
Chicago. The plan is expected to speed up some tax cuts and give
investors a break when they make money on corporate dividends. He'll
deny it's tilted toward the rich.
^

(Modesto, California-AP) -- Modesto, California, police say
the chances of finding Laci Peterson alive "are slim." Peterson is
eight months pregnant and has been missing since Christmas Eve.
Police want the public to help verify the whereabouts of her
husband last week.
^

(San Diego-AP) -- A California judge today decides the fate of
David Westerfield. Westerfield has been convicted of kidnapping and
murdering seven-year-old Danielle van Dam. A jury has already
recommended he be put to death. Prosecutors describe Westerfield as
"evil" and "cold-hearted."
^

(Washington-AP) -- The government is handing out grants to
promote marriage. The Department of Health and Human Services is
sending more than two (m) million dollars to religious and nonprofit
groups to emphasize marriage. Critics say marriage should be none of
the government's business.
^

(Islamabad, Pakistan-AP) -- Pakistanis are protesting a possible
U-S-led war against Iraq with a nationwide strike. Security is being
tightened around the U-S embassy in Islamabad. One hard-line
religious leader says an attack on Iraq would be "an attack on the
Islamic world."
^

(Washington-AP) — 2002 was a safe year to fly. No one was killed
flying on a passenger or cargo plane in the U-S last year. That's the

third time in a decade there hasn't been a commercial airline death.
Aviation officials attribute the safety record to better equipment
and improved training.

    by Chad Pergram

    (Copyright 2003 by The Associated Press. All Rights Reserved.)
    AP-NY-01-03-03 0351EST<

^AP-4th News Agenda
^<

            - - - - - - - - - - - - - -
                    ! NEWS AGENDA !
- -
Here are the top stories on the wire at this hour:
- -
^
    (Raleigh, North Carolina-AP) -- Another Democrat is jumping into
the presidential election ring.
    North Carolina Senator John Edwards broke the news to friends at
a New Year's gathering Yesterday and will make it public today on
the "Today" show.
    Friend and former North Carolina Democratic Party chief Ed
Turlington says those there had a feeling they were witnessing
something historic. In his words, "We believe he's ready. We believe
he has a great chance to win."
    Edwards is 49. He's a first-term senator, a former trial lawyer
and a (m) millionaire.
^
    (Beijing-AP) -- China says it will launch its first manned
spacecraft this year.
    State media say the Shenzhou (shen-JOH') Five spacecraft will
carry a human into space in the second half of 2003.
    The Shenzhou Four is orbiting the Earth now, three days into a
seven-day mission. It's testing life-support and other systems with
an eye toward a manned flight. Shenzhou means "sacred vessel."
    Only the United States and Russia have sent human beings into
space on their own.
    The Chinese government presents its space program as a symbol of
national pride, much as the United States did during the space race
against the Soviets in the '60's.
^
    (Detroit-AP) -- Auto executives are not a happy bunch.

A survey finds they're less confident about a return to profitability than they were a year ago, and most see foreign automakers continuing to take market share.

About 30 percent of the 100 senior auto executives interviewed by the accounting firm K-P-M-G say they expect lean times industrywide until at least 2005.

The director of K-P-M-G's automotive practice division says the gloomy outlook stems in part from consumer's new expectations for rebates, special pricing and similar deals.

Carmakers introduced the incentives after the terror attacks, but they've cut deeply into profits.

North American automakers hope to catch the consumer's eye with new styling and technology, allow them to put zero-percent financing to rest.

^

(Modesto, California-AP) -- California police are continuing their search for Laci Peterson.

The 27-year-old pregnant woman from Modesto hasn't been seen since the day before Christmas.

Officers on horseback combed the area along the Tuolumne (TWAH'-luh-mee) River yesterday, asking homeless people camped along its banks if they've seen her. But investigators report no leads.

Peterson's family, including her husband, Scott, worked the phones at a volunteer center. He reported her missing when he returned from a fishing trip.

Police think she was the victim of foul play, but relatives aren't giving up hope. Her father-in-law says, "I feel that she's still with us and has the baby and we're going to find her."

^

(Seoul, South Korea-AP) -- Anti-American sentiment is on the rise in South Korea, and North Korea sees that as an opportunity.

The reclusive Stalinist regime is asking South Koreans for their support in its confrontation with the United States over its renewed nuclear weapons program.

Washington is the South Korean government's chief ally, but Seoul (sohl) is criticizing the American plan to use economic sanctions against the North.

U-S-South Korean ties have frayed recently. Two American soldiers were cleared in military trials after they accidentally killed two teenagers in a traffic accident. Thousands of people have turned out to protest. Many also want to see the 37-thousand U-S troops posted in South Korea go home.

^

(Sydney, Australia-AP) -- It's hard to tell just what the situation is on two remote Pacific islands raked by a cyclone.

A photographer who flew over the islands says every tree has been shredded, almost every building has been damaged, and the sea has overrun some villages.

An aid worker who did a flyover reports seeing people going about their business, including fishing. He did see damage to crops and homes.

More than three-thousand people live on the specks of land in the Solomon Islands, about 14-hundred miles north of Sydney, Australia.

Cyclone Zoe, a Category Five storm, blasted through on Sunday with winds of up to 225 miles-an-hour.
^

(Cairo, Egypt-AP) -- Another allied airstrike inside Iraq's southern no-fly zone.

The U-S military says American and British warplanes attacked an Iraqi mobile radar system Wednesday when it entered the zone.

The official Iraqi News Agency says the planes attacked "civil and service installations," killing one civilian and wounding two others. There's no word of casualties from Central Command. Iraq routinely accuses the allied pilots of attacking civilian targets.

The no-fly zones were set up after the Gulf War to protect Kurdish rebels in the north and Shiite (SHEE'-eyet) Muslims in the south from the government.

Iraq considers the zone a violation of its sovereignty and frequently challenges the patrols, who respond in kind.
^

(Haifa, Israel-AP) -- Warships from Israel, the U-S and Turkey have completed a joint training exercise off Israel's coast.

The sea-rescue maneuvers, dubbed Operation "Reliant Mermaid," are held every year and Israel insists they were unrelated to the possibility of war with Iraq. As one naval commander puts it, they "are not intended to improve coordination during a military battle." He says the focus is humanitarian.

This year's Reliant mermaid involved three Israeli ships, two vessels from Turkey and one U-S ship.
^

(Undated-AP) -- Michigan's first female governor calls it "a great message for our daughters and our sons."

Jennifer Granholm was sworn in Wednesday, along with a number of other new leaders around the country.

George Pataki has been inaugurated to his third term as governor of New York. He says the dust has settled and the fires are out, but "we still face a crisis." New York's fiscal problems reflect both the national recession and the after-effects of the terror attacks.

In New Mexico, Bill Richardson is the new governor. He's outlining proposals to save money and boost teachers' pay. The former member of the Clinton cabinet is asking people to judge him on his results, not his promises.
^

(Tokyo-AP) -- The Tokyo fire department reports at least three people have died from choking on traditional New Year's holiday rice cakes.
Twenty-two other people have been hospitalized—ten of them in comas.
The gooey treats are usually served in a broth or are grilled and wrapped in seaweed.
The rice cakes are typically blamed in several deaths a year -- usually among the elderly.
Fire officials issued a reminder warning this week, urging rice-cake eaters to take small bites, chew well and wash them down with lots of liquids.

(Copyright 2003 by The Associated Press. All Rights Reserved.)
AP-NY-01-02-03 0358EST<

^AP-NY—2nd News Agenda<
^

            - - - - - - - - - - - - - - - - - -
                   ! ASSOCIATED PRESS !
- -
^Here are the top stories in New York at this hour<
- -
^

(Albany-AP) -- Ready for more snow?
Forecasters say parts of upstate New York could get well over a foot of snow between today and Saturday afternoon, with eastern parts of the state expected to bear the brunt of the latest storm.
Eastern New York is still recovering from the Christmas Day storm that dumped two feet of snow on Albany and nearby communities, while some parts of the Mohawk Valley got three feet or more.
Today's storm could bring as much as 18 inches to the Schoharie, Mohawk and Hudson Valleys and the Catskills.
Central and western New York are expected to get less snow — up to seven inches in some counties east of Rochester — while Buffalo will get only a few inches.
Many schools are closed or are sending students hope early because of the slippery driving conditions.

(Buffalo-AP) -- James Kopp's confession that he killed a Buffalo-area abortion provider has resulted in a sharp drop in donations to his defense fund.

As a result, taxpayers will now pick up the tab for the attorney assigned to defend the anti-abortion extremist in federal court.

A federal judge has assigned western New York's chief federal public defender to represent Kopp at his trial.

The move comes after Kopp's former attorney informed court officials that donations for the defendant's case stopped coming in after Kopp confessed to The Buffalo News that he killed Dr. Barnett Slepian in October 1998.

William Clauss will defend Kopp against the federal charges.

The 48-year-old Kopp also faces state murder charges in Erie County Court. He's being represented by private-practice attorneys in that case.
^

(Niagara Falls-AP) -- New York state's newest casino is barely three days old and already it's sparking potential spin-off development in Niagara Falls.

That's according to business and development officials in Niagara County.

Officials at the county's County Industrial Development Agency tell The Buffalo News that the Seneca Niagara Casino is beginning to stir interest from local hotels looking to either renovate or expand their facilities.

The agency had already received several proposals for hotel improvements even before had its grand opening on Tuesday.

Since then, the Niagara Falls Chamber of Commerce says it has received numerous calls from out-of-town interests. Chamber officials say many of the callers are seeking demographic information about Niagara Falls.

(Dannemora-AP) -- A former guard at a state prison in northern New York faces rape, contraband and bribery charges.

State correctional services officials say 49-year-old Lucy Godfrey of Peru has been charged with promoting prison contraband, bribe receiving, official misconduct and rape.

Godfrey has resigned from her job. She had been a guard since 1988 and had been working at Clinton Correctional Facility near Plattsburgh for the past two years.

Corrections department officials aren't releasing any other information on the charges, saying that it might jeopardize an on-going investigation at the maximum-security prison.

Godfrey is being held in Clinton County Jail on one-thousand dollars bail.

(Albany-AP) -- U-S Senator Charles Schumer says he will fight to keep Wall Street's biggest firms in Manhattan despite a federal proposal that would require some to branch outside the New York. The federal measure would aim to protect the world's financial markets in the event of another terrorist attack.

(Le Roy-AP) -- A 48-year-old western New York man has been charged with selling heroin to another man who overdosed and died New Year's Day.

Police in the Genesee County village of Le Roy say John Michael Stewart of Le Roy is also charged with providing heroin to two other men, including one who overdosed but was revived in November.

Stewart faces two counts of third-degree criminal sale of a controlled substance and one count of criminal possessing of a hypodermic needle.

On New Year's Eve, Stewart allegedly sold heroin to two men in the village, including 44-year-old Robert Slaven of Le Roy, who died the next day.

(Syracuse-AP) -- Onondaga County Executive Nicholas Pirro is pledging to turn the Syracuse area into an international tourist destination if voters return him to office for a fifth term.

The Republican announced last night during a political pep rally that he would seek another term in office.

Pirro says he wants to see the Destiny U-S-A project completed.

Destiny U-S-A is a two (b) billion-dollar proposal to expand the existing Carousel Center into the nation's largest retail and entertainment complex.

Pirro has been a major supporter of the project and the mall developer's requests for tax breaks.

Developers say the mall will attract between 40 (m) million and 50 (m) million visitors annually.

(Syracuse-AP) -- Police in Syracuse say an 18-year-old woman committed suicide last night by jumping off a bridge over Interstate 81 in downtown Syracuse.

The woman was pronounced dead at the scene after being struck by at least three vehicles, including a tractor-trailer.

Syracuse police spokesman Tom Connellan says police are investigating what led the woman to jump off the bridge.

The woman's name hasn't been released yet.

Northbound traffic on I-81 through downtown Syracuse was shut down for about two hours following the incident, which occurred shortly after 7:30 p-m.

(Binghamton-AP) -- A Binghamton-area convenience store clerk apparently tried to get lucky -- illegally.

Twenty-two-year-old Derek Harlec has been accused of using stolen credit card numbers to buy hundreds of dollars worth of lottery tickets.

Authorities say Harlec -- who lives in the town of Chenango -- faces a felony grand larceny charge.

Police say Harlec allegedly used credit card numbers illegally obtained on the Internet.

He's accused of making a half-dozen lottery ticket purchases using the purloined card numbers.

Police don't know whether any of the tickets were winners because they haven't been found.

(Copyright 2003 by The Associated Press. All Rights Reserved.)
AP-NY-01-03-03 1140EST<

^AP-11th News Agenda
^<

                - - - - - - - - - - - - - - -
                      ! NEWS AGENDA !
- -
Here are the top stories on the wire at this hour:
- -
^

(San Diego-AP) -- David Westerfield learns his fate later this hour.

He's the San Diego neighbor convicted of snatching and killing seven-year-old Danielle van Dam last year.

A jury recommended a death penalty -- and a judge is expected to go along.

The slain girls' mother says she's just happy Westerfield is off the street.

Brenda van Dam tells N-B-C's "Today" show that the life of David Westerfield "is over."
^

(Crawford, Texas-AP) -- The head cheerleader leads a big pep rally at Fort Hood, Texas today.

President Bush today fires up the troops at the nation's largest military base.

Fort Hood is home to the First Calvary Division -- a highly mobile unit that relies on helicopters and tanks. With 41-thousand

troops overall, the base will probably play a key role should the U-S go to war against Iraq.
^

(Baghdad, Iraq-AP) -- Iraq isn't buying it.

Baghdad's official newspaper says it doesn't believe President Bush has "suddenly become rational" when he says he hopes the U-S doesn't have to go to war.

The paper accused Bush of trying to cool international criticism of U-S war planning.

Meantime, U-N arms inspectors today looked at two sites outside Baghdad.

One makes fuel for missiles. The other produces chemicals.

The inspectors say they're not finished with their weapons checks and need more time to look at other sites.
^

(Scranton, Pennsylvania-AP) -- It's the cost of terrorism.

A Scranton, Pennsylvania, water company wants to jack up its prices to pay for added security around reservoirs and filtration plants.

The surcharge would cost customers an extra four cents a day.

The company says it's spent more than eight (m) million dollars to tighten security. It's also hired more security guards.

Natural gas company P-G Energy is also considering imposing a similar fee.
^

(Washington-AP) -- For the second straight day, the economic news is better than expected.

The Commerce Department reports construction spending rose by three-tenths of one percent in November, helped by record activity in the red-hot housing market.

The Commerce Department says building activity totaled 843 (B) billion dollars at an annual rate in November.

There's also word that October was revised to show a one percent gain, instead of the three-tenth's increase earlier indicated.

Low interest rates have been credited for fueling continued demand for homes, both new and existing.

The stock market rallied on the first session of the new year, as investors reacted to a report indicating an upturn in the manufacturing sector.
^

(New York-AP) -- A fairly quiet session so far for stocks, after yesterday's 265-point gain for the Dow Industrials average. The broader market has been little changed in this morning's trading.
^

(Paris-AP) -- There's word the parents of a baby alleged to be the first human clone are afraid their child might be taken away from them.

So says the head of Clonaid (KLOHN'-ayd), the company that claims to have produced the clone. Brigitte Boisselier (bwah-suh-lee-AY') says the parents are rethinking whether to allow D-N-A testing to determine if what Clonaid says is true.

She tells a French T-V station (France-2) the parents fear some recent legal action could end up in the baby being taken away. A Florida lawyer is asking a court to turn the baby over to state care if it finds the baby's health is in danger.

Clonaid is linked to a group that believes aliens created life on Earth.

The group's founder -- who calls himself Rael (ray-EHL') -- tells C-N-N he urged Boisselier not to allow any testing.

He says a Florida judge had "signed a paper" saying the baby should be taken from the family. But in fact, there's no indication the court has made a decision.
^

(Albany, New York-AP) -- One of the nation's largest state police agencies has pulled its fleet of Ford Crown Victoria cruisers off the road.

New York State Police Superintendent James McMahon has ordered the cars removed from patrol duty and retrofitted with gasoline tank shields.

The shields can prevent fires resulting from rear-end collisions.

Two weeks, ago a New York state trooper died after his Crown Victoria patrol car was struck from behind on the New York State Thruway in Yonkers.

The decision to idle the Crown Victorias came after the union representing New York's troopers urged its members to refuse to patrol in those vehicles.

At least 13 police officers nationwide have died over the past two decades following crashes in which their Crown Victorias caught fire.
^

(London-AP) -- Monty Python members are remembering Ian MacNaughton as a "wild Scotsman" who loved trying something new.

The T-V director who helped bring "Monty Python's Flying Circus" to the screen died last month in Germany from injuries he suffered in a car crash. He was 76.

MacNaughton directed all but the first four episodes of the comedy show, which ran on B-B-C television from 1969 to '74.

He also directed one of the comedy troupe's feature films, "And Now For Something Completely Different," and a German version of the series.

In an obituary in The Guardian newspaper, group member Terry Jones says there was friction at first between the director and the comedians.

But he says MacNaughton was later credited with shaping their wild talents, and defending them to skeptical T-V executives.

Python member Michael Palin tells The Times newspaper that MacNaughton appreciated the group's "touch of anarchy."
^

(Lantana, Florida-AP) -- Nothing like leaving your wallet during a robbery to get police on your tail.

A Florida man is behind bars after police found his wallet at the scene of an armed robbery.

Authorities say a man went into a gas station in Lantana Wednesday night, opened his wallet and asked the clerk for change. He then set the wallet down on the counter and pulled a gun from his waistband.

The robber fled with about 200 dollars.

When deputies arrived on the scene, they found the wallet still on the counter.

They used several traffic citations inside to track the suspect down.
^

^AP-Israel-Politics

- - - - - - - - - - - - - - - - -
                                 !   GENERAL NEWS   !
- -
Prime Minister Sharon's party hurt by corruption charges ahead of election
- -
^

(Jerusalem-AP) -- Polls indicate support for Israeli Prime Minister Ariel Sharon's Likud (lee-KOOD') party is slipping away amid allegations of bribery and corruption.

The polls show Likud losing nearly a quarter of its support since last month. But the surveys also show the party and its hard-line allies will win enough seats to form a government and give Sharon another term in office in this month's election.

Meantime, police say charges are being considered against four Likud activists who were allegedly involved in arranging bribes during the party primary.

The scandal is overshadowing the main issues in the campaign —
the ongoing conflict between Israel and the Palestinians and
strengthening Israel's defenses in the face of an American-led war
with Iraq.
^

    %@AP Links

    <<APPHOTO JRL104 (01/02/03)>>
    I: Israeli Prime Minister Ariel Sharon, left, views a painting
by Pablo Picasso during a visit to the Tel Aviv Museum Thursday
Jan. 2, 003.
^

    (Copyright 2003 by The Associated Press. All Rights Reserved.)
    AP-NY-01-03-03 0936EST<

^AP-Medical Malpractice
^<

                              - - - - - - - - - - - - - - - - -
                              ! GENERAL NEWS !
- -
No progress reported in ending walkout
- -
^

    (Charleston, West Virginia-AP) -- There's no end in sight to a
walkout by surgeons protesting high malpractice insurance costs in
West Virginia.
    One surgeon says the strike will continue indefinitely because
Governor Bob Wise and state lawmakers aren't doing enough to address
the problem.
    A state official says Wise plans to reveal a new insurance plan
in a speech next week. A group of surgeons had met with state
officials yesterday.
    The walkout involves more than two dozen orthopedic, general and
heart surgeons who serve four hospitals in northern West Virginia.
Some started 30-day leaves of absence on Wednesday, while others
plan to start leaves in the next few days.
    They want the state to make it harder to file malpractice suits,
a move they say would lower their premiums.
    The affected hospitals are keeping their emergency rooms open --
but except for plastic surgeons, they have almost no emergency
surgeons on duty.

Five patients have had to be taken elsewhere.
^

^AP-Three Found Dead
^<

```
                          - - - - - - - - - - - - - - - -
                                          !  GENERAL NEWS  !
- - - - - - - - - - - - - - - - - - - - - - - - - - - - - - - -
```
Suspect in deaths of wife, daughters is jailed
```
- - - - - - - - - - - - - - - - - - - - - - - - - - - - - - - -
```
^

    (Harrisburg, Pennsylvania-AP) -- A Pennsylvania man police say
is a suspect in the Christmas Eve murders of his wife and two
daughters is now in jail in connection with another charge.
    The Harrisburg Patriot-News reports that authorities were afraid
Ernest Wholaver would flee before they were able to try him for
allegedly sexually abusing his daughters.
    At the time his wife and daughters were killed, he had been free
on 100-thousand dollars bond with the condition that he stay away
from his family.
    Each of the women died from a single gunshot to the head and
were found at their home near Harrisburg Christmas morning.
    Wholaver's attorney says his client is not a flight risk.
    While Wholaver remains a suspect, police say they are
investigating other scenarios.
^

^AP-Midday BusinessMinute
^<

```
                          - - - - - - - - - - - - - - - -
                                          !  AP BUSINESSMINUTE  !
- - - - - - - - - - - - - - - - - - - - - - - - - - - - - - - -
```
  Quiet stocks...Construction spending rises...Home Depot tanks
```
- - - - - - - - - - - - - - - - - - - - - - - - - - - - - - - -
```
^

(New York-AP) -- A fairly quiet session so far for stocks, after yesterday's 265-point gain for the Dow Industrials average. The broader market has been little changed in the first hour of trading.
^

(Washington-AP) -- The Commerce Department says construction spending has now risen for four straight months. Not only were outlays better than expected in November, but October was revised higher.
^

(Detroit-AP) -- The world's largest automaker is extending its zero-percent financing offer through the end of February. G-M has been attempting to take additional market share through aggressive incentives.
^

(New York-AP) -- Home Depot shares have dipped more than ten percent in early trading. The home improvement giant warned about earnings for the fiscal year ending next month in the face of lackluster sales.
^

(Fort Worth, Texas-Dow Jones/AP) -- The holiday shopping season wasn't as strong as Radio Shack expected. It has trimmed the fourth-quarter earnings outlook, citing disappointing sales of a variety of items, including Sprint P-C-S phones and certain radio-controlled toys as well as batteries.
^

^AP-Morning BusinessWatch, take 2

```
                               - - - - - - - - - - - - - - -
                               !  MORE BUSINESS  !
- - - - - - - - - - - - - - - - - - - - - - - - - - - - - - -
```
Crude prices rise...Mortgage rates hit new lows...
```
- - - - - - - - - - - - - - - - - - - - - - - - - - - - - - -
```
^

(New York-Dow Jones/AP) -- Crude oil futures have jumped higher after the government reported that the monthlong strike in Venezuela had left a deep hole in U-S crude oil inventories in the past week.
On the New York Mercantile Exchange yesterday, February crude oil futures jumped as high as 32 dollars, nine cents a barrel before ending at 31-85 a barrel, up 65 cents.

February heating oil futures surged one-point-three to close at 88-point-oh-nine cents a gallon, while February gasoline ended the session at 88-point-30 cents up one and a-third cents a gallon.
^

(New York-Dow Jones/AP) -- If you thought mortgage rates couldn't go any lower -- you were wrong.

The mortgage company Freddie Mac says rates have dropped to yet another new low, averaging five-point-85 percent this week for a 30-year fixed-rate mortgage.

That's down from last week's average of five-point-93 percent, the previous record low in the Freddie Mac survey, which dates back to 1971.

The company's chief economist says worries about war and terrorism and an unexpected drop in consumer confidence have helped to drive down interest rates over the past week. He expects rates to hover around six percent for at least another few months.

Rates on 15-year fixed-rate mortgages also are lower, but the average for one-year adjustables is higher this week.
^

(Murray Hill, New Jersey-AP) -- Lucent Technologies has settled a lawsuit with a former sales chief.

Nina Aversano had sued the company, alleging she was forced out in 2000 for criticizing sales goals as too aggressive.

In a press release, the New Jersey-based telecommunications gear maker and Aversano announced a settlement to her breach-of-contract claim and that her lawsuit has been dismissed.

The terms weren't disclosed, and both sides said there would be no comment.

Aversano sued under New Jersey's whistleblower statute, contending that some of Lucent's sales goals were far too optimistic and that Lucent pushed her out for saying so.

Lucent responded that Aversano was responsible for many of the accounting and forecasting discrepancies cited in her complaint.
^

(Tempe, Arizona-AP) -- Recent cutbacks in airline food may be followed by a new trend: in-flight meals you pay for.

America West Airlines says it will begin a three-week test on Monday. On a dozen flights each day, the nation's eighth-largest airline will offer meals costing between three and ten dollars.

A spokeswoman says if the experiment proves successful, the airline may begin selling meals on all its flights longer than two and a-half hours.

With the industry under tremendous pressure to cut costs, other airlines acknowledge that they're considering following American West's lead.

Some analysts predict passengers will balk at the idea of paying for airline food.

But industry consultant Terry Trippler says the effort could improve the quality of the food. He says in some cases, it couldn't get much worse.
^

(Undated-AP) -- Wall Street may have kicked off the new year with a big rally, but that doesn't mean investors' jitters are gone.

A new survey finds that regret, fear, anger, bitterness and pessimism are the tone of conversations most people have had about the stock market lately.

When the subject of investing arises, 47 percent of investors said the tone of the talk was pessimistic, 44 percent said it's laden with regret and 35 percent said there is a tinge of fear among the participants. Only 22 percent of people said there was any sense of optimism about the market.

The data were pulled from an online survey of about a thousand people this fall for the brokerage Harrisdirect.
^

^AP-Construction Spending
^<

```
                                      - - - - - - - - - - -
                                      !  BUSINESS  !
- - - - - - - - - - - - - - - - - - - - - - - - - - - - - - - -
```
Construction better than thought
```
- - - - - - - - - - - - - - - - - - - - - - - - - - - - - - - -
```
^

(Washington-AP) -- For the second straight day, the economic news is better than expected.

The Commerce Department reports construction spending rose by three-tenths of one percent in November, helped by record activity in the red-hot housing market.

The Commerce Department says building activity totaled 843 (B) billion dollars at an annual rate in November.

There's also word that October was revised to show a one percent gain, instead of the three-tenth's increase earlier indicated.

Low interest rates have been credited for fueling continued demand for homes, both new and existing.

   The stock market rallied on the first session of the new year, as investors reacted to a report indicating an upturn in the manufacturing sector.
^

   %@AP Links

   <<GRAPHICSBANK 663157 (05/02/98)>> 1500x1125
   Carpenters work on new house, photo

   On the Net:
   Commerce Department: www.doc.gov
^

   (Copyright 2003 by The Associated Press. All Rights Reserved.)
   AP-NY-01-03-03 1015EST<

^AP-Wall Street-Midday-Take 2
^<

                                      - - - - - - - - - - - - - - -
                                      ! MORE BUSINESS !
- -
   Here the ten most active Big Board issues traded before noon (eastern time):
^<
  Home Depot   down   3.340
21.540
  Lucent Technologies Inc   up   .020
1.440
  Nortel Networks Corp (Holding Co)   up   .040
1.900
  Cadence Systems   down   2.420
9.240
  EMC Corp   down   .100
6.250
  Lowes Companies Inc   down   2.600
36.750
  AOL Time Warner Inc   up   .240
13.550
  General Electric Co   down   .380
25.100
  Pfizer Inc   up   .090
31.620
  JP Morgan Chase & Company   up   .010
25.450

^

The ten volume leaders on the American Stock Exchange:
^<
Nasdaq 100 Trust Series I   up   .030
25.430
Standard & Poors Depositary Receipts   down   .300
90.770
Semiconductor HOLDRs Trust   up   .180
23.900
DJIA Diamonds Trust   down   .190
85.990
Wheaton River Minerals Ltd   up   .090
1.100
Bema Gold   up   .050
1.340
SPDR Technology Sector   down   .070
15.530
iShares Trust Russell 2000 Index Fund   down   .270
77.630
Kinross Gold   up   0.20
2.460
Nabors Industries   down   .190
36.500
^

And the ten most active issues in Nasdaq trading:
^<
Cisco Systems   up   .071
13.711
Intel Corp   down   .150
16.540
Sun Microsystems Inc   up   .100
3.480
Applied Materials   up   .310
14.290
Oracle Corp   up   .075
11.285
Microsoft Corp   down   .640
53.080
JDS Uniphase Cp   up   .030
2.780
Dell Computer   down   .310
27.400
Qualcom Inc   down   1.101
36.039
Brocade Communications Systems Inc   up   .100
4.650

^

^AP-AM Prep-Entertainment History
^<

- -
      MORNING PREP - MORNING PREP - MORNING PREP - MORNING PREP
- -
^<
               -
               ! TODAY IN ENTERTAINMENT HISTORY !
               -
^

On January third, 1967, Carl Wilson of The Beach Boys refused to be sworn in after receiving a U-S Army draft notice. Wilson said he was a conscientious objector.

In 1969, John Lennon and Yoko Ono's "Two Virgin's" record sleeve, which showed them posing nude, was declared pornographic in New Jersey. Police seized copies of the album.

In 1970, members of The Beatles recorded their last song together, "I Me Mine." George Harrison later used that title for his autobiography.

Also in 1970, singer Davy Jones announced he was leaving The Monkees, a year after Peter Tork quit the group.

In 1974, Bob Dylan and The Band opened a brief tour. Several dates were recorded for a live album.

In 1980, singer Amos Milburn, known for the song "Chicken Shack Boogie," died in Texas.

In 1989, country legend Johnny Cash was released from a Nashville hospital two weeks after undergoing double-bypass heart surgery. At the time, he said he had no plans to cancel any of his tour dates that year.

Also in 1989, "The Arsenio Hall Show" made its premiere on Fox.

In 1991, the sit-com "Blossom" premiered on N-B-C.

In 1992, singer Jim Kerr of Simple Minds married actress Patsy Kensit in London. They have since split up.

Today's Birthdays: Record producer George Martin is 77. Actor Robert Loggia is 73, Actor Dabney Coleman is 72. Singer Stephen Stills is 58. Bassist John Paul Jones of Led Zeppelin is 57. Actress Victoria Principal is 53. Actor Mel Gibson is 47. Jazz saxophonist James Carter is 34. Actor Jason Marsden ("Ally McBeal") is 28.

Actress Danica McKellar ("The Wonder Years") is 28. Actor Nicholas
Gonzalez is 27. Actor Alex D. Linz is 14.

     Sound:
^sound from 'Queen For A Day'
^T-V premiere, 1956.
     <<CUT *269 (01/02/03)>> :11

^Peter, Paul and Mary, singing 'Leaving On A Jet Plane'
^Among the most popular songs this date, 1970.
     <<CUT *273 (01/02/03)>> :37

     (Copyright 2003 by The Associated Press. All Rights Reserved.)
     AP-NY-01-03-03 0824EST<

^AP-Network 3:32 aes, 01-02-03 (two takes)
^
^

     Entertainment: 'Two Weeks Notice' - Hugh Grant (COPY: V4306
Segue) <<CAT: egZ>>
^

     1-q-15-New York-(Hugh Grant, actor, with reporters)-"day,
actually"-Grant's asked if there are days where he doesn't want to
be witty for people like he is in the movies.
^<<CUT *1 (01/02/03)>>
     2-a-15-(Hugh Grant, actor, with reporters)-"met Sandy"-Grant
says being a giggler ended his stage career. (refers to Sandra
Bullock, his co-star in Two Weeks Notice)
^<<CUT *2 (01/02/03)>>
     3-a-14-(Hugh Grant, actor, with reporters)-"of mine"-Grant says
he has no interest in doing drama, even if someone wrote the part
just for him.
^<<CUT *3 (01/02/03)>>
     4-a-17-(Hugh Grant, actor, with reporters)-"the movie"-Grant
says he wishes he could do physical comedy as well as Sandra
Bullock. (refers to screenwriter Marc Lawrence)
^<<CUT *4 (01/02/03)>>
^

     Entertainment: 'The Wild Thornberrys' - Danielle Harris (COPY:
V4306 Segue) <<CAT: egZ>>
^

5-a-15-New York-(Danielle Harris, actress, with reporters)-"that's wonderful"-Harris says little kids can't believe she's the voice of Debbie Thornberry when they meet her.
^<<CUT *5 (01/02/03)>>

6-a-14-(Danielle Harris, actress, with reporters)-"hang out"-Harris says the key to speaking for Debbie is not being easily embarrassed.
^<<CUT *6 (01/02/03)>>

7-a-16-(Danielle Harris, actress, with reporters)-"really annoying"-Harris says she's picked up one of Debbie's habits of raising one of her eyebrows.
^<<CUT *7 (01/02/03)>>

8-a-14-(Danielle Harris, actress, with reporters)-"stuff in"-Harris says she's come up with some of Debbie's trademark phrases herself.
^<<CUT *8 (01/02/03)>>
^

Entertainment: Howie Day (COPY: V4305 Rock) <<CAT: eoZ>>
^

9-a-17-Fairfax, VA-(Howie Day, musician, in A-P interview)-"Howie Day (second reference)"-Day says he's eager to do a new album because he's grown so much since the first one.
^<<CUT *9 (01/02/03)>>

10-a-12-(Howie Day, musician, in A-P interview)-"every night"-Day says the main difference between his first album and the one he'll write next is that he's more mature.
^<<CUT *10 (01/02/03)>>

11-a-13-(Howie Day, musician in A-P interview)-"the lyrics"-Day says he plans to put more of himself into his music in the future.
^<<CUT *11 (01/02/03)>>

12-a-14-(Howie Day, musician, in A-P interview)-"for music"-Day says he may try taking a more positive turn on his future songs.
^<<CUT *12 (01/02/03)>>
^

Entertainment: Obit-Macmichael (COPY: V4305 Rock) <<CAT: eoZ>>
^

13-r-46-Undated-(Excerpt of Cutting Crew performing '(I Just) Died In Your Arms')-for production purposes.
^<<CUT *13 (01/02/03)>>

AP-NY-01-02-03 0456EST<

```
^AP-ConsumerWatch
^<
                     - - - - - - - - - - - - - - - - - - - -
                                      !  CONSUMERWATCH  !
- - - - - - - - - - - - - - - - - - - - - - - - - - - - - - -
Airlines continue to find more ways to make you pay more
- - - - - - - - - - - - - - - - - - - - - - - - - - - - - - -
^
```

   (Undated-AP) -- Major airlines have begun the year extending or launching fare sales as they keep working on trying to win back business lost since the nine-eleven terrorist attacks.
   But as air fares stay down, other charges continue to rise. Last year brought new fees for security and much steeper costs for making ticket changes, and industry analyst and consultant Robert Mann of R-W Mann and Company says America West's plan to experiment with charging for meals suggests the nickel-and-diming of air travelers is ongoing.
   Mann says that would be unfortunate. And, he says the industry may go too far with add-on costs and ending up riling passengers, as it has done many times in the past.
   Together, the airlines lost around nine (b) billion dollars in 2002, and analysts expect them to try to keep squeezing out savings by hiking fees and offering fewer perks for travelers.
^

   %@AP Links
^

   <<GRAPHICSBANK 442757 (07/17/96)>> 512x486
   Airline ticket over jet in flight, AIR FARES lettering, finished graphic
^

   On the Net: R.W. Mann & Co.: http://www.rwmann.com
^

   (Copyright 2003 by The Associated Press. All Rights Reserved.)
   AP-NY-01-03-03 0350EST<


```
^AP-Morning SportsWatch, take 3
^<
                              - - - - - - - - - -
                                     !  SPORTS  !
- - - - - - - - - - - - - - - - - - - - - - - - - - - - - - -
Chicago's love affair with Jordan continues...Blue Devils roll
- - - - - - - - - - - - - - - - - - - - - - - - - - - - - - -
```

^

   (Chicago-AP) -- Michael Jordan remains a hero in Chicago, and
Bulls fans reminded him of that last night. Jordan received a long
ovation before colleting ten points, five rebounds and five assists in
the Washington Wizards' 107-to-82 blowout over the Bulls.
   Jordan played 30 minutes before sitting out the fourth quarter
of his second game back in Chicago. Jerry Stackhouse poured in
28 points and Kwame Brown added 20 points and 12 rebounds as the
Wizards climbed within two games of .500.

   Dallas and Phoenix also won last night.
   Steve Nash scored 24 point and the Mavericks built a 24-point
lead in the second half before holding off the Los Angeles Clippers
102-to-92. Michael Finley and Dirk Nowitzki added 20 points apiece
as the Mavs improved to a league-leading 26-and-5.
   Shawn Marion scored 16 of his 24 points in the second half of
the Phoenix Suns' seventh straight home win 96-to-78 over
Philadelphia. Sixers guard Allen Iverson missed 13 of his 17 shots
and finished with just 12 points.

   (Undated-AP) -- Miami guard Travis Best could land on the
injured list after spraining his right ankle during Wednesday's win
over Atlanta. Best is expected to miss at least a week.
   And New Orleans guard Baron Davis will sit out today's game
against Orlando because of recurring back spasms. Davis has been
playing with a herniated disk.

   (Undated-AP) -- Duke appears to be on its way to a number-one
ranking in The Associate Press men's basketball poll. Dahntay Jones
scored 22 points and J.J. Redick added 20 as the third-ranked Blue
Devils handled Fairfield 86-to-58.
   Duke was given a chance to rise to the top of the poll following
losses by top-ranked Alabama and number-two Pittsburgh earlier this
week.

   Yesterday's college basketball slate included a battle of top-
ten teams, won by fourth-ranked Arizona 81-to-72 over number-nine
Oregon. Jason Gardner's 21 points helped the wildcats end the Ducks'
23-game home winning streak.
   Fifth-ranked Connecticut is 9-and-0 after slamming St.
Bonaventure 95-to-78. Ben Gordon scored 25 points and Emeka Okafor
(OH'-kah-fohr) added 18.
   Number-eight Mississippi State beat Alabama-Birmingham 68-to-52,
behind Mario Austin's 13 points and 12 rebounds.

Nick Collison hit for 20 points and Wayne Simien had 19 points and nine rebounds as 18th-ranked Kansas blasted North Carolina-Asheville 102-to-50.

Kentucky's Chuck Hayes scored 15 points and the 20th-rated Wildcats forced a season-high 28 turnovers in crushing Alcorn State 94-to-63.

^

^AP-AM Prep-Scores and Skeds
^<
- -
       MORNING PREP - MORNING PREP - MORNING PREP - MORNING PREP
- -
                        - - - - - - - - - - - -
                        ! SCORES AND SKEDS !
                        - - - - - - - - - - - -
^<
  College Football Bowls
    Thursday's Score
    <
  Orange Bowl at Miami
(5) Southern Cal 38   (3) Iowa 17

    Today's Game

    Fiesta Bowl At Tempe, Ariz.
    <
(1) Miami vs (2) Ohio State 8:00 p.m.
    <
N-B-A

    Thursday's Scores
    <
Washington Wizards   107   Chicago Bulls   82
Dallas Mavericks   102   Los Angeles Clippers   92
Phoenix Suns   96   Philadelphia 76ers   78

```
    Today's Games
    <
Cleveland Cavaliers        at    Toronto Raptors        7:00 p.m.
Portland Trail Blazers     at    Boston Celtics         8:00 p.m.
New Jersey Nets            at    Miami Heat             8:00 p.m.
Indiana Pacers             at    New York Knicks        8:00 p.m.
Los Angeles Clippers       at    Memphis Grizzlies      8:00 p.m.
Utah Jazz                  at    Milwaukee Bucks        8:30 p.m.
Orlando Magic              at    New Orleans Hornets    8:30 p.m.
Golden State Warriors      at    San Antonio Spurs      8:30 p.m.
Denver Nuggets             at    Seattle SuperSonics   10:30 p.m.
^<

N-H-L

    Thursday's Scores
    <
Ottawa Senators            8    Atlanta Thrashers      1
Chicago Blackhawks         4    St. Louis Blues        1
Florida Panthers           4    Colorado Avalanche     1
Minnesota Wild             2    Edmonton Oilers        1, OT
Calgary Flames             4    Tampa Bay Lightning    1
Philadelphia Flyers        4    Los Angeles Kings      1
Vancouver Canucks          3    Montreal Canadiens     2
Dallas Stars               3    San Jose Sharks        1

    Today's Games<
Carolina Hurricanes        at    Buffalo Sabres         7:00 p.m.
Boston Bruins              at    New York Islanders     7:00 p.m.
Columbus Blue Jackets      at    Washington Capitals    7:00 p.m.
Phoenix Coyotes            at    Detroit Red Wings      7:30 p.m.
Pittsburgh Penguins        at    Atlanta Thrashers      7:30 p.m.
Toronto Maple Leafs        at    New Jersey Devils      7:30 p.m.
Philadelphia Flyers        at    Anaheim Mighty Ducks  10:30 p.m.
    <
Top 25 College Basketball

    Thursday's Scores
    <
( 3) Duke                 86        Fairfield              58
( 4) Arizona              81   ( 9) Oregon                 72
( 5) Connecticut          95        St. Bonaventure        78
( 8) Mississippi State    68        Alabama-Birmingham     52
(18) Kansas              102        North Carolina-Asheville  50
(20) Kentucky             94        Alcorn State           63
```

Today's Games

No Games Scheduled
<
Women's Top 25 College Basketball

Thursday's Scores
<

(2)	L-S-U	74		North Texas	43
(7)	Purdue	76		Tulane	66
(8)	Texas Tech	94		Rutgers	81
	Oklahoma State	60	(9)	Arkansas	58
(10)	Minnesota	98		Michigan	70
(11)	North Carolina	72		Georgia Tech	67
	Louisville	92	(12)	Vanderbilt	82
(15)	Penn State	86		Wisconsin	55
(17)	Texas	64		Texas A&M-Corpus Christi	37
(18)	Mississippi State	78		Xavier	64
(20)	Arizona	96		Oregon	65
(21)	Wisconsin-Green Bay	93		Cleveland State	73
(22)	UC Santa Barbara	65		B-Y-U	51
(25)	Colorado	76		Buffalo	47

Today's Games
<

(4)	Kansas State	vs		Western Illinois	8:00 p.m.
(6)	Stanford	vs	(19)	Oklahoma	10:00 p.m.

^AP-The Sunriser
^<

- - - - - - - - - - - - - - -
                                                            ! AP AGWATCH !
- -
        Canadian feeder imports up...StarLink troubles continue
- -
^

     (Calgary, Alberta-AP) — Exports of Canadian feeder cattle to the United States are at record levels.
     The Canadian Cattlemen's Association says feeder cattle and calf exports to the United States reached 450-thousand head in 2002. That's more than double exports in 2001.

Drought in the Canadian prairies created a surge in shipments as feedlots emptied in Alberta and Saskatchewan.

The president of the Canadian cattle group says the group would have preferred to have their cattle fed in Canada. But feed prices in Canada went so high, and supply went so low, that some feedlots were importing U-S feed corn. And American importers were snapping up Canadian cattle.
^

(Washington-AP) -- StarLink is the corn controversy that doesn't go away. The U-S Agriculture Department says Japan has told the United States that StarLink has been found in a shipment of U-S corn.

The Agriculture Department approved StarLink for animals but not humans to eat. When it was found anyway in U-S food two years ago, recalls resulted. U-S-D-A and StarLink's developer also instituted a wide-ranging attempt to keep keep StarLink from being mixed with corn for food use. The corn was withdrawn from the market, but the United States and other countries still check for it in shipments.

A U-S-D-A spokesman says it's too soon to know how StarLink could have gotten mixed into the shipment in Japan. Exporter Harvest States Grain of Minnesota says it's waiting for more information from Japan.
^

(Los Angeles-AP) -- California officials want to destroy one (M) million chickens infected with exotic Newcastle disease.

Authorities say the virus was found in hens at an egg farm in San Bernardino County. The virus also was found in a commercial flock in San Diego County. State officials set quarantines in both counties, and added another as a buffer area to try to block the expansion of the epidemic.

The disease is highly infectious and threatens the state's three (B) billion-dollar poultry industry. A statewide outbreak in the 1970s threatened the entire U-S poultry and egg supply.
^

(Mexico City-AP) -- The Mexican government and farm groups will hold talks on a farm accord. The decision avoids protests that had threatened to block the country's border with the United States.

In addition to the talks, Mexico's economy secretary also left open the possibility that he would renegotiate some North American Free Trade Agreement requirements. Those rules require tariffs on U-S farm products to be lifted. Mexican farming groups had threatened to shut down the border on the day the tariffs are to be lifted, which was January first.

Farm groups now want to continue talks with the government until January 20th.

^

(Columbus, Ohio-AP) — Managers of a troubled egg megafarm say a federal complaint that its air emissions are a health hazard are bad for business.

The managers of Buckeye Egg Farm in Ohio say the possibility of a federal lawsuit could derail attempts to sell the farm.

One Buckeye official says E-P-A informed the company that it is prepared to go to court. And the company official says that's not fair. He says any air pollution problems are industry problems, not Buckeye's.

An E-P-A spokesman says Buckeye's problems are longstanding, and the notice of violation should be no surprise.
^

^AP-NY—Upstate Snow<
^

- - - - - - - - - - - - - - - - -
 ! AP NEWSWATCH !
- -
^More snow coming, eastern New York expected to beat brunt<
- -
^

(Albany-AP) -- Ready for more snow?

Forecasters say parts of upstate New York could get well over a foot of snow between this afternoon and Saturday afternoon, with eastern parts of the state expected to bear the brunt of the latest storm.

Eastern New York is still recovering from the Christmas Day storm that dumped two feet of snow on Albany and nearby communities, while some parts of the Mohawk Valley got three feet or more.

Today's storm could bring as much as 18 inches to the Schoharie, Mohawk and Hudson Valleys and the Catskills.

Central and western New York are expected to get less snow — up to seven inches in some counties east of Rochester — while Buffalo will get only a few inches.

Meteorologists say the system will be moving from the mid-Atlantic states today and along the southern New England coast tomorrow morning.

Television News Script

The following section contains an opening and three stories from the script for the evening television newscast of a medium-market CBS affiliate, WHP-TV in Harrisburg, Pennsylvania. Note the split between the video cues (to the left) and the audio (on the right).

11/23 21:36 JHE 2:20 # 15+1101 990LI-1
SUPTZ

TALENT-2-SHOT	(***GENE***)
	GOOD EVENING, COMING UP NEXT ON NEWSNIGHT 21 . . .
ENG-AOA	
VONAT (***VONAT***)	THE PRESIDENT AND CONGRESSIONAL LEADERS LOOK HAPPY TONIGHT, AS A STOPGAP SPENDING MEASURE IS SIGNED . . .
ENG-AOB	
SOT (***SOT***)	
RUNS-:06	((I'M EVAN FORRESTER . . .))
ENG-AOC	
VONAT (***VONAT***)	(***ROXANNE***)
	AND A STRIKE LOOMS AT THE STROEHMAN BAKERY IN HARRISBURG . . .
ON CAM	(***GENE***)
	THE TWO-LIVE CRUE OBSCENITY TRIAL HAS JURORS LAUGHING . . .
	(***ROXANNE***)
	AND JIM HAS A NICE WEEKEND WEATHER FORECAST, AND DOUG HAS LOTS OF HIGH SCHOOL FOOTBALL ACTION. . . .
	STAY WITH US, NEWSNIGHT 21 IS NEXT!
	(-0-)
BREAK-1	
RUNS-1:00	(***BREAK-1***|)
COLD	
TALENT-2-SHOT	
ENG-A1	
VONAT (***VONAT***)	(***GENE***)
	A MORE CONTENT PRESIDENT BUSH MEETS WITH CONGRESSIONAL LEADERS AS THE ATMOSPHERE CHANGES IN WASHINGTON.
	(-0)
FEDERAL	
TALENT-2-SHOT	(***GENE***)
	GOOD EVENING.

LAWMAKERS ARE NO LONGER PRESSING TO MEET A MIDNIGHT DEADLINE.

(***ROXANNE***)
   PRESIDENT BUSH HAS SIGNED A MEASURE TO KEEP THE GOVERNMENT
FUNDED THROUGH NEXT WEDNESDAY.

(***GENE***)
   BUT THE FIGHT'S NOT OVER. HOUSE AND SENATE MEMBERS WILL BE
TRYING TO AGREE ON A COMPROMISE BETWEEN THE TWO BUDGET PACKAGES
THEY'VE APPROVED.

(***ROXANNE***)
   PRESIDENT BUSH HAD SOME ADVICE FOR RANK-AND-FILE LAWMAKERS
THIS AFTERNOON.

ENG-A2
SOT (***SOT***)
RUNS-:13
   ((I WOULD SAY TO DEMOCRATS AND REPUBLICANS . . . PLEASE HEED WHAT
YOUR LEADERS ARE SAYING . . . THE LEADERS IN THE SENATE AND THE
LEADERS IN THE HOUSE . . . WE SHARE THIS VIEW AND
UH . . . THAT'S WHAT I SAY TO THEM.))

ON CAM
FULLSCREEN
CG-SENATE VERSION
GASOLINE TAX: 49 CENTS
INCOME TAX: LIMITS
DEDUCTIONS
MEDICARE INCREASED TAXES

(***ROXANNE***)

   THE SENATE VERSION OF THE BUDGET DEFICIT-REDUCTION BILL WOULD
DOUBLE THE GASOLINE TAX . . . FROM THE PRESENT 9-CENTS A GALLON TO
18-CENTS. ON INCOME TAX, THE SENATE VERSION LIMITS DEDUCTIONS FOR
PEOPLE WHO MAKE OVER 100-THOUSAND DOLLARS A YEAR.

FULLSCREEN
CG-HOUSE VERSION
GASOLINE TAX: NO INCREASE
INCOME TAX:
WEALTHY-33%
MEDICARE: INCREASED TAXES

   THE HOUSE VERSION HAS NO INCREASE IN THE GASOLINE TAX, BUT HITS
THE WEALTHY HARD. IT INCREASES THE TOP TAX BRACKET PAID BY THE
WEALTHIEST FROM 28 TO 33 PERCENT. BOTH VERSIONS INCREASE MEDICARE
TAXES.

ON CAM
   (***ROXANNE***)
CONGRESS NOW MUST WORK OUT THE DIFFERENCES.

   (-0)

11/23 00:16 JHE 2:20 # 15+1WAGNER-1

TALENT-GENE (***GENE***)

A YORK COUNTY BABYSITTER IS STILL ON TRIAL FOR THE MURDER OF A CHILD SHE WAS WATCHING.

TODAY, PROFESSIONAL TESTIMONY BACKS THE STORY OF 23-YEAR-OLD THERESA WAGNER THAT THE CHILD FELL.

THE PROSECUTION CHARGES WAGNER HIT THE CHILD AT LEAST TWICE.

BUT A DOCTOR TESTIFIED 18-MONTH OLD CRYSTAL SEACHRIST HAD PRIOR SKULL SURGERY FOR A DEFORMITY, AND THAT CONTRIBUTED TO THE SEVERITY OF INJURIES SUFFERED IN THE FALL.

THE BABY'S MOTHER DISAGREES.

ENG-A3

SOT (***SOT***)

CG-ELLEN SEACHRIST/

CHILD'S MOTHER

RUNS-:09 ((YOU KNOW IT HURTS WHEN YOU HEAR SOMEONE SAYING SOMETHING THAT'S NOT TRUE ABOUT YOUR DAUGHTER . . . SHE WAS A VERY NORMAL GIRL.))

VONAT (***VONAT***)

WAGNER MAINTAINS WHAT HAPPENED WAS AN ACCIDENT.

THE TRIAL CONTINUES TOMORROW.

(-0)

11/23 00:17 JHE 2:20 # 15+1GMRECALL-1

TALENT-ROXANNE (***ROXANNE***)

GENERAL MOTORS SAYS IT'S RECALLING 520-THOUSAND 1989 AND 1990 MODEL CARS FOR POTENTIALLY DEFECTIVE BRAKE LIGHTS.

A G-M SPOKESMAN SAYS THE CARS MAY HAVE A FAULTY ELECTRICAL SWITCH THAT COULD RESULT IN FAILURE OF THE BRAKE LIGHTS . . . BUT HE SAYS THE PROBLEM DOESN'T AFFECT THE BRAKES.

CG-FULLSCREEN

CG-GENERAL MOTORS RECALL

CG-1989 AND 1990 MODELS:

CG-GRAND PRIX

CG-CUTLASS SUPREME

CG-REGAL

CG-LUMINA THE MODELS INVOLVED IN THE RECALL ARE THE 1989 AND 1990 PONTIAC GRAND PRIX, OLDSMOBILE CUTLASS SUPREMES, BUICK REGALS, AND 1990 CHEVROLET LUMINA CARS.

G-M SAYS IT KNOWS OF TEN ACCIDENTS IN WHICH THE LIGHT DEFECT MAY HAVE BEEN A FACTOR.

OWNERS OF THESE CARS CAN GET THE DEFECT FIXED AT NO COST FROM G-M DEALERS.

(-0)

Working Television News Script

This script is the working copy of a script used for the television news class at New York University. The large type allows it to be easily read by anchors who use it in conjunction with a duplicate script fed through a prompting device.

There is also a log of the events in the newscast used by control room personnel.

TELEVISION NEWSCASTDATE 11/17/94

TIME 8:00 p.m.

No.	Slug	Anchor	VTR	Graph	Reptr	Seg	Accum
1	Open VTR		VTR				
2	Live Open	HA PA					
3	Irish leader Resigns	PA	ADV	SOT			
4	White House Gunman	HA	VTR	V/O			
5	Tropical Storms	PA					
6	Miami Crops	HA	ADV	V/O			
7	Lede to Smoke out	PA					
8	Smoke out package		VTR			1:30	
9	Governor	HA					

No.	Slug	Anchor	VTR	Graph	Reptr	Seg	Accum
10	Republi can conven tion	PA					
11	Dodd	HA	ADV	SOT			
12	Lede to Music	PA					
13	Music Package		VTR				
14	Beaujo lais	HA	ADV	V/O nat			
15	Nobel Prize Winner	PA					
16	Tuberc ulosis	HA					
17	lede to Jason	HA					
18	lede Dr. Sex	JB					
19	Dr. Sex package		VTR				
20	Intervi ew w/ Dr. Judy	JB DS					
21	Lede to Playgr ound	PA					
22	playgro und package		ADV			1:10	
23	Lede to Enterta inment	PA					

No.	Slug	Anchor	VTR	Graph	Reptr	Seg	Accum
a.	NYU Jazz Festival	GC	VTR	V/O-SOT			
b.	Museum	GC					
c.	Whitney	GC	ADV	V/O-SOT			
d.	Letter man	GC					
e.	Star Trek	GC	VTR	V/O-SOT			
24	FBI mob round up	HA					
25	Rikers	PA					
26	Lede to Sports	PA					
a.	volleyball	CL	ADV	V/O			
b.	crew team	CL					
c.	Basket ball	CL	VTR	V/O-SOT			
d.	Giants	CL					
27	Thanks giving News	PA					
28	Weather	HA					
29	Live Close	HA PA					
30	VTR Close		ADV				

Open VTR

Pia Alexander
Live Open

o/c   Good evening and welcome to NYU Tonight. It's Thursday, November 17th.
I'm Henry Abbott
And I'm Pia Alexander. Here is tonight's top story.

Lede   Irish 1
Abbott
Irish leader
11-17

Ireland's Prime Minister is stepping down, and the peace agreement
in Ireland may be threatened. Albert Reynolds was about to face a no-
confidence vote in the Parliament, which he was sure to lose, so today he
and his deputies submitted their resignations to President Mary Robinson.
Reynolds, who spearheaded recent peace agreements in Northern Ireland,
told Parliament today he was resigning to keep the agreements from being
derailed by the collapse of his government.

      S-O-T   S-O-T
IN: "I have taken"
runs: :11
out: "peace process"

o/c   Reynolds has been the head of a coalition government formed between
his party, FIANNA FAIL, and the Labor party. Recently the Labor party
withdrew its support of Reynolds because they were dissatisfied with his
handling of the case of a Catholic priest accused of molesting children. By
resigning, Reynolds has cleared the way for his pro-peace party to attempt
a revival of the coalition with the Labor party, which might allow them to
maintain the top office.

Sinn Fein leader Gerry Adams said he is willing to work with whoever is
in power, and that Reynolds' resignation will not alter his group's
commitment to peace. Meanwhile a Protestant leader in Northern Ireland
says he is not sure the peace process can survive Reynolds' resignation.

Jeanie Bae
"White House"
11/17/94

The White House gunman is charged with 11 counts in the October 29th
shooting. 26-year old Francisco Duran is charged with an assassination
attempt of President Clinton—as well as assaulting Secret Service officers,
possession of a firearm, and carrying a firearm during a violent crime. A
federal grand jury is letting prosecutors seek the maximum penalty. Duran
already has a 1991 conviction for assault when he was in the Army.

Jeanie Bae
11/17/94
"Storm"

About 400 people have died in Haiti, Cuba, and Jamaica from tropical storm "Gordon."

At 4 a-m Eastern time, Gordon's center was about 185 miles east of Daytona Beach and is moving northeast. North Carolina is preparing for strong winds and high seas as "Gordon" heads up the coast.

Forecasters say its path could be close enough to cause coastal flooding tonight and tomorrow. A gale warning is also in effect for the region.

MORE

"Gordon" has already destroyed dozens of homes in Florida and damaged thousands of acres of the nation's winter vegetable crop.

Charlotte Kullen
11/17/94
Miami Crops
O/C
V/O

Tropical Storm Gordon swept across southern Florida flooding tens of thousands of acres of farmland. In the last two days heavy rains have covered vegetable fields with nine inches of water. The flooding ruined most of the winter's supply of fruits and vegetables for the Eastern seaboard. Crops in Dade County . . . just south of Miami . . . suffered most from the floods and wind. The loss will force eastern stores to ship produce from California and Mexico. So New Yorkers will be paying higher prices this winter.

Smokeout Lede

If you're fond of the Marlboro Man, Joe Camel or the leggy Virginia Slims models, today was not your day. It was annual Great American Smokeout day and Christine Lim found out what the American Cancer Society is doing to clean up America's lungs.

Abbott
Governor
8pm
11-17

A week and a half after the election, Governor-elect George Pataki is readying his administration for Albany.

Today the Governor-elect announced his transition advisory group at his New York City headquarters. I spoke to his office, who told me that the bi-partisan group includes Dean Mary Scmidt Campbell, of Tisch School of the Arts, and NYU Medical Center Trustee Thomas Tisch. Other notables on the 53-member team include former Mayor Koch, Henry Kissinger, the Reverend Calvin Butts, Staten Island Borough President Guy Molinari, former

Governor Carey and Bernadette Castro who recently failed in her attempt to unseat Senator Moynihan. In preparation for his move to Albany, Pataki bought a hundred and fifty two acre farm near Albany, which he will use as an escape from the rigors of being governor.

Meanwhile Governor Cuomo is pondering his next move. Cuomo has earned over one million dollars making public speeches in the last 12 years, and says he will probably continue to speak for money. Cuomo is also known to be considering job offers from Major League Baseball, universities, and television networks. A spokesman for the state comptroller's office says Cuomo is eligible for a state pension worth over fifty seven thousand dollars.

Anne Cassigneul
Republican Convention
11/17/94

San Diego is a favorite with the Republicans. The city has a good chance of hosting the 1996 Republican national convention. It is the front runner because California has fifty four electoral votes in presidential elections.

In the meantime, the city of New York has been dropped from the running, to punish Republican Mayor Guiliani, for supporting Democratic governor Cuomo in the last week's election.

Joon Jang
Dodd/Reform

Video
V/O

Connecticut's Democratic Senator Christopher Dodd held a news conference today in Washington, calling for reform.

Dodd S-0-T

In: "We clearly have to reform . . .
Runs:
Out: . . . on those issues."

Dodd will challenge South Dakota's Tom Daschle for the Democratic leadership.

MUSIC LEDE IN
MALLETT/PLACERES
11/17/94

Feeling nostalgic for the sounds of old Broadway? Reporter Karin Mallett tells us that we don't need to go very far.

Music VTR

WINE
Maher, Denise

| | V/O | There was quite a celebration in New York today. Dancing, drinking and music highlighted the spirited event. |

(NAT- :08)

fade audio/

| | V/O | This year's vintage of (bow-joe-lays) new-vo wine made its debut—to the delight of many wine connoisseurs. Because of French law, the fruity young wine could not be opened until today. |

Nure Akdemir
November 17, 1994
nobel prize winner

Nobel prize winning poet Joseph Brodsky will be at NYU. He will read from Fleur (Flerr) Jaeggy's (Jaggies) Sweet Days of Discipline, on November 21st at 6 P.M.

The reading will be held at Casa Italiana located at 24 West 12th Street.

Brodsky is a poet and winner of the 1987 Nobel Prize for Literature.

He is also a former visiting professor at N.Y.U.

The reading is free and open to the public.

For further information call (212) 998-3859.

alicia
tuberculosis

Tuberculosis is spreading rapidly worldwide, due to a failure to develop new drugs.

According to the World Health Organization, new drug-resistant strains of the disease threaten to make it completely incurable.

WHO program manager, Araata Koch-ee warned that by using existing anti-TB drugs improperly, we are creating an epidemic and avoiding the search for a cure.

Tuberculosis kills an average of three million people annually . . . but WHO expects the death toll to rise to three and a half million within the next five years.

In New York City about a third of all TB cases are resistant to at least one of the six anti-TB drugs that are available.

- 0 -

INTERVIEW–Dr. Judy Kuriansky
LEDE-IN TO INTERVIEW

O/C Anchor

Now joining us is Jason Belkin with a special guest LIVE in the NYU Tonight studio . . . Jason . . .

INTERVIEW–Dr. Judy Kuriansky

        O/C Jason

                Thank you _____. Before we meet our guest, let's take a behind-the-scenes look at one of the New York area's hottest radio call-in shows. . . .

DR. SEX VTR
VTR–Package
IN: (film clips/music)   VTR
runs: 1:30
out: (standard out)

        O/C   And here in the studio with me is Dr. Judy Kuriansky, known to her fans as "Dr. Judy," the host of "Lovephones." Dr. Judy, welcome to NYU Tonight. . . .

                (Q&A)

                Thank you very much for joining us, Dr. Judy. I'm sure you've gotten a lot of viewers interested in your show which will actually be airing in about an hour and a half from now on Z-100 radio. Thanks for stopping by.

                #####

lede
playground

                Do little kids fly south for the winter? Not really. Reporter Wendy Wo found them wandering around in Playspace.

VTR

Entertainment Lede

> From the NYU campus to a galaxy far, far away, Gina Chai has this week's star-studded entertainment report. Gina . . .

Burruss
NYU Jazz Fest
11/17/94

          O/C

> NYU Jazz Series continues to provide quality artists from diverse backgrounds.

          V/O

> Santi DeBriano and the Panamaniacs performed at Loeb on Tuesday night as part of this series. Santi DeBriano captivated the audience with his spicy, upbeat style.
> > SOUND UP
> > about 10 sec

FADE, V/O

> This concert . . . cosponsored by NYU Program Board, the School of Continuing Education and the General Studies program . . . was also part of "La Herencia Latina"—Latin Heritage month. This celebration of Latin heritage lasts the entire month of November.

          O/C

> Check the office of student activities for information about other events.

Jeanie Bae
"Museum"
11/17/94

> The Museum of Modern Art has a new director after a 14-month search.
> Glenn Lowry, the 40-year old director of the Art Gallery of Ontario and a specialist in Islamic Art takes over next July.
> Mr. Lowry is a surprise choice succeeding Richard Oldenburg who announced his retirement last September 1993. The costly and time-consuming search actually began months before Mr. Oldenberg's announcement.
> Mr. Lowry will be the first director of the MOMA to have come to the job from another directorship.

Whitney Houston

> A concert entitled, "Whitney Houston celebrates a new South Africa," marked the new wave of peace in the country.
> The November twelfth concert was televised by HBO world wide.
> The seventy thousand seat arena for the five time grammy award winner sold out in one hour.

          v/o

> This makes it the biggest international music event in the history of South Africa.
> Houston performed to honor President Nelson Mandela.
>
> (sot)

Amanda Block
Letterman

> For all of you who just can't get enough of David Letterman, CBS will be airing an hour long video of Late Show favorites.

Among the classic Letterman gags are Dave filling drive-through orders at McDonald's, Dave and Paul golfing with a Sumo wrestler as their caddy, and Dave and Zsa Zsa Gabor partaking in an L.A. fast food pigout.

The special was taped in front of a live audience at the Ed Sullivan Theater which should add to the excitement. The "Late Show video special" will air on CBS at 10 p.m. Eastern time tonight.

Star Trek
Brittany Abbott

Movie audiences will have another chance to 'boldly go where no one has gone before' when <u>Star Trek-Generations</u> opens in theatres everywhere tomorrow.

v/o

Since its network debut in 1966, Star Trek has entertained millions of viewers around the world. <u>Generations</u>, the seventh Star Trek film, brings together the casts of the original <u>Star Trek</u> television series and the more recent <u>Next Generation</u> show.

(SOT) "Warp speed . . ."

Entertainment out

Looks like a great movie . . . well that's all for entertainment this week. Now back to you _____.

Joanna Goldenberg
Mob Incident

The tri-state area is cracking down on crime by breaking up two unrelated organized crime families. In New York, U-S Attorney Zachary Carter uncovered a murderous crime network led by Salvatore Candela of the Candela Bensonhurst Crew. The Crew was accused of smuggling guns, truck hijackings, robberies, drug dealing, and murder.

In Philadelphia, three men have been added to an indictment against mob boss, John Stanfa.

Giuseppe Palazzolo, Santo Bravata, Gaestano Scafidi, and 22 others were accused of racketeering and other crimes including murder.

Officials are continuing investigations and proceeding with the arrests.

Riker's Island

Tensions are high at Riker's Island. The Chairman of the City's Board of Corrections warns that the Guiliani Administration plans to cut 1,300 prison guards and social workers, fostering conditions similar to those in 1990 when inmates rioted. William Booth, Chairman of the Nine Member Board that monitors prison conditions feels the proposed budget cuts could lead to disaster.

There have never been such drastic cuts in the prison system. The 1990 cuts led to a riot in which 140 inmates and 20 officers were injured.

The correction officer's union says that inmate gangs are gaining power and violent incidents are on the rise.

Lede-IN to Sports
Carissa Lawson

The N-Y-U women's volleyball team ended their season heartbroken last weekend while the men's basketball team gets geared up for another championship run. Carissa Lawson is here to tell us more.

Volleyball
Lisa Heydet
o/c

The women's volleyball season ended on a sour note last weekend.

B-roll team   v/o

They missed their first chance ever to claim an N-C double-A division-three title after losing to Ithaca College. Ithaca sported a fifty and two record going into the tournament, before they shut-out the Violets three games to one.

Although Ithaca went on to win the title, the Violets were left with an impressive forty-three and six season record.

o/c

Senior Gabrielle Loop and Anna Sadleck both set NYU records for the year. Loop set it for digs at four hundred and eighty-six, and Sadleck set the kills record at six hundred and twelve.

Sailing into a more successful championship was NYU's rowing teams.

Best, Marcia
Crew Team

The NYU women's crew team rowed their way to a successful finish at the Metropolitan rowing championships by placing first. The women's varsity four came in first beating out SUNY Maritime, Kings Point, and Manhattan College. The Varsity eight led by Jen Salerno and Emily Johnson also placed first. The women's novice four placed third. The men's varsity eight crew team also had a successful finish; they captured third place. The men's novice eight did even better by placing second in the championships.

Basketball
Lisa Heydet

O/C

Only two days to go until the start of NYU's basketball season. The men's tip off tournament begins this Saturday at one o'clock at Cole's gym.

B-roll team   V/O
(:00-:12)

After two scrimmage games and six weeks of practice, the countdown is on. Players like Mike Farrell aren't letting anything or anyone stand in their way, nor are they making any promises.

Sound on tape
(:12-:30)

(Mike :18)
IN: "It's really competitive . . ."
OUT: ". . . you just never know."

more . . .

estab of coach   V/O
(:30-:33)

Even Coach Joe Neci is staying low-key.

Sound on Tape
(:33-:49)

(Joe Neci :16)
IN: "Our players . . .
OUT: ". . . focus right now."

players sitting   V/O
(:49-:56)

Well, players take advantage of the break, cause we are looking forward to a long and successful season.

O/C

The women's season also begins this weekend with a tournament at Muhlenberg College.

Joon Jang
Sports: Football
:30 sec

Video   Audio

These days the position of Quarterback on the New York Giants is a seesaw affair. During the Giants horrendous six game losing streak, Coach Dan Reeves has gone from starting quarterback Dave Brown to backup Kent Graham.

But following Sunday's seventh straight loss to the Arizona Cardinals, Coach Reeves switched back to Dave Brown. This, after promising to give Graham every opportunity to prove himself.

The move stunned teammates as well as Graham, who responded by saying "I feel the decision wasn't fair."

The Giants and Dave Brown are set to play the Houston Oilers, this Monday.

THANKSGIVING
Maher, Denise

Staying in town for Thanksgiving weekend? Bobst library, and the Academic Computing Facilities will be closed on November 24th and 25th. All dining halls will be closed for the entire weekend, but students on meal plans with a plus account can use the Violet Cafe or order in from Domino's and Mama Mia pizzerias.

Coles Sports Center will not be open on Thanksgiving Day, but will have regular hours for the rest of the weekend . . .

Looking for a way to celebrate Turkey Day in the city? The NYU community is invited to attend the Macy's Day Parade together. The group will leave from Hayden Residence Hall at 8am.

On Friday, November 25, Tisch School of the Arts will host a potluck international Thanksgiving dinner. Call Dan Stanford at 998-1914 for reservations (that's 998-1914).

The American Arts and Crafts Alliance will hold a crafts fair at Loeb from 12 to 7 Friday and Saturday and 12 to 6 Sunday.

Finally, on Sunday, November 27th, the Trolley will take students to the Frick Museum collection at 12:30 pm. The trip costs $3 with ID.

Pia Alexander
weather

o/c   And now for the weather. It's 49 degrees in Central Park. Tonight it will be cloudy with the low near 45.

Tomorrow's forecast calls for mostly cloudy skies, showers possible, with a high in the fifties.

Pia Alexander
Live Close

o/c   That concludes this week's edition of NYU Tonight. I'm Pia Alexander. And I'm Henry Abbott, good night.

Drill Material: Scripts and Commercial Copy

*T*his section of drill material gives you a variety of commercial copy, station promos, and other scripts. The material has been selected to give you practice in reading copy in several different forms requiring different approaches and techniques.

The distinguishing feature of the copy in this section is that it was written to persuade. Commercial copy is designed to get people to spend money on a product or service. Station promos are intended to get people to watch or listen to your station and not others. The AV script is intended to induce people to travel to the Caribbean. All have a message that seeks to persuade.

The best way to approach copy that is intended to persuade is to read through it several times and try to distill for yourself the central purpose intended by the copywriter. Try to identify the techniques used to make the message clear. Once you understand what the writer intends, and how copy has been structured to achieve a purpose, you will have a better idea of what techniques you as the announcer can bring to the job.

Radio Commercial Copy and Station Promos

The following is commercial and promotional copy written for radio. There is material from both small- and large-market stations. (Copy courtesy of the William Cook Agency. Copyright the William Cook Agency, Inc.)

THE
WILLIAM COOK
A G E N C Y

CLIENT: FIRST UNION FLORIDA
JOB TITLE: CUSTOMIZED BANKING RADIO - PERFORMANCE BANKING
JOB NUMBER: FUFL-R-00091-4
DATE: DECEMBER 3, 1990
COMMERCIAL #:   FFLR-30CBR-00091
RUN DATES: TBD

:30

SNG: WE'RE FIRST UNION BANK...

(:22)
ANC: To get more than checking out of your checking account, First Union recommends
        Performance Banking. It's customized, with smart-money features. Like a no-fee
        credit card, lower rates on auto loans, interest on your checking balance, and service
        that's guaranteed. Compare First Union Performance Banking to other bank
        accounts, and get more for your money.

SNG: SERVICE BANKING SERVING YOU
        WE'RE FIRST UNION NATIONAL BANK

ANC: Member FDIC.

(FFLR00091A)
KJ/ag

THE
WILLIAM COOK
AGENCY

CLIENT: FIRST UNION FLORIDA
JOB TITLE: DODGER SPONSORSHIP RADIO (50)
JOB #:   FUFL-42242
DATE: JANUARY 26, 1989
COMMERCIAL #: FUFL-60-029B (TO ROTATE WITH FUCORP-60SS-00068)
RUN DATES: AS INSTRUCTED

:60 TRACK #4 (:33.6 BED)

SNG: WE'RE FIRST UNION BANK
            OUR COMMITMENT TO SERVICE
            IS SOMETHING THAT WE GUARANTEE
            WE DELIVER PERFORMANCE
            IN A WAY NO OTHER BANK CAN BEAT

ANC: By the time you reach 50, you've made a real contribution through a
            lifetime of productivity. And FIRST UNION thinks you deserve some
            privileges. That's why we offer you the special privileges of Benefit
            Banking when you're only 50! Benefit Banking gives you a free
            interest checking account, free travelers' checks, notary service,
            estate planning, a bonus rate on CDs ... and so much more. So if
            you're 50 or over, call or visit FIRST UNION today. And let the
            privileges of Benefit Banking benefit you.

SNG: WE'RE FIRST UNION NATIONAL BANK.

(FLR42242B)
5/2/lmj

T H E
WILLIAM COOK
A G E N C Y

CLIENT: FIRST UNION FLORIDA
JOB TITLE: SPORTS RADIO -- THE GAME :60
JOB #:   FUFL-R-00140-5
DATE: SEPTEMBER 28, 1990
COMMERCIAL #: FUFLR-60G-00140
RUN DATES: TBD

ANC: First Union salutes Florida's athletes
      Because they don't just come to play
      They come to win.

SFX: (SLIGHT CROWD NOISE BUILDING)

ANC: It happens every year
      In stadiums packed to capacity
      Young athletes take to the field
      And learn the difference between good and great
      While we cheer, and cry "Go, go, go!"
      Willing them onward toward the goal.

SFX: (ROAR OF CROWD PEAKS, FADES)

ANC: Because at First Union we know what it takes to win
      And we give you everything we've got
      The muscle to move forward
      The strategies to get ahead
      And the commitment to go on when the going gets tough.

SFX: (CHEER RISES AND FADES, MUSIC MAY BE UNDER)

ANC: For the game is tough and exciting
      And we don't come to play.
      We come to win. For you.
      First Union salutes Florida's athletes.
      First Union, committed to Florida
      And what it takes to help you win.

FIRST UNION
SPORTS RADIO -- THE GAME :60
FUFL-R-00140-5
PAGE 2

          (PAUSE)

ANC: Service. We guarantee it.

          (PAUSE)

          First Union National Bank of Florida.
          Member FDIC.

(00140-60)
KJ/bh:lmj:bh

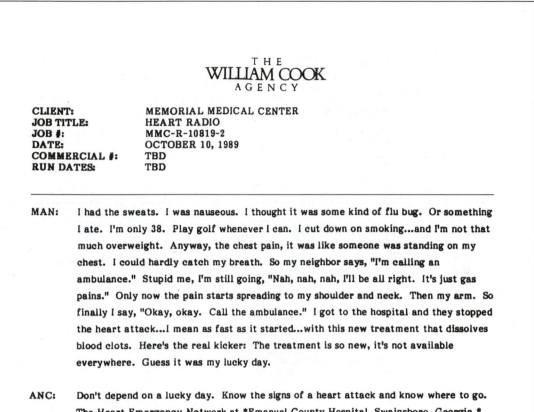

THE
WILLIAM COOK
A G E N C Y

CLIENT: MEMORIAL MEDICAL CENTER
JOB TITLE: HEART RADIO
JOB #:   MMC-R-10819-2
DATE: OCTOBER 10, 1989
COMMERCIAL #: TBD
RUN DATES: TBD

MAN: I had the sweats. I was nauseous. I thought it was some kind of flu bug. Or something I ate. I'm only 38. Play golf whenever I can. I cut down on smoking...and I'm not that much overweight. Anyway, the chest pain, it was like someone was standing on my chest. I could hardly catch my breath. So my neighbor says, "I'm calling an ambulance." Stupid me, I'm still going, "Nah, nah, nah, I'll be all right. It's just gas pains." Only now the pain starts spreading to my shoulder and neck. Then my arm. So finally I say, "Okay, okay. Call the ambulance." I got to the hospital and they stopped the heart attack...I mean as fast as it started...with this new treatment that dissolves blood clots. Here's the real kicker: The treatment is so new, it's not available everywhere. Guess it was my lucky day.

ANC: Don't depend on a lucky day. Know the signs of a heart attack and know where to go. The Heart Emergency Network at *Emanuel County Hospital, Swainsboro, Georgia,* and Memorial Medical Center.

MAN: I still can't believe it. I was having a heart attack and didn't even know it.

ALT TAGS:

    *Evans Memorial Hospital, Claxton, Georgia,

    *Jenkins County Hospital, Millen, Georgia,

    *Liberty Memorial Hospital, Hinesville, Georgia,

    *Live Oaks Hospital, Ridgeland, South Carolina,

    *Screven County Hospital, Sylvania, Georgia

(HATTACK)

3/lmj

THE
WILLIAM COOK
A G E N C Y

CLIENT:	JNO. H. SWISHER
JOB TITLE:	HOCKEY RADIO
JOB #:	SWSH-R-10029-2
DATE:	OCTOBER 3, 1988
COMMERCIAL #:	TBD
RUN DATES:	TBD

:60 RADIO

MAN: Okay, first, pucker up.

WOMAN: (playfully suspicious) I thought you were going to teach me about hockey.

MAN: I am. I'm demonstrating a faceoff.

WOMAN: Faceoff! I think you're offsides.

MAN: Looks like I'm starting off in the penalty box.

WOMAN: So, been a Ranger fan long?

MAN: Since the ice age.

WOMAN: So why aren't we <u>at</u> the Garden?

MAN: I always listen to the game on the radio so I can sit back, relax and enjoy my cigar. You don't mind, do you?

WOMAN: No. Not at all.

MAN: Could you hand me my Rangers jersey, please?

WOMAN: Cold?

MAN: No, it's a ritual.

WOMAN: Ritual?

JNO. H. SWISHER
HOCKEY RADIO
SWSH-R-10029-2
PAGE 2

MAN: Yeah. Every time the Rangers play,
                  I wear my lucky jersey and light up a Bering.

WOMAN: I understand the jersey, but why the Bering cigar?

MAN: Nowadays I can't find the time or place to smoke
                  as often as I like, so when I can do it, I do it right with Bering.

WOMAN: (Playfully) You look pretty good in that jersey.

MAN: (grizzly voice) Oh yeah, well how 'bout a body check?

WOMAN: How 'bout a slap shot?

ANC: Bering long-filler cigars...made from 100% imported tobacco with
                  natural leaf binder and wrapper. When you can do it, do it right.

(HOCKEY5)
GH/JS/bp

THE
WILLIAM COOK
A G E N C Y

CLIENT: WINN-DIXIE HEADQUARTERS
JOB TITLE: EDLP PHASE IV :30 RADIO "YOU'LL NEED SOMETHING"
JOB #:   WDH-R-10151-3
DATE: JANUARY 24, 1991
COMMERCIAL #:   WDHR-30Y-10151
RUN DATES: TBD

ANC: Sometimes it's easier to make money than to keep it. But shop

            at WINN-DIXIE and you'll need something to keep your savings

            in.

SFX: **SOUND OF LOOSE CHANGE GOING INTO JAR**

ANC: At WINN-DIXIE, you save a few cents on just about every

            item. So nearly everything you put in your cart puts a few

            cents back in your pocket.

SFX: **CHANGE GOING INTO JAR**

ANC: And those nickels and dimes will add up

SFX: **CHANGE GOING INTO JAR**

ANC: to a lot of dollars.

SFX: **A LOT OF CHANGE GOING INTO JAR**

ANC: Which is great. Because at WINN-DIXIE, what you save

SFX: **CHANGE GOING INTO JAR**

ANC: is what you keep.

SFX: **CHANGE GOING INTO JAR**

ANC: WINN-DIXIE, low prices every day.

SFX: **CHANGE GOING INTO JAR**

ANC: That's a promise.

SFX: **CHANGE GOING INTO JAR**

(WDHR10151D)
KJ/ag:bh

THE
WILLIAM COOK
AGENCY

CLIENT: WINN-DIXIE HEADQUARTERS
JOB TITLE: EDLP PHASE IV - :60 RADIO "NICKELS AND DIMES"
JOB NUMBER: WDH-R-10151-3
COMMERCIAL #: WDHR-60N-10151
DATE: JANUARY 24, 1991
RUN DATES: TBD

ANC: Question: What do you do with loose change -- you know, those nickels and dimes that collect in your pocket or the bottom of your handbag?

SFX: **SOUND OF HANDFUL OF LOOSE CHANGE**
JANGLING
Right. You save them --

SFX: **CHANGE GOING INTO CONTAINER**
in a can, in a jar -- whatever.

SFX: **MORE CHANGE GOING INTO CONTAINER**
-- And you let them add up to dollars.

SFX: **MORE CHANGE GOING INTO CONTAINER**
And you've noticed they can add up to a lot of dollars?

SFX: **MORE CHANGE GOING INTO CONTAINER**
then **MORE CHANGE GOING IN**
Good.

SFX: **MUSIC UP**
Because it shows how saving a few cents on just about every item every day at WINN-DIXIE really adds up. Now, imagine doing your grocery shopping where just about every time you put something in your cart, it's like putting a few cents back in your pocket.

SFX: **LOOSE CHANGE JANGLING**
And those nickels and dimes can add up fast.

SFX: **CHANGE GOING INTO A CONTAINER**
So when you get home, put your WINN-DIXIE savings in a BIG jar, because you'll save on every aisle every time you shop.

SFX: **COIN INTO CONTAINER**
And that adds up to a lot of dollars.
WINN-DIXIE. Low prices every day.

SFX: **CHANGE JANGLING**
That's a promise.

SFX: **CHANGE INTO CONTAINER**

(WDHR10151N)
KJ/ag:bh

THE
WILLIAM COOK
AGENCY

CLIENT: WINN-DIXIE STORES, INC.
COMMERCIAL #:   WDAR-60V1-10769 (aka: 60ALP-10769)

:60   SARAH 6   (:12.5 BED) (RELATIVES VISIT/LOW PRICE)

BAR: Every time my relatives visit, they eat me out of house and home. There's my Uncle

Louie. Whenever we have a cookout, he has two double cheeseburgers, three helpings

of baked beans, half a dozen hot dogs and a diet soda. It's ridiculous. Oh, and talk

about "like father like son." You should see Cousin Freddie. Every time I turn around

he's got his face in the fridge. This guy doesn't just snack between meals. He snacks

between the salad and the entree. I'm sure glad I shop at WINN-DIXIE, because they

have low prices on everything in the store. Meat, produce, baked beans, everything.

Hey, it's important for me to save money on groceries. Especially when my Aunt

Sophie's idea of a light lunch is anything she can pick up with a fork. So, from the

bottom of my pocket book, WINN-DIXIE, I thank you.

(:12.5)

ANC: ?

(SARAH6)

THE
WILLIAM COOK
A G E N C Y

CLIENT: WINN-DIXIE STORES, INC.
COMMERCIAL #: WDAR-60F-10769

:60 SARAH 5 (:12.5) (FLOWERS)
_____

BAR: I'm kind of a hopeless romantic. My husband, he's just kind of hopeless. But I discovered

a surefire way to get him to bring me flowers. All I do is call him up at his office at

about ten o'clock in the morning and say, "Hi, Honey, do you know what today is?"

Silence. Then I say, "You (SFX: sniff) don't know?" "Uh, uh" he says. Then I go, "Well, I

don't want to talk to you until you can tell me what today is!" And I hang up. Then, just

when he's ready to go home, I call him and say, "If you don't know what today is, maybe

you can remember to pick up some potatoes at WINN-DIXIE on the way home." Potatoes

are right next to the flowers. It never fails. He walks in the door with a sack of

potatoes, a bouquet of flowers and says, "Honey, I'm sorry. I just can't remember what

today is." So I tell him, "It's Tuesday."

(:12.5)

ANC: ?

(SARAH5)

THE
WILLIAM COOK
AGENCY

CLIENT: WINN-DIXIE STORES, INC.
COMMERCIAL #: WDAR-60RV-10199

:60 SARAH 3 (:8.5 BED) (COUCH POTATO/DELI)

WIF: My husband is a couch potato. In fourteen years, he's worn out three recliners. Can't

remember our anniversary, but he's got the TV schedule memorized. One time I took

the batteries out of his remote control. He called 911. Last week he comes home from

work, plops down in his recliner, throws it into liftoff position and tells me that his boss

is giving a dinner party and we're supposed to bring dessert. So I said, "Great. What are

you gonna make?" That brought him to his feet. He goes, "Gee, honey, I thought you'd

make your famous strawberry shortcake." "Think again," I said. "He's your boss. You

cook something." He was smarter than I thought. Went to the WINN-DIXIE

Deli/Bakery and picked up a cheesecake. Well, his boss's wife raved over it. So he says,

"Thank you. I made it from scratch." Then she asked for the recipe.

(:8.5)

ANC:

(SARAH3)

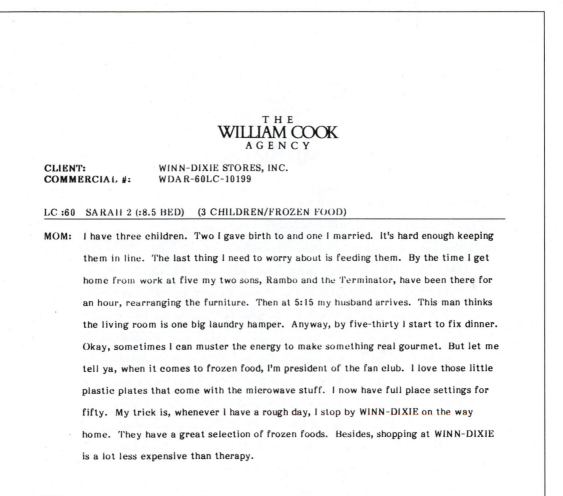

T H E
WILLIAM COOK
A G E N C Y

CLIENT: WINN-DIXIE STORES, INC.
COMMERCIAL #:   WDAR-60LC-10199

LC :60   SARAH 2 (:8.5 BED)   (3 CHILDREN/FROZEN FOOD)

MOM: I have three children. Two I gave birth to and one I married. It's hard enough keeping

them in line. The last thing I need to worry about is feeding them. By the time I get

home from work at five my two sons, Rambo and the Terminator, have been there for

an hour, rearranging the furniture. Then at 5:15 my husband arrives. This man thinks

the living room is one big laundry hamper. Anyway, by five-thirty I start to fix dinner.

Okay, sometimes I can muster the energy to make something real gourmet. But let me

tell ya, when it comes to frozen food, I'm president of the fan club. I love those little

plastic plates that come with the microwave stuff. I now have full place settings for

fifty. My trick is, whenever I have a rough day, I stop by WINN-DIXIE on the way

home. They have a great selection of frozen foods. Besides, shopping at WINN-DIXIE

is a lot less expensive than therapy.

(:8.5)

ANC: ?

(SARAH2)

THE
WILLIAM COOK
AGENCY

CLIENT: WINN-DIXIE STORES, INC.
COMMERCIAL #: WDN-60CR-10630 CS

:60 SARAH 18 (:6 BED)   (STAFF MEETING/CHEESE)

BAR: Last week the boss put me in charge of food for the big staff meeting. She says, "Don't

forget Camembert and Gorgonzola." I said, "Who?" She said, "Go to the Cheese Shop at

WINN-DIXIE." So there I was, with all of those cheeses. And I wouldn't know a Swiss

from a Gouda if it yodeled. They had sharp cheese, round cheese, blue cheese, yellow

cheese, cheeses from all over the world! Switzerland, France, New Zealand, Kenosha.

Good thing they had a cheese expert to help me. She said, "How 'bout Monterey Jack?" I

said, "The name is Barbara and I've never been to California." So she says, "How about a

dip?" I said, "Nah, we've got plenty of those back at the office." Anyhow, to make a

long story short, that WINN-DIXIE cheese girl fixed me up with everything I needed.

Now the boss calls me the "Gouda Gourmet." To think that just last week I thought a

fine Muenster was Frankenstein with good table manners.

(:6)

ANC: ?

(SARAH18)

THE
WILLIAM COOK
AGENCY

CLIENT: WINN-DIXIE STORES, INC.
COMMERCIAL #:   WDN-60CR-10630 P

:60 SARAH 17 (:6 BED)   (EMMA'S CURE/PHARMACY - LOCATION TAG ONLY)

WOM: It never ceases to amaze me. Get sick, and everybody's got a home remedy. My Aunt

Emma's cure-all is crushed garlic and Limburger cheese in a sock hung around her

neck. "I never catch a cold," she says. That's because nobody gets within fifty yards

of the woman. Then there's Cousin Moonbeam from California...swears by frozen tofu

daiquiris. And my mother, who, every time she hears me sneeze, wants to give me an

oil and vinegar rubdown. It's great if you don't mind smelling like a salad bar for a

week. Me, I just go to the Pharmacy at WINN-DIXIE. Their low prices alone will

make you feel better. But what I like most is the convenience. By the time I pick up

some chicken soup, my prescription's ready. That's because they have a computer with

my file in it. They know everything: my doctor's name, my allergies, the medicine I'm

taking. And not once did they tell me to gargle with guacamole.

(:6 BED)
ANC: ?

(SARAH 17)

FM 102 WHYL

Making Your Money Talk

P.O. Box WHYL
Carlisle, PA 17013

717-232-3126 or 717-249-1717

RADIO COPY

Client: **BRENNEMAN'S FURNITURE**

Length: **:30**

Today's date **5/25**

Start date **6/1-2** End date _____

Copy by: **RAY THOMAS**

Salesman: **LINCOLN**

Co-op Brand: **LANE**

Subject: **FATHER'S DAY**

1 A LANE RECLINER FROM BRENNEMAN'S FURNITURE IS A GREAT WAY TO SAY "HAPPY FATHER'S
2 DAY." THE LANE "SPOILER" FEATURES HEAD TO TOE COMFORT WITH SOFT, OVERSTUFFED
3 CUSHIONS. REGULAR $525, NOW A LOW $419. GIVE DAD THE GIFT OF COMFORT HE DESERVES
4 AND SAVE ON THE LANE RECLINER OF YOUR CHOICE. (BRING IN THE SALE CARD FROM
5 SATURDAY'S CARLISLE SENTINEL AND SAVE AN ADDITIONAL 10-PERCENT!) (HURRY, BECAUSE
6 THE NATIONAL LANE FATHER'S DAY SALE ENDS SOON!) THERE'S FREE DELIVERY AND YOUR
7 MAJOR CREDIT CARD IS WELCOME.)
8   (JINGLE)
9 JUST OFF THE PLAINFIELD EXIT OF I-81, CARLISLE.
10
11
12
13
14
15
16

This announcement was broadcast .... times, as entered in the station's program log. The times this announcement was broadcast were billed to this station's client on our invoice(s) numbered/dated .... at his earned rate of:
$... each for .... announcements, for a total of $...
$... each for .... announcements, for a total of $...

....
Signature of station official

....
(Notarize above)

....
Type name and title   Station

FM 102 WHYL

Making Your Money Talk

P.O. Box WHYL
Carlisle, PA 17013

717-232-3126 or 717-249-1717

RADIO COPY

Client: _____ CARLISLE TRUCK PLAZA

Length: _____ :60

Today's date _____ 5/31

Start date _____ 5/31   End date _____ 6/30

Copy by: _____ RAY THOMAS

Salesman: _____ LINCOLN ZEVE

Co-op Brand: _____

Subject: _____ SUMMERS HEAT

1   HI FOLKS, THIS IS PAUL ROGERS OF THE CARLISLE TEXACO TRUCK PLAZA FAMILY RESTAURANT
2   WITH SOME THOUGHTS ON THE SUMMER'S HEAT. YOU KNOW THERE'S NOTHING I HATE WORSE
3   THAN SLAVING OVER A HOT STOVE IN THE HEAT OF SUMMER. AND YOU CAN BEST BELIEVE MY
4   WIFE HATES IT EVEN MORE THAN I DO. THAT'S WHY SUMMER IS THE PERFECT TIME TO GET THE
5   LITTLE LADY OUT OF THE KITCHEN AND BRING THE WHOLE FAMILY IN FOR DINNER AT THE
6   CARLISLE TEXACO TRUCK PLAZA FAMILY RESTAURANT. ENJOY ALL YOUR DINNER FAVORITES IN
7   AIR-CONDITIONED COMFORT. THERE'S SOMETHING ON THE MENU FOR EVERY TASTE . . . EVEN
8   SUMMERTIME DESSERTS LIKE OUR SCRUMPTIOUS COLOSSAL, HUGE BANANA BOATS! AND THE
9   COLDEST SOFT DRINKS IN TOWN. SO THIS SUMMER, LEAVE THE SLAVING OVER A HOT STOVE TO
10 US. COME COOL OFF WITH DINNER TONIGHT AT THE CARLISLE TEXACO TRUCK PLAZA FAMILY
11 RESTAURANT, WHERE WE ALWAYS KEEP THE GRILL HOT FOR YOU.
12 ANNOUNCER: THE CARLISLE TEXACO TRUCK PLAZA FAMILY RESTAURANT, 1 ½ MILES NORTH OF
13 I-81 ON ROUTE 11 NEAR NEW KINGSTON. JUST LOOK FOR THE TEXACO SIGN.
14
15
16

This announcement was broadcast........ times, as entered in the station's program log. The times this announcement was broadcast were billed to this station's client on our invoice(s) numbered/dated ....at his earned rate of:
$........................... each for .... announcements, for a total of $..
$........................... each for .... announcements, for a total of $..

....
Signature of station official

....
(Notarize above)

....
Type name and title   Station

FM 102 WHYL

Making Your Money Talk

P.O. Box WHYL
Carlisle, PA 17013

717-232-3126 or 717-249-1717

RADIO COPY

Client: _____ FIRST BANK AND TRUST _____

Length: _____ :30 _____

Today's date ____ 7/1 _____

Start date _____ 7/1 _____ End date ___ 7/30 ___

Copy by: _____ RAY THOMAS _____

Salesman: _____ LINCOLN _____

Co-op Brand: _____

Subject: _____ SAVINGS PLANS _____

1 SECURING YOUR FUTURE BEGINS WITH A SMART SAVINGS PLAN FROM FIRST BANK AND TRUST!

2 FIRST BANK C.D.'S ARE THE PERFECT FINANCIAL PLANNING TOOLS. EARN HIGH RATES WITH

3 GOVERNMENT-INSURED SECURITY WITH A C.D. SAVINGS PLAN TO MEET YOUR GOALS AND

4 NEEDS . . . OR GET THE SAVINGS <u>HABIT</u> WITH A FIRST BANK STATEMENT SAVINGS ACCOUNT

5 THAT OFFERS HIGH RATES AND FREE 24 HOUR ACCESS TO ANY MAC MACHINE. FROM C.D.'S TO

6 SAVINGS TO TRUST AND ESTATE PLANNING, DEPEND ON 1ST BANK AND TRUST'S 130 YEAR

7 RECORD OF SERVICE. 5 LOCATIONS TO SERVE YOU. A PNC BANK AND MEMBER FDIC.

·8

9

10

11

12

13

14

15

·16

This announcement was broadcast .... times, as entered in the station's program log. The times this announcement was broadcast were billed to this station's client on our invoice(s) numbered/dated .... at his earned rate of:

$.. each for .... announcements, for a total of $..

$.. each for .... announcements, for a total of $..

....

Signature of station official

....
(Notarize above)

....

Type name and title   Station

BARBEAU PRONOUNCED BAR-BO
ANNCR:ATTENTION HOMEOWNERS AND WOULD-BE HOMEOWNERS! ARE HOME
MAINTENANCE CHORES GETTING THE BEST OF YOU? IS REPAIRING A BROKEN
STEP NOW AN IMPOSSIBLE STEP? THEN LISTEN TO THESE IMPORTANT FACTS
ABOUT THE RUSSELL BARBEAU COMPANY. FOR OVER 14 YEARS, THEIR
EXPERIENCED CRAFTSMEN HAVE DONE IT ALL . . . REPAIRS, REPLACEMENTS,
ADDITIONS . . . YOU NAME IT. NO JOB IS TOO SMALL. DO YOU NEED BROKEN
SASH CORDS REPLACED, BROKEN PANES REPAIRED, LOCKS INSTALLED, OPEN OR
ROOF DECKS ADDED, OR YOUR CELLAR CONVERTED? THE RUSSELL BARBEAU
COMPANY CAN HELP. JUST CALL 1-800-826-5000 FOR A FREE CUSTOM
ESTIMATE. THEY EVEN WORK EVENINGS TO FIT YOUR BUSY SCHEDULE.
ANYTHING FROM CELLULOSE INSULATION ON AN EXISTING BUILDING, TO A NEW
PORCH OR DECK ON YOUR EXISTING PROPERTY. THE RUSSELL BARBEAU COMPANY
PROS ARE YOUR EXPERTS . . . FROM WINDOW REFURBISHMENT, DOORS, SHEET-
ROCK INSULATION AND SIDING, TO FIXING DRAFTY HOLES, CRACKS AND SO
MUCH MORE. RUSSELL BARBEAU IS LICENSED, BONDED AND INSURED. CALL
1-800-826-5000 FOR A FREE ESTIMATE. THEY EVEN WORK EVENING HOURS AND
WEEKENDS. THAT'S 1-800-826-5000. YOU'LL BE PLEASANTLY SURPRISED AT
THE AFFORDABLE PRICES . . . SO CALL NOW. 1-800-826-5000.

SPON ID: THIS (FEATURE) IS SPONSORED BY ACCOUNTEMPS . . .

ANNCR:HERE'S A QUESTION FOR EXECUTIVES. HOW DO YOU HANDLE A BUSINESS
EMERGENCY? AN EMERGENCY THAT PUTS YOU IN IMMEDIATE NEED OF A
TEMPORARY ACCOUNTANT, BOOKKEEPER, DATA ENTRY OR CREDIT/COLLECTIONS
PERSON. IF YOU'RE RUNNING AN EFFICIENT BUSINESS, NO ONE HAS THE TIME
TO FILL IN FOR AN ABSENT EMPLOYEE. YOU'LL NEED A RELIABLE,
EFFICIENT, PROFESSIONAL TEMPORARY HELP SERVICE . . . ACCOUNTEMPS.
ACCOUNTEMPS ARE THE SPECIALISTS IN TEMPORARY ACCOUNTING,
BOOKKEEPING, DATA ENTRY AND CREDIT/COLLECTIONS PEOPLE AND THEY ARE
AVAILABLE ON A HALF DAY'S NOTICE TO WORK IN YOUR OFFICE AS LONG AS
YOU WANT . . . A DAY, A WEEK, A MONTH OR MORE . . . TO HELP YOUR
ACCOUNTING, BOOKKEEPING OR CREDIT DEPARTMENT RUN SMOOTHLY. SO THE
NEXT TIME YOU HAVE A PERSONNEL EMERGENCY, CALL ACCOUNTEMPS IN
BOSTON, BRAINTREE, LEXINGTON AND DANVERS. THEY UNDERSTAND WHAT YOU
NEED. IN FACT, YOU CAN CALL THE PRESIDENT, HERB MYERS AT 951-4000 IN
BOSTON, ALSO BRAINTREE, LEXINGTON AND DANVERS. ACCOUNTEMPS IS A
DIVISION OF THE ROBERT HALF ORGANIZATION—ACCOUNTEMPS.
ANNCR:DID YOU KNOW THAT WOBURN FOREIGN MOTORS NOW HAS NEW ENGLAND'S
FINEST SELECTION OF QUALITY PREOWNED VEHICLES? YES, YOUR PREMIERE
JAGUAR AND TOYOTA DEALERSHIP IS NOW THE LEADER FOR LATE MODEL
HIGH-LINE USED CARS. CHOOSE FROM AN INCREDIBLE SELECTION OF TOYOTAS,
JAGUARS, MERCEDESES, BMWS, PORSCHES, VOLVOS, SAABS, CADILLACS,
LINCOLNS . . . YOU NAME IT. OVER 50 AVAILABLE FOR IMMEDIATE
DELIVERY. HOW ABOUT A 1987 JAGUAR XJ6 . . . 4 DOOR SEDAN, FINISHED
IN RICH REGENT GRAY COMPLEMENTED BY A PLUSH BURGUNDY LEATHER
INTERIOR, ONE OWNER, LIKE NEW, ONLY 32,000 MILES, NOW AT WOBURN

FOREIGN MOTORS WITH THE REMAINDER OF THE FACTORY WARRANTY FOR ONLY
$26,900. EACH AND EVERY CAR IS HAND PICKED FOR ITS QUALITY AND MUST
PASS A FULL 40 POINT SERVICE FROM BUMPER TO BUMPER. LIKE A 1989
MAXIMA 4 DOOR SEDAN FULLY APPOINTED FOR ONLY $17,900, SAVE ALMOST
EIGHT THOUSAND DOLLARS. CALL 933-1100. FOR MORE DETAILS, THAT'S
933-1100. TAKE EXIT 36 ON 128 TO WOBURN FOREIGN MOTORS ONLY MINUTES
FROM DOWNTOWN BOSTON. STOCK NUMBER 3548A.
ANNCR:THIS ANNIVERSARY SWEEP HER OFF HER FEET WITH A DIAMOND
ANNIVERSARY RING FROM ALPHA OMEGA JEWELERS OF CAMBRIDGE. WHILE OTHER
GIFTS MAY SAY, "I LOVE YOU" IT'S THE DIAMOND ANNIVERSARY RING, A
SIMPLE BAND OF DIAMONDS, THAT SAYS YOU'D MARRY HER ALL OVER AGAIN.
AND ISN'T THAT WHAT ANNIVERSARIES ARE ALL ABOUT? AT ALPHA OMEGA
JEWELERS YOU'LL FIND DIAMONDS, EMERALDS, SAPPHIRES, AND RUBIES FROM
ALL OVER THE WORLD OF THE VERY FINEST QUALITY AND PRICE. QUALITY,
BECAUSE SHE DESERVES THE BEST. YOU'LL FIND THE LARGEST SELECTION OF
DIAMOND ANNIVERSARY RINGS . . . 14 KARAT, 18 KARAT, 22 KARAT, GOLD
JEWELRY AND WEDDING BANDS. YOU CAN VISIT ALPHA OMEGA AT THE GALLERIA
MALL IN HARVARD SQUARE AT 57 JFK STREET OR CALL 864-1227. THAT'S
864-1227. AND THERE'S VALIDATED PARKING AT UNIVERSITY PLACE. THIS
YEAR TELL HER YOU'D MARRY HER ALL OVER AGAIN WITH A DIAMOND
ANNIVERSARY RING FROM ALPHA OMEGA JEWELERS.

08/14/90 14:22 MMC ?:80 #12+1SPORTSN

SPORTSNIGHT PROMO . . . . . .

(M) I'M CRAIG MUSTARD
(B) AND I'M RON BARR
(M) TONIGHT AND EVERY WEEKNIGHT AT SEVEN IT'S WEEI SPORTSNIGHT,
(B) THEN AT 11, IT'S MY TURN: SPORTS BYLINE USA.
(M) TONIGHT ON SPORTSNIGHT . . . _____ AND THEN,
(B) TONIGHT ON SPORTS BYLINE USA . . . _____.
(M) AND I'LL HAVE THE LATEST SCORES AND NEWS, PLUS YOUR CALLS AND
    COMMENTS. PLEASE JOIN US TONIGHT, WEEI SPORTSNIGHT AT 7 . . .
(B) AND SPORTS BYLINE USA AT 11 . . . EXCLUSIVELY ON THE NEWS STATION.
(M) NEWSRADIO 590 WEEI.

08/07/90 11:36 MMC 0:80 #12+1WEATHER

WEATHER PROMOS

   EXPERIENCE IS THE KEY INGREDIENT TO THE WEEI WEATHER WATCH
FORECAST . . . HI THIS IS WEEI METEOROLOGIST DICK ALBERT . . .
TODAY, EVERYONE HAS RADAR AND SATELLITE PICTURES TO HELP PREDICT THE
WEATHER BUT OFTEN EXPERIENCE IS MISSING . . .
   BOB COPELAND AND I HAVE SEEN JUST ABOUT EVERY WEATHER CONDITION
NEW ENGLAND CAN THROW AT US. THAT MEANS, WHEN WE ANALYZE THE
COMPUTER DATA, WE KNOW WHAT THAT MEANS FOR THE BOSTON AREA.

EXPERIENCE YOU CAN DEPEND ON . . .

THE WEATHER WATCH FORECAST, EXCLUSIVELY ON THE NEWS STATION, NEWSRADIO 590 WEEI.

WEATHER PROMO #2

<u>EXPERIENCE</u> CAN MAKE THE DIFFERENCE WHEN IT COMES TO FORECASTING THE WEATHER IN NEW ENGLAND . . .

HI THIS IS WEEI METEOROLOGIST BOB COPELAND . . .

DICK ALBERT AND I HAVE ALL THE MODERN TOOLS LIKE SATELLITE AND RADAR, BUT WE ALSO HAVE ONE OTHER KEY INGREDIENT, DECADES OF EXPERIENCE . . .

WHEN WE ANALYZE THE WEATHER DATA COMING OFF THE COMPUTERS, WE KNOW EXACTLY WHAT IT MEANS FOR THE BOSTON AREA, BECAUSE WE'VE SEEN IT ALL BEFORE.

EXPERIENCE YOU CAN DEPEND ON . . .

THE WEATHER WATCH FORECAST, EXCLUSIVELY ON THE NEWS STATION, NEWSRADIO 590 WEEI.

08/10/90 14:42 MMC 7:80 #12+NEWSTIP

NEWSTIP PROMO . . . .

IF YOU SEE NEWS HAPPENING CALL 241-9959 . . .

THE WEEI NEWSTIP LINE.

EVERY WEEK WEEI NEWSRADIO AWARDS 59 DOLLARS TO A LISTENER WHO CALLS THE WEEI NEWSTIP LINE WITH THE BEST NEWSTIP OF THE WEEK.

241-9959, WRITE THE NUMBER DOWN AND KEEP IT HANDY.

THE WEEI NEWSTIP LINE, FROM THE NEWS STATION, NEWSRADIO 590 WEEI . . . .

06/19/90 10:43 MMC 0:80 #12+1SUMMER

SUMMER PROMO #2

THROUGHOUT THE SUMMER OF 90 STAY WITH NEWSRADIO 5-90, BECAUSE THURSDAY THRU SUNDAY WEEI'S SUMMER CALENDAR WITH BILL LAWRENCE WILL FEATURE FESTIVALS, CONCERTS, MOVIES, THEATER, PLUS EVENTS FOR THE WHOLE FAMILY.

AND FRIDAY THRU SUNDAY, THERE'S WEEI'S BEACH AND BOATING REPORTS WITH TOM WENDELL.

PLUS WEEI'S EXCLUSIVE WEATHER WATCH FORECAST WITH METEOROLOGISTS BOB COPELAND AND DICK ALBERT.

AND WE'LL GET YOU FROM HERE TO THERE WITH WEEI'S ALL DAY TRAFFIC WATCH.

FOR THE SUMMER OF 90, IT'S NEWSRADIO 5-90, THE NEWS STATION, WEEI.

06/13/90 15:49 BOA 0:80 #12+1PROMO

PROMO

    POLITICS IN MASSACHUSETTS. IT'S NOT ALWAYS PRETTY, BUT IT'S NEVER DULL.

    THIS IS WEEI'S BOB OAKES. THURSDAY AFTERNOONS AT 4:50 PM AND FRIDAY MORNINGS AT 7:50 AM, CAMPAIGN JOURNAL TAKES YOU BEHIND THE HEADLINES, TO GIVE YOU A CLOSE-UP VIEW OF CAMPAIGN 90.

    THE CANDIDATES . . . THE ISSUES . . . THE MONEY, THE MOVERS AND SHAKERS. JOIN US AS WE CHRONICLE THE FIGHT FOR YOUR VOTE.

    CAMPAIGN JOURNAL. THURSDAY AT 4:50 PM, FRIDAYS AT 7:50 AM. ONLY ON THE NEWSTATION, NEWSRADIO 590, WEEI.

Television Commercials

The following TV commercials were written by advertising agency writers for several different clients. They include copy that requires a "voice-over" announcer, who reads copy off camera, and other spots that feature short dramatic situations in which the performers play a role. In some dramatic spots, the talent appears on camera. In others the performance is off the camera. (Courtesy of the William Cook Agency. Copyright the William Cook Agency, Inc.)

THE
WILLIAM COOK
A G E N C Y

CLIENT: ORLANDO DAA
JOB TITLE: 1990 YEAR-END CLEARANCE
JOB #:   DDAO-T-10241-2
DATE: DECEMBER 3, 1990
COMMERCIAL #:   DDAO-30YE-10241 B
RUN DATES: TBD

:30 YEAR-END MUSIC

Open on graphic of months popping on screen.	VO:	You waited all year long for the best deal.
"December" blooms.		Now is your time to save big...
SUPER appears from top left corner of screen: NEW DODGE		on a new Dodge at your Gold Star Dodge Dealer.
75-million-dollar GRAPHIC flips up from infinity to full screen.	SFX: VO:	(POWEE/ZOWEE) (STACK & REVERB) The seventy-five-million-dollar Dodge Clearance.

Cuts of SUPER:
  Up to
  $2500
  Cash Back
	VO:	Get up to $2500 cash back.

Cut to quick cuts of Dodge cars and trucks.		Plus huge year-end savings.
Cut to crash of video excitement. Special-effect graphic: $75 MILLION DODGE CLEARANCE	SFX: VO:	(POWEE/ZOWEE) (STACK & REVERB) The seventy-five-million-dollar Dodge Clearance!
Cut to Dodge Caravan.		Get $1000 cash back on Caravan.
Cut to clocks & super: Sale ends Dec. 31.		Time is running out.
Cut to quick cuts of Dodge cars, trucks and vans.		Eight thousand vehicles must be sold before the first.
Cut to crash of video excitement. Special-effect graphic: $75 MILLION DODGE CLEARANCE	SFX: VO:	(POWEE/ZOWEE) (STACK & REVERB) The seventy-five-million-dollar Dodge Clearance!
Cut to Gold Star Dodge dealer logo.		Get the biggest savings of the year right now...at your Gold Star Dodge Dealer.

(DDOT10241)
GH/Gl/ag

THE
WILLIAM COOK
A G E N C Y

CLIENT: ORLANDO DAA
JOB TITLE: 1991 DODGE ANNOUNCEMENT (RATED)
JOB #: DDAO-T-10111
DATE: NOVEMBER 29, 1990
COMMERCIAL #: DDAO-30R-10111 B
RUN DATES: TBD

Open on graphic:
    WARNING: The following scenes are rated
    "R."
	VO:	Warning: The following scenes are rated "R."

Cut to clapboard.

Cuts to series of shots of the Dodge Stealth Twin Turbo RT & SUPER: RACY	MUS: VO:	(Hot music track throughout) The RACY Dodge Stealth,

---

Cut to series of shots of the Dodge Caravan EL & SUPER: REFINED		REFINED Caravan,

---

Cut to series of shots of the Dodge Shadow convertible & SUPER: REFRESHING		REFRESHING Shadow convertible,

---

Cut to series of shots of the Dodge Spirit RT & SUPER: RESPONSIVE		RESPONSIVE Spirit RT,

---

Cut to series of shots of the Dodge Viper & SUPER:
    RADICAL
    (Coming Soon)
		And the RADICAL new Viper.

Cut to clapboard.

Cut to Gold Star Dodge Dealer logo.		RUN to your Gold Star Dodge Dealer and see the hot new cars RIGHT NOW.

(DAOT10111R)
GDH/MC:ag:bh

THE
WILLIAM COOK
A G E N C Y

CLIENT: FIRST UNION CORPORATE
JOB TITLE: "MY JOB DEPENDS ON IT" TV SPOT/VERSION B
JOB #:   FUCORP-T-0070
DATE: JANUARY 24, 1991
COMMERCIAL #: FUB-30MJ-0070 B
RUN DATES: TBD

(:30)

Open on female customer service representative at computer terminal.	CSR #1:	Hello, Mrs. Jennings? This is First Union.
Quick cut of computer screen and busy office.		
Cut to male customer service representative.	CSR #2:	We'd like to ask you a few questions about service.
Quick cut to computer screen.		
Cut to Branch Manager.	BM:	We're tough on ourselves at First Union.
Pan of two male customer service representatives.	CRS #3:	Were you pleased with our service?
Cut to computer screen.	CRS #2:	Do you find our 24-hour banking machine reliable?
Cut to Branch Manager.	BM:	I'm a Branch Manager...
Quick cut to male and female customer service representatives.	CSR #2:	Did we greet you with a smile?
Cut to computer screen then female customer service representative.	CSR #4:	How long did your transaction take?
Cut to Branch Manager with "Member FDIC" in lower left corner.	BM:	...and I'm going to see to it that you get service that no other bank can equal.
Quick cuts to busy office, female customer service representative and computer screen.	CSR #4:	Did we have the information you needed?
Cut to Branch Manager.	BM:	My job depends on it.
Cut to First Union logo. Fade up: Service. We Guarantee It. Member FDIC	ANC:	First Union service. We guarantee it.

(MYJOB)
/lms

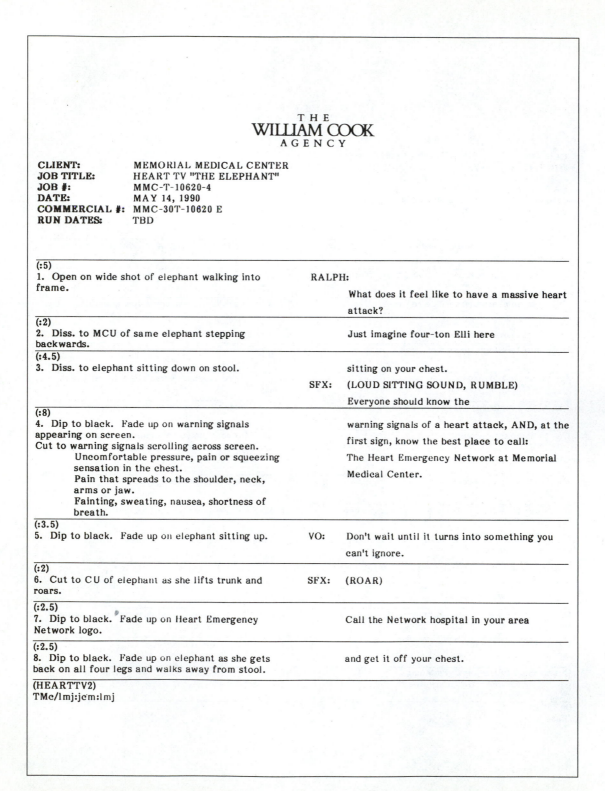

THE
WILLIAM COOK
AGENCY

CLIENT: MEMORIAL MEDICAL CENTER
JOB TITLE: HEART TV "THE ELEPHANT"
JOB #: MMC-T-10620-4
DATE: MAY 14, 1990
COMMERCIAL #: MMC-30T-10620 E
RUN DATES: TBD

(:5)
1. Open on wide shot of elephant walking into frame.

RALPH:

What does it feel like to have a massive heart attack?

(:2)
2. Diss. to MCU of same elephant stepping backwards.

Just imagine four-ton Elli here

(:4.5)
3. Diss. to elephant sitting down on stool.

sitting on your chest.

SFX: (LOUD SITTING SOUND, RUMBLE)

Everyone should know the

(:8)
4. Dip to black. Fade up on warning signals appearing on screen.
Cut to warning signals scrolling across screen.
    Uncomfortable pressure, pain or squeezing sensation in the chest.
    Pain that spreads to the shoulder, neck, arms or jaw.
    Fainting, sweating, nausea, shortness of breath.

warning signals of a heart attack, AND, at the first sign, know the best place to call:
The Heart Emergency Network at Memorial Medical Center.

(:3.5)
5. Dip to black. Fade up on elephant sitting up.

VO: Don't wait until it turns into something you can't ignore.

(:2)
6. Cut to CU of elephant as she lifts trunk and roars.

SFX: (ROAR)

(:2.5)
7. Dip to black. Fade up on Heart Emergency Network logo.

Call the Network hospital in your area

(:2.5)
8. Dip to black. Fade up on elephant as she gets back on all four legs and walks away from stool.

and get it off your chest.

(HEARTTV2)
TMc/lmj:jcm:lmj

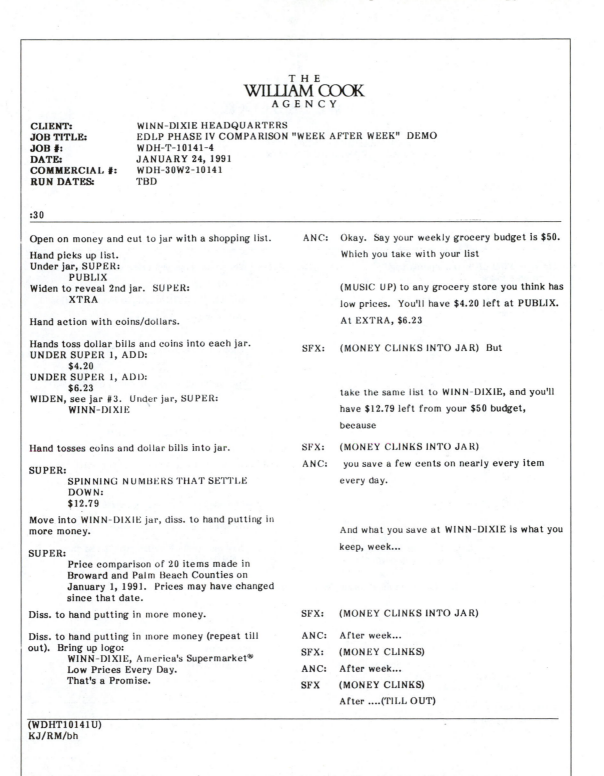

T H E
WILLIAM COOK
A G E N C Y

CLIENT: WINN-DIXIE HEADQUARTERS
JOB TITLE: EDLP PHASE IV COMPARISON "WEEK AFTER WEEK" DEMO
JOB #:   WDH-T-10141-4
DATE: JANUARY 24, 1991
COMMERCIAL #:   WDH-30W2-10141
RUN DATES: TBD

:30

Open on money and cut to jar with a shopping list.	ANC: Okay. Say your weekly grocery budget is $50. Which you take with your list

Hand picks up list.
Under jar, SUPER:
    PUBLIX
Widen to reveal 2nd jar. SUPER:
    XTRA
	(MUSIC UP) to any grocery store you think has low prices. You'll have $4.20 left at PUBLIX. At EXTRA, $6.23

Hand action with coins/dollars.	

Hands toss dollar bills and coins into each jar.
UNDER SUPER 1, ADD:
    $4.20
UNDER SUPER 1, ADD:
    $6.23
WIDEN, see jar #3. Under jar, SUPER:
    WINN-DIXIE
	SFX: (MONEY CLINKS INTO JAR) But
	
	take the same list to WINN-DIXIE, and you'll have $12.79 left from your $50 budget, because

Hand tosses coins and dollar bills into jar.	SFX: (MONEY CLINKS INTO JAR)

SUPER:
    SPINNING NUMBERS THAT SETTLE
    DOWN:
    $12.79
	ANC: you save a few cents on nearly every item every day.

Move into WINN-DIXIE jar, diss. to hand putting in more money.	And what you save at WINN-DIXIE is what you keep, week...

SUPER:
    Price comparison of 20 items made in
    Broward and Palm Beach Counties on
    January 1, 1991. Prices may have changed
    since that date.	

Diss. to hand putting in more money.	SFX: (MONEY CLINKS INTO JAR)

Diss. to hand putting in more money (repeat till out). Bring up logo:
    WINN-DIXIE, America's Supermarket®
    Low Prices Every Day.
    That's a Promise.
	ANC: After week...
	SFX: (MONEY CLINKS)
	ANC: After week...
	SFX (MONEY CLINKS)
	    After ....(TILL OUT)

(WDHT10141U)
KJ/RM/bh

THE
WILLIAM COOK
AGENCY

CLIENT: WINN-DIXIE HEADQUARTERS
JOB TITLE: EDLP PHASE IV POWER BUY "TRAINLOAD"
JOB #: WDH-T-10141-4
DATE: JANUARY 24, 1991
COMMERCIAL #: XXCX-1148
RUN DATES: TBD

:30

Open on ECU of W-D shopping bag. Hand pats bag.	BVO: When you shop, you bring groceries home in one of these.
Widen to reveal Burt walking down street with grocery bag.	But WINN-DIXIE shops for over 2 million customers every day.
	SFX: (DISTANT SOUND OF TRAIN)
	They bring groceries home in one of these.
Freight train roars in front of camera.	SFX: (ROAR OF FREIGHT TRAIN)
	SFX: (TRAIN SOUNDS UNDER FOOTAGE)
Cut to existing computer footage.	BVO: WINN-DIXIE constantly tracks down the best deals,
Cut to roaring freight train.	then uses volume buying power
Cut to printout footage.	to lower the price even more.
Cut to series of ECUs of Power Buy stickers and products on shelf. Hands pick up products.	They call them POWER BUYS. So shop WINN-DIXIE.
	SFX: (TRAIN OUT)
Cut to Burt putting items away in his kitchen. W-D bag in frame.	BURT: And you'll never miss the best deal.
Cut to ECU of train zooming by, revealing JAR LOGO. Hand drops dollars and coins into jar. SUPERS: WINN-DIXIE, America's Supermarket® Low Prices Every Day. That's a Promise.	BVO: Power Buys save you money on every aisle, every day.
	SFX: (TRAIN AND/OR WHISTLE)

(WDHT10141K)
KJ/RM/bh:ag:bh:ag

T H E
WILLIAM COOK
A G E N C Y

CLIENT: WINN-DIXIE HEADQUARTERS
JOB TITLE: EDLP PHASE IV DISCOUNT "SEE RED"
JOB #:   WDH-T-10141-7
DATE: JANUARY 24, 1991
COMMERCIAL #:   XXCX-1149
RUN DATES: TBD

:30

Open on white screen.	ANC:	You know how you feel when you pay full price and
Screen slowly begins to turn red, by either slowly deepening all over or with strong swashes of red.	SFX:	(ANGER SOUND) then find out everybody else paid less?
Red fades to sunny blue sky with puffy white clouds.	SFX:	(MUSIC UP, BIRDS TWEET, ETC.)
	ANC:	Well, it won't happen at WINN-DIXIE.
Coins, dollar bills and items such as magazines, snack packs, greeting cards, pantyhose packages, etc., start to fall in slo-mo through sky.		Forget the package price, forget the cover price, because you won't pay them. With WINN-DIXIE discounts, you save 5 to 25% off the full price of snacks, magazines, greeting cards, pantyhose...
Start to follow one of the coins down.		And what you save
Coin lands in jar with other coins and dollar bills, some additional money follows until out. BRING UP LOGO:		is what you keep.

BRING UP LOGO:
     WINN-DIXIE, America's Supermarket®
     Low Prices Every Day
     That's A Promise

(WDHT10141J)
KJ/RM/bh

THE
WILLIAM COOK
AGENCY

CLIENT: WINN-DIXIE HEADQUARTERS
JOB TITLE: EDLP PHASE IV - "30 POUNDS"
JOB #:   WDH-T-10141-5
DATE: JANUARY 24, 1991
COMMERCIAL #: XXCX-1144
RUN DATES: TBD

:30

Open very wide on Burt walking with his puppy through a park. An overweight jogger runs by, huffing and puffing.	BURT: I have a friend who once asked me, "What's the best way to lose 30 pounds?"
Cut to MCU of Burt and DOLLY with Burt, still walking, not looking directly into camera, but glancing at it as if it were a companion. (Documentary feeling.)	So I told him (GLANCES AT CAMERA, LITTLE SMILE) -- one pound at a time.
He pauses on his walk, slow move in to Burt.	(QUIETLY, SINCERE, FATHERLY ADVICE.) A pound isn't much, but lose one every week...and it becomes a lot.
He pats his tummy.	Tried and true advice.
He resumes walking, camera stays close.	Same at WINN-DIXIE. Saving a few cents isn't much, but save it on just about every item every day -- and it adds up to a lot.
Diss. to Mason jar in limbo. Hand drops bunch of coins plus a couple of dollar bills into jar.	SFX: (CLINKING OF COINS)
SUPER: WINN-DIXIE, America's Supermarket® Low Prices Every Day. That's A Promise.	
Cut back to Burt CU. He's on park bench with dog. Puppy jumps on him, licks him.	

(WDHT10141I)
KJ/RM/bh:ag

THE
WILLIAM COOK
A G E N C Y

CLIENT: WINN-DIXIE HEADQUARTERS
JOB TITLE: EDLP PHASE IV "BASEBALL GLOVE"
JOB #:   WDH-T-10141-6
DATE: JANUARY 24, 1991
COMMERCIAL #: XXCX-1143
RUN DATES: TBD

:30
_____

Open very wide on Burt walking down neighborhood street. Kids (boys and girls) are playing baseball in the street.

BURT: Years ago, my son told me he wanted to buy a baseball glove with his own money.

Cut to ECU of Burt and DOLLY with him. He strolls along, talking, not looking directly into camera, but glancing at it as if it were a companion. (Documentary feeling.)

(JOKING, MAYBE HAND TO HEART OR HEAD) When I regained consciousness, I told him

He pauses a moment to make his point.

*(THOUGHTFULLY, FATHERLY) "Start saving your pennies, and the dollars will take care of themselves."

He resumes walking, camera dollies with him.

He got the glove and the message. It's WINN-DIXIE's message, too. Save a few cents on nearly every item -- every day -- and you'll end up with a lot of dollars you wouldn't have had.

Diss. to Mason jar in limbo. Hand drops a bunch of coins and a couple of dollar bills into jar.

SFX: (CLINKING COINS)

SUPER:
    WINN-DIXIE, America's Supermarket®
    Low Prices Every Day.
    That's A Promise.

Cut back to Burt, MCU. He sits on front porch steps wearing ball glove, has ball, or tosses ball with one of the kids.

BURT: Little things add up to a lot at WINN-DIXIE.
_____

(WDHT10141E)
KJ/RM/bh:ag

THE
WILLIAM COOK
AGENCY

CLIENT:	WINN-DIXIE HEADQUARTERS
JOB TITLE:	EDLP PHASE IV "GONNA NEED 'EM"
JOB #:	WDH-T-10141-7
DATE:	JANUARY 24, 1991
COMMERCIAL #:	XXCX-1141
RUN DATES:	TBD

:30

Open on dolly through attic. There are old family items like tricycle, hat rack, old porch rocker, doll house, etc. In background Burt rummages in an old cupboard like an antique armoire or dry sink. There is a large black leather trunk nearby. Stacked on it are some dusty Mason jars. Light streams through rafters from a high window.

SFX: AMBIENT SOUND OF RUMMAGING.

BURT: I like to save things, because -- well, I might need them.

Burt walks over to trunk, picks up Mason jar. He looks at it, glancing at camera now and again as if it were a companion.

I use these for pocket change.

He reaches into his pocket and pulls out a handful of loose change and tosses it into the jar.

Toss in a little every night, and it really adds up.

Burt moves to the stairs and starts down. Camera follows from behind.

Same thing happens at WINN-DIXIE. Save a nickel or dime on one thing, it's not much. But save it on just about everything and you come out with a fistful of savings from WINN-DIXIE every time you shop.

Diss. to Mason jar. Hands put coins and dollar bills into jar.

SFX: (CLINKING COINS.)

SUPER:
  WINN-DIXIE, America's Supermarket®
  Low Prices Every Day.
  That's A Promise.

BURT VO:

  That's a promise.

Cut to Burt in front of open cupboard. Jar full of coins is there. He places second jar (the one from the attic) next to it.

BURT: So get one of these, because,--well--you're gonna need it.

(WDHT10141A)
KJ/RM/bh:ag:bh:ag

Audiovisual Script

This audiovisual script is representative of the work broadcast performers are often hired to do and has several features that make it an excellent exercise for polishing your skills. The rapid change of visual elements calls for the narrator to be precise. You must be constantly aware of the changing visuals, while taking care that your attention to this concern does not cause your concentration on your presentation to lapse.

This narration is difficult because it is not one continuous thought, but rather a series of individual thoughts, most of them relating specifically to the picture being displayed at a particular moment. The challenge is to avoid a choppy style in your delivery. A trick that helps here is to identify the central message of the presentation and keep it focused in your mind as you read.

This script demands that narrators communicate both a sense of the fun of traveling to this resort and the carefree atmosphere of the unhurried lifestyle. The writing is descriptive, and the style of the narration should be evident to the listener/viewer.

Look for key words that convey images of beauty, fun, and relaxation. Take care to emphasize these key words so that they come through clearly. You might try going through the script and highlighting all the descriptive words you see. (Courtesy of the William Cook Agency. Copyright the William Cook Agency, Inc.)

T H E
WILLIAM COOK
A G E N C Y

CLIENT: SANDALS
JOB TITLE: A V PRESENTATION
JOB #:   SR-C-11730
DATE: JANUARY 17, 1990
COMMERCIAL #:   NA
RUN DATES: NA

Up from black to title slide: Dear Sandals,	**FEMALE VO:** Dear Sandals,
Diss. to couple walking on the beach at twilight.	I think perhaps we began to come back together that very first night, while we strolled down the beach.
Diss. to closeup of couple above.	The Caribbean sky just seemed to dwarf our problems.
Diss. to aerial of the property.	But I'm getting ahead of myself.
Diss. to second shot.	I'm really writing to tell you what we liked so much about Sandals.
Diss to couple in wicker chairs.	For starters, we really liked the "couples only" idea.
Diss. to second couple.	It's not that we don't like kids. We do. But you guys devote all your energies...
Diss. to third couple.	to just one group - couples - and it's great.
Diss. to couple at swim-up bar.	The swim-up pool bars, for instance. They're perfect for couples.
Diss. to couple at piano bar.	And without a bunch of singles on the loose... well, you know what I mean.
Diss. to snorkeling.	I can't begin to tell you all the things we did. I think we did it all. We snorkeled.

SANDALS
A V PRESENTATION
SR-C-11730
PAGE 2

Diss. to skiing.	skied...
Diss. to cabaret.	danced...
Diss. to dining.	dined...
Diss. to toga dancing.	danced...
Diss. to dining.	and dined again.

Diss.to chefs with beautiful food.	The restaurants were fantastic...
Diss. to snacking.	and the round-the-clock snacks filled in where the dining ended.

Diss. to couple with waiter behind them.	Most importantly, we really liked being able to order what we wanted.

Diss. to health club.	Oh, yes, and thanks for putting in a health club.

Diss. to second health-club shot.	The workouts kept me from gaining even a pound.

Diss. to entertainment.	Unlike a lot of other vacations, this wasn't a
Diss. to couple.	he or she vacation...it was a "we" vacation.

Diss. to Montego Bay.	But rather than me telling you about the other side of this story,
Diss. to interior shot.	I'll let him tell you himself.

Diss. to Royal Caribbean.	MAN:	Well, here goes. To be honest, I picked
Diss. to Negril.		Sandals because of the all-inclusive pricing.
		I was just fed up with making decisions.

Diss. to zoom in on Ocho Rios.	So I took the easy way out. Pure convenience. To begin with, that is.

SANDALS
A V PRESENTATION
SR-C-11730
PAGE 3

Diss. to pool.	It wasn't until we actually got there that I discovered the biggest benefit of all.
Diss. to couple with two waiters offering plates of food.	Not once, not even a little, did we discuss money again.
Diss. to couple in whirlpools with drinks.	For the entire vacation.
Diss. to couple in paddle boat.	We knew everything...
Diss. to couple playing tennis.	was included.
Diss. to sunfish.	So we just did...
Diss. to boat bike.	what we wanted.
Diss. to cognac after dinner.	If we wanted a cognac after dinner, we ordered it.
Diss. to midnight snack.	If we wanted a midnight snack, we had one.
Diss. to couple in canoe at twilight.	If we felt like doing something, we did it.
Diss. to couple in a hammock.	And if we didn't, well, then we didn't.
Diss. to couple in rattan swing.	I can't tell you how relaxed you can get when...
Diss. to couple having drinks with banjo player in background.	you don't have to carry your wallet or even a few bucks for tips.
Diss. to couple under a straw hut.	For once in my life, I really did smell the roses.
Diss. to drink with hibiscus.	
Diss. to couple with yellow drinks and hibiscus on the table.	I even noticed the flowers...
Diss. to couple with conch shell and waiter pouring the water.	the water....

SANDALS
A V PRESENTATION
SR-C-11730
PAGE 4

Diss. to moonlight scene.		the moon.
Diss. to man looking at his sweetheart.		But most of all, I noticed her. Again. You know, I hadn't done that for some time.
Diss. to closeup of above.		And what I saw was worth all the money in the world -- all inclusive or not.
Diss. to room with two couples.	WM:	I just wanted to say one more thing. The rooms were beautiful...
Diss. to room with view of ocean and couple looking out.		so close to the ocean and all.
Diss. to empty room with spiral staircase. Diss. to couple at white table.		And although we didn't spend...well, a whole lot of time in ours, the little niceties were really nice.
Diss. to room revealing vanity and king-size bed.		The king-sized bed...even the blow dryers in the rooms...were nice surprises.
Diss. to couple on a veranda. Diss. to couple on a pier. Diss. to peacock. Diss. to couple with palm tree in background. Diss. to couple on beach with sunfish in background.		You knew nothing could detract from the rest and relaxation of a trip to such a beautiful place.
Diss. to gazebo. Diss. to aerial of Negril.		We're already planning our next trip. We took you up on your offer... and played a little at the other three Sandals Resorts on the island.
Diss. to fronts of buildings at Negril with beach.		We can't decide if next time we'll stay at Negril with its fantastic seven-mile beach...

SANDALS
A V PRESENTATION
SR-C-11730
PAGE 5

Diss. to Royal Caribbean, front of building.	Or try Royal Caribbean. We really were taken with its British Colonial charm.
Diss. to Monetgo Bay beachfront with two-story veranda.	We liked the Jamaican style of Montego Bay, too.
Diss. to building with boat in foreground.	Then again, we might just stay at Ocho Rios again.
Diss. to Dunn's River Falls. Diss. to artist's rendering.	But who knows? We heard there's a new Sandals at Dunn's River Falls opening soon. We might just be your first guests there.
Diss. to Carlyle, front of building. Diss. to Carlyle interior. Diss. to third Carlyle amenity shot.	While we were visiting, we heard about your Carlyle Hotel on Montego Bay. Everyone says it's smaller, more intimate, and bit different that your other resorts. You know, it's hard to decide.
Diss. to Montego Bay.	But WHEREVER we stay, you can be sure of one thing...it won't be long before we come back.
Diss. to people around a piano. Diss. to couple having a candlelight dinner.	Because at Sandals we found something we were never able to find at any other resort in the world...

SANDALS
A V PRESENTATION
SR-C-11730
PAGE 6

Diss. to silhouette.	each other. Sincerely, Kenny
Diss. to Sandals slide.	Tricia McCauley.
	Sandals

(TONY)
GDH/bh:lmj

Pronunciation by the Book

*N*o portion of a textbook can provide you with anything approaching a complete guide to foreign pronunciation. We have, however, condensed two valuable tools in this section; although they are not the answer to all pronunciation problems, they can lead you to the answers.

First, we have included a simplified guide to the International Phonetic Alphabet (IPA). The IPA reproduces most sounds found in human speech.

Second, we provide an all-purpose chart outlining the fundamentals of foreign pronunciation. This chart, which we have developed over a period of years, will serve as a quick reference: find the letter, read across the chart to the appropriate language, and you'll see the most common pronunciation.

The IPA was developed by the International Phonetic Association, which is headquartered in London. Originally, the alphabet was created by a small group of teachers in France interested in transcription of language sounds, and in the 1880s a journal was published using only phonetic transcription.

Soon, the idea of an alphabet that would apply to all languages became a reality; it has proven useful to linguists, speech scientists, and others.

However, the IPA has never achieved the widespread acceptance its developers had hoped for. It is more complex than traditional phonetic transcription (such as wire-service transcription used in this book) and is still rather limited in its accuracy. The editors of the latest edition of the *Principles of the International Phonetic Association* note that fine regional variations are impossible to discern using the alphabet, and some American dictionary editors, such as the editors of The *NBC Handbook of Pronunciation,* dropped the IPA in the volume's 1984 edition in favor of more practical standard dictionary transcription.

The *NBC Handbook* editors also noted that it is simply impossible for Americans to mimic sounds native to other languages from a printed reference; also, it is extremely difficult for Americans to make sounds found, say, in Arabic or Chinese without special training.

The editors recommend in some circumstances that you consult a native speaker of the language to hear the sounds.

And that is one reason why we titled this section "By the Book." There are some outstanding CD-ROM reference "books" on the market that not only give you the written (phonetically transcribed) version of the word but also a computer-synthesized pronunciation.

You will often find that the transcriptions are in simplified form (similar to wire-service transcriptions) and in IPA. Standard foreign-language dictionaries (the printed kind) also use the IPA.

So while the IPA's use in the newsroom and air studio is limited, it can be handy for those looking to develop fluency in native or near-native pronunciation. This IPA table provides all the English sounds. (If you want to pursue study of nonnative speech sounds, we second the advice given above and suggest you contact a native speaker, or an infinitely more patient CD-ROM and foreign-language dictionary, which will tutor you on the special IPA characters used for native sounds.)

In the meantime, though, you may find IPA transcription handy for certain applications. We have attempted to remove one obstacle often encountered in learning the IPA: the fact that the sounds are presented out of any typical order and you must memorize the whole system before it makes sense. Instead, we present the IPA by listing the native American English sounds in the order we learn them: by alphabetized consonants, by alphabetized vowels, and then by alphabetized consonant pairs and alphabetized vowel pairs.

You can now learn the rudiments of the IPA in less than an hour.

The IPA: Single Consonants

Common consonant sounds listed by the English letter usually asociated with that sound. This table lists single consonants.

B	/b/	boy
C	/k/	cat
	/s/	cell
D	/d/	dog
F	/f/	fan
G	/g/	gone
H	/h/	hot
J	/dʒ/	judge

Continues

K	/k/	kill
L	/l/	low
M	/m/	man
N	/n/	night
P	/p/	pig
Qu (kw)	/kw/	queen
R	/r/	rain
S	/s/	stop
T	/t/	toy
V	/v/	vest
W	/w/	want
X (ks)	/ks/	box
Y	/j/	young
Z	/z/	zebra

The IPA: Paired Consonants

Paired consonants, listed by the English letters usually associated with their sounds.

CH	/tS/	chew
NG	/ŋ/	sing
SH	/S/	shoe
TH (unvoiced)	/ə/	thin
TH (voiced)	/ð/	then
WH	/HW/	when
ZH (voiced SH)	/ʒ/	pleasure

The IPA: Single Vowels

Common single vowel sounds. The long *a* in "ate" and the *i* in "ice" are actually combinations of two vowels sounds.

These sounds are listed by the English letter usually associated with that sound.

A (long)	/ei/	ate (diphthong)
A (long)	/e/	age
A (short)	/ae/	back
E (long)	/i/	meet
E (short)	/ɛ/	bed
I (long)	/ai/	ice (diphthong)
I (short)	/I/	hit
O (long)	/o/	open
O (short)	/a/	hot
U (long)	/u/	tube
U (short)	/ʌ/	up

The IPA: Complex Vowels

Common complex vowels and diphthongs (vowel combinations) listed by the English letter(s) usually associated with the sound.

AW	/ɔ/	th<u>aw</u>
er	/ɚ/	winn<u>er</u>
ir	/ɛ˞/	th<u>ir</u>d
OO (long)	/u/	b<u>oo</u>m (same as t<u>u</u>be)
OO (short)	/ʊ/	l<u>oo</u>k
OW	/aʊ/	n<u>ow</u>
OY	/ɔi/	b<u>oy</u>
uh	/ə/	<u>a</u>bout, b<u>a</u>n<u>a</u>na
yu	/Iu/	acc<u>u</u>se (within word)
yu	/ju/	<u>u</u>se (at start of word)

Transcribing words with the IPA

Now, you can simply choose the sounds and place them together within slashes //—which signify IPA transcription.

For example:
effort = /ɛfɚt/
think = /əIŋk/
come = /kʌm/
For multisyllable words, place an accent (') before the stressed syllable:
above = /əˈbʌv/
A secondary stress is indicated by an accent (') on the lower part of the letter before the syllable that receives secondary stress:
renewing = /ˌriˈnuiŋ/

Foreign Language Pronunciation Chart

Vowels	FRENCH	GERMAN	ITALIAN	SPANISH
a	as in: "f<u>a</u>ther"	as in: "f<u>a</u>ther"	as in: "f<u>a</u>ther"	as in: "f<u>a</u>ther"
aa		"g<u>a</u>te"		
ae, ai	"ai," "b<u>e</u>t," or "g<u>a</u>te"	"ai," "r<u>i</u>de"		"ae," "ai," "r<u>i</u>de"
au	"s<u>o</u>"		"c<u>ow</u>"	"c<u>ow</u>"
e	"b<u>e</u>t" or "<u>up</u>"	"g<u>a</u>te" or "b<u>e</u>t"	"g<u>a</u>te" or "b<u>e</u>t"	"g<u>a</u>te"
é	"g<u>a</u>te"		"g<u>a</u>te"	
ê	"b<u>e</u>t"			
è	"b<u>e</u>t"		"b<u>e</u>t"	
eau	"s<u>o</u>"			
ei	"b<u>e</u>t"	"r<u>i</u>de"		"g<u>a</u>te"
eu	"b<u>ur</u>n"	"s<u>oi</u>l"		

Continues

Vowels	FRENCH	GERMAN	ITALIAN	SPANISH
ey	"y<u>e</u>t"	"r<u>i</u>de"		
i	"gr<u>ee</u>t"	"gr<u>ee</u>t" or "k<u>i</u>ss"	"gr<u>ee</u>t" or "y" (before or after vowels)	"gr<u>ee</u>t"
ie		"gr<u>ee</u>t"		"y<u>ea</u>"
o	"sh<u>o</u>re" or "<u>u</u>p"	"s<u>o</u>" or "s<u>a</u>w"	"s<u>o</u>" or "s<u>a</u>w"	"s<u>o</u>"
ô	"s<u>o</u>"			
ö, oe		"t<u>u</u>rn," "s<u>a</u>y" (pursed lips)		
oi	"w<u>a</u>ft"		"b<u>oy</u>"	"b<u>oy</u>"
ou	"st<u>oo</u>l"			

Consonants*	FRENCH	GERMAN	ITALIAN	SPANISH
b		sounded as "p" when at the end of a word		
c	as "k" when final sound in word; "s" before <u>e</u>, <u>i</u>, <u>y</u>; "k" elsewhere	"kh" before <u>a</u>, <u>o</u>, <u>u</u>	"ch" before <u>e</u>, <u>i</u>, <u>y</u>; "k" before <u>a</u>, <u>o</u>, <u>u</u>	"s" before <u>e</u>, <u>i</u>, <u>y</u>; "k" otherwise
ch	"sh" "ck"	(aspirated)	"k"	
ck			"kk"	
d		"t" when at the end of a word		"th" within or at the end of a word
dt		"t"		
f	as in English	as in English	as in English	as in English
g	"zh" before <u>e</u>, <u>i</u>, <u>y</u>; elsewhere as in "get"	as in "get" when first sound in word; sometimes guttural "ch"	"j" before <u>e</u>, <u>i</u>, <u>y</u>; as in "get" before <u>a</u>, <u>o</u>, <u>u</u>	"h" before <u>e</u>, <u>i</u>, <u>y</u>; as in "get"
gh			as in "get" before <u>i</u>, similar to "bi<u>ll</u>iards"	
gl				
gn	"ny" as in "onion"		"ny" as in "onion"	
h	silent	as in English	silent	silent
j	"zh"	"y"	often as "i"	"h"
ll				"y"
m, n, ng	when preceded by vowel, in the same syllable, the vowel is nasalized			

Continues

Consonants*	FRENCH	GERMAN	ITALIAN	SPANISH
ñ				"y" added before following vowel sound
q	"k"			
qu	"k"	"kv"	"qw"	"k" before e, i
r	guttural rolled, or trilled	guttural or trilled		
s	as in "see"; "z" between vowels	"z" when beginning word or before vowel; as in "see"	as in "see"	
sc	"sk" before a, o, u; "s" before e, i		"sk" before a, o, u; "sh" before e, i	
sch		"sh"	"sk"	
sp		"shp" at beginning of a word		
st		"sht" at beginning of word	"t"	
t	as in English	as in English	as in English	as in English
th	"t"	"t"		
v		"f"		"b"
w	"v"	"v"	rare, like "v"	
x				"s" when preceded by consonant
z		"ts"	"ts" as in "cats" or "dz" as in "fin<u>ds</u>"	

*Pronounced very much as they are in English; exceptions are noted here.

RECOMMENDATION   Ideally, you must know the **convention.** Use pronunciation guides, the dictionary, wire service pronouncers, and the pronunciations you have heard from network newscasters. Be aware that the network standard in foreign pronunciation is not always infallible, and often those at the very top levels of the networks cannot come up with a definitive pronunciation, either. Coverage of the Iranian hostage crisis involved widely different pronunciations of names for a period of months until conventions were established. Use the convention favored by the most authoritative source you have.

PROBLEM   Assuming you know the convention to use, is the word or phrase (not a proper name or place name) pronounced with foreign inflection? If so, how much?

RECOMMENDATION   Attempting to pronounce foreign words and phrases with the inflection used by a native speaker of that country can sound affected in many circumstances. For example, an announcer reading a commercial for a Mexican fast-food restaurant would appear affected if he or she trilled the *r*'s in *burrito,* unless that announcer were adopting a character role. On the other side of the issue, American announcers do not have the flexibility to anglicize pronunciations as severely as the British, who pronounce Quixote as *Kwiks'-oht.* The American announcer must come up with compromises depending on the situation.

1.   Most foreign pronunciations sound natural, unaffected, and acceptable when rules of foreign pronunciation are followed. However, the word is pronounced *as an educated native English speaker would say it,* not as a native would say the word. An American speaker, for example, knows that the *au* configuration in German is pronounced *ow,* and would use that pronunciation. The speaker would not, though, try to reproduce a German accent precisely. Likewise, the speaker following this rule would not trill *r*'s in Spanish words and would not make the *n*'s in French words too nasal.

2.   The most notable exception is announcing for classical music programs, for here the announcer is expected to be an expert. Typically, the classical music announcer should give full inflection to the words, using native pronunciation.

PROBLEM   What about proper names and place names?

RECOMMENDATION   Follow convention; use American pronunciations for names of well-known people or places according to these guidelines:

1.   The names of major cities and countries are spoken according to American convention (for example, Munich, not München). In most cases, an American-flavored pronunciation, rather than an imitation of native inflection, is best. The final *ch* in Munich, then, would be pronounced like an American *k,* not gutturalized, as in German.

2.   Proper names of newsmakers are usually pronounced without foreign inflection. However, it is always correct to pronounce a person's name the way he or she says it, whether that person is foreign or American. Many names in classical music are by custom pronounced with foreign pronunciation and full inflection.

3.   It is good form to pronounce names of people and places with foreign inflection if those people or places are not famous. A story about a small wine-producing town in France, for example, could be read with native French inflections given to the words.

It is difficult to decipher foreign pronunciations from tables of vowels and consonants. Moreover, a table is not always available, so it is worthwhile to memorize the *general characteristics* of the major languages. It is also worthwhile to listen to recordings of foreign speakers.

FRENCH   At the end of a French word, the letter *e*, without an accent, is not pronounced (étoil*e*). This is also the case for final *es* (étoil*es*) and for the ent ending on verbs (ils parl*ent*).

Most final consonants are not pronounced. A phonetic approximation of *"Parlez-vous français?"* ("Do you speak French?"), for example, is *"Pahr-lay voo frahn-say'?"*

Most of the consonants are pronounced like English consonants. Some vowels before *n* and *m* are nasalized (*en*fant, so*nt*, fi*n*, *en*chanter, *un* ameri-cain. In short, a vowel or diphthong is nasalized when it is followed by *n* or *m* in the same syllable; *en*/fant, *em*/ployer, *am*/bu/lance.

J is pronounced *zh*, like the sound in *beige*. Accents usually fall on the last syllable: *bataille, terminée.* Otherwise syllables receive about equal stress: *in-té-res-sant, Mon-a-co.*

GERMAN   There are few if any silent letters in German. Some sounds are not approximated in English, such as the *ö* (the mark above the letter is an umlaut). This vowel can be either short or long, in the same sense that the English *a* is long in "lake" but short in "bat." The long *ö* can be approximated by rounding the lips as though you were going to say "oh" but saying "ay" as in "say" instead. To shorten the vowel, don't say "ay" as in "say" but rather "eh" as in "bed."

Two main indicators of a long vowel are that it is before only one consonant (much the same as in English) or that it is at the end of a word.

Other major facets of German vowel pronunciation are that *au* is pronounced *ow; eu* is pronounced *oy; ei* is pronounced like the word *"eye"*; and *ie* is pronounced *ee.*

Common consonant pronunciations: *d* is pronounced as *t* when occurring at the end of a word. Another common word ending substitution is *p* for *b*. The letter *j* is pronounced as a *y; s* is pronounced as *z; w* is pronounced as *f.* Native German speakers will pronounce a beginning *s* as *sh* when words start with an *st* or *sp* cluster; *ch* is pronounced as *kh*, a guttural *k.*

"Sprechen sie Deutsch?" ("Do you speak German?") would be approximated as *"Shprek'h-en zee Doytch?"*

Accents in German are most commonly on the first syllable. It is also helpful to know that all nouns are capitalized in written German.

SPANISH   Spanish is very regular in its pronunciations, and you can figure out many Spanish words and names by remembering that *i* is pronounced *ee*, and *e* is pronounced *ay*. Typically, *a* is pronounced *ah* as in "father" rather than *a* as in "apple" (a convention that applies to many languages).

For consonants, remember that *ll* is pronounced as a *y*.

Caballero ("gentleman") is pronounced *cahb-ah-yay'-row.*

In Spanish, the *r* is trilled, but in most cases you will not try to approximate this in English pronunciation. *J* is pronounced like an English *h*. Accents usually fall on the last or next-to-last syllable; occasionally accent marks tell you what syllable to stress.

ITALIAN Italian words are pronounced much as they are spelled. Unlike English, double consonants are pronounced as in ca*pp*ello (hat) and ca*rr*o (cart) in contrast to ca*p*ello (hair) and ca*r*o (dear).

Be aware that Italian *ci* and *ce* take on a *ch* sound, as in *cibo* (food) and *cena* (supper). Also, as often in English, Italian *gi* and *ge* take on a *j* sound (*Giovanni, gelato*). The letter *h* is silent and is mainly used to change *ci, ce, gi, ge* sequences from *ch* and *j* sounds to *k* and *g* sounds (Cec*ch*etti, *Gh*ia).

The letter combinations *gn* and *gl* are pronounced something like the first *n* in *onion* (og*n*i, meaning "every") and the *ll* in *billiards* (fi*gl*io, meaning "son").

Keep in mind that *i* is pronounced *ee* but that *e* can be *ay* (m*e*no) or *e* (*E*lena) and that *o* can be *oh* (s*o*le) or *aw* as in English *law* (f*o*rte).

The letters *i* and *u* before and after another vowel (with the exception of the *ci, ce, gi, ge* sequences) are generally pronounced *y*, as in *yes* (ch*i*amo), and *w*, as in *wet* (b*u*ono).

Next-to-last syllables frequently receive stress in Italian words, but there are many words with stress on other syllables.

RUSSIAN Russian language copy written in the Cyrillic alphabet is transliterated for English speakers. This means that in broadcasting, the words have been converted to English equivalents, although the pronunciations still are somewhat irregular. The *ev* in Gorbachev, for example, is usually pronounced *off* by American speakers who transliterate.

GLOSSARY

acted delivery   Speaking lines in the guise of a character, such as assuming the role of a tired husband in a headache-remedy commercial. Opposite of *straight delivery,* in which a reader delivers lines as an announcer, not as a character.

actuality   An interview segment recorded on tape for later use, sometimes in a voice actuality or voice wrap. The term *actuality* is most commonly used in radio. Television producers tend to call interview segments *sound bites* or *SOT* (sound-on-tape) *segments.*

actuality interview   An interview conducted expressly for the purpose of gathering an actuality.

additions   In speech, the interjection of extra sounds within a word, such as saying "ath-a-lete" instead of "athlete."

ad-lib   Material spoken spontaneously without being read from a script. Literally, "at pleasure."

adult contemporary   A radio format that usually consists of a mix of softer rock (compared with "hard" rock) and often includes a heavy component of news and information.

AFTRA   American Federation of Television and Radio Artists, a union that represents certain on-air personnel.

agent   A businessperson who represents a performer in contract negotiations. The agent re-ceives a percentage of the performer's salary in return for negotiating the terms of the contract.

aircheck   Audio or video recording of a performer when he or she is on air. Often used as a critiquing tool or an audition tape.

album-oriented rock (AOR)   A radio format featuring longer cuts, usually of fairly "heavy" rock, although AOR is split into several segments, including "classic" AOR.

amplification   The process of boosting a signal's strength, one function of the audio console.

anchor   In current usage, anyone who delivers news on air, in radio and television, from a studio. Generally reserved to refer to the main announcer who reads the newscast from start to finish. Also used, on occasion, to refer to "sports anchor."

AOR   *See* album-oriented rock.

Arbitron   A firm that, among other types of research, is noted for its radio ratings. In informal usage, *Arbitron* is used as a noun to denote the ratings report.

area of dominant influence (ADI)   A ratings term that delineates a broadcast market by size. There are slightly more than 200 ADIs in the United States.

443

articulation In informal usage (usage by performers rather than speech scientists), the clarity of sound production by a person speaking.

attribution A reference, within a story, to the source of the story or information.

audition channel A separate channel on the audio console that lets the operator hear the output of the board without having that output go over the air. It is useful for doing production work off air and for hearing off-air sources through the main speaker.

automation Using mechanized devices to carry out certain operations in the broadcast or cable studio. For example, some radio stations have equipment that automatically plays back a sequence of recordings. Many television studios have preset, mechanized control of the cameras, thus eliminating the need for a camera operator.

bidirectional pickup pattern A mic pattern that picks up sounds from the front or rear but rejects sounds from the side.

billboard A listing of audio or video cuts to be fed by a news service.

cardioid A type of microphone with a one-direction, heart-shaped pattern. (Note that the root *cardi-*, as in *cardiac,* means *heart.*)

cartridge machine A unit that plays or records cartridge tapes, which are continuous loops of tape housed in a plastic case that is usually called a *cart.* The units are called *cart machines.*

cassette A plastic device that holds tape internally. Both audio and video tape come in cassette format.

CD Compact disc.

CHR Abbreviation for *contemporary hit radio,* a format that features a rotation of a fairly small number of the most popular songs.

cluttering In informal usage, the tendency of some announcers to push sounds together in a too-rapid jumble.

compressing copy Speeding up the reading to shorten the time needed to read copy.

console The device used by an audio operator to route, amplify, and mix audio sources.

condenser A microphone that uses an electrical element called a capacitor to store an electrical charge. The vibration of the diaphragm produces a change in capacitance, which is transduced into an electrical signal. Condenser mics provide the highest quality of sound reproduction with excellent sensitivity.

contemporary hit radio *See* CHR.

copy Any written material to be read on tape or over the air.

country/country western A format featuring songs of a distinctly rural character. There are many varieties of country, some of which are quite close to rock. "Western" music often features steel guitars and cowboy-type themes; "country western" is a variety of country.

cue channel A channel on the audio console that allows the operator to hear a source without having it go over the air. Cue is generally routed through a small speaker in the console, as opposed to audition, which is played back over the studio speaker.

cutaway In video production, a segment (usually a shot of the reporter or some other image relevant to the news story) that is used to cover an edit during an interview.

daypart In radio, a section of the day that has particular audience characteristics. Morning drive time, for example, is a daypart.

dead air Silent time on radio, generally something announcers try to avoid at all costs.

dialect In informal usage, a peculiarity of speech based on either region or social status. A distinctive variation of a language in which pronunciation, usage, and grammatical structure differ from the theoretical standard. Usually refers to a geographic difference (for example, a Cajun dialect) but also refers to differences caused by the social class of the speaker.

diaphragmatic breathing Inhalation and exhalation using the full expansion and contraction of the diaphragm, a sheet of muscle between the chest and the abdomen; the diaphragm is responsible for motion of air through the breathing apparatus and vocal tract.

diction The formation of individual sounds.

digital audiotape (DAT) An audio tape that records signals in the on-off language of computers.

distortion In speech, the improper alteration of sound, such as saying "intertainment" instead of "entertainment" (the initial "e" sound is distorted). In broadcasting, *distortion* often refers to unacceptable deviations in the sound caused by the electronic equipment; for example, when a tape is played too loudly over a speaker.

drive time Periods of heavy listening when many radio audience members are in their cars. Morning drive time and afternoon drive time are two important dayparts.

dub To copy an audiotape or videotape.

easy listening A radio format usually featuring orchestrated versions of popular and standard songs along with vocals.

EFP (electronic field production) The use of portable equipment to gather and/or edit material outside of the studio.

ENG (electronic newsgathering) Basically the same as EFP, but applied to news operations.

erase head The part of a tape-recording unit that eradicates any signal laid down on tape.

fact sheet A listing of brief items from which the announcer will ad-lib a commercial.

fader A variable resistor that governs the loudness of the audio signal.

field producer An executive in charge of the artistic and technical elements of a program produced outside the studio.

field report A news item filed from outside the studio.

fluency In informal usage, the area of speech concerned with either cluttering or stuttering, or both.

format The overall programming structure of a radio station.

frequency response The range of frequencies that can be reproduced by a microphone or audio system.

fricative A speech sound produced by forcing air through a narrow vocal passage, therefore producing the sound by friction (hence the term *fricative*). The sound of "f," for example, is produced by the friction of air being forced between the top lip and the bottom teeth.

general American speech The speech pattern used by an educated American, free from regional accents. A more precise and common term is *network standard.*

hard news News that is "breaking"—that is, happening currently—and is of immediate importance. Soft news is generally considered to be "human interest" news, which is not necessarily current or breaking.

hard sell A type of delivery that involves a very deliberate, forceful approach.

inflection The announcer's use of tone and pitch.

International Phonetic Alphabet (IPA) A comprehensive system of symbols used to describe the full range of speech sounds, of primary use to linguists, speech clinicians, and other scholars.

lead The opening sentence or sentences of a news story.

libel A published ("published" means put in print or stated over the air) statement that is provably untrue and causes hardship to someone's reputation and/or finances.

lite A music format characterized by easy listening standards. Stations use the word, attached to their call letters, to provide easy identification for the listener.

market A term indicating the locality served by a station.

melody (in reading) The rise and fall of pitch among words in a sentence.

microphone A device for picking up sounds and changing the motional energy of sound waves (a vibration in the air) into electrical energy.

mixing The process of taking two or more audio outputs and blending them together.

monitor An audio speaker or a studio-quality television set that is used to listen to or watch the signal in studio.

moving coil mic A microphone using a coil that moves through a magnetic field in response to the movement of a diaphragm, which vibrates in response to sound waves. The movement of the coil produces an electrical signal.

NABET National Association of Broadcast Employees and Technicians, a union that represents some technical and certain other employees in broadcasting.

narration The process of reading a script off the camera.

network A linkage of organizations-in our frame of reference, primarily broadcast stations-in which a central source of programming supplies material to the individual stations that make up the system.

network standard The unaccented (that is, lacking regional accents) speech patterns, pronunciation, and grammatical construction used by most announcers broadcasting over radio and TV networks.

news director The executive in charge of the news department.

news feed A series of reports "fed" from a network to local stations, usually by satellite or telephone line.

news/talk A format that features listener call-in combined with heavy news programming.

omission In speech, the failure to pronounce a sound within a word, such as saying "maket" instead of "market."

omnidirectional pickup pattern A microphone pickup pattern in which sound sources are picked up equally well in all directions regardless of their position in relation to the microphone.

outcue The last words (or other visual or auditory cue) in a taped presentation. Knowing the outcue helps an anchor or announcer to know when the piece is ending.

package A complete report filed by a television journalist for inclusion in a newscast. Usually the rough visual equivalent of a radio voice actuality.

patter A word used primarily by radio staff announcers to describe their spoken delivery. Usually ad-libbed humorous material.

phonation The act of producing a speech sound by vibrating vocal cords.

phrasing The way an announcer uses timing and pitch to communicate a message clearly.

playback head The electromagnetic sensor that picks up signals on an audio tape and translates them back to sound.

plosive A speech sound produced by an explosion (a word that uses the same root as the word *plosive*) from the mouth. The *p* sound, for example, is produced by building up air behind the closed lips and then allowing it to "explode."

privileged communication A certain type of statement that is immune from a libel charge. Privileged communication takes place on the floor of legislative bodies, in courts, and in most official proceedings.

program channel The on-air channel. During off-air production work, the program signal is generally fed to a tape recorder.

prompting device A device that projects the script on a one-way mirror in front of the television lens. The announcer can see the script, but it won't show up on the camera.

pronouncer A written reference explaining how to say an unfamiliar word. Wire services include pronouncers in their copy.

proximity effect The way some mics tend to boost bass frequencies when a person speaks very close to the mic's diaphragm.

public figure (defense) The concept that someone who actively seeks public office or, to a lesser extent, public notice, has less protection against libel.

ratings Statistical measurements of the audience viewing or listening to a particular broadcast station or network. These measurements are made by specialized ratings firms and reported to the stations. The ratings report is then often referred to as "the book."

record head The part of a tape-recording unit that lays a signal down on the tape.

reel-to-reel A recording unit that uses tape spooled on open reels, rather than on cassettes.

regionalism A speech pattern characteristic of a particular geographical location, such as a New England accent or a Southern accent. Regionalisms are generally a handicap to on-air performers, even within the regions from which they derive their accents.

résumé   A document that outlines experience and education. Sometimes called a "vita" in other professions, but almost always called a résumé in broadcasting.

reverse shot   A video picture of a reporter, usually taken from the opposite angle of the shot of the newsmaker. The reverse shot serves two purposes: to show the reporter on the scene and to provide a piece of cover video to facilitate an edit. A reverse shot must never change the context of the actual questions as posed during the interview.

ribbon mic   A microphone using a thin element that vibrates in response to the velocity of sound waves. The ribbonlike element is suspended in a magnetic field that converts the sound to an electrical signal.

rip and read   The practice of allowing news coverage to become nothing more than the printing of service copy off the computer and reading it on the air. The term is anachronistic because copy is generated on a computer as opposed to a wire service teletype.

running the board   Operating the broadcast console.

share   The percentage of the available audience tuned in to a particular radio or TV station. (A rating reflects the percentage in relation to the total of all households that have radio or TV in a given area.)

shock jock   Slang term for *disk jockey* who uses outlandish material to amuse the audience.

social dialect   A peculiarity of speech that is primarily related to one's social and/or educational background.

soft news   Nonbreaking news, such as feature news or human interest stories.

spot   Colloquial term for a commercial.

standard English   The type of English spoken and written by an educated person of the upper class or upper-middle class. Applied particularly to the United States, the term "standard American English" is often used. Note that this term applies mainly to usage, vocabulary, and sentence structure. *Network standard* is the term generally applied to unaccented speech.

stand-up   A report done with the journalist reading straight to the camera, usually standing before some recognizable landmark or landscape that figures in the news event.

station sound   The underlying strategy of the station, the "sound" into which all elements must fit.

stop   A speech sound caused by completely shutting off the flow of air. A stop is a component of a plosive. The lips in the "p" sound come together to impede the flow of air and then come apart to release the "explosion."

straight reading or **straight delivery**   A reading in which the announcer delivers the copy as an announcer, not in the guise of a character. Opposite of acted scene or acted delivery.

studio interview   An interview conducted in studio as part of a show that has a beginning, a middle, and an end. Distinct from an actuality interview, in which only a piece of the interview is to be used.

stuttering   A complex group of speech problems stemming from a variety of causes and offering many manifestations, one of which is stammering or spasmodic repetition of a sound. Stuttering can also involve "blocking" on words, not being able to initiate pronunciation.

style   An unusual or unique way of doing things; a method of presentation that differentiates one's work from that of others.

substitution   A speech term describing a situation in which an improper sound is used in place of the proper sound, such as saying "wabbit" instead of "rabbit."

tally light   The light on a camera that shows when the camera is on air.

tight board; running a tight board   Industry jargon for adeptly operating the console and butting program elements up against each other in rapid succession with no blank time or "dead air."

top 40   A radio format that may include many of the most popular songs or heavy dayparting (specially designed formats for the changing listenership during the day). Also called *contemporary* or *current hit radio*.

transduction   Converting energy from one form to another. A microphone transduces the motional energy of sound into electrical energy; a loudspeaker transduces electrical energy into sound.

voice-actuality   A report from a journalist in which an actuality (the sound of an event or recording of an interview) is included.

voicer   An oral report of a straight news item, spoken by a journalist who signs off with a name ("this is Ted Baxter reporting from City Hall").

voice-over   Narration placed over video.

waveform   In audio editing software, the waveform is the sound file displayed on the computer screen.

wild sound bite   A recorded piece of sound, such as the sound of fire engines, used in an edited news piece.

wire service   A service, such as the Associated Press or United Press International, that provides news from a central source to client affiliates.

wrap or **voice wrap**   A radio report in which the reporter's narration "wraps" around the actuality. Same as a *voice actuality*.

SUGGESTED READINGS

Some of the more traditional selections in the study of broadcasting are listed here, along with some nontraditional works that give valuable insight into the world of on-air performance. A number of the following works are now out of print but are readily available in libraries and through interlibrary loan.

Books

Stanley R. Alten. *Audio in Media.* 6th ed. Belmont, CA: Wadsworth, 2002. The definitive guide to audio; contains answers to any questions an announcer might ask about mics, audio consoles, and other equipment.

Terri Apple and Gary Owens. *Making Money in Voice-Overs: Winning Strategies to a Successful Career in TV, Commercials, Radio and Animation.* Los Angeles: Lone Eagle, 1999. Practical and interesting career advice.

Brad Kalbfeld. *The Associated Press Broadcast News Handbook: Incorporating the AP Libel Manual,* 3rd ed. New York: Associated Press, 2001. Thorough guide to writing and staying out of trouble.

Eric Barnouw. *Tube of Plenty: The Evolution of American Television.* Rev. ed. New York: Oxford University Press, 1982. Readable history based on *A Tower in Babel, The Golden Web,* and *The Image Empire,* by the same author.

Cicely Berry. *Voice and the Actor.* New York: Macmillan, 1974. Although primarily intended for the stage actor, this is a valuable book for any performer.

Shirley Biagi. *Interviews That Work: A Practical Guide for Journalists.* 2nd ed. Belmont, CA: Wadsworth, 1992. Leading journalists discuss the art of interviewing. Text includes a chapter on broadcast interviewing, and examples related to broadcast appear throughout.

Broadcasting/Cablecasting Yearbook. Washington: Broadcasting Publications. Names, addresses, phone numbers, and other valuable information on job hunting and the industry in general.

Joe Dominick, Fritz Messere, and Barry Sherman. *Broadcasting, Cable, the Internet and Beyond.* McGraw-Hill. 2003. Authoritative survey work with valuable insights.

Bruce E. Gronbeck (Editor), **Kathleen German** (Contributor), **Douglas Ehninger, Alan Monroe.** *Principles of Speech Communication.* New York: Addison-Wesley, 1997. Interesting and informative.

Jon Eisenson. *Voice and Diction: A Program for Improvement.* 7th ed. New York: Macmillan, 1996. Useful guide.

James E. Fletcher, ed. *Handbook of Radio and TV Broadcasting: Research Procedures in Audience, Program and Revenues.* New York: Van Nostrand Reinhold, 1981. Useful for understanding ratings and the broadcast business in general.

Uta Hagen, with Haskel Frankel. *Respect for Acting.* New York: Macmillan, 1973. One of the classic acting texts.

Jeffrey C. Hahner. *Speaking Clearly: Improving Voice and Diction with pronunciation CD-ROM,* McGraw-Hill, 2001. Authoritative guide to improving voice; good pronunciation guide accompanies the text.

Carl Hausman. *Crisis of Conscience: Perspectives on Journalism Ethics.* New York: HarperCollins, 1992. Broad-based study of some of the modern problems facing the journalist.

Carl Hausman. *Crafting the News.* Belmont, CA: Wadsworth, 1999. Standard broadcast journalism text but with heavy emphasis on news judgment and what makes news.

Carl Hausman. *The Decision-Making Process in Journalism.* Chicago: Nelson-Hall, 1990. Case histories of how experienced journalists made decisions; a useful introduction to news judgment.

Carl Hausman, Philip Benoit, Fritz Messere, and Lewis B. O'Donnell. *Modern Radio Production.* 6th ed. Belmont, CA: Wadsworth, 2004. Contains several selections on techniques of the announcer in various production duties.

William Hawes. *The Performer in Mass Media: In Media Professions and in the Community.* New York: Hastings House, 1978. Well-written guide with special focus on dramatic performance.

Vangie Hayes and Gloria Hainline. *How to Get into Commercials.* New York: Harper & Row, 1983. Authoritative and detailed, with good sections on commercial delivery.

Stuart W. Hyde. *Television and Radio Announcing.* 9th ed. Boston: Houghton Mifflin, 2003. Detailed study of announcing field.

Kathleen Hall Jamieson. *Eloquence in the Electronic Age.* New York: Oxford University Press, 1990. Primarily a treatise on political speechmaking, yet contains valuable insights into what makes a message work in the mass media.

Michael C. Keith. *The Radio Station,* 5th ed. Focal Press. 2000. Good overall look at the operations of broadcast radio.

Lauren Kessler and Duncan McDonald. *When Words Collide: A Journalist's Guide to Grammar and Style.* 6th ed. Belmont, CA: Wadsworth, 2004. Practical and easy-to-use guide.

Tim Logan. *Acting in the Million Dollar Minute: The Art and Business of Performing in TV Commercials.* Washington, DC: Communications Press, 1984. A comprehensive how-to book; good advice on performance techniques.

Barbara Matusow. *The Evening Stars: The Making of the Network News Anchor.* Boston: Houghton Mifflin, 1983. Enlightening behind-the-scenes look at the news business.

Lewis B. O'Donnell, Carl Hausman, and Philip Benoit. *Radio Station Operations: Management and Employee Perspectives.* Belmont, CA: Wadsworth, 1989. Includes highly detailed information on radio formats and radio news and the announcer's role in station operations.

Dan Rather. *Datelines and Deadlines.* New York: Morrow, 1999. A wonderful insight into the world of broadcast reporting.

Everett M. Schreck. *Principles and Styles of Acting.* Reading, MA: Addison-Wesley, 1970. Concise, easily digested book on basic acting techniques.

Gini Graham Scott. *Can We Talk? The Power and Influence of Talk Shows.* New York: Insight Books, 1996. Interesting inside view of one of radio's hottest commodities.

Constantine Stanislavski, Elizabeth Hapgood (translator). *Building a Character.* Theater Arts Books, 2002. Excellent study of what makes a charcater real to the audience.

Ann Utterback. *Broadcast Voice Handbook: How to Polish Your On-Air Delivery,* 3rd ed. Chicago: Bonus Books, 2000. A practical voice-training manual useful to broadcasters.

Mike Wallace and Gary Paul Gates. *Close Encounters.* New York: Morrow, 1984. Actual transcripts from Wallace interviews highlight a master in action.

Gilbert A. Williams. *Legendary Pioneers of Black Radio.* New York: Praeger, 1998. An interesting and readable work about black disc jockeys, often unheralded shapers of the industry.

Periodicals

Broadcasting and Cable (www.broadcastingcable.com). The trade journal of the broadcast industry. For the performer, of most interest for its help-wanted ads. Note, though, that most positions advertised are not for beginners.

College Broadcaster (Box 1955, Brown University, Providence, RI 02901). Addresses wide range of issues of interest to college TV and radio station personnel. Announcing and related areas—such as programming—receive clear and relevant treatment.

Communicator (The Magazine for the Radio-Television News Directors Association, Suite 615, 1717 K Street, Washington, DC 20006). Frequent articles on improving performance. One of the most valuable publications for the news announcer. Membership in the RTNDA (you don't have to be a news director to join) also entitles you to a twice-monthly job information service listing and a code number to access a jobs data bank.

The Quill (Society of Professional Journalists, P.O. Box 77, Greencastle, IN 46135). Geared toward print and broadcast journalists. Articles of general interest to the news announcer.

CREDITS

This page constitutes an extension of the copyright page. We have made every effort to trace the ownership of all copyrighted material and to secure permission from copyright holders. In the event of any question arising as to the use of any material, we will be pleased to make the necessary corrections in future printings. Thanks are due to the following authors, publishers, and agents for permission to use the material indicated.

Foreword. Photo courtesy of KGO-TV, ABC 7

Chapter 1. Figure 1.1: ©Bettmann/CORBIS. Figure 1.2: ©Bettmann-UPI/CORBIS. Figure 1.3: ©Bettmann-UPI/CORBIS. Figure 1.4: ©Bettmann-UPI/CORBIS. Figure 1.5: ©Bettmann-UPI/CORBIS. Figure 1.6: AP/Wide World Photos. Figure 1.7: AP/Wide World Photos. Figure 1.8: Photo courtesy of NBC/Globe Photos. Figure 1.9: ©Bettmann/CORBIS. Figure 1.10: ©Bettmann/ CORBIS. Figure 1.11: ©Bettmann/CORBIS. Figure 1.12: Courtesy of Clear Channel Radio/WHTZ-FM, NY. Figure 1.13: ©2003 Cable News Network LP, LLLP. All Rights Reserved. Used by permission of CNN. Figure 1.14: Courtesy of C-SPAN

Chapter 2. Page 44 David Blair McClosky and Barbara McClosky, Voice in Song and Speech (Boston: Boston Music Company, 1984). Figure 2.4: Photos by Philip Benoit. Figure 2.5: Photos by Philip Benoit

Chapter 3. Page 60: Quotes used with permission. Figure 3.1: Photos by Philip Benoit

Chapter 4. Figure 4.1: Photo by Philip Benoit. Figure 4.2: ©Richard T. Nowitz/CORBIS. Figure 4.3: Photo by Zuma Archive/ZUMA Press. Copyright © 2000 by Zuma Archivea week. Figure 4.4: Photo courtesy of CBS News. Figure 4.5: Photo by Philip Benoit. Figure 4.6: Source: CBS Photo Archive. Figure 4.8 (a, b): Photos by Philip Benoit. Figure 4.8 (c): Courtesy of Gotham Audio Corporation. Figure 4.10: Photos by Philip Benoit. Figure 4.11: Photos by Fritz Messere

Chapter 5. Figure 5.1: Photo by Fritz Messere. Figure 5.2: OnTheAir Software, used by permission. Figure 5.3: Photo by Fritz Messere. Figure 5.4: Photo by Fritz Messere. Figure 5.5: Courtesy of Smarts Broadcast Systems. Figure 5.6: Photo courtesy of Sony Corporation of America. Figure 5.7: Photo by Fritz Messere. Figure 5.8: Photo courtesy of TASCAM. Figure 5.9: Photo by Philip Benoit. Figure 5.10: Photo by Fritz Messere. Figure 5.11: Photo by Philip Benoit. Figure 5.12: Photo by Fritz Messere. Figure 5.13: Photo courtesy of Broadcast Electronics, Quincy, IL

Chapter 6. Figure 6.1: AP/Wide World Photos. Figure 6.2: Photo by Philip Benoit. Figure 6.3: Photo by Fritz Messere. Figure 6.4: Used by permission of Syntrillium Software. Figure 6.5: Photo by Carl Hausman. Figure 6.6: ©Bettmann/CORBIS

Chapter 7. Figure 7.1: Photo by Philip Benoit. Figure 7.2: Photo by Philip Benoit. Figure 7.4 (a–f): Screen shots by Fritz Messere. Figure 7.5: Photo by Carl Hausman. Figure 7.6: Photo by Fritz Messere. Figure 7.8: Photo by Philip Benoit. Figure 7.9: Photo by Philip Benoit. Figure 7.10: Photo by Carl Hausman. Figure 7.11: Photo by Philip Benoit. Figure 7.12: Photo by Fritz Messere. Figure 7.13: ©AFP/CORBIS. Figure 7.14: AP/Wide World Photos. Figure 7.15: Screen shot of E-Z News courtesy of Automated Data Systems. Figure 7.16: Copyright © 2003 ABC Photography Archive

Chapter 8. Figure 8.1: Photo by Philip Benoit. Figure 8.2: Photo courtesy of XM Satellite Radio

Chapter 9. Figure 9.1: Photo by Aaron Rappaport/FOX. Figure 9.2: Photo courtesy of Accu-Weather, Inc. Figure 9.5: Photo courtesy of Will Lyman

Chapter 10. Figure 10.1: Photo courtesy of Nick Schatzki

Chapter 11.. Page 318: From the November 1994 RTDNA Communicator. Reprinted with permission. Page 324: Excerpts reprinted with permission. Figure 11.1: Janaette Beckmann/CORBIS Outline

Chapter 12. Page 329: Excerpts reprinted with permission. Figure 12.1: Photo courtesy Raycom Media, AL. Figure 12.2: Photo by Carl Hausman. Page 338: Courtesy of Professor Richard E. Labunski, University of Washington

INDEX